RHOD

CW00405351

The Dodecanes
& Pireaus

including
Rhodes, Chalki, Kastellorizo, Karpathos,
Kasos, Simi, Tilos, Nisiros, Kos, Pserimos,
Kalimnos, Leros, Patmos, Lipsos, Arki,
Marathi & Angathonisi islands
with excursions to Yialos & Telentos islands

For the package & villa holiday-maker,
backpacker & independent traveller,
whether journeying by air, car, coach, ferry-boat
or train

by
Geoffrey O'Connell

Published by

Ashford, Buchan
& Enright
31 Bridge Street
Leatherhead
Surrey KT22 8BN

CONTENTS

ILLUSTRATIONS

The series is now in its eleventh year of publication, and I would appreciate continuing to hear from readers who have any additions or corrections to bring to my attention. As in the past, all correspondence (except that addressed to 'Dear filth', or similar endearments) will be answered. I hope readers will excuse errors that barge their way into the welter of detailed information included in the body text. My only excuse is to hide behind the fact that in order to ensure the volumes are as up-to-date as possible, the period from inception to publication is often kept down to some six months, which results in the occasional slip up...!

The cover picture of the caique, floating at a Dodecanese harbour mooring is reproduced by kind permission of GREEK ISLAND PHOTOS, Willowbridge Enterprises, Bletchley, Milton Keynes, Bucks.

The unique
'GROC's Greek Island Hotline'

Available to readers of the guides, this service enables a respondent to receive a bang up-to-the-minute update, to supplement the extensive information contained in a particular GROC's Candid Guide.
To obtain these paraphrased computer print-outs, all that is necessary is to:-

Complete the form, enclosing a payment of £2.00* & a large SAE (50p) and send to:-
Willowbridge Publishing, Bridge House, Southwick Village, Nr Fareham, Hants. PO17 6DZ.

This only allows for postage & packing to a UK address.

Note: The information will be of no use to anyone who does not possess the relevant, most up-to-date GROC's Candid Greek Island Guide. We are unable to dispatch the Hotline without details of the guide AND the specific edition, which information is on the Inside Front Cover.

Clients who take out **SURETRAVEL INSURANCE**, at the same time as requesting a Hotline, will receive the Hotline Free of Charge.

Issue: Spring 1993

Planned departure dates..................................
....
Mr/Mrs/Miss...
of...
....
I possess: I require:
GROC's Greek Island Guides   Edition   GROC's Greek Island Hotline
to:................................ .... to:..................................
....
....
....
....
....
and enclose a fee of £2.00 & a large SAE (50p).
Signature........................ .... Date..............................
I appreciate that the 'Hotline' may not be dispatched for up to 7-10 days from receipt of this application.

GROC's Candid Guides
introduce to readers

Suretravel '93

A comprehensive, cost-effective holiday insurance plan that 'gives cover many other policies do not reach', to travellers all over the world, AND at a reduced cost to previous years! In addition to the more usual insurance, the

SURETRAVEL HOLIDAY PLAN

offers legal expenses, and up to double the cover in some categories. It also includes (where medically necessary) 24 hour world wide medical emergency service and, where appropriate, repatriation by air ambulance. Also incorporated are personal accident, medical and emergency expenses, EVEN while hiring a bicycle, scooter or car, as well as other wide-ranging holiday activities.

An example 1993 premium, for a 10-17 day holiday in Greece, is £16.00 per person.
Note: all offers & terms are subject to the Insurance Certificate Cover

For an application form please complete the cut-out below and send to: Willowbridge Publishing, Bridge House, Southwick Village, Nr Fareham, Hants. PO17 6DZ

Mr/Mrs/Miss...Age.............

of..

....

I request a **SURETRAVEL** application form

Date of commencement of holiday....................Duration.............

Signature...Date............

FOREWORD

This guide is the third edition of **GROC's Candid Guide to Rhodes & The Dodecanese Islands**. It is a long-overdue rewrite of one of the most popular in the existing, extremely successful, well-proven series of nine Candid Guides to Greece and the Greek islands. The continuing rationale, the *raison d'etre* behind their production is, in the case of the islands, to treat each administrative and geographical island grouping on an individual and comprehensive basis. The course of action followed obviates attempting to do justice, to any one island of a specific chain, and having to lump it together, in amongst an aggregation of many others. It allows a much more detailed treatise in respect of each and every island, which is 'no bad thing'. If for no other reason, the vast distances involved, preclude visitors stopping-off at more than a small number of islands, even if travelling for a great many weeks.

Hopefully, the considerations of all vacationers have been borne in mind. Package hotel or villa holiday-makers want an unbiased description of the chosen resort, and its surroundings, rather than the usual, extravagant hyperbole to be found in almost all sales brochures. On the other hand, independent travellers, arriving by air, coach, ferry-boat, hydrofoil or train, have rather different requirements. They want accurate and specific information concerning their immediate whereabouts, as well as sleeping and dining opportunities, in addition to the availability of sundry other facilities, services and supplies. To cope with these diverse needs, factual and forthright location reports are combined with accommodation and dining particulars, itemised travel timetables, a comprehensive A to Z, coupled with detailed plans and regional maps, and full route narratives.

A few of the most important archaeological sites are accompanied by a plan of the layout, a brief elaboration covering the main features, as well as particulars of relevant historical and mythological interest. The serious student should purchase an individual site guide. They are usually excellently illustrated and well produced, even if the English is often rather quaint.

This GROC's guide, as all the others in the series, is researched as close to the planned publication date as is possible. On the other hand, to facilitate production, it is not always feasible to wait for information, only available in the year of publication. To overcome this awkward fact, as well as to keep an already produced guide up-to-date, year-on-year, any relevant alterations and changes in information, including current travel timetables, are 'punched' into a *Hotline* information pack, for particulars of which read on.

Part One introduces the Dodecanese, Part Two describes Piraeus, the universal ferry-boat port from which many travellers will set forth, whilst Part Three heralds the individual chapters detailing each island in the group.

As has become the routine, all general information about Greece, including travel, to and from the country, as well as Athens City, is covered in a separate guide. The necessary division of the material was first implemented in 1989. From then on these preliminaries, and a thoroughly redrafted account of the capital, still the hub for much Hellenic travel, have been treated in a separate guide. This decision had to be made to ensure the continued improvement and expansion of each guide's contents, as the sheer volume of information had become rather unwieldy. Countless readers, who wished to take along two or three guides, were humping about hundreds of pages of duplicated information. Furthermore, in years gone-by, it was almost mandatory to include the city in any Greek guide book, as the capital was pivotal to most travellers. With the ever-increasing number of direct island flights available, it became feasible to reach a particular destination, without recourse to Athens. Even if Athens has to be used, as a transfer point, many travellers' only sight of the Greek capital will be the facilities, and tarmacadam of the airport. And then, only whilst swapping over from an international to a domestic flight, for the onward leg of a particular journey.

The exchange rate has, over the years, tended to gently slide in favour of other currencies, with the Greek drachma constantly devaluing. Unfortunately, this decline in the value of the drachma has not been as much as it would, were it not a 'managed' money. At the time of writing the final draft of this guide, the rate to the English pound (£) was 'lurking about' in the region of 320drs. Lamentably, Greek prices are subject to fluctuation, upward. Annual increases in the last few years have exceeded 15/20%, and the drachma has ceased to devalue sufficiently to compensate for these uplifts.

Recommendations and personalities are almost always based on personal observation and experience, occasionally emphasised by the discerning comments of readers and or colleagues. They may well change from year to year, and, being such individual, idiosyncratic judgements, are subject to different interpretation by others!

The series continues to incorporate two services, evolved over the years, one of which remains both innovative and unique. They are:

GROC's Greek Hotline: An unrivalled benefit available to purchasers of a current guide. Application enables a reader to obtain a summary print-out, listing all relevant comments and information, that have become available, since the publication of that particular book. The Hotline is constantly updated and revised, incorporating bang up-to-the-moment intelligence, not only culled from our own resources, but from readers' correspondence. Completion of the form incorporated in the book, accompanied by the relevant fee and a SAE, is all that is required to receive the specific Hotline.

Travel Insurance: A comprehensive holiday insurance plan that 'gives cover that many other policies do not reach....' See elsewhere for details.

Enjoy yourselves and 'Ya Sou'.   Geoffrey O'Connell 1993

ACKNOWLEDGEMENTS
Over the years, the list of those to be thanked has remained remarkably similar. As always, my constant travelling companion, Rosemary, who can unfailingly be relied on to add often unwanted, uninformed comments and asides, requires especial thanks for her unrelieved, unstinting (well, almost unstinting) support. Some of those who assist me, year in and year out, require specific acknowledgement - if only for effort, far beyond the siren call of vulgar remuneration! These worthies include: Graham Bishop, who continues to draw splendid maps and plans; Ted Spittles who does clever things with the process camera, and the paste-up; Viv Grady, previously Hitie, who now not only controls the word processor, but the laser printer - soon she will write the wretched things; and Richard Joseph, a long-standing friend, who encouraged me to 'put pen to paper', some fourteen or fifteen years ago, and continues to guide, help and motivate me.

Lastly, but not least, I must extend my sincerest thanks to Paola Dell'Olio, who thoroughly researched the lastest 'Dodecanese state of play', in an inimitable style.

1 PART ONE
INTRODUCTION TO THE DODECANESE
ISLANDS (Dodekanes, Dhodhekanisos)

You asked me for the beauty of ages past, for the beauty of land and sea, for the beauty of human beings, for the beauty of tradition, for the beauty of contemporary luxury, for every kind of beauty, and I brought you to the Dodecanese.

Of all the island groupings perhaps the Dodecanese can be 'all islands to all men and women'! The essential difference between the Dodecanese and most of the other Aegean islands is, in the main, due to comparatively recent historical associations. The fortuitous twist of fate that caused the Knights of St John to settle throughout the group, had far-reaching consequences. For instance, in their increasingly determined efforts to hang on to their acquisitions, the Knights caused to be built a series of fortified island city settlements. In so doing, they demonstrably transformed the architecture, if not the culture. A further throw of fate's dice, resulted, at a much later date, in the comparative 'blink of an eyelid' suzerainty exercised by the Italians. Their presence, between 1912 and 1943, completed a transformation that gave the Dodecanese a municipal order and living-museum ambiance that is manifestly obvious. This is especially so when comparing the Dodecanese to almost any Cycladean island. The only Greek island group that reflects a similar refinement is the Ionian. Here, centuries of successive Venetian and British involvement had a similar, civilising affect, an introduction of 19thC Western European overlay, which added a gloss of urban refinement.

But back to the Dodecanese, the maze-like shambles chanced upon in the average Cyclades Chora, wildly contrasts with the spacious municipal order to be found on many of the Dodecanese islands. Here wide avenues, spacious parks and art Deco administration buildings are the 'order of the day'. The latter features were introduced by the Italians. They were also responsible for carrying out the imaginative and widespread restoration of much of the crumbling castle-architecture, that had been the provenance of the Knights. Il Duce's almost heroic, but, more prosaically, megalomaniacal dreams of recreating a Mediterranean 20thC Roman Empire, were at the root of this rush to preserve and reinstate to their former glory, some of the more magnificent of the medieval constructions. It is only necessary to wander round the Old Quarter of Rhodes to appreciate the immensity of the assignment the Italians undertook, and their unqualified success in achieving the task. So, it is unarguable that these foreign adventurers fundamentally affected, not only the architecture, but the very fabric of these islands' culture.

The grouping referred to as the Dodecanese, which means the twelve islands, and confusingly covers at least seventeen, includes Astipalaia. The latter's official inclusion owes more to the niceties of 'administrative illogicality' than adjacency to the Dodecanese. Astipalaia's geographical location and life-style is Cycladian. As if to reinforce this disparity, there are few direct ferry-boat connections with the Dodecanese. For these reasons Astipalaia is to be found in the GROC's Guide to the Cyclades.

Generally, ferry-boat links between the islands in the chain are relatively good, with a regular number of craft travelling the length of the group. Out of the height of summer season months, the frequency of the schedules falls off, more especially to the more far-flung islands. It must not be forgotten that

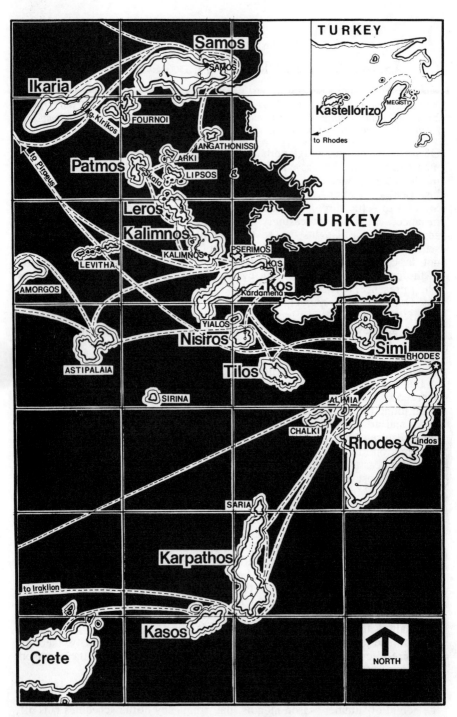

Illustration 1 The Dodecanese islands

inclement weather,   and sea-state, can severely curtail a particular ferry's operation.   Yes, they do have storms in the Aegean! A limited hydrofoil service links Rhodes with a few other islands.

The long established international and domestic scheduled air services, to and from Rhodes and Kos, have been supplemented by a number of other island airfields. These are only able to accept the smaller aircraft, but allow flights between Athens and Karpathos, Kasos, Kastellorizo and Leros.

The proximity of the group to the Turkish mainland has, over the centuries, not unnaturally, resulted in their being strongly influenced by this close, and powerful neighbour. In fact, the history of the Dodecanese is one of almost constant invasion and conquest. These commenced with the reliably documented Phoenicians,   then the Minoans of Crete (2500 and 1440 BC), followed by the Achaians of the Peloponnese (1550-1150 BC). The Dorians ruled from 1150-1000 BC and promulgated the change-over from female dominated gods, to a more chauvinistically masculine role for the divinity. After Rhodes had sided with the losing Persians, the Athenians took over, in 480 BC. This relationship changed to that of allies, after which the Rhodians, by judicious sitting on the fence and constant switching of allegiances, managed to build a position of wealth and power. The eminence of Rhodes was such that even Alexander the Great allowed the island to engage in flourishing Egyptian trade links, without hindrance. On Alexander's death, Rhodes was powerful enough to rebuff a Macedonian siege. The beginning of the end of this period of pre-eminence was heralded when Rhodes signed a treaty with Rome, in the 2ndC BC. The Romans, to bring their wealthy and independent ally into line, declared the Cycladean island of Delos a free port.

From hereon it was downhill for Rhodes. This fall from grace culminated, after the death of Caesar, in the plundering, sacking and firing of the island. This despoliation was carried out on the instructions of Cassius (he of the lean and hungry look!), after Rhodes had declined to side with him. The first thirteen hundred or so years of anno Domini did not result in any marked improvement in the island's fortunes, despite coming under Byzantine rule. Forts were built, regardless of which Rhodes was the subject of endless raids and invasions by, amongst others, the Goths, Arabs, Saracens, Venetians, Franks and Genoese. After a Crusader visit, in 1097, followed by Richard Coeur-de-Lion (our Lionheart), in 1191, the Knights of St John of Jerusalem, who had been ousted from Jerusalem,   requested the then Genoese overlords to allow them to settle. On being turned down, the Knights conquered Rhodes in 1309, and ruled for two hundred and thirteen years.

The Knights repulsed two serious sieges, in 1444 and 1480. Nonetheless, in 1522, the Turkish sultan, Suleiman 1st, or the Magnificent, decided to sort out, once and for all, 'those turbulent Knights' (to thoroughly misquote Henry II). Mind you, the magnificent Turk required some one hundred thousand men (one report mentioning double that number) to overcome the Rhodes garrison. And they totalled the huge number of six hundred and fifty Knights, assisted by about four hundred Candians (from Crete, not Canadians, which would have resulted in a historical reassessment, methinks), two hundred Genoese, fifty Venetians, and an assortment of town citizens. After six months, weakened but not bowed, the courageous Knights were reputed to have been betrayed by one of their own, a Portuguese Knight. Suleiman's regard for the besieged was such that the surviving one hundred and eighty Knights, and their supporters, were allowed to leave, unmolested. This was a rare privilege, for the Turks normally rewarded the vanquished with such

'Turkish delights' as death at the sword, boiling and skinning alive, or simple, straightforward burning. The Knights retired, at first to Crete, and then to Malta, in 1530, where they remained as a force to be reckoned with, until the French captured the island, in 1748. Recently, a strange quirk of history brought the Knighthood to public notice. In 1988, an English Benedictine schoolmaster was elected to the pre-eminence of Grand Master of the Order. He now presides over a couple of acres, and a Roman palace, within sight of Vatican City - all that remains of the once powerful kingdom.

Turkish dominance over the Dodecanese islands lasted three hundred and ninety years but, surprisingly, their influence was restricted to a mosque here, and a minaret there. Arguably their four hundred or so years of rule had less impact and influence than the thirty one years of occupation exercised by the Italians, in the early 20th century. Certainly the Turks were overtaken by a gentle, slow, languid decline, presiding over the gradual deterioration of the islands' infrastructure and buildings. Fortunately, as elsewhere, the Turks allowed the Greek religion and culture to continue, if not prosper. In fact, they had a habit of distancing themselves from the indigenous population. In the case of Rhodes, they excluding the Greeks from living in the Old Quarter, forcing them to remain beyond the walls. Thus came about the Nea Chora, now submerged in modern-day Rhodes City. The by-product of this partition was to help preserve the Greek identity and their way of life.

The Turkish occupation ended in 1912, when the Italians drove them out of the Dodecanese, during a Turko-Italian conflict. This was a bit of a side-show, a spin-off resulting from a period during which Italy wished to expand its overseas territories, especially in the Mediterranean. A number of international conferences failed to unseat them. Although from their 'taverna seat', the Greeks may find it difficult to appreciate, on balance the Italian occupation must be considered beneficial. The undue, if benign repression, experienced throughout the Mussolini fascist period, has to be weighed against the civil engineering, architectural and archaeological works they put in hand. Unfortunately, the Second World War collapse of the Mussolini government, in 1943, left an 'overlord void'. To take advantage of this situation, the German and British forces fought a number of bitter and troop-costly battles, with much suffering incurred by the locals. After the collapse of the Third Reich, in 1945, the islands were freed by British and Greek troops, and formally ceded to the Greek nation in 1947.

Greek Orthodoxy is the religion of the Dodecanese, with tiny enclaves of Turkish Muslims and Jews on Rhodes, and Turks on Kos.

Symbols, Keys & Definitions Below are some notes in respect of the initials and symbols used in the text, as well as an explanation of the possibly idiosyncratic nouns, adjectives and phrases, found throughout the book.

Keys The key *Tmr*, in conjunction with grids, is used as a map reference to aid easy identification of this or that location on port and town plans. Other keys used in the text include *Sbo* - 'Sea behind one'; *Fsw* - 'Facing seawards'; *Fbqbo* - 'Ferry-boat quay behind one'; *DTs* - Day-trippers; *BPTs* - 'British Package Tourists' and *OTT* - 'Over The Top'.

GROC's definitions, 'proper' adjectives & nouns: These may require some elucidation, as most do not appear in 'official' works of reference and are used with my own interpretation, as set out below.

Backshore: the furthest strip of beach from the sea's edge. The marginal rim separating the shore from the surrounds. *See* **Scrubbly.**

Chatty: with pretension to grandeur or sophistication.

Dead: an establishment that appears to be 'terminally' closed, and not about to open for business, but... who knows?

Donkey-droppings: as in 'two donkey-droppings', indicating a very small hamlet. *See* **One-eyed.**

Doo-hickey: an Irish based colloquialism, suggesting an extreme lack of sophistication and or rather 'daffy' (despite contrary indications in the authoritative and excellent *Partridges Dictionary of Slang!*).

Ethnic: very unsophisticated, Greek indigenous and, as a rule, applied to hotels and pensions. *See* **Provincial.**

(Ships) Galley Cooking: used to describe 'tired' rows of metal trays 'lurking' under the glass counters of tavernas, containing the exhausted, dried up, overcooked remnants of the lunch-time fare.

Gongoozle: borrowed from canal boat terminology, and indicates the state of very idly and leisurely, but inquisitively staring at others involved in some vital and busy activity.

Graze: Dine out or eat.

Great unwashed: the less attractive, modern-day mutation of the 1960s hippy. They are usually Western European, inactive loafers and layabouts 'by choice', or unemployed drop-outs. Once having located a desirable location, often a splendid beach, they camp under plastic and in shabby tents, thus ensuring the spot is despoiled for others. The 'men of the tribe' tend to trail a mangy dog on a piece of string. The women, more often than not, with a grubby child or two in train, pester cafe-bar clients to purchase items of home-made jewellery or trinkets. This genre appears to be incurably penniless (but then who isn't?).

Grecocilious: Describes those Greeks, usually bank clerks or tour office owners, who are making their money from tourists but are disdainful of the 'hand that feeds them'. They appear to consider holiday-makers are some form of small intellect, low-browed, tree clambering, inferior relation to the Greek *homo sapiens*. They can usually converse passably in two or three foreign languages (when it suits them) and habitually display an air of weary sophistication.

Grelish: Greco-English accented chat.

Grine: Expatriate Greeks who have lived a number of years in Australia, and thus have a Greek -Australian, or 'Grine' accent.

Hillbilly: similar to 'ethnic', but applied to describe countryside or a settlement, as in 'backwoods'.

Hippy: those who live outside the predictable, boring (!) mainstream of life and are frequently genuine, if sometimes impecunious travellers. The category may include students, or young professionals, taking a sabbatical and who are often 'negligent' of their sartorial appearance.

Hose down: Have a shower.

Independents: vacationers who make their own travel and accommodation arrangements, spurning the 'siren calls' of structured tourism, preferring to step off the package holiday carousel and make their own way.

Kosta'd: used to describe the 'ultimate' in development necessary for a settlement to reach the apogee required to satisfy the popular common denominator of package tourism. That this state of 'paradise on earth' has been accomplished, will be evidenced by the 'High St' presence of cocktail or music bars, discos, (garden) pubs, bistros and fast food. 'First division' locations are pinpointed by the aforementioned establishments offering inducements, which may include wet T-shirt, nightdress or pyjama bottom parties; air conditioning; space invader games and table top videos; as well as sundowner, happy or doubles hours.

Local prices: *See* **Special prices.**

Mr Big: a local trader or pension owner, an aspiring tycoon, a small fish trying to be a big, one in a 'small pool'. Despite being flashy with shady overtones, his lack of sophistication is apparent by his not being Grecocilious!

Noddies or nodders: the palpable, floating evidence of untreated sewage being discharged into the sea.

One-eyed: small. *See* **Donkey-droppings.**

Poom: a descriptive noun 'borrowed' after sighting on Crete, some years ago, a crudely written sign advertising accommodation that simply stated POOMS! This particular place was basic with low-raftered ceilings, earth-floors and windowless rooms, simply equipped with a pair of truckle beds and rickety oilcloth covered washstand - very reminiscent of typical Cycladean cubicles of the 1950/60s period.

Provincial: usually applied to accommodation and an improvement on **Ethnic.** Not meant to indicate, say, dirty but should conjure up images of faded, rather gloomy establishments, with a mausoleum atmosphere; high ceilinged, Victorian rooms with worn, brown linoleum; dusty, tired aspidistras, as well as bathrooms and plumbing of unbelievable antiquity.

Pump ship: To 'ablute'.

Richter scale: borrowed from earthquake seismology and employed to indicate the (appalling) state of toilets, on an 'eye-watering' scale.

Rustic: unsophisticated, unrefined.

Schlepper: vigorous touting for customers by restaurant staff. It is said of a skilled market schlepper that he can 'retrieve' a passer-by from up to thirty or forty metres beyond the stall.

Scrubbly: usually applied to a beach or countryside, and indicating a rather messy, shabby area.

Special prices: A phrase employed to conceal the fact that the price charged is no more, no less than that of all the other bandits! No, no - competitors.

Local prices: is a homespun variation designed to give the impression that the goods are charged at a much lower figure than that obtainable elsewhere. Both are totally inaccurate, misleading misnomers.

Squatty: A Turkish (or French) style ablution arrangement. None of the old, familiar lavatory bowl and seat. Oh, no, just two moulded footprints edging a dirty looking hole, set in a porcelain surround. Apart from the unaccustomed nature of the exercise, the Lord simply did not give us enough limbs to keep a shirt up and control wayward trousers, that constantly attempt to flop down on to the floor, awash with goodness knows what! All this has to be enacted whilst gripping the toilet roll in one hand and wiping one's 'botty', with the other hand. Impossible! Incidentally, ladies should (perhaps) substitute blouse for shirt and skirt for trousers, but then it is easier (I am told) to tuck a skirt into one's waistband! A minor defect in the transition from Turkey, is that the close-to-the-floor tap, installed to aid flushing a squatty, is noticeable by its absence, in Greece. Well, it would be wouldn't it?

Way-station: mainly used to refer to an office or terminus in the sticks, and cloaked with an abandoned, unwanted air.

Dodecanese islands described include:

Island	Capital	Ports (at which Ferry-boats & Hydrofoils dock)	Ferry-boat/Hydrofoil connections (FB = boat; H = Hydrofoil EB = excursion boat; M = Mainland)
Angathonisi (Agathonisi, Gaidaros, Gaidharos)	Megalo Chorio	Ag Georgios	FB: Arki, Patmos,Lipsos, Leros, Kalimnos, Kos, Nisiros,Tilos, Simi, Rhodes; Samos. EB: Samos, Leros, Patmos.
Arki		Port Augusta	FB: Angathonisi, Samos;Patmos, Lipsos, Leros, Kalimnos, Kos, Nisiros, Tilos, Simi, Rhodes.
Chalki (Chalkis, Khalkia, Khalki, Halki)	Nimborio (Emborio, Skala)	Nimborio	FB: Rhodes,Simi,Tilos,Nisiros, Kos, Karpathos, Astipalaia, Piraeus(M); Diafani(Karpathos), Karpathos, Kasos, Sitia(Crete), Ag Nikolaos(Crete); Kamiros, Skala(Rhodes).
Kalimnos (Kalymos, Calymnos)	Kalimnos (Pothia)	Kalimnos	FB: Leros, Lipsos,Patmos, Arki, Angathonisi, Samos, Kos, Nisiros, Tilos, Simi, Rhodes, Karpathos, Kasos, Sitia(Crete), Ag Nikolaos(Crete); Astipalaia, Amorgos, Paros, Piraeus(M). EB: Pserimos, Kos, Mastichari (Kos), Patmos, Turkey.
		Myrtes	EB: Xerokampos(Leros), Telentos.
Karpathos (Scarpanto)	Karpathos (Pighadia)	Karpathos	FB: Kasos, Sitia(Crete), Ag Nikolaos(Crete), Anafi, Santorini, Folegandros, Milos; Diafani(Karpathos), Chalki, Rhodes, Simi, Tilos, Nisiros, Kos, Kalimnos, Astipalaia, Amorgos, Paros, Piraeus(M).
		Diafani	See Karpathos.
Kasos (Kassos)	Fry (Phry, Fri, Ophrys)	Fry/Emborio	FB: Sitia(Crete),Ag Nikolaos (Crete),Anafi,Santorini, Folegandros, Milos, Piraeus(M); Karpathos, Diafani(Karpathos), Chalki, Rhodes, Simi,Tilos, Nisiros, Kos, Kalimnos, Astipalaia, Amorgos, Paros, Piraeus(M).
Kastellorizo (Kastelorizo, Kastellorizon, Kastellorizo, Castelorizo, Megisti)	Kastellorizo (Kastellorizon, Megisti)	Kastellorizo	FB: Rhodes.
Kos (Cos)	Kos	Kos	FB: Kalimnos, Leros, Lipsos, Patmos, Arki, Angathonisi, Samos Chios, Mitilini(Lesbos), Kavala(M); Astipalaia, Limnos, Amorgos, Paros, Piraeus(M); Nisiros, Tilos, Simi, Rhodes. FD: Simi, Rhodes; Patmos. EB: Nisiros,Kalimnos,Pserimos.
		Mastichari	EB: Kalimnos, Pserimos.
		Kardamena	EB: Nisiros.

Island	Capital	Ports	Ferry-boat/Hydrofoil connections
Leros	Platanos	Lakki	FB: Lipsos, Patmos, Arki, Angathonisi, Samos; Kalimnos, Kos, Nisiros, Tilos, Simi, Rhodes; Patmos, Piraeus(M).
		Ag Marina	EB: Lipsos, Patmos, Angathonisi.
		Xerokampos	EB: Myrtes(Leros).
Lipsos (Lipsi, Lipso Lipsoi)	Lipsos	Lipsos	FB: Patmos, Arki, Angathonisi, Samos; Leros, Kalimnos, Kos, Nisiros, Tilos, Simi, Rhodes. EB: Patmos.
Marathi (Marathos, Maranthi)		Marathi	EB: Patmos.
Nisiros (Nisyros, Nissiros)	Mandraki	Mandraki	FB: Tilos, Simi, Rhodes; Kos, Kalimnos, Leros, Lipsos, Patmos, Arki, Angathonisi, Samos; Patmos, Piraeus(M).
Patmos	The Chora	Skala	FB: Arki, Angathonisi, Samos, Chios, Mitilini(Lesbos), Limnos, Kavala(M); Lipsos, Leros, Kalimnos, Kos, Nisiros, Tilos, Simi, Rhodes; Piraeus(M); Katakolon(M), Venice. FD: Kos, Rhodes. EB: Kos, Samos, Lipsos, Leros, Ikaria, Paros, Kalimnos.
Pserimos	Pserimos	Pserimos	EB: Kos, Mastichari(Kos), Kalimnos.
Rhodes (Rhodhos, Rodos)	Rhodes	Rhodes	FB: Simi, Tilos, Nisiros, Kos, Kalimnos, Leros, Lipsos, Patmos, Arki, Angathonisi, Samos, Chios, Mitilini(Lesbos), Limnos, Kavala(M); Astipalaia, Amorgos, Paros, Piraeus(M); Chalki, Karpathos, Kasos, Sitia(Crete), Ag Nikolaos(Crete), Anafi, Santorini, Folegandros, Milos; Megisti(Kastellorizo); FD: Kos, Simi, Patmos. EB: Lindos(Rhodes), Simi.
		Kamiros Skala	FB: Chalki.
Simi (Symi, Syme)	The Chora	Gialos/Simi	FB: Tilos, Nisiros, Kos, Kalimnos Leros, Lipsos, Patmos, Arki, Angathonisi, Samos; Astipalaia, Amorgos, Piraeus(M); Rhodes. FD: Kos, Rhodes. EB: Rhodes.
Tilos (Telos, Episkopi)	Megalo Chorio	Livadia (Levadhia)	FB: Nisiros, Kos, Kalimnos, Leros, Lipsos, Patmos, Arki, Angathonisi, Samos; Simi, Rhodes; Astipalaia, Amorgos, Paros, Piraeus(M).
Yialos (Giali)			EB: Nisiros.

2 PART TWO

PIREAUS (Pireas, Pireefs)

Fortune and hope farewell! I've found the port you've done with me; go now with others sport. From a Greek epigram

Tel prefix 01. Piraeus (Illus 2 & 3) is the port of Athens and the usual ferry-boat departure point for most of the Aegean islands. Unfortunately, it is a wearisomely large town, with a confusing layout on first, second and third acquaintanceship. One thing is for certain, and that is that the modern-day port bears very little resemblance to the Piraeus of old, as portrayed in the film *Never on a Sunday*. The bawdy seaport cafes, hashish dens, tavernas and seedy waterfront have been replaced by smart shipping offices, banks, tree planted thoroughfares, squares and parks. It has to be admitted that the sleazy, south end of the parallel, canyon-like streets of Filonos and Notara are the 'Soho' of Piraeus, and remain rather rich in low-life. I suppose fairly typical of this downtown area is the *Clapcabana Cabaret* (which is probably what a client will get from over-zealous attendance). Other, not to be forgotten hot-spots, are the *Seamens Bar/Nightclub* and the *Moulin Rouge*! The other side of the coin is the very smart, rinky-dinky, east flank of the peninsula. This is edged by a neat Esplanade, which chicanes gently and leisurely, rising and falling, following the cove, bay and harbour indented coastline.

ARRIVAL BY AIR *See* GROCs Candid Guide to Athens &...

ARRIVAL BY BUS From Syntagma Sq (Athens), Bus No 40 arrives at Plateia Korai (*Tmr* C3), but in truth that is rather an over-simplification. For a start, the bus is absolutely crammed, especially early morning, and secondly it is very difficult to know one's exact whereabouts. The first mentioned drawback makes it difficult to leap up and down, looking for telltale signs, whilst the latter impediment is germane, as the bus hurtles on down to the south end of the Piraeus peninsula. The initial indicator, that the end of the ¾ hour journey is imminent, is when the bus runs parallel to the Metro lines. The next is crossing the wide avenue of Leoforos Vassileos Georgiou, after which signposts for the Archaeological Museum indicate that it is time to bale-out. From Plateia Korai: north-west down Leoforos Vassileos Georgiou (Yeoryiou) leads to the Main (Grand or Central) Harbour (*Tmr* B4); south-east progresses towards Limin Zeas (Pasalimani) Harbour (*Tmr* D3/4); and east makes off towards Limin Mounikhias (Tourkolimano) Harbour (*Tmr* E2). Limin Zeas is where the hydrofoils (Flying Dolphins - *Ceres*) that service the Argo Saronic islands dock (*Tmr* 26E4), that is except for the Aegina island craft, which berth (*Tmr* 24A/B3/4) alongside Plateia Astigos (Karaiskaki).
  The airport Express buses terminus on Plateia Astigos (*Tmr* 2A/B3/4); from Omonia Sq (Athens), Bus No 49 arrives at Plateia Themistokleous (*Tmr* 21B/C3); and a number of other services (including for instance Bus No 101) arrive at Kleisovis St (*Tmr* B/C5/6). From the latter, head north-east along Hatzikiriakou to Sakhtouri St, at which turn left, in a northerly direction, to reach the southern end of the Main Harbour waterfront.

ARRIVAL BY FERRY Re-orientate using the above information. Bear in mind

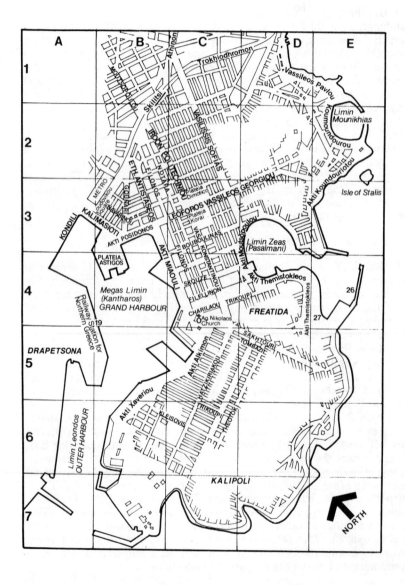

Illustration 2 Piraeus - Port & Town detail

that the various ferries dock all the way round the eastern periphery of the Grand Harbour, from the area of Plateia Astigos (*Tmr* 2A/B3/4) to a point south of the relatively new Passenger Ferry-Boat terminal (*Tmr* 25B/C4). This facility is set in a pleasantly paved and landscaped section of Akti Miaouli.

ARRIVAL BY HYDROFOIL A limited inter-island service operates in and around the Dodecanese islands, but none connect with the mainland.

ARRIVAL BY METRO The Piraeus Metro station (*Tmr* 1A/B2/3) is the end of the line and hidden away in a large, but rather inconspicuous building, flanked by Plateia Loudovikou. Passengers emerge opposite the quayside, towards the north end of the Grand Harbour.

Those catching a ferry-boat, almost immediately, might consider establishing a temporary headquarters. To do so, turn right out of the Metro building, cross the mainly paved Plateia Loudovikou to the waterfront, follow the Esplanade round to the left, and traverse Plateia Astigos (*Tmr* 2A/B3/4). This square is pleasantly shaded with trees, planted with bench seats, displays an old wooden railway carriage, and is dominated by a tall, multi-storey waterfront building. Apart from size, it is noticeable for the advertising slogan that tops off the block. Set into the south, harbour-facing side are a number of cafe-bars, any one of which makes a convenient base camp. Refreshments are not inexpensive, at any of the harbour establishments. The Port police (*Tmr* 3A/B3/4) are located at the rear of the large Plateia Astigos building and must be regarded as 'favourites' to dispense accurate information in respect of ferry-boats. Any knowledge received is best tucked away, for future comparison with the rest of the advice acquired!

ARRIVAL BY TRAIN Peloponnese trains pull up at the same terminus building as the Metro (*Tmr* 1A/B2/3), whilst trains from Northern Greece. 'steam' into the far (north-west) side of the Grand Harbour (*Tmr* 19A/B4/5). The station for this latter terminal is almost like a country halt - even if it is plonked down alongside a squalid, industrial section of the waterfront.

THE ACCOMMODATION & EATING OUT
The Accommodation Although I have never had to doss (or camp) out in Piraeus, I am advised that it is not to be recommended. Incidentally, all accommodation prices, throughout the book, are listed on a per night basis, and rarely include breakfast, which will be charged as an extra amount.

Close by the Metro station, are the:
Hotel Kentrikon (*Tmr* 29A/B3) (Class D) 16 Loudovikou Sq   Tel 417 9497
Directions: From the Loudovikou Sq entrance to the Metro building, turn left (*Sea to the right*). The hotel edges the square.
All rooms sharing, a single priced at 3190drs & a double at 5320drs.

Hotel Ionion (*Tmr* 4B3) (Class C) 10 Kapodistrion   Tel 417 0992
Directions: Turn left from the Metro station (*Fsw*) along the quay road, Akti Kalimasioti, and left again at the first side-street.
The hotel, halfway up on the right, has a prominent sign promising 'Economical Prices'. Rates as for the *Kentrikon*.

To the north-east of the *Ionion*, along the street and over the crossroads of Kapodistrion and Navarinou, is the:

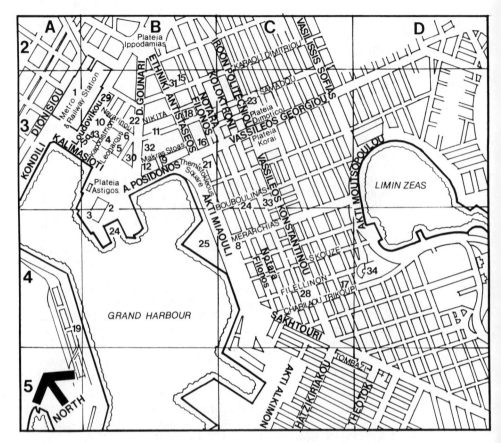

Tmr

1A/B2/3	Metro & Peloponnese Railway Station
2A/B3/4	Plateia Astigos (Karaiskaki)
3A/B3/4	Port Police
4B3	Hotel Ionian
5B3	Hotel Delfini
6B3	Hotel Elektra
7C4	Hotel Capitol
8B/C3/4	Olympic Airline Office
9B3	Macedonia & Thrace Bank
10	Bread Shops
11B3	Main shopping street
12B3	J.S. Travel
13A/B3	Porto Ferry-boat Tickets
14B/C4/5	Customs Office
15B2/3	OTE
16B/C3	Ag Triada Cathedral
17C/D4	Archaeological Museum
18B/C3	Post Office
19A/B4/5	Northern Greece Railway Station Terminus
20E2	Delligiannis Taverna
21B/C3	Plateia Themistokleous
22B3	Ionian Bank
23B/C2/3	Town Police
24A/B3/4	Aegina Hydrofoil Dock
25B/C4	New passenger Ferry-boat Terminal
26E4	Argo-Saronic/Peloponnese Hydrofoil Dock
27D/E4	Naval Museum
28C4	Coin-op Launderette
29A/B3	Hotel Kentrikon
30B3	Hotel Acropole
31B2/3	Hotel Aenos
32B3	'Market' Square
33C3/4	'First Aid Station'
34C/D4	Ancient Theatre

(Tmr) = *Town map reference*
(Fsw) = *Facing seawards*
(Sbo) = *Sea behind one*
(Fbqbo) = *Ferry-boat Quay behind one*

Illustration 3 Piraeus inset

Hotel Sparti (*Tmr* B3) (Class E) 18 Kapodistrion   Tel 411 0402
Directions: As above.
Outwardly a 'bit-of-a-sleaze', with 'share-a-bathroom' rates of 2000drs for a single & 3000drs for a double.

The Delfini (*Tmr* 5B3) (Class C) 7 Leoharous   Tel 412 3512
Directions: As for the *Ionion*, but the second turning left.
Singles cost 4000/4500drs & doubles 5000/6000drs, bathroom en suite.

The other side of the street to the *Delfini* is the:
Hotel Ikaros (*Tmr* B3) (Class E) 18 Leoharous   Tel 417 7094
Directions: As above.
Only doubles, sharing the bathroom, at a cost of 2480drs.

Hotel Elektra (*Tmr* 6B3) (Class E) 12 Navarinou.   Tel 417 7057
Directions: At the top of Leoharous St is the 'Esplanade parallel' Navarinou St. Turn right, and the hotel is at the end of the block.
Comfortable, and convenient. Rates as for the *Kentrikon*.

Whilst in this neighbourhood, there are two smarter options. One is the relatively new *Hotel Acropole* (*Tmr* 30B3) (Class C, tel 417 4190), right at the junction of Navarinou and Gounari Sts, and on the right (*Fsw*). The other is across D. Gounari St, on the north-east side of the Makras Stoas Market, and is the:
Hotel Triton (*Tmr* B3) (Class B) 8 Tsamadou   Tel 417 3457
Directions: As above.
A single room, sharing, costs 3940/4330drs & with an en suite bathroom 4860/5345drs, whilst a double room sharing is priced at 5235/5760drs & en suite 6170/6785drs.

A seedy, rather slovenly, but cheaper choice is the:
Hotel Aenos (Enos) (*Tmr* 31B2/3) 14 E. Antistaseos   Tel 417 4879
Directions: From Odhos Navarinou cross over D. Gounari St, along Tsamadou St, as far as the junction with E. Antistaseos, where turn left. The hotel is up the street, and on the right (*Sbo*).
An old style building, all rooms sharing. A single costing 1600drs & doubles 2400drs, but use of a shower is charged an extra 300drs, per head.

For a rich (in numbers), if somewhat questionable sector, in and around the 'Old Quarter' of Piraeus, follow the quay road of Akti Posidonos and the waterfront of Akti Miaouli in a southerly direction, towards the Custom's office (*Tmr* 14B/C4/5). This passes by the:
Hotel Piraeus (*Tmr* B/C3/4) (Class D) 1 Bouboulinas   Tel 417 2950
Directions: As above, at the corner of the Esplanade and Bouboulinas St, in a building of Victorian appearance.
Rates as for the *Aenos*.

South along Akti Miaouli, leads to the outset of C. Trikoupi Ave (*Tmr* C4), which runs east and is amply furnished with cheaper hotels, including the:
Capitol Hotel (*Tmr* 7C4) (Class C) C. Trikoupi/147 Filonos   Tel 452 4911
Directions: As above, on the right, across the street from a cinema.
A single costs 4000drs & a double 5000drs, both en suite.

Ranged along Filonos St, which is wider and cleaner than the next, parallel street of Notara, are the: *Hotel Lux* (Class E, tel 452 0354), all rooms sharing, with singles at 1200drs & doubles 1730drs; *Hotel Adonis* (Class D, tel 452 0330), the minder of which is of Far Eastern appearance, and popular with the more   impecunious backpackers, with a single costing 2000drs & a double 2600drs, both sharing; and the *Hotel Cavo* (Class C, tel 411 6134), all rooms en suite, with a single costing 2800/3100drs & doubles 3780/4300drs.

Back down on Leoforos C. Trikoupi, there are the: *Glaros Hotel* (Class C, tel 452 7887), with singles en suite costing 3015/3325drs,   doubles sharing costing 3545/3990drs & doubles en suite 4255/4700drs; *Serifos Hotel* (Class C, tel 452 5075), all rooms en suite, with a single priced at 2405drs & a double 3540drs; and the *Santorini Hotel* (Class C, tel 452 2147), wherein all rooms are en suite, singles priced at 3015/3325drs & doubles 4255/4700drs.

The next side-street off to the left of Leoforos C. Trikoupi is Notara St, on which are sited a number of hotels, all bedrooms of which have en suite bathrooms, and include the: *Hotel Atlantis* (Class C, tel 452 6871), singles costing 3500drs & doubles 4500drs; *Faros Hotel* (Class D, tel 452 6317), a single costing 2260drs & a double 3370drs; and the *Hotel Ideal* (Class C, tel 451 1727), singles charged at 3960/5200drs & doubles 5700/7200drs.

Again at right angles to Leoforos C. Trikoupi, is Kolokotroni St, on which is, amongst others, the *Aris Hotel* (Class D, tel 452 0487), a single room, sharing, costing 1780drs & en suite 2260drs, whilst a double sharing costs 2400drs & en suite 3370drs.

Hotel Diana (*Tmr* C4) (Class C) 11 Filellinon   Tel 452 5020
Directions: Towards the south of Akti Miaouli, and to the left.
    Recommended as 'quiet for a city'. A single room sharing is charged at 1175drs, a double sharing 2290drs & en suite 3235drs.

It will not go amiss to point out that a few of the accommodation opportunities here and abouts are nothing more than doss-houses, for seamen and ladies of the night. I am of the opinion that most merchant men are the salt-of-the-air, and 'pay-as-you-earn ladies' are..., but...!
    For a complete change of ambiance, and price, those wishing to spend a leisurely time at Piraeus might consider staying on the east coast of the peninsula. It always seems to be sunny thereabouts (!), but the sheer volume of traffic that courses along the narrow road is a bit of a problem. From Limin Zeas Harbour, the Esplanade snakes along the coastal strip, passing the 'Town beach', **Stalis islet** close inshore, as well as the Royal Yacht Club of Greece. On the inland side, is the:

Hotel Cavo D'Oro (*Tmr* D/E1) (Class B) 19 V. Pavlou   Tel 411 3744
Directions: As above.
    Charges for their en suite rooms are 7000/7700drs for a single & 10625/11580drs for a double.

Yet another recommendation, on 'this side of the tracks' is the:
Hotel Lilia (*Tmr* C/D3/4) (Class C) 131 Limin Zeas   Tel 417 9108
Directions: As above.
Looks good, and beside a quiet street. All bedrooms are en suite, with a single charged at 3280/4000drs & doubles 4435/5000drs.

The Eating Out Piraeus is not noted for outstanding dining places around the Grand Harbour, or the encircling terrain, despite the numerous restaurants, tavernas and cafes that line the quayside. Apart from the cafe-bars ranged along the Plateia Astigos building (*Tmr* 2A/B3/4), the main streets, avenues and Esplanade are sprinkled with fast food outfits. Some of the best value places are to found in, and about, the Makras Stoas Market Sq (*Tmr* 32B3). Returning to Plateia Astigos, a correspondent has confirmed that there is a single storey, more modern building, to the rear of that which dominates the square. The latter contains a cafe-snackbar, a waiting room and 'some of the cleanest loos in all of Greece'. Thus it is ideal for an 'on the spot, wash and brush up', before or after a ferry-boat trip. To escape these generally lacklustre offerings, there are some excellent dining establishments spaced out along the eastern coastline of the peninsula. That is the stretch bounded by Akti Moutsopoulou (*Tmr* C/D3/4) and Akti Koumoundourou (*Tmr* E1/2), encircling (respectively) the Zeas and Mounikhias Harbours. The latter is a more intimate location, with an 'off-the-main-drag', tree lined, harbour encircling Esplanade. The tables and chairs of the various awning covered patios are spread around the waterfront.

Especially recommended are:
Delligiannis (*Tmr* 20E2) 1 Akti Koundouriotou   Tel 413 2013
Directions: A very pleasant setting, in the 'pretty' part of Piraeus, up on the hill to the south-west of, and overlooking Limin Mounikhias.
    A change of ownership, a couple of years ago, might well have modified the critical acclaim, but the selection of food was excellent.

A few doors down is an Italian restaurant, the:
Taverna Kpanah
Directions: As above.
    Offers enjoyable food and service, and a fixed price menu. A very large, nicely cooked meal, for two, of an aperitif each (an ouzo or Martini), a plate of small fried fish, fried kalamares & shrimps, a Greek salad, a taramosalata, tzatziki, 1 red snapper, 1 sole fried in butter, cherries, a bottle of dry white wine, bread, coffee & ouzo, and service, cost 6000drs.

THE A TO Z OF USEFUL INFORMATION
AIRLINE OFFICE & TERMINUS (*Tmr* 8B/C3/4) The Olympic office is about half-way along Akti Miaouli, at the junction with Merarchias St. Open weekdays 0800-1900hrs & Sat 0800-1500hrs, but closed on Sun & 'idle days'.

BANKS The most impressive is the **Macedonia & Thrace** (*Tmr* 9B3), housed in a vast, imposing emporium which towers over the Akti Posidonos. Should this establishment induce a state of awe, then, in the same block, is the **Commercial Bank**, which carries out all necessary transactions. Incidentally, behind this 'Manhattan', tinted glass glitz, hides away the Market. Around the corner, south along D. Gounari St, and on the left (*Sbo*), is an **Ionion Bank** (22B3). Bordering Loudovikou Sq, the elongated plateia alongside the Metro station (*Tmr* 1A/B2/3), is a **Credit Bank** (orange in colour) that deals in Eurocheques and *Visa* transactions. A number of British banks have a presence, including **Barclays, Midland** and **National Westminster**, but they are at the international, cruise liner, south end of the waterfront.

BEACHES There is a 100m long, broad stretch of beach (*Tmr* E2/3), between Zeas and Mounikhias Harbours, opposite Stalis islet. The shore is mainly pebble, with a sandy middle and backshore. It is fine for a bathe - if the general pollution of the bay can be ignored.

BREAD SHOPS Quite widely spaced out, but one (*Tmr* 10A/B3) is conveniently situated by Loudovikou Sq. There are others: one across D. Gounari St from the *Acropole* (*Tmr* 30B3), actually a General store; one on the corner of the junction of Dimothenous St and Akti Posidonos, to the west of the Macedonia Bank (*Tmr* 9B3); yet another, only a few clothes shops further west on Akti Posidonos; and one more next door to the OTE (*Tmr* 15B2/3), on Karaoli Dimitriou St.

BUSES The two buses that circulate around the peninsula (in opposite directions) are the Nos 904 and 905. The terminus for both is on Plateia Loudovikou, beside the Metro terminus (*Tmr* 1A/B2/3), and they connect the Metro station to the Zeas Marina (*Tmr* 26E4).
No 904 proceeds to Navarinou, Tsamadou, Leoforos Iroon Polytechniou, Chatzikyriakou, Ralli, Athanasiou, Akti Themistokleous, Akti Moutsopoulou, Lampraki, Leoforos Vassileos Georgiou.
No 905 proceeds to Navarinou, Tsamadou, Leoforos Vassileos Georgiou, Lampraki, Akti Moutsopoulou, Akti Themistokleous, Athanasiou, Ralli, Chatzikyriakou, Leoforos Iroon Polytechniou.
Plasteia Astigos (*Tmr* 2A/B3/4) is the 'Bus Sq' for the Express buses to the West and East Airport terminals. There is a ticket office bordering Plateia Astigos. The 'Night Bus', No 050, for Athinas/Akadimias Sts, Athens leaves from Sotirosdios/Filonos Sts, south of Themistokleous Sq (*Tmr* 21 B/C3).
Trolley Buses
No 16 Drosopoulou (Ag Triada Cathedral, *Tmr* 16B/C3), Ag Ioannis Rentis (NE Piraeus suburb).
No 17 Skouze St, Akti Miaouli, Ag Georgios (NW Piraeus suburb).
No 20 Skylitsi(Neo Faliro), Leoforos Vas Pavlou, Akti Kountourioti, Leoforos Vas Georgiou, Akti Kondili, Drapetsona (W Piraeus suburb).

COMMERCIAL SHOPPING AREA There is a flourishing, noisy, busy Market and Market Sq (*Tmr* 32B3), in the area bounded by Makras Stoas St (behind the Macedonia Bank) and D. Gounari St. Adjacent to the Market Sq, is an excellent **Supermarket**, on the corner of Makras Stoas St, useful for the shopper who cannot be bothered to visit the various market shops and stalls. The right-hand (*Sbo*), south end of D. Gounari St is awash with provisions stores, and Odhos Tsamadou (*Tmr* 11B3) is a main shopping street. Towards the D. Gounari St end of Navarinou St, on the north side of the road, and close to the *Sparti*, is what can only be described as a **Drinks Supermarket** (*Tmr* B3). Established in 1932, the choice and prices are absolutely excellent, if not unrivalled, and the owners/staff are most helpful. For those with a container, there are a wide range of 'from the barrel' possibilities.
Prices in Piraeus are generally higher than elsewhere in Greece and shop hours are the 'standard' for large cities.

FERRY-BOATS Most ferry-boats leave from the quay, between Akti Kondili (at the north end of the Grand Harbour), via Plateia Astigos and Akti Posidonos, round to Akti Miaouli (towards the south end of the Grand Harbour). Dodecanese boats tend to depart from the quay bordered by A. Posidonos and the north end of Akti Miaouli (*Tmr* B/C3/4).

Ferry-boat timetables (Mid-season)

Day	Departure time	Ferry-boat	Ports/Islands of Call
Mon-Sat	1300hrs	Ialyssos/Kamiros	Patmos, Leros, Kalimnos, Kos, Rhodes.
Mon/Wed/ Fri	1800hrs	Rodos	Rhodes.
Wed/Fri	600hrs	Rodanthi	Paros, Santorini, Iraklion(Crete), Karpathos, Rhodes.
Tue	0900hrs	Kimolos	Siphnos, Milos, Folegandros, Sikinos, Santorini, Ag Nikolaos(Crete), Sitia (Crete), Kasos, Karpathos, Diafani (Karpathos), Chalki, Simi, Rhodes.
	1530hrs	Daliana	Paros, Santorini, Iraklion(Crete), Karpathos, Rhodes.
Thur	2030hrs	Daliana	Paros, Santorini, Iraklion(Crete), Rhodes.
Fri	1200hrs	Ag Raphael	Patmos, Leros, Kalimnos, Kos, Simi, Rhodes.
Sun	1200hrs	Ag Raphael	Patmos, Leros, Kalimnos, Kos, Rhodes.

One-way 3rd class fares Piraeus to: Chalki 4500drs; Kalimnos 3250ds; Karpathos 4250drs; Kasos 4250drs; Kastellorizo 4500drs; Kos 3850drs; Leros 3250drs; Nisiros 3850drs; Patmos 3550drs; Rhodes 4250drs; Simi 3850drs; and Tilos 3850drs.

FERRY-BOAT TICKET OFFICES Without doubt, they are 'extremely thick' on the waterfront. My favourite offices continue to be the same two, geographically not far from each other, but poles apart in presentation and style. They are:
Jannis Stoulis Travel (*Tmr* 12B3) 2 D. Gounari   Tel 417 9491
Directions: On the right (*Sbo*) of the outset of D. Gounari St.
    The owner, who has a rather disinterested air, is extremely efficient and speaks three languages, including English. Business has been good enough to allow the employment of a manager. The doors open Mon-Fri 0900-1900hrs & Sat 0900-1430hrs.
    And his fast talking, ever-smiling, 'speedy Gonzales' counterpart is now dressed in a sharp suit and occupies a carpeted, as distinct from a linoleumed, wall-to-wall stairway, alongside Akti Kalimasioti (*Tmr* 13A/B3). It has to admitted that my regard for the latter operator is entirely due to the fact that he was the man who sold me my first ever Greek island ferry-boat ticket, more years ago than I am willing to concede.
    There are 'batches' of ticket offices spaced out around the ground floor of the Plateia Astigos Building (*Tmr* 2A/B3/4), as well as a 'reader recommended' firm in the Metro station concourse (*Tmr* 1A/B2/3). Those prospects aimlessly wandering along the quayside may be accosted by an enterprising vendor of tickets who lurks, from early morning, amongst the ferry-boat stalls on Akti Posidonos. It is probably best to make enquiries about the exact location of a particular ferry's departure point, prior to paying for the tickets. It has to be admitted the vendors tend to refer to a ship's point of departure with an airy wave of the hand. When searching the quayside, do not go beyond the junction of Kondili and Kalimasioti, to the north, or the Port offices & Custom house (*Tmr* 14B/C4/5), to the south. A comparatively new facility is the Passenger terminal (*Tmr* 25B/C4), to the sea wall side of Akti Miaouli. The waiting room is up a shallow flight of steps, whilst the basement reveals evidence of an Information/Tourist police office, which, unfortunately, appears 'dead'.

LAUNDRY A **Launderette** (*Tmr* 28C4) on the 'up', or south side of Kolokotroni St, between Filelinon and C. Trikoupi Sts, at No 133.

LUGGAGE STORE This facility has an incredibly garish hallway, and is on the north corner of the Plateia Astigos building (*Tmr* 2A/B3/4).
Some ticket offices allow the purchasers of ferry-boat tickets to store their luggage - for free.

MEDICAL CARE Apart from the usual chemists, there is a 'First Aid Station' (*Tmr* 33C3/4), alongside a square bounded by Leoforos V. Konstantinou (Iroon Politechniou), Kolokotroni & Bouboulinas Sts.

METRO *See* Arrival by Metro. Purchasers of a ticket must validate it in the ticket machine - or face a fine.

NTOG Apart from the 'maybe-maybe not' office, in the basement of the Ferry-boat passenger terminal (*Tmr* 25B/C4, *See* Ferry-boat Ticket Offices), there is, or was, a somewhat inconveniently situated facility at Limin Zeas Harbour (*Tmr* D3/4). This is on the way round to the hydrofoil dock, but if and when it functions, it only does so weekdays, between 0700-1500hrs.

OTE (*Tmr* 15B2/3) The office is beside Karaoli Dimitriou St, close to the junction with Filonos St. It is open seven days a week, 24hrs a day.

PLACES & EVENTS OF INTEREST
Archaeological Museum (*Tmr* 17C/D4) Situated between Filellinon and Leoforos C. Trikoupi Sts. Well laid out, with easy to identify exhibits. Open daily 0830-1500hrs, but closed on Mondays, with entrance costing 400drs.
Ag Triada Cathedral (*Tmr* 16B/C3) The Cathedral was rebuilt in the early 1960s, having been destroyed in 1944. It has a distinctive, mosaic tile finish.
Battleship Averoff This legendary craft, dear to the Greek nation, is now located at the Paleon Faliron Marina, along the coast to the east of Piraeus. The boat and its fame perhaps, helps to illustrate the Greeks' need for tangible proof of their modern, military might. The Italian built warship was purchased in 1911. The vessel was rather out of date, at the outbreak of the First World War, but joined in sea battles against the Turks, between 1912-13, at Eli and Limnos. During the Second World War it was loaned to the Allies and carried out escort duty in the Indian Ocean, to be 'pensioned off' in 1945. The ship can be viewed Tue-Sat between 0900-1230hrs, with entrance costing 100drs. These opening hours are subject to alteration, without notice.
Ancient Theatre (*Tmr* 34C/D4) Adjacent to the Archaeological Museum, close to Limin Zeas Harbour. The remains date from the 2ndC BC.
Limin Zeas (Pasalimani) (*Tmr* D3/4) This semicircular harbour is of great antiquity, but is now lined by expensive, high-rise buildings. The modern port shelters fishing boats and caiques; provides a marina basin for the larger, modern yachts, some of them extremely expensive boats; contains a hydrofoil terminal; as well as a base for yacht charterers. Immediately to the south of the harbour is a small triangle of sand and pebble beach. In addition to the NTOG office, there is a National Bank, which transacts all exchange requirements. Excavations have shown that, in ancient times, there were several hundred boat sheds radiating out around the edge of the waterfront. These were used to house the *triremes*, the great, three-banked warships, that ruled the Aegean, centuries ago.

The Naval Museum of Greece (*Tmr* 27D/E4) Tucked into a horseshoe of land bounded by the Esplanade Akti Themistoleous and the south, outer end of Limin Zeas Harbour. On display are varied exhibits of naval history, through the ages. Open Tue-Sat 0830-1300hrs, entrance costing 100drs.

Limin Mounikhias (Tourkolimano or Mikrolimano) (*Tmr* E2). From Limin Zeas, continue north-east along the constricted, winding, coast hugging Esplanade. The main road circles about 50m above the attractive, intimate, quayside promenade that edges the semicircular, old Turkish harbour. The picturesque waterside is tree shaded and 'chattily' ringed with awning covered patios of cafe-bars, tavernas and restaurants, the latter forming a backcloth to the multi-coloured sails of the assembled yachts crowded into Limin Mounikhias. Racing yachts are believed to have slipped their moorings, for regattas in Saroniko Bay, as far back as the 4thC BC, as they do to this day.

The Hill of Kastela Overlooks Mounikhias Harbour and has a modern, open-air, marble amphitheatre, wherein theatre and dance displays are staged, more especially during the Athens Festival.

POLICE
Port (*Tmr* 3A/B3/4) Tucked away behind the Plateia Astigos building.
Tourist & Town (*Tmr* 23B/C2/3) To the north of Plateia Dimotico, in amongst various other Municipal buildings and offices.

POST OFFICE (*Tmr* 18B/C3) The main office is on the corner of Tsamadou and Filonos Sts. There is another office in the Metro (*Tmr* 1C1/2) concourse, but rather hidden by some stalls, and only open between 0730-1415hrs.

RAILWAY STATIONS *See* Arrival by Metro & Arrival by Train.
Metro (Underground) (*Tmr* 1A/B2/3).
'Steam' Station 1 (*Tmr* 1A/B2/3) The terminus for the Peloponnese, which is on the far, north side of the Metro.
'Steam' Station 2 (*Tmr* 19A/B4/5) The terminus for Northern Greece, situated on the far, west side of the Grand Harbour.

TAXIS They rank at all the major places and squares. Amongst such a 'people honest' nation, it is sad to have to warn anyone hiring a cab, to ensure they ascertain the exact fare, prior to getting in, and allowing their luggage to be shut away in the boot. You have been warned. An early morning trip to the airport costs at least 3000drs. Why not catch a bus?

TELEPHONE NUMBERS & ADDRESSES
NTOG (*Tmr* D3/4) Zeas Marina	Tel 413 5716
Port Authorities	Tel 451 1311
Taxi rank	Tel 417 8138

TOILETS There are some old-fashioned, large 'door-gap', 'squatties' in the Metro concourse (*Tmr* 1A/B2/3).

TRAVEL AGENTS & TOUR OFFICES *See* Ferry-boat Ticket Offices.

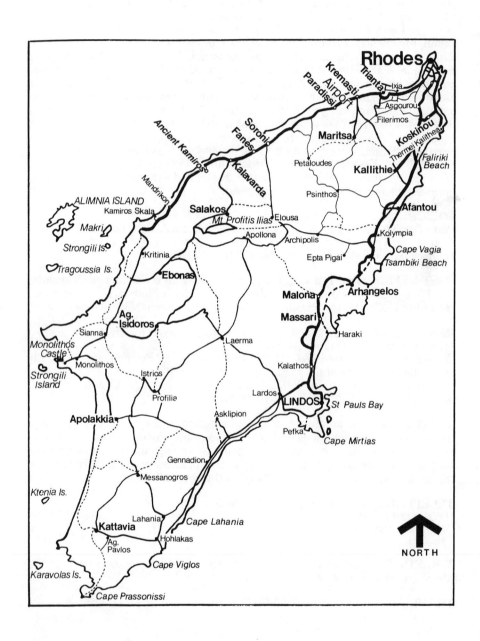

Illustration 4 Rhodes island

3 PART THREE
RHODES (Rhodos, Rodos)
Dodecanese Islands

North island **
South island ***

FIRST IMPRESSIONS Beautiful medieval old town; a package tourists' mecca - Kosta'd atmosphere; uninteresting, overcrowded coastal villages; overcrowded beaches - all people, sun-beds & umbrellas; African parrots; public toilets - some of them regularly cleaned.

SPECIALITIES Spirits & perfumes; package tourists.

LOCAL RELIGIOUS HOLIDAYS & FESTIVALS incl: 7th Jan - Feast of St John the Baptist; 23rd April - Feast of St George, Afantou; 15th June - Ag Amos, near Faliraki; 17th June - Festival at Asgourou, Koskinou & Paradissi (Paradision); 29th-30th July - Ag Soulas, Soroni; 6th-31st Aug - Dance Festivals at Ebonas, Kallithea & Maritsa; 26th Aug - Ag Fanourios, Rhodes Old Quarter; 8th Sept - Fertility Festival, Tsambika Monastery; 14th Sept - Feast, Apollona, Damatria & Malona.

VITAL STATISTICS The island, largest of the Dodecanese, is 77km from top to bottom, up to 37km wide, with an area of some 1400sqkm. Of the population of some 80,000, about 35,000 are domiciled in the capital.

HISTORY The history outlined in Chapter 1 refers mainly to Rhodes island. In the main, the other Dodecanese islands tended to mirror that of Rhodes. Where the detail and facts differ, then the dissimilarities have been recorded.

The Turks did not interfere with the basics of Greek life, during an occupation lasting some four hundred years. On the other hand, the Italians, in a tenth of the period, made themselves very unpopular, by ordering the banning of the Orthodox church and the imposition of Italian as the official language? It just didn't do a lot for their standing in the community!

GENERAL Rhodes is a green and pretty island of comparatively low mountains and relatively flat land, in nearly all the areas bordering the coastline. The richness of the architecture owes much to the Knights, some to the Turks, and a lot to the Italians, who had an insatiable desire to rebuild and reconstruct, everything.

The island is famed for roses and deer, but the latter are now limited to a few herds penned in enclosures on the slopes of Mt Profitis Ilias, and in a section of the Old Quarter moat, close to the Marine Gate.

Rhodes must vie with Corfu as the most international holiday target of all the Greek islands. The constant coming and going of aircraft is supplemented by a tidal wave of cruise liners, which daily disgorge and 'hoover' back on board 'mega-waves' of all manner of shipborne sightseers. Whereas, until even five years ago, it was possible to draw attention to some plus points, the continued tourist development has, at last, left little to praise. Working down from the northernmost, Rhodes Town capped point, the uncontrolled holiday building has continued almost unabated. Many new hotels have been built further and further from the relevant beach, and more often than not on the wrong side of the main, ribbon coastal road. There are a tremendous number of partially completed buildings, which bear every appearance of being a long way from ever being topped off. Surely the ultimate absurdity in this 'Kosta destruction' of the island's coastline and environment, must be the enormous *Rhodes Hilton*, at Ixia, which has been finished - and closed!

Most of the roads are now asphalted, even that stretch down to Monolithos Castle, although, whatever the maps detail, that between Maritsa and Psinthos remains unsurfaced.

Despite the reputation of being a duty-free port, with cheap prices, even alchohol and perfumery are not that inexpensive, being more costly than Heathrow Airport. Generally, the prices of all goods are high, if not the most inflated of any of the Greek islands.

One unalterable geographical feature are the beaches. A reader has taken me to task for not pointing out that those on the east are infinitely superior to those on the west coast. That is apart from the very first few miles of the topmost coastline. To escape the worst excesses of the tourist industry, it used to be sufficient to travel south of an imaginary line drawn from Monolithos village, in the west, to Gennadion, on the east side, but... It is to be regretted that the ubiquitous beach-buggy has put most of the island within the reach of seemingly all and sundry. To some extent, below this 'tourist line', the passage of the fun-seeking, pleasure-seeking hedonists remains transitory.

In 1992, once again, the island suffered a devastating forest fire, this one 'carbonating' much of the southern island countryside.

RHODES (Rhodos, Rodos): capital city & main port (Illus 5 & 6) Tel prefix 0241. The city is really two towns, one a large, rambling, medieval Old Quarter, which is encircled by the other, the New Town or Nea Chora. This configuration results in a rather confusing layout. The difficulties are compounded as the Old Quarter can only be entered via a number of Gates, spaced out around its periphery.

Much of the New Town reflects a Western European ambience, rather than that of a traditional island capital. For instance, the occasional department store is scattered about the inner zone, with the suburban outskirts degenerating into a high-rise sprawl.

The flourishing Old Quarter appears, at first and possibly second glance, to be a maze of incoherent, directionless narrow lanes, passages, alleys and streets which drunkenly wind their way in between a glorious admixture of dwellings, of all descriptions,   shapes and sizes. Interspersed throughout this confusion are a tangle of squares, churches, mosques and the occasional minaret, all crowded and packed inside the great walls encircling the area. The sometimes   lifeless, tomb-like street of the Inns of the Knights (Odhos Ippoton) contrasts absurdly with the crowded, constantly shifting, dawdling, scurrying and harried swarm of tourists who ebb and flow up and down Odhos Socratous. Perhaps the most unacceptable manifestation of the worldly-wise nature of the inhabitants occurs in Socratous St. The length of this pedestrian way appears to be lined with predatory, schlepping shopkeepers selling furs, as well as a full range of 'tourist-forgetabilia'. To restore a sense of balance, of great enjoyment and pleasure, it is only necessary to wander through the quieter backwaters of the medieval Old Quarter. On the east side, both New Town and the Old Quarter are edged by the waterfront. This runs from the small bluff alongside Kountouriotou Sq (*Tmr* 1D3) all the way down to Acandia Harbour (*Tmr* G6). Mandraki Harbour (*Tmr* D/E4) hosts the excursion trip boats, skippered by highly vociferous owners, some private yachts and the hydrofoil craft. A substantial mole closes off the eastern side of

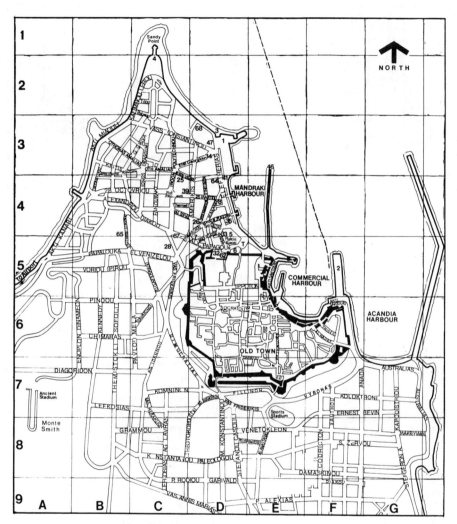

Illustration 5 Rhodes City

the harbour, on which still stand three ancient, but now redundant windmills, as does the Fort of St Nicholas (*Tmr* 46E3/4). The windmills have been refitted with sails, for the titillation of tourists. Beyond St Paul's Gate (*Tmr* E5), the quay road borders the Commercial Harbour and is edged by massive fort walls, pierced only by the Marine Gate (*Tmr* E6) and St Catherines Gate (*Tmr* F5/6). The latter harbour accommodates the smaller, more local ferry and excursion craft, commercial fishing boats and the larger private yachts.

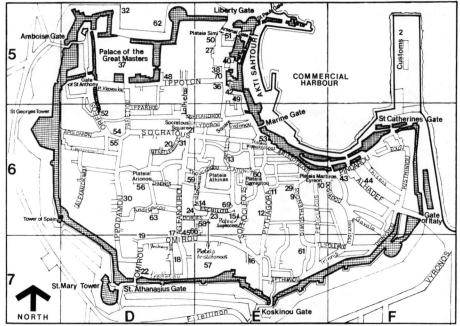

Illustration 6 Rhodes Old Quarter

The east side is dominated by the Customs Hall Quay (*Tmr* 2F5), the far side of which is Acandia Harbour (*Tmr* F/G5/6) utilised by the larger ferry-boats and cruise liners. Beyond and south of Acandia, the city degenerates into an industrial mess, or 'East End', with a large wine making factory at the centre of the activity and squalor.

The seaboard cafe society of Rhodes only fronts Mandraki Harbour. Only is an unfairly pejorative word, as the cafes line the   ground floor of an immense building. This may not be so grand as the Liston, Corfu Town, but, nonetheless, is an excellent facility. A   coffee can be spun out for an hour or more, from dawn to early the following morning, with the constant activity providing more than adequate entertainment.

North of Mandraki Harbour, Rhodes peaks out to the narrow bluff of Sandy Point, around which the most popular beach wraps itself. The   very sandy foreshore commences alongside the *Elli Club* (*Tmr* 3D3),   continues round the point of the headland, whereon is The Aquarium (*Tmr* 4C1/2), and down the west side of the point. The west shore is narrow, more pebbly, and is edged by the main road which is bordered by high-rise buildings, many of them hotels. This avenue, Akti Miaouli, is probably the busiest road on the island leading. Holiday-makers along this stretch should bear in mind that to reach the beach, the sun-beds and umbrellas, requires crossing the traffic-laden, noisy highway. Nasty!

ARRIVAL BY AIR (& BUS) This is one of the few Dodecanese international airports. In the summer months, when the package tourist flights are added into the melee, planes arrive and depart almost continuously. At night-time, the stream of aircraft flashing lights can be seen as far away as Chalki island.

The Airport is some 14km distant from the city, on the west coast road, immediately prior to the village of Paradissi (Paradision). The Olympic bus is for 'dedicated' national airline travellers only. Municipal buses to Rhodes City, stop across the main road. For the 3min walk, turn left out of the main concourse, proceed up the access slip road to the thoroughfare, across which is the bus shelter. A single fare costs 650drs and buses run every 30/45mins, between 0630-2230hrs.

At Rhodes City, buses pull in alongside the New Market (*Tmr* 5D4/5). Accommodation is rarely 'on offer' at the Bus terminals, due to the large number of arrivals, departures and general confusion. Worry not. Close by is the City Tourist office (*Tmr* 6D5), beside Plateia Rimini. Ascending the fairly steep climb of Odhos Alexandrou Papagou and, after four side-streets, to the right of a traffic light junction, is the NTOG office (*Tmr* 7C/D4/5).

Taxis rank thickly alongside the airport building, but charge more than those cabs which randomly pull-up by the bus shelter. The fare is some 1500drs, and if no definite destination is in mind, passengers should request the driver to proceed to the vicinity of the NTOG or City Tourist offices. The affluent might consider hiring a vehicle from one of the row of car rental offices, lined up within   the airport building. Other airport services and facilities available include the 'hutches' of a bank, Post Office, and OTE, in addition to the usual shops.

ARRIVAL BY FERRY The main inter-island ferry-boats berth in Acandia Harbour, against Customs House Quay (*Tmr* 2F5). The smaller ferries (such as the **FB Nissos Kalymnos**) dock in the Commercial Harbour. The direction to proceed depends whether or not visitors intend to seek accommodation in the Old Quarter. St Catherines (*Tmr* F5/6) and Marine (*Tmr* E6) Gates allow access to the Old Quarter. Otherwise, follow the Esplanade round to the area of the New Market (*Tmr* 5D4/5). Rooms are usually offered at both points.

THE ACCOMMODATION & EATING OUT

The Accommodation The prodigious number of tourists, including swarms of backpackers, places a great strain on accommodation at the height of the season. Neither the City Tourist office (*Tmr* 6D5) nor the NTOG (*Tmr* 7C/D4/5) hand out lists of accommodation, though the latter's brochure does list some hotels. On the other hand, they operate a splendid service, first establishing an enquirer's requirements and price bracket, and then telephoning round to locate and book a suitable room.

The choice rests between the New Town and the Old Quarter. Most hotels are located in the New Town, but are tour operator block booked, whilst the majority of *Rooms* are scattered about the traffic-free Old Quarter.

New Town An area rich with D and E class hotels is the truncated wedge created by the streets of Othonos Amalias and Apolloniou Rodiou (*Tmr* B/C3/4) as well as Amalias St. Hotels herein, all with en suite bathrooms, include, in alphabetical order, the: *Ambassadeur* (Class C, tel 24679) & *Aphrodite* (or *Venus*) (Class C, tel 24668), both about 6500drs for singles & 9000drs for doubles; *Atlas* (Class D, tel 24022) and *D'Or* (Class D, tel 22911), with rates about 3000drs for singles & 4000drs for doubles. The package tourist *Hotel International*, which can usually offer a bedroom, except at the height of season, has en suite doubles for 5000drs, including breakfast. The well regarded *Efrossyni* (Class D, tel 24629), has bedrooms sharing the bathrooms, with singles priced at 2000drs & doubles 3500drs.

Hotel Psaroupoula (*Tmr* B/C4) (Class E) 43 Alex. Diakou   Tel 27494
Directions: Two blocks in from the western coast road.
   A basic hotel but clean, some bedrooms sharing, others en suite, charging the going rates for the New Town. The shower water may not always be hot.

Rooms Loukourias (*Tmr* C7) 51 Komninon.
Directions: To the west & south of St Athanasius Gate.
   The accommodation comprises a double and triple-bedded room, sharing a bathroom, with endless hot water, as well as a kitchen, all extremely clean, on the top floor of a modern apartment block with a roof terrace. The double bedroom is charged up to, the not inconsiderable sum, of 5000drs per night.

Old Quarter Well endowed with acceptably priced pensions and *Rooms*. The Square of the Jewish Martyrs (*Tmr* E/F6) is a congenial lounging location, and a 'happy-hunting' ground for accommodation seekers.

To the left of this square (*Acandia Harbour behind one*), a step or three along Odhos Pericleous is:
Pension Ipapanti (*Tmr* 10E/F6) 15 Pericleos.
Directions: As above.
   A double room costs 3000drs, rising to 4000drs.

Hotel Spot (Class E) 21 Pericleous   Tel 34737
Directions: As above, and further along the street.
   All rooms share bathrooms, and double rooms are charged at 3000drs.

The next street to the west of Odhos Pericleous includes:
Pension Alekka (*Tmr* 9E6) 8 Dimosthenous.
Directions: As above, situated in a quieter area, with the roof mounted pension sign observable from the square.
A family run concern, with the accommodation on the ground floor and the family living on the first floor. This is a rickety, decaying building, the tumbledown appearance of which is not concealed by the gaily painted, pink woodwork. During the day, swallows and swifts swoop and dive around the 'country' courtyard, whilst at night the family television and energetic activities reverberate through the medium of the ceiling floorboards. The bedrooms, as well as their fixtures and fittings, accurately reflect the dilapidated external appearance! Double bedrooms share the toilet and cold water shower, for a charge of 3000/4000drs per night. The landlady is likely to omit to mention the 200drs levy, for use of the shower!

Pension Artemis Pissa 12 Dimosthenous.
Directions: Further along the same alley as *Alekka*.
Rates as for *Alekka*.

Turning left (*Plateia Eyreon behind one*) from Dimosthenous, along Odhos Deosthenou, leads to *Pension Eleni*, at No 19, and the *Pension Fantasia*, at No 21. The latter is NTOG approved, clean, spacious, and the bedrooms have en suite bathrooms.

From Plateia Eyreon, bordering the western wall from St Catherines Gate to the Gate of Italy, is Odhos Kisthiniou, beside which is:
Kava d'Oro Hotel (*Tmr* F6) 15 Kisthiniou   Tel 36980
Directions: As above.
Reader recommended, and the owner, Thanasais, meets ferry-boat arrivals. The house was originally built in the 13thC, and restored by Thanasais and his German wife. The rooms are comfortable and the breakfast excellent. It is quiet, convenient and inexpensive, a double being charged 3000drs.

Return to and proceed from Plateia Martirion Eyreon along Odhos Aristotelous to Plateia Hippokratous (*Tmr* E6). On the left (*Acandia Harbour behind one*) is paved Odhos Pythagora which climbs, not so gently, towards Koskinou Gate (*Tmr* E7) past:

Pension Athinaea (*Tmr* 11E6) (Class C) 45 Pythagora/Palea Agora Tel 23221
Directions: As above, under the curved archway that spans the lane, and along the narrow, closed-in alley.
Inexpensive, but the rooms are small and full of excess furniture, resulting in the strong impression of sleeping in a store cupboard. Although bedside lamps are fitted, there aren't any electric sockets. The shared bathroom is cramped. A single room costs 1480drs & a double 2110/2500drs.

Pension Rena (*Tmr* 12E6) 62 Pythagora   Tel 26217
Directions: Further along from the *Athinaea*, on the right.
Shares the frontage with the *Taverna Kostas*, both run by the friendly Mr Costa Hagicotsas who, in good English, enthusiastically 'encourages' both prospective diners and 'overnighters' to patronise his establishments. The simple, clean bedrooms share the bathroom. The smaller, double bedrooms cost 2000drs, the slightly larger ones, with a wardrobe, are charged 3000drs.

Lots of hot water and a washing machine, that works.

Pension Lia (Class C) 66c Pythagora   Tel 20371/26209
Directions: The next turning off to the left, beyond the *Rena*.

Dark and pungent, offering basic double bedrooms, sharing the bathrooms, at a per night price of 4000/5000drs.

Although it is possible to proceed 'cross country', it is easier to return to Hippokratous Sq, from whence Socratous St climbs, in a westward direction.

Hotel Sydney (*Tmr* 13E6) (Class E) 41 Apellou   Tel 25965
Directions: One-third of the way along Socratous St, turn left on to Apellou St, and the hotel is on the left.

A to-be-recommended establishment, run by a Frenchman and his Greek wife. The pension has a 'roof garden', or more accurately a large, flat rooftop, over which are scattered tables and chairs, and across which is stretched a washing line. Passing, late-night revellers can prove a nuisance, as the hotel is close to 'the action'. En suite double room rates are 3000/4500drs. Breakfast costs an extra 400drs.

A little further to the south, and Apellou St opens out on to the Rhodes equivalent of a wartime bomb site, or Plateia Athinas. Diagonally opposite Apellou St is Odhos Aristofanous, a narrow lane that swings left on to the small Aristofanous Sq. One possibility to be avoided, off to the right of Aristofanous St, is *Rooms Yianni*. That is unless a traveller wishes to 'luxuriate' in all the delights of a truly old-fashioned, 1950s City Pooms (*sic*). Yianni is able to offer a total gamut of the genre, an almost perfect time warp, amongst the treasures of which are: medieval, cramped conditions - inside and out; a 'Steptoe' courtyard; bed-crammed sleeping quarters; a utility room in which lurk two rather smelly toilets and a shower, in addition to a washbasin and scruffy kitchen area; a landing-based, museum worthy refrigerator, which struggles to keep the contents a degree or two beneath the ambient temperature; a landing relaxation area sporting a mattress, many years past the 'has seen better days', as well as a pile of long abandoned papers and magazines, which appear to have been tramp-discarded; and, as is entirely appropriate for an establishment of this quality, an endless litany of rules and regulations. Yianni explains often, very often, that the various ailments and general incapacity of his elderly mother makes his life one endless round of toil - which may well explain the dirty state of the place. To appreciate the awesomely dedicated approach to squalor, it is only necessary to peek beneath a bed or two! Despite the social history interest of this accommodation, Yianni has 'forced' rates down to the applicable 'pension average'!

Pension Dora (*Tmr* 14D/E6) (Class C) 37 Aristofanous   Tel 25214/24523
Directions: As above, and on the left-hand side, prior to the lane describing a sharp left-hand turn.

The garden gate opens on to a pretty, profusely flowered and be-shrubbed patio, with the entrance to the pension up the stairs. A reader has kindly pointed out that the *Dora* should only be listed in a guide for down-and-out 'doss houses'. The catalogue of criticisms was impressive, but included: wall murals framed with fluorescent orange curtains; 1960s wallpaper; a total lack of electric sockets, apart from a straggle of bare wires leading to an outside light switch; a once white, now grey washbasin with a length of hose, in place of a tap; and a shared toilet and shower, which had to be seen to be believed, and cost an extra 250drs! I have dreamt about rooms with wallpaper ...! All bedrooms share the bathroom, with a single charged 1625drs & a double 2710drs, which rates rise for the height of summer.

Aristofanous St swings round to the east, becoming Odhos Eschilou and thence to Plateia Sophocleous, which yields up the:
Hotel Teherani (*Tmr* 15E6/7) (Class E) 41B Sophocleous   Tel 27594
Directions: As above, and on the edge of the square, almost hidden   behind the large *Taverna Trata*, in an ethnic, rather noisy area.   It is not only hemmed in by a number of tavernas, but borders a small park, boasting a couple of bench seats. These are put to good use by the local winos, whilst carousing and slurping the night away.
A clean and comfortable hotel, only offering double rooms, sharing the bathroom, with prices of 2220/3045drs.

Proceeding from Plateia Sophocleous, on to Odhos Sophocleous, as if heading south towards Omirou St, and close to Sophocleous Sq is:
Niki's Rooms (*Tmr* E6/7)   Tel 25115
Directions: As above.
Niki, the friendly, honest proprietor, speaks good English, and often   vies for business, down at the ferry-boat quay. Niki offers clients a lift in his tiny, blue Nissan van. The building is pleasantly located, is set in its own courtyard, and has an agreeable suntrap of a breakfast terrace. The bedrooms occupy both the ground and first floors. Those at ground level have en suite bathrooms, and are more expensive than the upper storey alternatives, which share the bathroom, but have the compensation of cheaper rates, as well as a good view of the old town, and the castle. Sharing doubles cost 3500drs a night & en suite doubles 3900drs.

Pension Apollon (& Andrea's Bar) (*Tmr* 16E7) 28C Omirou   Tel 35064
Directions: Continuing south along Sophocleous St, the street run's   into the transverse street of Omirou St. Almost directly across from this junction is a small side-street leading to the whitewashed steps of the pension, on the left.
The rather basic accommodation is priced at 900drs per head, bedrooms sharing the bathroom, and having use of some kitchen facilities. If the very friendly and helpful landlady is not at home, callers should make themselves at home, or enquire next door, at *Andrea's Bar*, wherein are a launderette and a television set. Posted in the hall are current bus and ferry timetables.

West along Omirou St advances to the sometimes motor cycle noisy junction with Ag Fanouriou St, alongside which is the:
Hotel Paris (*Tmr* 17D6/7) (Class D) 88 Ag Fanouriou/Omirou Tel 26356
Directions: As above.
The congenial hotel has a large patio garden to one side of the building. Compared to the pension alternatives, the rates are rather expensive. Some bathroom sharing bedrooms have the proportions of a broom cupboard. Single bedrooms share a bathroom at a cost of 4000/5600drs, double rooms sharing are priced at 5600/6600drs & doubles en suite 6200/7800drs.

Pension Rooms Paris
Directions: Next door to, and owned by, the *Paris*, but there ends   any similarity. This 'doss' house has a large *Rooms* sign.
Not to be recommended, for apart from the appalling state of the

establishment, the manageress is quite possibly a 'nut-nut'. The sole bathroom, shared by the occupants of the six bedrooms, is clean. There is a communal fridge. A double room costs 2000drs.

Pension Maria Massari (*Tmr* 18D7) (Class C) 42 Irodotou   Tel 22469
Directions: From the junction of Ag Fanouriou and Omirou Sts, proceed west along Omirou. The first, narrow turning, to the left, leads beneath a massive archway, beyond which the lane opens out, with the pension on the left.
    This is a pleasant and quiet location. Maria is a friendly, matronly mama, but her husband can turn rather unpleasant, should a casual enquiry not result in a 'firm booking'. The spotless establishment is laid out on two floors, in a square around the ground floor courtyard. The simple rooms share the bathroom facilities and the showers are very hot. A double costs 3000drs.

Steve's Pension (*Tmr* 19 D6/7) 60 Omirou   Tel 24357
Directions: Situated further along Omirou St, on the right-hand side, close to the point at which the lane turns sharply left. A signboard heralds the accommodation. This is situated down a small alley, which disappears beneath a large, beautiful hibiscus tree overhanging the passage.
    Steve Kefalas is the mild, very pleasant proprietor of this friendly, lively, if somewhat dank, ancient and malodorous pension. He spent a number of years in the New World, as a floor show manager, and speaks excellent 'Canadian'. The ground floor rooms and bathrooms are haphazardly arranged throughout the building, and have the 'group user' feature of 'dormitories', allowing up to 4 people to a room (Ugh!). Beyond them is a bush and tree shaded courtyard, which makes an attractive meeting place for the polyglot and cosmopolitan clients - and mosquitoes. Steve's familiarity with their language, combined with the 'Times Sq' ambiance of the quadrangle and the provision of some multi-bedded rooms, acts as an outstanding draw to young North Americans. The windows of the somewhat shabby rooms are, in the main, without mosquito screens, a drawback as these winged marauders are a great nuisance in this area. The per head nightly charge is 1500drs.
    In addition Steve owns overflow facilities at *Rooms No 77*, just round the corner. There is a 'downstairs' bedroom. This has to be traversed, whether occupied, or not, to gain the rickety stairs, which have to be negotiated to reach the two, first floor, cell-like bedrooms. The sizeable door key of these 'cubby holes' seems rather superfluous, as neither has any glass in the large, inward facing, 'stolen light' window frames. On the other hand, the absence of window panes assists with ventilation. To further aid this, it is best to ensure that the rooftop door, approached by an even more unsafe flight of steps, is left open. The fairly squalid, shared bathroom is also on the first floor, but lacks any hot water. Adjacent is *Rooms No 65*, another 'interesting', but 'friendly' location. The bedrooms are all on the ground floor. The toilet (or what's left of it) and the shower are the other side of a small, courtyard, which has the usual clutter. The doo-hickey bathroom is rather public, with a hole in the wall for a window, and the waste water draining into the courtyard, via a hole in the floor.
    Also in this neck of the woods is *Jimy's Rooms* (*Tmr* 22D7). From *Steve's*, Omirou St angles to head south towards St Athanasius Gate. To the left, inside the Old Quarter wall, stretches Irodotou St, and *Jimy's* is on the left, facing the wall. The usual rates.

From anywhere in the surrounding area, proceeding in a northerly direction, for instance along Odhos Ag Fanouriou, spills on to Odhos Socratous, at a crossroads and tree shaded square. Turning left, facing up the steeply inclined pedestrian way, and almost immediately left again, alongside a pie, cake and bread shop, leads on to Odhos Menecleous. Incidentally, this continues on towards the fascinating Plateia Arionos, in the middle of which is a large, crippled tree, a section of its tortured trunk supported by a foreshortened Doric column! One flank of the square is bordered by the splendid, communal Turkish Baths (*Tmr* 56D6).

Pension 'Mamas' (*Tmr* 20D6) 28 Menecleous   Tel 25359
Directions: As above, situated on the right, beside a widened section of the street, prior to where it climbs up on to Plateia Arionos, and immediately prior to the Moustafa Mosque, on the left.
     Yet another friendly, lively, if rather basic pension, with not overly clean, shared, somewhat smelly bathroom facilities, boasting an ethnic courtyard, across which are the bedrooms. The shower water is hot and the rooms are acceptable, costing the to-be-expected 3000drs for a double.

Hotel Kastro (*Tmr* D6) (Class E) 14 Plateia Arionos   Tel 20446
Directions: As above, and on the right of the square, facing the Turkish Baths (*Tmr* 56D6), beyond the *Kastro Taverna*, in a fascinating, 'local colour' location. There can be quite a lot of 'coming and going'.
     A standard, simple, clean E class hotel. Only double bedrooms, those sharing costing 2710/3160drs & those en suite 3160/3615drs. To book in advance, telephone 25993. This is the number of the ground floor restaurant at which works the owner, Mr Philimonas.

The Eating Out There are no shortage of establishments, more a surfeit of poor, average and expensive choices. As always, the trick is to sort out the 'mezes from the hotdog', the acceptable from the overwhelm of pap. Rhodes is a comparatively expensive place to 'break bread', and many restaurants accept payment by credit cards! Those simply seeking liquid refreshment must be selective, as cafe-crawling can work out to be extremely costly. There are listed 'the good and the bad', with the appropriate comments. The idea is to ensure that all need not be 'gloom and dyspepsia'.
     As a starting-off location, probably there is no better than the 'Old Quarter-central' Plateia Socratous, about half-way up, or down, Socratous St, depending from whence you set out. To the left (*Facing east*), down the slope of the thoroughfare, which battles through massed fur shops, and on the right of the junction with Lathetos St, is an inviting looking, tree shaded *Cafe* (*Tmr* 21D/E5/6). Beneath the spreading branches are spaced out a huge number of white painted metal chairs and tables. Unfortunately, not only is it very touristy, but the prices border on the extortionate. The speciality is a non-alcoholic 'fruit cocktail', costing in excess of 1600drs. Yes, 1600drs... An ouzo works out at a less breathtaking 850drs (only just less...). The inordinately high prices results in a constant turnover of customers, more especially those lucky enough to grasp what is going on, prior to ordering.
     In strict contrast, two or three buildings along Odhos Lathetos is a small *Kafeneion*, on the same side as the latter cafe. This is an inexpensive, good quality, traditional Greek style kafeneion, mainly frequented by locals, where, for instance, a Nes meh ghala & can of soda costs 180drs. There's better! Returning to the Socratous Sq crossroads, to the right, at the junction with

Menecleous St, is the *Express Pastry shop* (*Tmr* 31D6). An excellent choice for a 'take-away' breakfast, selling freshly made pies and croissants, at reasonable prices. There are other Socratous St opportunities, but none to compare, thus the *Express* is very popular with locals, and tourists alike.

A few metres down Odhos Socratous and on the left is a traditional, men only *Kafeneion*, at No 76. It is attractive enough to feature on some of the more artistic of the city postcards, and is a bastion of the 'village' elders, thus few, if any, tourists enter its dark and mysterious world. Descending Socratous St, in an easterly direction, and on the left, is a souvlaki stall *Fast Food*, close to the junction with Odhos Apellou. Also to the left is a shaded Square (*Tmr* E6), formed by the junction of Apellou and Evdimou Sts, whereon are two cheek by jowl, dirty and expensive tavernas, notable for rude and slow service, despite much schlepping at the outset. They practice a form of chicanery in which a waiter maintains that they have 'run-out' of this, or that, inexpensive item, in order to be able to offer a very much more expensive alternative. Mmmh!

The Plateia Hippokratous (*Tmr* E6) cafe-restaurants are expensive, as are those around Plateia Martiron Eyreon (*Tmr* E/F6). Of the latter square's prospects, probably the best of the bunch is the *International Cafe-bar*. An advantage of a Plateia Martiron Eyreon location is the opportunity to establish a vantage point from which to watch the antics of the cruise liner clients. Some of them, when on their 'run ashore', wander up to the square, in order to hire a scooter from one of the firms hereabouts. Without doubt, one of the to-be-avoided spots is the *Cafe bar Zorba*, at the far side of the plateia from the fountain. The perfunctory service is supplemented by a 'greasy' menu. The house speciality is a fat-swimming omelette & chips. A plate of 'special', dry bread, with a watery Nes meh ghala, cost about 950drs per head.

One location, at which to have a coffee, a snack or sandwich, and watch the hurly-burly of commercial life, is 'without' or within the very large, many sided New Market (*Tmr* 5D4/5). Inside the big, inner courtyard are a number of workaday, greasy spoon, fast food snackbars, cafes and kafeneions, all squeezed in amongst the stalls, shops and the fish market. Unfortunately the quality tends to be poor and the prices high. Despite these more than apparent shortcomings, the location remains tourist-popular. A greasy English breakfast, at one of the cramped cafes, comprising a plate of fried egg, a spoonful of cold tinned beans & 2 tomato slices, a small roll, some butter & jam, with tea, cost 800drs. Not an enjoyable experience, but there you go. To enjoy a superior coffee, and if feeling very 'flush', wander around to the arcaded exterior of the building, where it borders the Mandraki Harbour Esplanade. Here a row of expensive and trendy cafe-bars and restaurants, table by table, are open from morning to early the next morning, serving a full menu range, as well as truly enormous ice-creams. A Nescafe costs 280drs, a tea 240drs, a slice of milopita 750drs, with the long drinks and cocktails proving very pricey. In the evenings, the tables are more than likely to be monopolised by Scandinavian package tourists, who probably consider the charges trifling, compared to the cost of similar goodies, back at home.

Despite the shortage of reasonable priced drinking and eating places, those that receive the *GROC's Stamp of Approval* really do make up for their paucity. Small in number they may be, but my goodness one or three of them are really excellent! I hope readers agree. One of the few is the:

Taverna Kostas (*Tmr* 12E6).
Directions: See *Pension Rena*, The Accommodation.

Kostas is very friendly, the menu is good value, thus the establishment remains extremely 'independent tourist' popular.

Pandesia Restaurant (*Tmr* 23D/E6/7) Aristofanous Sq.
Directions: Located to one side of the plateia, and approached from either Ag Fanouriou or Sophocleous Sts. A sign fastened to the wall, facing the square, proclaims *Souvlaki Pandesia*.

Not always open until the end of May, but probably the best value 'meal in town', if not the island, even on their off-nights. The *Pandesia* is squeaky clean, but prospective clients must not be put-off by the entrance mounted photographs, depicting the various dishes, a usual pointer to an establishment being a tourist trap. Nothing could be further from the truth. The patron, George, is a wild-eyed, high cheek-boned, moustachioed gentleman, who gets increasingly bothered as the split-level patio of his taverna fills with clients. The friendly, initially efficient service and George's English become more and more chaotic, as the evening wears on. This is a family concern with the women, dressed in traditional costume, working in the kitchen, tucked away a door or two along the narrow side-street, and the children helping to serve at the tables. The dishes are tasty and traditionally Greek. On occasions these are out-of-the-ordinary, and might include grilled piperies (green peppers), fried melitzanes (aubergines), or the house speciality of stuffed chicken, which has to be ordered in advance. Other offerings might be chicken in the pot, or stifado, and retsina is served. A meal for two of skordalia (garlic sauce), 1 baked green peppers, 1 moussaka in a clay bowl, 1 fried zucchini, 1 plate of stuffed tomatoes & peppers, excellent village bread, 2 Heineken beers, 1 ouzo & service, cost 2495drs - plus 2 ouzos, on the house. A diner, for two, of 2 special omelettes, 2 plates of chips, a Greek salad, 1 tzatziki, 4 bottles of Amstel (200drs each), bread & service, cost 2790drs.

Just around the corner, on the elbow of Eschilou St is the:
Spilia Taverna (*Tmr* 24D/E6) 24 Eschilou.
Directions: As above.

Last year it was closed each time we chose to call, and there were conflicting reports. These varied from " ...he opens when he feels like it", to " ...all the family were killed in a car crash". Bearing in mind that this is a late night eatery, and assuming the doors do open... At first sight this appears to be an unremarkable little place, but diners should hope their luck is in, and the music starts. The patron's neat wife is a good chef(ess), preparing most enjoyable, freshly cooked dishes. If 'Paganini' turns up it will most likely become a very lively evening, with 'your actual dancing in the streets'! When the bespectacled virtuoso plays the violin and sings, the patron reaches for his accordion. The action really swings if their bouzouki playing friend arrives, for the trio may well perform, right through the night. It is best to 'bag' a table on the tiny patio, just across the narrow lane from the taverna building, before the action gets underway, at about 2200hrs. After this, patrons flood-in and tables and chairs fill the street. The menu is individually cooked, and no one night is any particular dish available, although kalamares are a house speciality, and are they good? A Greek salad, a plate of beans, two large plates of kalamares, two bottles of retsina and bread costs about 2000drs.

Sea Star Taverna (*Tmr* 69E6) Sophocleous Sq.
Directions: Opposite the *Teherani*, on the corner of the lane, Odhos Eschilou.

The taverna opens lunchtimes, as well as evenings, and is popular with both locals and tourists 'put in the know'. The house speciality is fish 'grilled while you wait', seated outside. The wizened, tyrannical old patron, Mr Kiriako, resembles a weather beaten fisherman, and runs a tight ship, priding himself on his fish. He speaks elementary English, French and German, and good Italian, but at first might well appear rather brusque. With the energetic help of his friendly assistant Francesca, the service is quick. Naturally fish is that much more expensive, but a simple meal, for one, of Greek salad, octopus, bread & a bottle of retsina, costs 1350drs.

Archangelos Cafe-bar Restaurant (*Tmr* 66D/E6/7) Aristofanous Sq.
Directions: Just to the left of the junction of Omirou St with Plateia Aristofanous, in a lovely, quiet, very large tree shaded setting, alongside a mosque dominated square.

There can be no doubt that the owner is more than a little laid back and taciturn in respect of prospects. When John Cleese tires of running *Fawlty Towers*, or making training films, perhaps the casting directors should consider this gentleman for the role. His uncompromising approach involves ignoring customers - entirely. There is a rumour that he can be so minded as to hand out little gifts of appreciation - such as wine glasses. When business is at a low ebb, he might well be found catching up on his 'shut-eye', slumped face down on one or other of the tables. Those that persevere will find the huge choice of drinks and food 'Rhodes reasonably' priced. The *Archangelos* is both a breakfast and dinner establishment. A morning's toast, butter & tea costs 300drs, whilst an Amstel beer is 200drs and a Heineken 250drs. A meal for two of olives, tzatziki, giant beans, aubergines in tomato sauce, tomato/cucumber salad, an expensive imported beer, 1 litre of Ilios wine & bread, cost 2900drs. The service is rapid, and the food piping hot, the latter probably due to the microwave oven, lurking in the 'hole in the wall' kitchen.

Restaurant Oasis (*Tmr* 66D/E6/7) Aristofanous Sq.
Directions: As above.

Due to the slick, pre-dinner sales technique, and obsequious post-prandial solicitations of the owner, the restaurant enjoys success, more especially with German and Scandinavian tourists. Taped bouzouki music echoes over the tables and chairs, whilst the jolly, smiling proprietor entertains the guests, giving every appearance of being a 'real taverna find' (in the heart of Rhodes!). What we have here is 'your actual' tourist trap, serving small portions of tasteless and not inexpensive food. The 'packaging' ensures a 'regular' tourist clientele, happy to photograph and video each other, eating 'typical' Greek dishes. Oh goody!

Both Omirou and Ag Fanouriou Sts spawn a number of night-time tavernas that are invisible during the day, being nothing more than caverns or cellars. Their offerings may well be reasonable in quality and price.

Mandraki Harbour hosts a very fashionable, floating restaurant, where impossibly high prices purchase nicely presented, but small portions, from an extensive menu. To further spoil the fun, the meals are served in strict European order, and on hot plates! Not surprisingly, credit cards are accepted.

THE A TO Z OF USEFUL INFORMATION
AIRLINE OFFICE (*Tmr* 25C/D3/4). The Olympic premises are on the left of

Odhos Ierou Lochou, beyond the *Plaza Hotel*. Open Mon-Fri 0900-1600hrs. there is often only one desk 'manned'. In 1992, the Olympic coach link had been discontinued, but there is a more than adequate bus service (*See* Buses). There are clean toilets down the stairs, as well as a cold drinking water fountain.

Aircraft timetable (Mid-season)
Rhodes to Athens
Daily	0735(except Wed/Sat), 1120, 2315hrs
Wed	2230hrs.
Sat	1935hrs.

Return
Daily	0600 (except Wed/Sat), 0945, 1800, 2120hrs.
Wed/Sat	1715hrs.

One-way fare 17800drs; duration 55mins.
Rhodes to Santorini
Mon/Wed/Thur/Sat	2115hrs.

Return
Mon/Wed/Thur/Sat	1950hrs.

One-way fare 12300drs; duration 1hr.
Rhodes to Thessaloniki
Thur/Sun	2120hrs

Return
Thur/Sun	2040hrs

One-way fare 23500drs; duration 1hr 10mins
Rhodes to Iraklion (Crete)
Daily	2205hrs (not Tue/Thur)

Return
Daily	2045hrs (not Tue/Thur)

One-way fare 13200drs; duration 40mins.
Rhodes to Karpathos
Daily	1530, 1740hrs.
Daily	1030, 1240hrs (not Tue/Thur/Sat)
Tue/Thur/Sat	0945hrs.

Return
Daily	1630, 1840hrs.
Daily	1130hrs. (not Tue/Thur/Sat)
Tue/Thur/Sat	0835, 1045hrs.

One-way fare 8200drs; duration 40mins.
Rhodes to Kasos
Daily	1240hrs. (not Tue/Thur/Sat)
Tue/Thur/Sat	0700hrs.

Return
Daily	1415hrs. (not Tue/Thur/Sat)
Tue/Thur/Sat	0800hrs.

One-way fare 8200drs; duration 40mins.
Rhodes to Kastellorizo
Mon/Wed/Fri/Sun	0810hrs.

Return
Mon/Wed/Fri/Sun	0915hrs.

One-way fare 7900drs; duration 45mins.
Rhodes to Kos
Tue/Thur/Sat	1155hrs.

Return
Tue/Thur/Sat	1245hrs.

One-way fare 7500drs; duration 30mins.

Aircraft timetable (Mid-season) (Contd)
Rhodes to Mykonos
Wed/Fri/Sat   2145hrs.
Return
Wed/Fri/Sun   2020hrs.
One-way fare 12500drs; duration 50mins.
Rhodes to Sitia (Crete)
See Karpathos & Kassos.
Rhodes to Syros
Mon   1750hrs.
Return
Mon   1625hrs.
One-way fare 15600drs; duration 55mins.

BANKS In the Old Quarter are the: **National Bank** (*Tmr* 70E5), at the outset of Ippoton St, open extended hours Mon-Thur 0800-1400 & 1800-2000hrs, Fri 0800-1330 & 1800-2000hrs & Sat 1000-1200hrs; **Ionian & Popular** (*Tmr* 27E5); and the **Commercial Bank** (*Tmr* 38E5).
In the New Town are the: **National Bank** (*Tmr* 26C/D4), at the apex of Vassilisis Sofias and Ethnarchou Sts, offering extended opening times - Mon-Thur 0800-1400 & 1430-2030hrs, Fri 0800-1330 & 1430-2000hrs, Sat 0800-1400hrs & Sun 0800-1200hrs, and changes Eurocheques; **Bank of Greece** (*Tmr* 35D4); several Banks behind the New Market; and a **Barclay's Bank** (*Tmr* C/D3) in V. Konstantinou St.

BEACHES
Beach 1: Starting at the *Elli Club* (*Tmr* 3D3), a splendid but extremely crowded and wind exposed beach, which wraps its way round Sandy Point headland. The sand is intermixed with very fine, grey pebbles, but it is necessary to keep an eye open for tar globules. There are beach showers and a diving board in the sea, as well as sun-beds and umbrellas (350drs per person). The *Elli Club* buildings include a restaurant, a small first-aid office and very clean 'No Pay' toilets, tucked into the corner. Unfortunately these latter, excellent facilities run out of toilet paper by midday, so 'clients' should carry their own, or 'borrow' paper napkins from the adjoining taverna. A well organised *Municipal Cantina* sells reasonably priced hot food, rolls, fruit, soft drinks and beer.
Beaches 2 & 3: Two other small, more often than not filthy, if sandy, beaches are located, one each, in the Commercial and Acandia Harbours. The Commercial Harbour beach is signposted 'Swimming Prohibited' and there is the possibility of a sewer outfall here. The beach at the bottom of Acandia Harbour, despite 'sporting' another swimming prohibited sign, has a beach shower and toilets.

BICYCLE, SCOOTER & CAR HIRE There are countless firms, but charges are expensive. Despite all the major car hire firms being present, including **Avis & Hertz**, in addition to many others, such as **RETCA** at 26 Dodekannision St (*Tmr* D4), cars often have to be booked ahead. Apart from wearing out sandal leather, it really does pay to 'shop around'. For instance, **Traffic** (*Tmr* G7), beside Australias St, asks 12500drs per day for a Fiat Panda, whilst **Smile**, alongside *Pension Ipapanti* (*Tmr* 10E/F6), beside Plateia Martiron Eyreon, rents the same make for some 8000drs. Hirers must remember to allow for the usually enormous daily damage deposit, varying between 10000-20000drs, which has to be left in the 'safe' hands of the rental firm! To cope with this latter necessity, it is   more often than not only practical to complete the formalities by paying with a credit card.

New Town bike and scooter hire outfits include: one alongside the aforementioned 1930s *Thermai Hotel* (*Tmr* 28C5), to one side of a grandiose gate structure; and another on Odhos Alexandrou Diakou (*Tmr*   B/C4). Scooter hire in the Old Quarter is centred on the Dimosthenous St side of the Square of the Jewish Martyrs (*Tmr* E/F6). The firm alongside the *International Cafe-bar*, run by a large, smiling old rogue, is up to 1500drs cheaper (for an automatic Suzuki/Yamaha 50cc moped) than his neater rival - I Mandar Scooters (*Tmr* 29E6) at 2 Dimosthenous St, Tel 30665. The latter outfit operates from a waste-lot, and charge 3000/3500drs for 2 seater scooters, some dating back to my last visit, others quite new. Generally in good condition, the inventory includes a spare wheel, as well as a   secure locker. The charges drop for punters prepared to negotiate a week's hire.

BOOKSELLERS There isn't a 'dedicated' bookshop. In the Old Quarter are one or two mixed goods shops, selling inexpensive, English language 'cheapos'. A wide variety of overseas newspapers and magazines are sold from two kiosk newsagents, which face each other across the wide entrance to the inner courtyard of the New Market (*Tmr* 5D4/5), on the harbour side of the building. The Library Academy (*Tmr* C3/4), 7 Dragoumi St, houses a vast selection of English language books, which cover such subjects as Ancient Greece, Byzantine studies, Rhodes, and the Knights, in addition to novels. Entrance is free, weekdays, between 1800-2100hrs.

BREAD SHOPS There is a Bread shop (*Tmr* D4/5) opposite the West terminal Bus stop (*Tmr* 33D4/5). Another is hidden away on Palama St, one up and west from Odhos Averoff, which circles the New Market (*Tmr* 5D4/5). There is no need to go round on to Odhos Alexandrou Papagou, as a little side-street leads to a flight of steps which emerge alongside the shop. An Old Quarter Baker (*Tmr* E6) is situated beside Pythagora St, close to the junction with Plateia Hippokratous. Other Bakers include: one at No 41 Ippodamou (*Tmr* 30D6); and *Express* (*Tmr* 31D6), situated on the junction of Menecleous and Socratous Sts, which is also a cake, pastry and pie shop.

BUSES The bus service is excellent, the depots are centrally located   and information is easy to come by, from the various tourist offices.

Bus timetable & Terminals
A. The East (side of the island) Terminal (KTEL) (*Tmr* 32D5). Located beside Odhos Alexandrou Papagou, alongside the park in which the Son   et Lumiere takes place.
NB All fares are quoted per person, one-way (unless otherwise stated)   & Sunday/holiday schedules are usually subject to variation.

Rhodes City to Lindos
Daily   0830, 0900, 0930, 1000, 1030, 1100, 1130, 1300, 1500, 1615hrs
Return journey
Daily   0700, 0800, 0940, 1000, 1030, 1045, 1130, 1145, 1215, 1300, 1430,
             1500, 1630, 1630, 1800hrs
One-way fare 650drs
Rhodes City to Arhangelos via Afantou
Daily   0700, 0900, 1000, 1130, 1300, 1430, 1500, 1630, 1700, 1800, 1930,
             2100hrs

Return journey
Daily   0600, 0615, 0630, 0700, 0730, 0820, 1000, 1100, 1145, 1215, 1245,
           1330, 1530, 1700, 1830hrs
One-way fare 370drs
Rhodes City to Tsambika Beach
Daily   0900hrs
Return journey
Daily   1530hrs
One-way fare 400drs
Rhodes City to Kolympia
Daily   0900, 1400, 1630, 1745, 1930, 2100hrs
Return journey
Daily   0630, 0800, 0945, 1000, 1130, 1330, 1445, 1715, 1835hrs
One-way fare 350drs.
Rhodes City to Faliraki Beach
Daily   0600, 0700, 0800, 0900, 0930, 1000, 1030, 1100, 1130, 1200, 1300,
           1400, 1430, 1500, 1530, 1600, 1630, 1700, 1730, 1800, 1900, 2000,
           2100, 2200hrs.
Return journey
Daily   0630, 0730, 0830, 0930, 1000, 1030, 1100, 1130, 1200, 1230, 1330,
           1430, 1500, 1530, 1600, 1630, 1700, 1730, 1800, 1830, 1930, 2030,
           2115hrs.
One-way fare 240drs
Rhodes City to Psinthos via Kallithie
Daily   0600, 1530hrs
Return journey
Daily   0645, 1610hrs
One-way fare 280drs
Rhodes City to Laerma via Malona, Massari, Kalathos, Pilon, Lardos
Daily   1500hrs
Return journey
Daily   0700, 0715hrs
One-way fare 800drs
Rhodes City to Kattavia via Malona, Massari, Kalathos, Lardos, Asklipiion, Lahania
Tue/Thur   1500hrs
  & Sat
Return journey
Tue/Thur   0700hrs.
  & Sat
One-way fare 1050drs.

B. The West (side of the island) Terminal (Roda) (*Tmr* 33D4/5). On Averoff
St, alongside the west side of the New Market
Rhodes City to the *Hotel Calypso* via Kallithie.*
Daily   0650, 0745, 0830 & every ½hr until 2300hrs.
Return journey
Daily   0715, 0815, 0900 & every ½hr until 2300hrs.
One-way fare 190drs.
Rhodes City to Koskinou*
Daily   0600, 0640, 0720, 0930, 1210, 1340, 1430, 1510, 1600, 1710, 1830,
           2010, 2110hrs
Return journey
Daily   0620, 0705, 0745, 0955, 1235, 1405, 1455, 1535, 1625, 1735, 1855,
           2035, 2130hrs
One-way fare 190drs
**I realise that these destinations are on the East side, but we are in Greece!*

Rhodes City to Paradissi(Airport) via Trianta, Kremasti
Daily   0650, 0730, 0845, 1000, 1410, 1600, 1800, 2000, 2110, 2300hrs
Return journey

Daily   0725, 0805, 0920, 1035, 1445, 1635, 1835, 2035, 2145, 2335hrs
One-way fare 200drs
Rhodes City to Ancient Kamiros
Daily   0910, 1200, 1830hrs (Note Ancient Kamiros is closed Mondays).
Return journey
Daily   1010, 1305, 1700, 1935hrs
One-way fare 600drs
Rhodes City to Petaloudes (Valley of the Butterflies)
Daily   0900, 1100hrs
Return journey
Daily   1150, 1430hrs
One-way fare 600drs
Rhodes to Ebonas
Daily   1315, 1440hrs
Daily   0600hrs
One-way fare 750drs
Rhodes City to Monolithos via Kamiros Skala
Sunday   1315hrs
Return journey
Sunday   0615hrs
One-way fare 900drs
Rhodes City to Kalavarda via Theologos
Daily   0930*, 1710*, 2045, 2200*hrs
Return journey
Daily   0545, 1010*, 1750*, 2240*hrs
One-way fare 240/340drs.
* Only to & from Theologos.
Rhodes City to Kremasti
Daily   0930, 1030, 1100, 1200, 1250, 1410, 1620, 1800, 1930, 2020hrs
Return journey
Daily   0955, 1055, 1125, 1225, 1315, 1435, 1645, 1825, 1955, 2045hrs
One-way fare 200drs.

Rhodes City Buses
From the New Market. Fare: 105drs.

No 1 Mitropoleos	Daily	0700-2030hrs, every 45mins.
No 2 Analipsi.	Daily	0615-2110hrs, every hour.
No 3 Rodini Park	Daily	0600-2110hrs, every 45mins.
No 4 St Dimitrios	Daily	0645-1405hrs, every 40mins.
No 5 St John	Daily	0550-1950hrs, every 40mins.
No 6 Mengavli	Daily	0530-2230hrs, every hour.

CAMPING *See* Faliraki & Lardos, Route One.

CINEMAS Up to six in the Nea Chora (New Town) including the: **Rodon**, to the rear of the National Theatre (*Tmr* 34D3); the **Esperia** (*Tmr* D4), on 25 Martiou; the **Metropol** (*Tmr* D/E7/8), beside variously Vyronas, Vass Friderikis, Dimocratias and the junction with Stefanou Casouli; and the **Titania** (*Tmr* F/G7), on Colokotroni St, east of the Stadium. The usual mix of Greek and foreign films, accompanied by Greek subtitles, with entrance costing 600/800drs for older films, and 900drs for new releases.

CITY TOURIST OFFICE *See* Municipal Tourist office.

COMMERCIAL SHOPPING AREA The Old Quarter appears to market almost all of the world's output of furs, an effort which is concentrated beside Socratous, Polydorou and Aghisandrou Sts (*Tmr* D/E6). These three streets and Odhos Orfeos (*Tmr* D5/6) also house a multitude of dress and souvenir shops. Additionally, the Old Quarter is well provided with shops and stores of every description, shape and size.

The major attraction must be the **New Market**, or **Nea Agora** (*Tmr* 5D4/5). In and around this shopping magnet, can be purchased almost all and every requirement. Entry to the inner courtyard is through various alleyways that pierce the facade of the building. A number of public lavatories are accessible from the courtyard. The main attraction of the many sided, white building is the Fish Market. This takes place to one side of a tree shaded internal courtyard, on a raised rotunda, beneath a pagoda-like temple roof, and wherein are some very clean toilets. All around and also crammed within the large area, are fruit and vegetable stalls, mini-stores, kafeneions, fast food cafeterias, souvlaki & pitta counters, and a sprinkling of tatty souvenir shops. The shops that occupy the arcaded, columned front facing Mandraki Harbour are, in the main, cafes and cake shops. Around the remaining sides of the external periphery of the building are gift, liquor, grocery and gift shops, as well as perfumeries, boutiques and a number of small supermarkets.

In the Nea Chora, or New Town, there are some smart departmental type stores (*Tmr* D4) centred on the streets of V. Sofias, Gallias and E. Makariou. An excellent souvenir shop is beside Vassileos Konstantinou Ave (*Tmr* C/D3), across the thoroughfare from a restored, Italian period hotel. The proprietor sells superb, inexpensive, imitation bronze pottery, as well as facsimile faces of Greek gods, urns, pots and jugs. The present owner claims his father spent forty years perfecting the process. Oh, yes!

CONSULATES *See* Embassies, ...

DISCOS To discourage the tourist excesses, and in line with the ruling Conservative party's efforts to restore family and national pride, all the Old Quarter discos have been closed. Despite this, a few 'red light district' music bars stay open, most of the night. There remains no shortage of New Town establishments. A number are based behind the Post Office (*Tmr* 64D3/4). Others are centred on and around Akadimias Sq (also known as Vass Georgiou A Sq - *Tmr* C4), as well as Iroon Politechniou, and nearby Alexandrou Diakou St.

EMBASSIES, CONSULATES & VICE CONSULS Usually these luminaries are only available for business, Mon-Fri, during the morning.

British: 23, 25th Martiou St	Tel 27247
Turkey: 10 Iroon Polytechniou	Tel 23362
USA: c/o Voice of America, Sgoura St.	Tel 24731

FERRY-BOATS & HYDROFOILS Many a greater intellect than my own has foundered on the uncertainties of Greek timetables. The summer schedules that follow are subject to all sorts of variations, but (hopefully) give an indication of the excellent coverage. The two Tourist offices (*Tmr* 6D5 & 7C/D4/5) are extremely helpful in this respect, as they are in most others. No attempt should be made to cross-reference one island's listings with another. Why? Because I have ceased to attempt to square the circle - that's why! Any enquiries made, even within the space of one week, will be enough to result in an 'all change'. The listings are maintained in order to give travellers a start, a foundation from and on which new information can be built-up.

Ferry-boat timetable (Mid-season)

Day	Departure time	Ferry-boat	Ports/Islands of Call
Mon	1000hrs	Alkeos	Kos, Kalimnos, Leros, Patmos, Vathi(Samos), Chios, Mitilini (Lesbos), Limnos, Kavala(M).
	1500hrs	Nissos Kalymnos	Kastellorizo.
Tue	1000hrs	Nissos Kalymnos	Simi, Tilos, Nisiros, Kos, Kalimnos.
	1200hrs	Kamiros/Ialyssos	Kos, Kalimnos, Leros, Patmos, Piraeus.
	1300hrs	Ionian Sun	Kos, Kalimnos, Astipalaia, Mykonos, Andros, Rafina (M).
	1300hrs	Sea Harmony	Limassol (Cyprus), Haifa(Israel).
	1800hrs	Symi 1	Simi.
	1800hrs	Rodos Express	Piraeus (in 14hrs).
Wed	1200hrs	Kamirios/Ialysos	Kos, Kalimnos, Leros, Patmos, Piraeus.
	1600hrs	Kimolos	Chalki, Diafani(Karpathos), Karpathos, Kasos, Sitia(Crete), Ag Nikolaos(Crete), Santorini, Sikinos, Folegandros, Milos, Siphnos, Piraeus.
	1600hrs	Daliana	Karpathos, Iraklion(Crete), Santorini, Paros, Piraeus.
	1800hrs	Symi I	Simi.
Thur	1100hrs	Alkeos	Kos, Kalimnos, Leros, Patmos, Piraeus.
	1200hrs	Kamiros/Ialysos	Kos, Kalimnos, Leros, Patmos, Piraeus.
	1300hrs	Ionian Sun	Tilos, Nisiros, Mykonos, Tinos, Andros, Rafina(M).
	1500hrs	Victory	Larnaca(Cyprus), Lebanon.
	1500hrs	Rodanthi	Iraklion(Crete), Santorini, Piraeus.
	1800hrs	Rodos Express	Piraeus (in 14hrs).
Fri	1200hrs	Kamiros/Ialysos	Kos, Kalimnos, Leros, Patmos, Piraeus.
	1500hrs	Nissos Kalymnos	Kastellorizo.
	1600hrs	Silver Paloma	Limassol(Cyprus), Haifa(Israel).
	1600hrs	Golden Vergina	Limassol(Cyprus), Haifal(Israel).
	2100hrs	Daliana	Iraklion(Crete), Santorini, Paros, Piraeus.
Sat	1000hrs	Nissos Kalymnos	Simi, Tilos, Nisiros, Kos, Kalimnos.
	1100hrs	Alkeos	Simi, Kos, Kalimnos, Leros, Patmos, Piraeus.
	1200hrs	Kamiros/Ialyssos	Kos, Kalimnos, Leros, Patmos, Piraeus.
	1300hrs	Ionian Sun	Kos, Mykonos, Tinos, Andros, Rafina(M).
	1800hrs	Rodos Express	Piraeus (in 14hrs).
	1800hrs	Symi 1	Simi.
	2000hrs	Rodanthi	Karpathos, Iraklion(Crete), Santorini, Paros, Piraeus.
Sun	1200hrs	Kamiros/Ialyssos	Kos, Kalimnos, Leros, Patmos, Piraeus.

Ferry-boat sailing durations:

Rhodes to		Rhodes to	
Astipalaia	10½hrs	Simi	2hrs
Chalki	2½hrs	Tilos	4½hrs
Kastellorizo	7hrs	Nisiros	7hrs
Kos	4½-9½hrs	Kalimnos	7-11hrs
Karpathos	7¼hrs	Leros	11hrs
Diafani	5½hrs	Patmos	15hrs
Kasos	9¼hrs	Angathonisi	17¾hrs
Piraeus	circa 18hrs	Arki	16¼hrs
Lipsos	13hrs		

See individual island details for further details of ferry-boats.

In addition to the scheduled ferry-boats, there are a number of comparatively expensive excursion & trip boats running regular services:

Day	Vessel	Depart	Return	Destination	Fare
Daily	Excursion Boat	0900hrs	1800hrs	Simi.	3000drs return.

Hydrofoil timetable (Mid-season)
Oh, dear God! If divining the enigma of the ferry-boat schedules is considered to require the patience of Job, the mind of Einstein and the memory storage of a mainframe computer, to unravel the riddle of the hydrofoils needs more of each! Even the owners, Ilio Lines, appear to have doubts about the operation of their fast, if expensive means of winging across the Aegean seas.

Daily 1800, 2000hrs Kos, Kalimnos
One-way fare Rhodes to Kos 7200drs

FERRY-BOAT & HYDROFOIL TICKET OFFICES

FB Rodos/Kamiros/Ialyssos	DANE (*Tmr* C/D4) 95 Amerikis St	Tel 30930
FB Paloma/Alkeos	Red Sea (*Tmr* D4/5) 13 Theodoraki St	Tel 27721
FB Daliana/Rodanthi	Kydon (*Tmr* D4) E. Dodekanision St	Tel 23000
N. Kalymnos.		
FB Ionian Sun	Skevos (*Tmr* C/D4) 111 Amerikis St	Tel 22461
FB Golden Vergina	Kouros (*Tmr* D4/5) 34 Karpathou (Haile Selassie) St	
		Tel 24377

HAIRDRESSERS There are a number in the New Town, amongst which is the **The British Salon**, behind Barclay's Bank (*Tmr* C/D3), on Vass Konstantinou St. Unsurprisingly the staff of the latter are 'Brits'. The Old Quarter, as would be expected, is a bastion of old-fashioned kourion, or barbers shops, with a preponderance beside Pythagora St, several of which are true, old-time establishments.

LAUNDRY Apart from a number of **Dry Cleaners**, there is a New Town launderette, the **Lavomatic** (*Tmr* C4) at 32, 28th Octovriou St. From Akadimias Sq (*Tmr* D3) proceed west along 28th Octovriou. The shop is between the side-streets of Fanouraki and Ionos Dragoumi. Open daily 0700-2300hrs, with a machine load costing 600drs and a machine drier 200drs, for 20mins. The machines consume 50drs coins.

LUGGAGE STORE A Pension on the left (*Facing east*) of Alex Papagou, about a 100m prior to the City Tourist office (*Tmr* 6D5), fulfils the function.

MEDICAL CARE
Chemists & Pharmacies There are countless numbers, in both Old and New Rhodes, with at least two on the periphery of the New Market (*Tmr* 5D4/5). A rota system is in operation for emergencies.
Dentists There are two 'circling' the Olympic office (*Tmr* 25C/D3/4).
Doctors The **Hiotakis Centre** (*Tmr* C/D3), beside the junction of Polytechniou and Efstathiou Georgiou St, has three doctors - administering, daily, between 0900-1300 & 1700-2000hrs.
Hospital (*Tmr* 65B/C4/5). An emergency clinic is at action stations 24 hours a day, whilst the visitors facility 'operates' daily, between 1400-1700hrs.

MUNICIPAL (or CITY) TOURIST OFFICE (*Tmr* 6D5) Conveniently close to the Bus termini and the New Market. The minimum opening hours are weekday mornings & afternoons and Saturdays until 1400hrs, closed Sundays. The staff are competent to cope with the usual city questions and enquiries, but are 'short' on Rhodes island generally, and out of their depth in respect of most other matters.

NTOG (EOT) (*Tmr* 7C/D4/5).Only open Mon-Fri 0830-1400hrs. Located beside the crossroads of Alexandrou Diakou, Alexandrou Papagou, Ethnarchou Gallias & Vass. Friderikis. A neat and well organised outfit. The elderly staff offer helpful, if stereotyped and impersonal attention, as well as operate an excellent accommodation finding service.

OTE The main office (*Tmr* 39C/D4) is beside the junction of Amerikis and 25th Martiou, and opens daily 0600-2300hrs. There is a small, Old Quarter office (*Tmr* 40E5), diagonally across from Ippoton St. It is tucked away beyond the first floor Tourist Police office, alongside a decorative gateway and to one side of 'Museum' Square, and opens Mon-Fri 0730-2200hrs.

PETROL Plenty. A Filling Station close to the KTEL terminus (*Tmr* 32D5).

PLACES & EVENTS OF INTEREST
Aquarium (*Tmr* 4C1/2) Open daily between 0900-2100hrs, closing at 1800hrs weekends, with entrance costing 300drs. This Italian built structure is at the northern end of the sandy bluff of Rhodes City. Most of the exhibits, as well as much of the complex have 'seen better days'. The ground floor is 'fished' with 'parrot dead' exhibits, many of which appear to have been 'stuffed' where they were found - mostly on the shores of the island. A staircase leads down to an aquaria, set in a dank, dark, dripping and mouldy circular grotto. The cases and tanks contain fish, marine turtles and associated underwater vertebrates. Some of the exhibits are difficult to see, due to tankside slime.
Churches & Cathedrals
Church of St John the Evangelist (*Tmr* 41D3/4) Nea Chora. The Archbishopric, and built by the Italians, in 1925. They modelled it on the St Johns Church that originally stood in the Old Quarter.
Orthodox Cathedral of St Mary (*Tmr* 42E5/6) Old Quarter. Sited at the bottom end of Ippoton St. This 13thC Byzantine church, first became the Cathedral of the Knights, was converted into a mosque (Enderoum Mosque) by the all-conquering Turks, who replaced the steeple with a minaret, and is now a Byzantine Museum.
Church of St Marie du Bourg (*Tmr* 43E/F6) Pindarou St. A road has been laid through some of the old foundations of the original church.
    Nearby, on Alhadef St, is the:
Hospice of St Catherine (*Tmr* 44F6) This was built, in 1392, to provide accommodation for Italian pilgrims.
On towards St Catherine's Gate, beyond the *Church of St Panteleimon*, are a few ruins that are all that remain of the:
Church of the Madonna of Victory Built to celebrate a famous victory, in 1480, over the Turks. The inhabitants made a spirited defence, after a vision of the Madonna appeared. The building was demolished, around 1520.
Church of St Fanourios (*Tmr* 45D/E6/7) On the right of Ag Fanouriou St (*facing north*), beyond the junction with Omirou St. It is entered via a narrow, wooden corridor and is now a regular place of worship. The original Byzantine church, was taken over by the Turks who, at first, used the building as stables, thus destroying the lower wall paintings. Later it was converted into the Pial-el-Din Mosque, only for the Greeks to take it back and reconvert it to the Orthodox faith. The Italians restored the paintings.
Gates, Harbours & Walls The walls of the Old Quarter are continuous. There are two guided tours a week (Mon & Sat), setting out at 1445hrs, from the Palace of the Grand Masters (*Tmr* 37D5), which last some 1¼hr, at a cost of 800drs. Seems expensive for a ramble.

The medieval wall, towers, gates and ditches were built, and the moats excavated, by the Knights. All were heavily modified during their 213 years of occupation (1309-1522), having been constructed, in part, on Byzantine foundations. After 1465 the fortress was divided into eight sectors, or bulwarks, which were allocated, for defence purposes, to the eight Tongues, or nationalities. After repulsing the Turkish siege of 1480, Italian engineers were commissioned to assist the then Grand Master (Pierre d'Aubusson) to strengthen the fortifications which, in places, resulted in wall thicknesses of up to 12m. The number of gates were reduced and the moat widened to 20m.

The busiest Gate must be Liberty or Eleftherias (once also named the New Gate), constructed as recently as 1924, and renamed in 1947, on the reunification of the Dodecanese with the rest of Greece. To the left is the medieval St Paul's Gate, which leads to the edge of the Commercial Harbour, originally defended by two moles. The north mole stretches out from close by St Paul's Gate, and was fortified by the siege Tower of Naillac, prior to its destruction in the middle 1800s. The eastern mole, on which stood thirteen or fifteen windmills (depending on which authority you believe), has sadly and unromantically been replaced by the Customs & Ferry-boat Quay.

The Esplanade roadway skirts the Commercial Harbour and is dominated by truly massive walls. The latter ramparts are pierced by three Gates, the Arsenal, Marine (sometimes mistakenly annotated St Catherines) and St Catherines (also known as Mills Gate, for obvious reasons), as well as a modern, arched roadway, driven through from Alhadef St. Particularly worth inspection is the bas-relief over the attractive Marine or Naval Base Gate. This includes figures of the Virgin Mary, St Peter, St Paul and the arms of Pierre d'Aubusson of France. This section of wall is reputed to have been the backcloth for some of the scenes in the film *Guns of Navarone*.

The battlements run from the Customs Hall Quay, along the west side of Acandia Harbour, to the Gate of Italy, built in 1924 as part of the orgy of aggrandisement indulged in by the Italians. From hereon the fortifications turn the corner, in the direction of Koskinou or St John's Gate, the gate through which the Italians triumphantly marched, in 1912. The section, or bulwark, between this latter Gate and St Athanasius Gate, alongside St Mary's Tower, was that allocated to the English order or Tongue. The tower has a bas-relief of The Virgin Mary and child. The Gate of St Athanasius (or St Athun), one of the weakest points of the walled city, was the place where Suleiman, the all-conquering Turk, breached the defences, in 1522. It is rumoured that Suleiman redoubled his efforts, due to the duplicity of a Portuguese Knight, who let him know just how ill the Knights were faring, exactly at the time when the Turks were considering giving up the siege.

Continuing in a clockwise direction, the wall turns past the Tower of Spain and on to the large Tower of St George, once also a Gate. Above the old entrance are bas-reliefs of St George, a Pope, a Grand Master and the Order of the Knights. The next fortified entrance, the grandest, is Amboise Gate which leads, via a triple arched bridge, over the outer moat and through the main part of the Gate, bedded in the enormous walls. Here the roadway snakes to a bridge over the inner moat and through an inner Gate, which opens out, at right angles, on to the tree shaded avenue of Odhos Orfeos. This traffic free thoroughfare is towered over by the walls of the Palace of the Grand Masters (*Tmr* 37D5), on the left, and leads to the last Gate, that of St Anthony, at the top of Odhos Orfeos. Left here leads to a large, paved

courtyard, to one side of the Palace, and the top of Odhos Ippoton, the Street of the Inns of the Knights.
Mandraki Harbour Outside the Old Quarter walls. The title is Greek for sheepfold, a pointer to one of the previous uses of the harbour. Mandraki accommodates private yachts, the excursion and trip boats, and the hydrofoil craft. At the narrow entrance are two pillars supporting, respectively, a statue of a stag and a doe, one of which replaced a column topping Italian she-wolf. It is popular belief that, in ancient times, the famous Colossus of Rhodes stood in the place of the more modest, modern-day pillars. One of the Seven Wonders of the Ancient World, the bronze statue of the Sun God Apollo, or Helios, supposedly some 30m tall, was erected by Chares of Lindos, circa 300 BC. Incidentally, the construction costs of the Colossus were reputedly funded by the sale of some abandoned Helepolis siege towers. These were left behind when a certain Demetrios Poliorketes gave up an abortive campaign to teach the citizens of Rhodes a lesson for failing to support his father, in some campaign of conquest - it's an ill-wind that blows somebody some good, isn't it? Supposedly the head of the Colossus was surrounded by sunrays and one hand held a torch which, when lit, acted as a guiding   light and signal for sailors. Unfortunately, some 70 years after its erection, an earthquake brought the remarkable statue to its knees,   the broken remains lying around for eight hundred years. In the 7thC AD the twenty tons of bronze scrap was sold to a Syrian merchant and   contemporaneous reports suggest that nine hundred camels were required to remove the booty. More recent calculations have suggested that ninety would have been a more likely figure. It has also been hinted, no doubt by some joker, that the Rhodians received their erstwhile scrap back, in the form of cannon balls fired by the Turks!

To protect the outer mole of Mandraki Harbour, St Nicholas Fort (*Tmr* 46E3/4) was constructed in 1464, on the site of an old chapel. This connection is maintained by the small church which is built within the walls of the fort, and dedicated to St Nicholas, the Greek Orthodox patron saint of sailors. Over the years, the structure was supplemented by a lighthouse and modified to accommodate Second World War gun positions, so maintaining an on and off war-footing, for nearly five hundred years. This eastern mole also supported three grain windmills, still extant, and which date back to the late 1400s.   The landward side of the harbour 'benefited' from the Italian treatment, but the Greeks maintain that the resultant buildings are alien in appearance. For my part, I am sure, were it not for the Italians, that Rhodes City would present a very different appearance, and not the magical and magnificent effect that must please most visitors. Generally, the guide books are dismissive of the majestic, 1930s, 'neo-municipal' Italian architecture, which buildings include   the Harbour Master's office, the Post Office, the 'home' of the Town police, the Town Hall, two theatres, Government House (or the 'Governors Palace'), and St John's Church. I admit there is an air of strange unreality about them, as if they have been constructed for a film set, but nonetheless they have style.

One construction in this vicinity, not reconstructed or newly built by the Italians, is the delightful and elegant Turkish mosque of Murad Reis (*Tmr* 47D3), and its cemetery. The minaret is particularly attractive and the tree shaded burial ground is littered with quaintly carved headstones. The type and fashion of the stone headwear is supposed to denote the particular person's trade or profession. The circular tomb, adjacent to the mosque, is the burial place of Murad Reis, Admiral to Suleiman the Magnificent, who met his death towards the end of the historic siege of 1522.

The Jewish Quarter Located in the south-east sector of the Old Quarter. The most touching memorials to the haphazard, but deadly quirks of Second World War fate must be the Plateia Matiron Eyreon (Square of the Martyrs) and the Synagogue, beside Odhos Dosiadou. More correctly, it is the plaque on the wall of this dignified building, not the Synagogue. The square, complete with a circular, tiled fountain, topped off with three cast sea-horses, was renamed after the Second World War. This act of remembrance commemorates the tragic twist of fortune that befell the Jewish population, in July 1943. It was then that the beneficient Italian regime was rudely replaced by the Nazis of the Third Reich, whom unexpectedly took over the administration of Rhodes. The poignant, wall-mounted memorial records that the two thousand Jews, still resident after the European apocalypse, were, in one year, transported to concentration camps, in the 'Fatherland'. Some fifty survived. Need one say more?

On a brighter note the 15thC Archbishops Palace overlooks the square and was the bishopric, prior to the Turkish take-over.

The Knights Quarter The two most attractive ways into this sector of the Old Quarter are through Liberty or Freedom Gate (*Tmr* E5), to Plateia Simi, or via Amboise Gate and St Anthony's (*Tmr* D5). On the other hand, cruise liner passengers wander in from the direction of the Commercial Harbour. As it is difficult to describe both routes, simultaneously, I have chosen to wander down the Street of the Knights, from the:

Palace of the Grand Masters (*Tmr* 37D5) Open daily, between 0830-1500hrs, entrance costing 800drs, but closed on Mondays. The palace, to the left of the large, paved Plateia Kleovoulou, is a splendid and imposing pile, if possessed of a rather sanitised appearance. This is not so surprising, as it was completely rebuilt by the Italians, only being completed a short time prior to their hurried and sudden departure.

The Knights originally completed this magnificent edifice in the 14thC. It served the dual purpose of a fort, in times of war, and the home of the reigning Grand Master, the 'top dog', in peacetime. For a man who was subject to vows of penury, I cannot but regard the place as a rather opulent and oversized residence. Despite the ravages inflicted by Suleiman the Magnificent's siege, the Palace suffered very little during the battles. Notwithstanding which, over the next few centuries, the languid Turks allowed the structure to deteriorate, which dilapidation climaxed in a horrendous explosion, in 1856. Some absent-minded dolts are reputed to have stowed explosives, possibly a long time previously, in the vaults of the palace and or the Loggia or Church of St John. Wherever and whatever, the initial blast and resultant holocaust destroyed much of this part of the city, killing some eight hundred people and reducing the palace to ruins. The Italian reconstructed building was intended to be used for state visits, by their pre-war King, Emmanuel III, and Il Duce, Benito Mussolini. In keeping with the grandeur of these personages, the rebuilding allowed for concealed lifts, central heating and electric lighting, modern prerequisites that I am sure the Knights would have found puzzling, to say the least. The courtyard, hallways and rooms open to the public, exhibit a number of Roman statues and display many magnificently restored mosaics, mostly from Kos island. The most famous of the mosaics is that titled the Nine Muses, dating from the 1stC AD.

Street of the Knights (Odhos Ippoton) (*Tmr* D/E5) Turning left, out of the palace entrance gates, descends the sometimes unbelievably quiet, stately, if not funereal street. The buildings seem to crowd-in on the narrow, cobbled lane that falls steeply towards the Commercial Harbour. It takes time to realise that there are no shops, no traders, no 'schleppers' and often no tourists.

The Knights were divided into three streams: the military Knights, enlisted from the aristocracy; soldiers-cum-nurses, who were drawn from more pedestrian backgrounds; and the brothers, who carried out the religious duties. The order was organised, originally, into seven, and subsequently eight Tongues, and each had its own 'hall of residence' (House), or Inn. The nomenclature Tongue related to the language, or nationality, of the particular Inn. The Knights were 'conscripted' from citizens of: France; Auvergne and Provence, which were both separate countries from France, at that time; Spain, consequently subdivided into Aragon and Castilian; Italy; Germany; and England. The English were recruited at the Clerkenwell Priory, still extant in the form of the Gate House in St John's Lane, the last remaining London medieval gate. Interestingly, the English Tongue, which ceased after Henry VIII's Reformation, was revived, about 1830, as the British Order of St John of Jerusalem. The Inns were located on either side of the Street of the Knights, which drops by the side-street of Panetiou, on the right, then beneath an archway spanning the thoroughfare. This latter structure, combined with its counterpart, further down, appears to draw the walls of the buildings even closer together. That on the right, on the corner of Panetiou St, is The Loggia of St John, or more correctly, the partly restored Loggia. This used to connect the palace with St John's Church and was destroyed, in 1856, by the 'big bang'. Much of the site is now occupied by a garden. It is followed by the Inn of Spain, dating from the 15thC and edging Ipparhou St, and the other archway. Opposite the Inn of Spain is the Inn of Provence, bordered by entrance ways to gated gardens, the furthest one of which has a small church built over the remains of a Temple to Dionysius.

Once through the second archway, the building on the left, which is now the official residence of the Italian Vice Consulate (*Tmr* 48D5), was the French Chaplain's House. Next door is the Chapel of France (or more correctly the Chapel of the French Tongue), complete with a statue of the Virgin and child, and the arms of a Grand Master of the period (1365-1374). Next down is the large Inn of France, well endowed with various coats of arms, and probably the most eye-catching of all the street's buildings. Incidentally, the reason for the preponderance of French associated edifices, was that they were the most numerous of the Knights. In fact, the French supplied fourteen or so Grand Masters (you know, senior prefect) out of the nineteen, elected in the two hundred and thirteen years of their rule. And this was prior to the EC self-perpetuating oligarchy, or was it simply a forerunner? Certainly the Inn of France, the construction of which started in 1492, is the grandest of the Inns and possesses the most heavily decorated facade, with various coats of arms and a very noticeable fleur-de-lis and crown. Opposite the latter is the 'Edifice of Unknown' (as one of the official guide books quaintly puts it). This is followed by the side-street, Odhos Lathetos, and a lovely, serene Turkish garden framed by the surrounding walls, in which is set a wrought iron gate. The tree shaded and shadowy garden attracts attention, if only because the mute tranquillity of the street is delightfully disturbed by the bubbling and splashing of the garden's fountain. Across the thoroughfare is the Palace of Villiers de L'Isle Adam, the last Grand Master of Rhodes, who finally had to concede defeat to Suleiman. Next down is the Inn of Italy, with the arms of the Italian Grand Master, Fabrizio del Carretto, who caused the structure to be rebuilt in 1519. One of the last buildings on the left is now occupied by The Commercial Bank of Greece.

It is thought that the Knights utilised the ground floor of the Inns as stables, the first floors being accessed by open stairs. The Turks, during their long occupation, as was their wont, festooned the upper story facades with a 'standard design', wooden balcony, which supported the 'carsey hut'.

The last structure on the right, the original door of which faced the Street of The Knights, is the:

Hospital of the Knights Archaeological Museum (*Tmr* 36E5) Open daily, except Mondays, between 0830-1500hrs, with entrance costing 600drs. It has been a museum since 1916, and is now the Archaeological Museum, facing on to Plateia Moussiou. In common with most of the Street of the Knights, it was 'Italian restored' in the early 1900s, the original hospital having been completed by 1489. The entrance archway opens on to a courtyard, enclosed on all sides by a vaulted frontage. The first floor housed the original infirmary. There are seven pillar roof supports, and one wall contains a number of small rooms without windows, the use of which has never been conclusively deduced. The courtyard display includes: a marble crouching lion, some 2000 years old; piles of cannon balls from the time of the Turkish invasion; catapult shot, supposedly dating back to the siege of Demetrios Poliorketes; and a mosaic, circa 650 BC, from Arkasa on the island of Karpathos. Other notable exhibits, amongst a number of interesting items, are: the Aphrodite of Rhodes, a statue of a kneeling woman, holding out the strands of her hair; the head of the Sun God Helios; and the Marine Venus, a statue of Aphrodite, dating back to the 3rdC BC, found on the foreshore off Sandy Point. Splendid public lavatories and a pleasant first floor garden.

Also on the periphery of Museum Sq, or more correctly a small plateia to one side of the larger square, is the totally restored Inn of England (*Tmr* 49E5/6). Built in 1482, the all but demolished Inn was rebuilt in the early 1900s, and restored by the British, after the Second World War.

Backtracking across bustling Museum Sq, towards Liberty Gate, progresses by The Inn of Auvergne, the first floor of which is occupied by the Tourist police. From here, beneath an archway, advances on to the busy pedestrian and vehicle 'ridden' Plateia Simi, with the small Argyrokastron Sq to the left. The latter square has an agreeable fountain, based on a font, and is bordered by the Armeria Palace. This building was possibly the first infirmary of the Knights, but now houses the Archaeological Department of the Dodecanese.

The Museum of Decorative Arts (*Tmr* 38E5) Open daily, apart from Monday, 0800-1500hrs. Entrance costs 400drs. Edges another side of the small square and, at one time, probably an Arsenal. This exhibition merits a visit. On show are a collection of clothes and costumes, embroidery, woodwork, including furniture, china, ceramics and plates, as well as the reconstruction of a typical, Greek village room.

On the square, as elsewhere throughout the Old Quarter, are piles of cannon balls, leftovers from the 1522 siege. Across Argyrokastron Sq, and on the same side of the larger Plateia Simi, is a long building, in which is situated the Ionian Popular Bank (*Tmr* 27E5). Steps ascend to the:

The Municipal Art Gallery (*Tmr* 50E5) Open daily, except Sunday, 0800-1400hrs. Entrance costs 150drs. Works of modern Greek painters. Opposite, in the direction of the Arsenal Gate, are all that is left of the Temple of Aphrodite (*Tmr* 51E5), more a pile of 3rdC BC stones.

Two other buildings belong in this section. The first is the Clock Tower (*Tmr* 52D5/6), which was erected on the top of the wall edging Orfeos St. The structure steeples upwards and was once used as a watch tower, or signal post. Abutting this, the Knights built an inner wall down to the seafront, which separated the Knight's Quarter (Collachium) from the rest of the Old Quarter. The other is the:

Tribune of Commerce (*Tmr* 53E6) Also known as the Palace of Castellania, and is on the left of the Square of Hippokratous (*Facing towards Acandia Harbour*). Completed in 1507, it was the Court House of the Knights. The first floor, reached by wide, external stone steps, is supported by columns which form a ground level arcade. The doorway is decorated with carved coats of arms.

Mosques (& the Turkish Sector of the Old Quarter) Probably the most noteworthy is the *Mosque of Suleiman* (*Tmr* 54D6), situated at the top of Socratous St. This pleasing mosque and minaret was originally constructed in honour of the Turkish conqueror, in 1522. Across the road is the *Turkish Library* (*Tmr* 55D6), built towards the end of the 1700s. The Persian and Arabic exhibits include two Korans, one of 1412, and the other, exquisitely illuminated, dated 1540, but it is never opened to the public. The *Mosque of Chourmali Medresse* is located beside Apolonion St, alongside the Turkish Library, and was a Turkish adaption of a Byzantine church, now in a ruined state. As with many other 'conversions', the traditional Byzantium dome shows up above and topping off the building. *Takkedji (Takkeci) Mosque* (*Tmr* D6), beside Ippodamou St, was also known as the Mosque of the Dervishes, and originally a Byzantine church, but not now in use. The *Moustafa (Mustupha) Mosque* (*Tmr* D6), also known as Sultan Moustafa Mosque, was completed in 1765, on one side of Plateia Arionos. It is now locked and deteriorating, despite which it retains a pleasing appearance. Arionos Sq appears to have more names than usual, which include Plateia Archelaou and the 'Square of the Baths'. The last mentioned is understandable, as one side is edged by the:

Turkish Baths (*Tmr* 56D6) Open daily 0700-1900hrs, but closed Sundays. Admission costs 500drs, with a cut price fee of 150drs, on Saturdays. Also built in 1765, the building was very badly damaged during the Second World War and subsequently rebuilt. The old marble floor remains and the reconstruction was sympathetically carried out. This is not an authentic Turkish bath, wherein an attendant, of the same sex, washes, scrubs and loofahs a client down, followed by a 'steaming' and massage. This is more a 'bring all your own requisites', such as soap and towel, and 'do it yourself'. The lady attendant hires towels, at a cost of 300drs, even if their appearance indicates that they have already been used - on a number of occasions! Once inside, there are some basins, with water coursing along runnels in the floor, all shrouded in steamy vapours. Clients sit on a chunk of marble, next to a marble bowl, and commence dowsing. Often there is an audience of curious locals, some of whom would seem to have purchased their toiletries - from a *Body Shop*. The cockroaches are probably the same ones that were present last time I visited, but even larger! Rated as a definite experience.

Abdul Djelil Mosque (*Tmr* D6) is sited on the edge of a small square beside

Andronicou St, and was a Byzantine church, prior to conversion, but is now in a poor state of repair. *Bourouzan Mosque* (*Tmr* 57D/E7) is south of Omirou St, close by the walls, and has a minaret. The *Retjep Pasha Mosque* (*Tmr* 58D/E6/7) is behind St Fanourios Church, once the Pial-el-Din Mosque, and beside elongated Dories Sq, which has a row of three trees, planted in a rectangular bed. The abandoned mosque, constructed in 1588, using, in part, bits and pieces of various Byzantine churches, was one of the principal and most decorative of the Turkish religious buildings. The imminence of final collapse, has persuaded the authorities to commence the very necessary and desirous reconstruction of the building. There is a small rotunda fountain to the front of the mosque, and the forecourt is a playground for the children of the area. The *Kavakly Mosque* (*Tmr* 59D/E6) has a pleasant little minaret, stretching up from behind a stone wall, to one side of the ruined square of Athinas. *Demerli Mosque* is beside Odhos Thoucididou Platonos, to the east of Ag Fanouriou. The building, once a large Byzantine church, is now in a bad state of repair. *Ibrahim Pasha Mosque* (*Tmr* 60E6) is to the side of the small Plateia Damagitou, located between Sophocleous and Pythagora Sts and the junction with Odhos Platonos. Originally built in 1531, it was restored by the Italians, in the 1930s, who also rebuilt the minaret. The very attractive interior may be inspected, as this mosque is open to visitors. A large plane tree alongside the building is said to have been the site for summary executions, during Turkish rule. The *Dolaplee Mosque* (*Tmr* 61E7) is situated at the south city wall end of Dimosthenous St, which runs parallel and two streets to the east of Sophocleous St. Once a Byzantine church, exhibiting the curious feature (admittedly shared with one or two others) of having longer cross arms than the nave and apse. *Ilk Mihrab Mosque* was also known as Mihram Mosque, and is beside Pericleous St, close to the Dolaplee Mosque. Very little now remains of what was originally a Byzantine church, once possessed of some very fine frescoes. The *Agha Mosque* is mounted on wooden pillars, close to the junction of Socratous and Ag Fanouriou Sts, and named after an erstwhile Turkish Commander.

Son et Lumiere (*Tmr* 62D5) The summer month, nightly performances take place in a municipal garden, edged on two sides by sections of the original city wall. The first show commences at 2015hrs, takes approximately one hour, and entrance costs 700drs. The tickets are available from the NTOG (*Tmr* 7C/D4/5), or at the gate. An English language version is performed every night, except Sunday, with Swedish, German, French and Greek versions on alternative evenings. It is sensible to ascertain what is happening to whom, and when!

Theatre (*Tmr* 63D6) More exactly the Folk Dance Theatre, situated in a pleasant, taverna-like garden, behind the Turkish Baths, alongside Odhos Andronicou. The performances of traditional Greek folk dances and songs commence at 2120hrs, every evening, except Saturday, and end at 2300hrs, entrance costing 2000drs. If asked, after a night's show, the staff will arrange to give lessons. Yes, dancing lessons...!

POLICE
Port (*Tmr* 64D3/4) To the left (*Sbo*) of the Post Office, and with a 'presence' at the bottom of the Ferry-boat Quay (*Tmr* 2F5).
Tourist (*Tmr* 40E5) A cosy little set-up, equipped with so many creature comforts that the staff can prove reluctant to cope with enquiries. The television set is a hurdle, for both inmates and intruders.

Town (*Tmr* 64D3/4) In the same municipal building as the Post Office.

POST OFFICE (*Tmr* 64D3/4) Open weekdays 0730-2200hrs, the main office is a splendid Italianesque affair, bordering Eleftherias St. The interior is gained by ascending a grand flight of steps, that sweep up from the pavement. The rumour that the Scandinavians have a postal slot all of their own is just not true! . There is an Old Quarter 'caravan' (*Tmr* D5/6) beside Orfeos St. The workaday hours of this 'mobile' vary - just a little! The not-so-busy summer months guarantee weekdays between 0800-1400hrs, whilst the height-of-panic period results in daily hours of Mon-Fri 0800-2000hrs, and Sat/Sun a minimum of 0900-1400hrs.

SPORTS FACILITIES There is possibly a wider choice here than anywhere else in Greece, other than Athens. There is even a Casino.
Boating & Canoeing Apply to the **Nautical Club of Rhodes (NOR)** (*Tmr* 1D3) at 9 Kountouriotou Sq (Tel 23287), close by the *Elli Club*.
Golf Some 19km distant is an 18 hole course (Tel 51121/51541) at *Xenia Golf Hotel*. Facilities include a club house, changing rooms and hire of clubs. The fees are reasonable, the grass sparse.
Horse Riding 'Mikes Stables' are close to and inland from Kallithie village, about 15km from the city. Also signposted from Filerimos.
Swimming There is a small, not so clean and always overcrowded outdoor swimming pool (*Tmr* 67C4/5) in the small park across the street from the *Hotel Thermai*, opposite which is an entrance. There is another entrance approximately across the way from the NTOG office (*Tmr* 7C/D4/5). The pool is surrounded by bars and restaurants, it costs nothing to get in, but a fee is charged for the sun-beds.
Tennis Various of the smarter hotels have courts, and there are a few public courts. The **Rhodes Town Tennis Club** (*Tmr* 68C/D2/3, tel 25705), at 20 Vass Konstantinou, faces on to Elli Beach and is about 300m north of the *Elli Club*. The Club has two courts, welcomes all visitors, is open between 0900-2000hrs, and it costs two players 4000drs for ¾hr. Rackets and balls can be borrowed in this charge. Prospective players must wear 'tennis suitable' clothes, not swimsuits. There is a bar and cafe facing the beach road.
Water Sports You dream about it, Rhodes can supply it. Apart from applying to the Nautical Club (*See Boating*), simply enquire of any of the lads in and around the beach. Most of the popular island beaches offer a minimum of windsurfing, water & para-skiing. Any number of craft moored in the Commercial Harbour offer scuba diving opportunities.

TAXIS (*Tmr* T) The main rank is beside Hristoforou Sq, the south side of the New Market (*Tmr* 5D4/5). The minimum fare is 200drs. In the city, the meter runs on tariff 1 and outside the limits, on tariff 2. The airport fare is about 1500drs, to Kamiros Skala 3000/4500drs, and to Lindos some 5000drs.

TELEPHONE NUMBERS & ADDRESSES

British Consulate, 17, 25th Martiou	Tel 27306
Bus Offices: RODA	Tel 27462
: KTEL	Tel 27706
City Tourist office (*Tmr* 6D5)	Tel 35645
Hospital (*Tmr* 65B/C4/5) Erithrou Stavrou (Helvetas or Red Cross St)	Tel 22222
NTOG (*Tmr* 7C/D4/5)	Tel 23255/23655
Olympic Airways (*Tmr* 25C/D3/4) Office: 9 Ierou Lochou	Tel 24571/5
Airport:	Tel 92981/6
Police (*Tmr* 64D3/4)	Tel 27423
Taxis (*Tmr* D4/5)	Tel 27666

TOILETS Rhodes City has almost a surplus, with: several clean ones in the New Market (*Tmr* 5D4/5); a busy, 'kept-clean' one beside Alex Papagou, close by the Bus terminus (*Tmr* 32D5); at the Olympic Airways office (*Tmr* 25C/D3/4); one opposite the *Hotel Sydney* (*Tmr* 13E6); a fairly clean one by Orfeos St (*Tmr* D5/6), between the Grand Palace Gates and the Clock Tower; a very dirty, smelly one next door to *Zorba's Cafe-bar*, Plateia Martiron Eyreon (*Tmr* E/F6); a filthy, busy one by Acandia Beach (*Tmr* G6/7); as well as the facility alongside the *Elli Club* (*Tmr* 3D3).

TRAVEL AGENTS & TOUR OFFICES In addition to those listed under Ferry-boat Ticket offices, there are any number of firms scattered about the New and Old Town, most of them unhelpful. An Old Quarter recommendation is **Kastellania Travel Agent** (*Tmr* E6, tel 24288), close to Plateia Hippokratous, in the right-hand corner (*Sbo*), at the end of the row of cafe-bars outside which are tables and chairs. It is run by a friendly young man who has lived in London for a number of years.

A New Town testimonial must be awarded to **Loucas Hatzigeorgiou** (*Tmr* D4/5) at No 4 Odhos Theodoraki, a street which cuts across between Kyprou Sq and Alex. Papagou St, to the west of the New Market (*Tmr* 5D4/5). Not only is the firm agent for many travel options, but they accept payment by *Visa*, are speedy, extremely co-operative, well-established and 'Greek popular'. Thoughtfully, there is a metered telephone on the counter.

For visitors who wish to have an overnight glimpse of Turkey, **Triton Tours** (*Tmr* D4, tel 30657), at 25 Plastira St, which runs from Kyprou Sq to the waterfront, beside Mandraki Harbour, offer a round-trip to the Turkish resort and port of Marmaris. The Triton office is open weekdays, between 0800-1400 & 1600-2100hrs and Sat 0900-1330 & 1600-2000hrs. The excursion boats depart at 1700hrs, for the 3hr voyage, returning at 0800hrs the next day. The return fare is 10800drs, and the boats run Mon-Sat, in the summer months. Inclement weather and the 'out of season' period 'severely' reduces the frequency of the trips. Participants must ensure the passport angle is properly covered. Where holiday-makers have arrived in Greece, on a charter flight, the Greek authorities can be difficult, if not obdurate about a trip to Turkey. They are perfectly within their rights (that is, their convoluted Greek rights) to declare any such visit illegal, and insist the person concerned leaves the country, on a scheduled flight - and pay! It is true to write that most travel agents have ways and means, but you have been warned!

EXCURSIONS TO RHODES CITY SURROUNDS
Excursion to Monte Smith (1½km) A quaint anomaly is the persistence in favouring the present name for the hill, also known as Mt Ag Stephanos. The English title is because one Sydney Smith, an English Admiral, used the prominence as a lookout, during 1802, whilst on watch for Napoleon's fleet.

The whole area is rich in archaeological remains, and is only a short bus ride (Bus No 5) from the city. For those of the 'mad-dog' variety, it is best approached via Vass Friderikis (*Tmr* C5), taking the right-hand fork on to Ag Ioannou, then turning right along Odhos Diagoridon.

To the left of Diagoridon St is the heavily restored Theatre, which is alongside and almost on the same plane as the Stadium, both set in a grove of olive trees. Above the Theatre, which was possibly a School of Rhetoric, and on a terrace reached up a large flight of steps, is the Temple of Pythios Apollo, marked by three restored columns. Above the Temple, the summit of

Monte Smith, site of an ancient Acropolis, allows magnificent views, especially at dusk, when the setting sun makes a resplendent sight as it dips dramatically beneath the far horizon. From the 120m crown of the hilltop, in a northerly direction, and turning east along Odhos Voriou Ipirou, advances past scattered remains, including a few discs of once huge pillars, lying around the Temple of Athena Polias.

Excursion to Rodini Park (3km) Bus No 3, and most east side buses, take the Asgourou village road out of Rhodes City, past the park. Rodini was formally laid out, by the Italians, on an ancient site which included the remains of a Roman aqueduct. Rodini is yet another pretender to the mantle of being the location of the legendary Rhodes School of Rhetoric.

The wooded park is criss-crossed with streams, shallow canals, paths, rustic bridges and laced with grottoes and ponds, all set in verdant grounds. A resident monkey has achieved some celebrity status over the years. Sadly he, or she, appears to be permanently sick, and plans are afoot for the animals removal to an animal welfare clinic. It is a shame to report that the park would (greatly) benefit from some 'tender loving care'. I am not suggesting that no investment has been outlayed. Oh, dear me, no. The real essentials have been taken care-of, as *in situ* are a restaurant and night club.

A walk of some 15mins, in a south-west direction, advances to a burial place, the Tomb of the Ptolemies. This is probably a misnomer as Ptolemy and his progeny were Kings of Egypt. The tomb is of the Hellenistic era, with columns carved into the rock.

Excursion to Thermei Kallithea (via the coast road, 10km) It is probably easiest to take the eastern coast road, and not the main east island route. The Old Quarter wall should be followed along Vass Friderikis (or Dimocratias - they are the same road), by the Police Training College, beyond St Athanasius Gate, to the junction by St Francis Catholic Church, and a derelict filling station. Turn right along Stefanou Casouli St to where the road divides around a traffic drum or small, circular, waist-high roundabout. The right fork heads towards the main east road, and the left fork to the coast road, which rejoins the main road at Faliraki. Take the coast road. Incidentally, it has been suggested, rather than follow my directions, it would be easier to track the signs from the main traffic light junction on Australias St!

AG MARINA (4½km from Rhodes) The first east coast tourist resort - developed entirely with package-holiday-makers in mind. The not-so-smart seaside expansion, almost part of the 'downtown' Rhodes City, East End sprawl, has a slightly tatty milieu. There are many large hotels alongside both the main and coast roads, as well as plenty of expensive restaurants and (pretend) tavernas. The beach is agreeably sandy, with a 1930s lido building, supplemented by backshore showers, as well as beach beds and sun umbrellas. An OTE van is open weekdays.

Between Rhodes City and the Koskinou junction are occasional clumps of gigantic hotel complexes set in not very prepossessing countryside.

THERMEI KALLITHEA (10km from Rhodes) The location's delights result in Thermei being overcrowded during the height-of summer-months, and most weekends. Some guide books list this as being quiet and unpeopled, but coach outings, trip boats, car hire and the ubiquitous scooter have changed all that.

The final approach is via a pleasantly well spaced-out park, planted with groves of trees, and terminating in a gravel car park. This is above the spa, and a pebble edged, small bay, encompassing a 'compact' sandy area, dotted with sun umbrellas, and separated from the sea by rocks. The North African appearance of the buildings is the result of an Italian whim. They enthusiastically constructed the complex, in the 1920s, as a health resort and watering place. The *raison d'etre* lost all relevance once they had departed - 'Built by the Italians, allowed to decay by the Greeks'. The neglect is more noticeable in the surrounding parkland, around which are scattered now unused, probably unusable, rainwater and rubbish filled, circular bathing pools. It must have been a beautiful spot, in Mussolini's days. A nod to the wise is that, while everybody else swarms towards the bay, the loggia makes an ideal, shady, quiet place in which to sit, and enjoy a contemplative read.

Steps descend, through formally laid out gardens, to the narrow shore, complete with a quay mounted shower and sun-beds. Flippers and face masks can be hired from an expatriate American couple, who work out of a small shop tucked into one of the buildings. There are also motor boats for rent. A further hazard is that Thermei is the chosen location for some three or four city diving schools to put into pupil practice, all their classroom instruction. The small beach is often so busy that there is no space on which to even place a tiny beach towel. It can be imagined the chaos that ensues on those days, 'when the divers call'.

Excursion to Petaloudes - the Valley of the Butterflies (25km) From Rhodes City, the main, west coast road is reached by: proceeding along Vas Konstantinou to emerge on Akti Miaouli, towards the north of the city; taking 25th Martiou across Plateia Akadimias (Vas Georgiou) to 28 Octovriou; or by heading up Alexandrou Papagou, through to Alexandrou Diakou, both of which spill out on to the coast road, lower down on Akti Kanari.

The first part of the road edges a continuation of the city headland beach. Not a sandy swathe, rather a thin foreshore of pebbly sand (with a preponderance of pebbles), and row upon row of regimented sun-beds and umbrellas. The inland side of the road is a polite'ish, seaside ribbon development, a 'cram' of tree lined, low and high rise, smart and not-so smart hotels, interspersed by the occasional restaurant and souvenir shop.

KRITIKA (3km from Rhodes) A once straggling, rather sad, pathetic strip of turn-of-the-century, look-alike housing, now being uprooted by the bulldozer. This destruction is to make way for the inevitable construction of - even more hotels. The village was originally settled by Turkish refugees from Crete, after the formal removal of the Sultan's right to rule that island, in 1898.

From Kritika the quality of the countryside improves, slightly, even if it is only at the expense of hotel development, commencing with the *Hotel Sirene Beach*. It is a sadness to report that the three *en route* resorts are being progressively 'Kosta'd'.

FANEROMENI (4km from Rhodes) The site of a small monastery. A road to the left, towards the interior, bends round, via **Kandilion** village, to Monte Smith. From this direction, the southern extremities of Rhodes City can beseen to be littered, with a mess of shanty smallholdings.

Through Ixia, the coast road approaches:

TRIANTA (8km from Rhodes) Almost a town, the settlement has been the subject of fairly massive hotel construction, despite which the frontage remains attractive, with small public gardens edging the beach. The landscaping helps offset such internationalism as *The Pink Panther Club,* Chinese restaurants, 'real' tavernas *ad nauseam.* The church, dedicated to the Assumption of the Holy Mary, has a splendidly carved, 18thC screen.

Alongside a centrally located filling station, a turning to the left leads to:
FILERIMOS (13km from Rhodes) Probably because it is distant from the coast, the village is quieter and less tourist despoiled.

The ascent of the mountain is long and hard enough, to suggest a 500drs taxi ride might be preferable. For those hell-bent on the outdoor life, the descent, through the forest clad mountainside, allows great views, and should assuage anyone's need to indulge in energetic hikes.

Ancient Filerimos The road cul de sac's on a car park. Alongside this is a large, tree shaded bar, selling cheese pies, sandwiches, coffee, drinks, postcards, and various other tourist items. The site opens daily, between 0830-1500hrs, except Mondays, with entrance to the monastery and various churches costing 400drs.

This is the site of the ancient City state of Ialysos, one of the sponsors, with Kamiros and Lindos, of Rhodes City. Ironically, the inexorable expansion of the latter once again reduced Ialysos to a village, by the end of the 1stC BC. The settlement was positioned on the irregular rectangular shaped flat surface, at the top of the thickly wooded hillsides of Mt Filerimos, some 276m above sea-level.

To the left, behind a wall with iron gates as an entrance, is the:
Church of Our Lady of Filerimos Originally a Knights church but the subject of much 'putting up and knocking down'. The Knights built it (or at least restored the building), the Turks then used it as stables (what did they not?), only for the Italians and Germans to indiscriminately 'rubble' the site. This was during a trifling disagreement between the Axis countries' soldiers, subsequent to Mussolini being forcibly retired'. After the Second World War, the church was rebuilt, once again.

Between the church and the car park, lie the remains of:
The Temple of Athena Poliados & Zeus Polieas There is little left, apart from a few bits of the original columns. This construction was laid over an earlier, probably Phoenician temple, of which there are even less fragments, at the top end of the Athena Temple.

In front of the temple site is the:
Chapel of Ag Georgios A very small, underground Byzantine church with restored, wall-to-wall 15thC frescoes, and a part exposed, earlier cross.

Behind the church are the cloisters of the:
Monastery Another substantially restored and agreeable, if small building. Beyond the cloisters leads to a place, from whence a fine view.

Back at the car park, to the left, from the steps, proceeds to a Doric fountain, on the one hand, and a public lavatory, on the other. The fountain was exposed by a landslide, after which the Italians (inevitably) restored part of this 4thC BC structure.

Straight ahead of the Church of our Lady of Filerimos, more steps climb to the Italian inspired Stations of the Cross.

The strategic desirability of the summit, with its splendid range and field of vision, did not escape the eyes of various commanders, down the ages. These included, reputably, the Genoese, when removing the Byzantines, the Knights, when removing the Genoese, and Suleiman the Magnificent, when removing the Knights - *c'est la vie*. Before departing the site, most visitors will not fail to observe the 'dragons', or, more correctly, the large lizards named Agamas, which are also to be seen in numbers, on the island of Mykonos.

Back at Trianta, the main road continues on to:
KREMASTI (11km from Rhodes) Rather overshadowed by the creation of an enormous mausoleum - okay, a church, surrounded by acres of marble paving. The village school building is also a curiosity, as the costs were met by citizens of Kremasti, who had emigrated to North America. They decreed that the architectural style should be American neo-colonial...! Well, I suppose, every expatriate to his own.

At a coastal road junction, an inland turning heads past the old civilian airport, which is now a military field, to:
MARITSA (16km from Rhodes) A large, pleasant village spread up the hillside, and somewhat off the tourist-beaten track. That is unless the little darlings' divert a 'Safari hire car trek' this way. A summer-dry river-bed courses the length of the village, and the local youth have a disco - maybe I am wrong about Maritsa being off the holiday-makers ambit!

It should be possible, according to many island maps, to proceed from Maritsa to **Kalamon**, on the road to Petaloudes, but the vivid imagination of the cartographers, combined with the presence of the military, have made this particular route a non-starter.

Back on the main route, many map makers indulge in perpetuating a myth, as most show the Airport as being beyond or alongside the village of Paradissi. In fact the Airport entrance is about 1km prior to the village.

PARADISSI (Paradision - 15km from Rhodes) Hardly a paradise now, with the extensive airfield so close, but the name is due to a nearby mountain. The road narrows down through this still pretty, agricultural settlement, but the runway has devoured much of the land that the villagers used to farm.

Some 3km beyond Paradissi, a side road climbs gently, via olive-groves, to **Kalamon** (5km) and then, after passing a substantial military camp, on to:

Petaloudes - The Valley of the Butterflies (25km from Rhodes) The approaches are infested with buses, coaches, tour guides and tourists. The valley is open daily, between 0900-1800hrs, and entrance costs 400drs.

It is common to develop a preconceived idea about how a particular landscape or place will look, and this much overworked tourist attraction was a specific instance. I imagined the valley to be wide and spacious, with granite rocks dotted about a sparsely vegetated ravine. Actually, the site is an extensively foliaged, steeply climbing, narrow defile down which a stream tumbles, in a series of rock pools and waterfalls. It is strongly reminiscent of a less savage Black Falls, in North Wales.

The fairly steep ascent is up a pathway, which criss-crosses the stream and pools, via rustic bridges and rock steps. The butterflies are dark brown and cream, when their wings are folded, and red, black, brown and white, when in flight. They are difficult to spot, whilst at rest, but a sharp sound sends clouds of them into the air in a darting, dipping, tumbling flight. Mind you, a very loud, sudden bang would probably send thousands of the tourists, that wend their way up and down the valley, into an aerial display of sorts.

The season for the butterflies, which are not indigenous to the island, is between June and September. It appears these natives of Turkey are attracted by the resinous trees.

The maps almost all detail a road to Psinthos, but...
Excursion to Psinthsos (30km) Psinthos is best reached from the east coast road, via Afantou. A spread out, agricultural village with a very large, open square, around which are dotted the mandatory tavernas, the owners of which indulge in some 'schlepping', when numbers permit. Travellers, picking their time of arrival, to ensure that the hordes have not mistakenly stumbled upon the settlement, will find this a pleasant spot at which to 'taverna'. Did you know - Psinthos is the unlikely place at which the invading Italians finally routed the Turks, in 1912?

ROUTE ONE
To Kattavia via Lindos (91km) The route involves taking the east coast road, the first part of which, as far as, and including Thermei Kallithea, has been described under **Excursions to Rhodes City Surrounds**.

From Thermei the road skirts the long, gently curving, fine shingle and very sandy beach of:

FALIRAKI BEACH (15½km from Rhodes) The Kosta Brava or Marbella of Rhodes - depending upon a visitors standpoint. From the 'top' end, a number of massive hotel complexes, such as the *Esperides Beach*, *Blue Sea* and *Rodos Beach* are edged by 'neat' beach, as well as all the necessary paraphernalia of sun-beds, umbrellas and beach showers. Unfortunately, for holiday-makers, what with the clutter of 'beds & 'brellas', even early or late in the summer period, it is difficult to spy any sand, let alone a sweep of the stuff!

Those who select Faliraki, must not be concerned that any 'delight has been left unturned'. Oh, no. The massed hordes of tourists are beset by every 'feel-good' factor known to the industry. These encompass a full range of (youthful) temptations, accompanied by the maximum amount of frenetic activity and noise. To ensure the complete success of Faliraki, the overwhelm of opportunities, at which to 'enjoy' oneself, are supported by a lavish supporting cast of: discos; disco-bars; disco-pubs; cocktail bars; music cocktail bars; bars; pubs; night clubs & fun-centres; restaurants of most hues, including at least one serving 'roast beef & Yorkshire pudding'; fast food (& slow food); and a gamut of water sport activities. Generally, prices reflect the more affluent holiday-makers backpocket (or purse).

As the far, southern crescent of the bay is approached, the development inexorably degenerates, from international 'package-set' to a more homespun, more 'typically shambolic', traditionally Hellenic mix of small hotels, villas and shopping precincts. Down here, a number of the villas are on the wrong side of the tracks - okay, the inland side of a very busy main road. I'm sure no one advises prospective clients, when they are booking their holiday! Some sections of the strip are backed by a reedy, marsh-like swathe in which frogs loudly croak and mosquitoes prepare themselves for their nightly forays.

Passing by Faliraki, on the main road, a sign to the left indicates *Faliraki Camping* (Tel 85358). A tidy set-up, with every facility - even a swimming pool. The per head charge is from 700drs, with a tent charged at 500drs.

Another 2km south along the coast road, and a side-turning shambles down to:
CAPE LADIKO (23km from Rhodes) Certainly, compared to Faliraki, this is a more tranquil location - but in comparison, so would be bedlam, or Beirut! Ladiko is a package resort, with a sandy, clean beach, and all the facilities.

Turning left off the approach road, leads, after a short drive, to the smart *Hotel Ladiko*. This tops a crest, from whence are views of the small, nearly circular bay, set in rocky surrounds, at the bottom of a steep slope. The sand is lovely and the water clear. In addition, there are beach showers, beach umbrellas, and the *Restaurant Ladiko*, where the prices are reasonable.

A side-road to the left can be negotiated, to rejoin the main road. On the right is the *Pension Sofi*, beyond which is a turning down to the north end of Afantou Beach. The *Pension Despina* is to the right. The *Sofi* and *Despina* charge about 4000drs, in mid-season, for an en suite double bedroom.

For a short distance the roadway becomes a very modern stretch of dual carriageway, with a flyover. The approach to this 'spaghetti' passes by the *Xenia Golf Hotel*, an 18 hole golf course, and the *Golf Taverna*. The latter's menu owns-up to serving kid, but, when requested, it is just as likely to be 'orf'. The proprietor has an agreeable way of giving 'selected' diners a cherry brandy, on payment of the bill, a gesture that looses some of its point, when it is observed that all the other clients receive a similar gesture.

Turnings inland, to the right, lead to:
AFANTOU (20km from Rhodes) The prescence of the golf course has resulted in almost every business adding the appellation 'Golf' this, or 'Golf' that. Despite being unexceptional, with apricots and carpets the local 'bill of fare', Afantou is extremely tourist popular. There are *Rooms*, a filling station at the outset to the settlement, a travel agent and a Post Office. Also on the right, beyond Afantou, is a hillock with the Stations of the Cross winding up a steeply inclined, tarmacadam drive.

To the left of the route is a 2km side-road to the very long, pebbly sand of:
Afantou Beach (22km from Rhodes) Alongside the junction of the access road with the beach, there skulks a camouflaged Army lookout post. The inland side of the road is signed to indicate the fact that the marshy area is sown with mines - as in mines that go bang, when they are 'disturbed'. I doubt that the Turks are too bothered. Sun-beds and umbrellas are supplemented by a snack-bar and beach showers. The beach is edged by a long, straight, narrow, backshore road, towards the south end of which are signs warning those wearing pacemakers to beware, due to the presence of possibly damaging radio waves. The road comes to a dead-end, up against the gates of a large radio station and transmitter, operated by The Voice of America. Bathers should note that the coast becomes rocky when swimming northwards.

There are some *Rooms*, beside the main road, which hereabouts bridges a large river-bed. The surrounding countryside sprouts some plastic green-houses, in addition to the olive groves, in which are dotted about numerous ceramic factories and warehouses - that old Spanish ambience.

Prior to reaching Kolympia (Kolibia), there is a right-hand turning towards the interior. This road is arguably one of the most beautiful of the Rhodes island routes. It proceeds through groves of firs and pomegranates, followed by a lush, green pine forest, without a dwelling, let alone a taverna, in sight. *En route* to Archipolis village, a lane sheers off to:

Epta Pigai (Seven Springs - 30km from Rhodes) Well not directly, as it is necessary to turn left again, which advances to a confluence of seven streams, running into an Italian-made lake, a waterfall and the mandatory restaurant. Some of the restaurant's tables are supported on flat-topped rocks, in and alongside the water, all set in densely wooded countryside. To reach the bright green lake, bordered by heavy foliage, rather similar to a jungle lagoon, it is necessary to walk through a long, narrow, stream-running tunnel - an odd and quite exciting sensation. It is safe to swim in the lake, but not advisable to get too close to the wall of the dam.

Further along the road to Archipolis, still surrounded by a lovely, green landscape, is a church, high on the left-hand side. To the front of this is a 'three spout' water fountain, shaded by a large, hollow plane tree.

ARCHIPOLIS (34km from Rhodes) Prior to reaching this unexceptional village, a road to the right heads off towards **Psinthos**, initially winding through attractive, pine tree clad scenery, which gives way to olive groves.

Straight on, or west from Archipolis leads to **Eleousa** and other villages, clinging to the sides of Mt Profitis Ilias, and described under Route Two.

Returning to the main route, proceeds to:
KOLYMPIA (Kolibia - 26km from Rhodes) The road is a wide stretch of highway, which rushes past an Italian built series of accommodation blocks. Alongside them is a side-road to the coast. This turning dodges round the old people's home (for that is what the 'accommodation' buildings are), after which 'jinking', there is an arrow straight, tree lined, majestic, three kilometre long avenue. On either side of this are dotted the occasional 1920s Italian forerunner of 'a Wimpy home', a standard design villa, with external ovens and a number of columns supporting the large first floor terrace.

Another unusual feature are the precast, water running, mini irrigation aqueducts lining the length of the road. They continue to be fed from a waterfall, the inland side of the main road, a source of irrigation tied-in with the system at Epta Pigai, and installed by the Italians to update the agriculture of the area. At the coast end, four or five nice looking *Pensions* border both sides of the avenue, as well as several Rent A Moped firms. This area is being developed, with mega-sized hotels completed, and under construction. A 'for instance' is a huge hotel being built to the left (*Fsw*), between the road and the previously mentioned Voice of America transmitter, about where the tree lined avenue divides around the headland of:

Cape Vagia (29km from Rhodes). This is a now a neighbourhood that must be written about 'in the same ink' as Faliraki - there's praise indeed.

A small hotel is on the right, beyond which a track proceeds round in that direction. This advances by a small, circular cove, with a childrens' holiday camp in the foreground, and table-like, sandstone rock edging the sea, and a small sandy shore. Further on is another, much larger and more pleasing bay. Here fine shingle borders the sandy sea's edge, the shore hosting beach umbrellas and a 'Surf Centre'. The far end of the beach is shut-off by a towering, rocky promontory. Beside the approach to this last detailed bay is a low, tawdry taverna, sprawling over a small, tree shaded hillock. There are outside toilets, and old, domed bread ovens, to one side of the main building, both still being pressed into service.

To the left of the (Cape Vagia) headland, a path meanders down to a small caique pier and boat repair yard, flanked by a taverna. To the left (*Fsw*) is a slab rock seashore, edged by a small, narrow, fine shingle swathe, in which is to be found some sand. A mimosa, some tamarisk trees and a few beach umbrellas border the clean beach. In the distance is the radio station end of Afantou Beach. This sea-shore collection of dwellings is possibly on the 'Evening out at a traditional fishing hamlet', coach excursion schedule. Certainly a canvas covered patio, opposite the taverna, is lined with a seemingly disproportionate number of chairs and tables.

Proceeding towards Arhanglos along the main route, after about 3km there is a left turning down to:
Tsambika Beach (31km from Rhodes) The paved, 2km long access road descends steeply to a geographically lovely location, but... Unfortunately, despite this or that guide book advising to the contrary, Tsambika becomes impossibly crowded during the day. The scheduled bus service is ably supplemented by coach tours and trip boats, in addition to swarms of scooters, motor bikes and hire cars. Two and four wheeled vehicles are ranked to one side of the sign-bestrewn rock, sited at the bottom of the access road. This extremely popular, large bay is edged, to the left (*Fsw*), by a vertical cliff, high up the rock face of which the sand is wind-blown. To the right is an extremely large, scrub-clad plain. To left and right stretches the long and beautifully sandy beach. If the crowds of happy, gambolling holiday-makers were insufficient to mar the gentle serenity of the spot, sun-beds and umbrellas are ably supported by an all-action cast of water sports, such as sea-rafts, pedaloes, parascending, and 'personal speedboats', to list but some of the opportunities available. The 'inner tourist' is well catered for, as would be expected. To the right (*Fsw*) are two *Cantinas* (more realistically old caravans) hunkered down on the huge backshore area, with their generators buzzing away in the background. To the left is a *Beach Taverna*, beside the patio of which is mounted a stalk-like shower head.

Tsambika Monastery (31km from Rhodes) A concrete path of a road angles off the Tsambika Beach road, towards the whitewashed, Byzantine monastery. It is surrounded by stone walls and, being set close by the mountain top, there are splendid views. The monastery is the site for a religious ceremony, or fertility rite, and on September 8th women wishing to conceive children climb the steep approach, on foot, and pray that they may give birth.
There is also a signed concrete road from the main highway.

Three kilometres further along the main road to Arhangelos, and a signpost indicates a rough stone track, which is negotiable by motor car, and zig-zags about in a series of hairpin bends, before joining a tarmac road descending to:
STEGENA (35km from Rhodes) Due to years of erosion, and localised movement of the earth's crust, the various access roads and tracks vary from bad to 'disappeared'. Stegena was once a delightful, unspoilt hamlet, set on the near side of a pretty bay, one of those places to which to direct travellers, in search of a 'find'. Continuing transformation into a totally developed resort is underway, but for the meantime Stegena remains quieter than its neighbours. The straggling settlement comprised old, adobe style dwellings, lining the sea-shore, and mainly bunched together at the outset of the cove. This 'core' village has been supplemented by the *Taverna Stegena*, where owner Vassilis is very friendly, a small block of four apartments for rent, and

a group of single storey dwellings. The original buildings were mainly
fishermen's shacks, occupied when the   fish ran, followed by moorings for
dinghies and outboard engined craft, in the mouth of a small river. Two more
side-by-side tavernas edge the   roadway which borders the fine shingle, sandy
foreshore. The sand gives   way to a small, smooth pebble sea-bed. The track
is lined by cultivated land, vegetation and trees, including olives and oranges,
and some gardens   fringing the backshore road. A large, irregular, rocky
protrusion divides   the bay, at the far right-hand end of which is a caique
cove. A small,   unpretentious restaurant, some *Rooms*, and beach showers
complete this still satisfying location.

For the time being, it is not possible to continue on round and up alongside
the mosquito infested, swamp of a river-bed (to Arhangelos), due to this track
having been completely washed away.
ARHANGELOS (33km from Rhodes) This very large, airless, sprawling,
inland village is not overly attractive. It has an 'Old Quarter', is set in fertile
countryside, and is famed for its distinctive leather boots. The winter 'fresh'
or flood runs strongly, and the river-bed and bridge are substantially
constructed - obviously the track was not. Masses of accommodation is
available, which includes: the modern *Hotel Fivos* (Class D, tel 22600),
wherein all rooms are en suite, singles priced at 2500drs & doubles 3600drs;
and *Hotel Archangelos* (Class D, tel 22925), with en suite singles costing
2500drs & doubles 4000drs. At least two tavernas 'dish-up' decent meals, and
one of the bars is just as likely to offer 'an ouzo on the house'. There is a
filling station. Above the settlement lurks a 15thC fort, built on the
instructions of Knight Grand Master Orsini.

There is a choice of routes from Arhangelos, as the New Road sweetly curves
about, almost paralleling the coastline, whilst the Old Road twists and turns
through verdant fields, thickly planted with fruit-laden trees and cypresses, all
the way to **Malona** (39km). Immediately prior to the village, a left-hand
turning crosses the New Road to:
HARAKI (43km from Rhodes) This small, comparatively quiet, still lovely
seaside village, remains a 'find'. This is despite the constant growl of the
cement mixer heralding the slow, but steady, only to-be-expected
transformation of Haraki into a resort. To the north side of the headland, into
which are tucked some caique moorings, is a slender, clean, curving, almost
circular, pebble beach. The tree lined Esplanade sweeps round to a sandy,
shingly beach, to the left, with 'ducks-a-bobbing'. There are *Rooms*,
bungalows and a few tavernas.

Back at Malona, the road leads on to **Massari** (41km). From this village yet
another side turning curves down across the New Road, then along an
unmade track, not to a village, but to:
Haraki Beach A long, gently curving bay edged by a pebbly sand sea-shore.
This is overlooked, on the left, by the ruined **Castle of Feraclos**, set on a low
promontory, the south side of the headland. The fort, used by the Knights as
a gaolhouse for prisoners of war and their own miscreants, was one of the last
to fall to the invading Turks.
The access track decants on to the beach backshore, alongside the almost
obligatory, tree shaded Army camp. The crystal clear sea more than makes up
for the pebbly beach. The Old and New roads merge, beyond where the New

Highway crosses a dry, very broad river-bed. The latter is subject to continual excavation for building materials. Where the roadway has been embanked, it cuts across an old, possibly wartime runway that almost spills into the sea.

KALATHOS (50km from Rhodes) A one-eyed hamlet, sited to the right of the main road, with a surprisingly large, Class E hotel, *The Mouratis*, and not one, but two filling stations. There is a very exposed, shingly beach.

Some 1½km further on the route forks. To the right proceeds to the villages of Lardos and Kattavia. To the left heads past a side lane dropping down to the splendidly sited *Lindos Beach Hotel*. This towers over a small cove, nestling in a crook of the headland in which is sited the legendary:

LINDOS (56km from Rhodes) (Illus 7) Tel prefix 0244. Whatever a visitor's lasting perceptions, it is unarguable, once the resort and acropolis first hove into view, that they present a breathtakingly beautiful sight. Closer, more detailed inspection will, without doubt, erode these idealistic, first impressions. Even if the outright tourist exploitation were not too much to stomach, the inhabitants will surely ensure that any initial delight is dashed. Almost all the Lindiots have become, oh so worldly-wise and bored to distraction, with the whole money-making treadmill on to which the holiday industry has enticed them. Oh dear me.

The steeply descending road spews on to a tree shaded, small, almost circular square, Plateia Eleftherias. Only mopeds and taxis are allowed to park here, cars having to proceed to a designated park, above the square, or down towards the bay. There is a small tourist office beside the plateia, and an acute left-hand turn plummets down, past two discos, to Grand Harbour Bay. The bay is bordered by a fairly small, sandy, tourist crowded beach.

The old village is entered from the far side of the aforementioned square, whence the visitor is absorbed into what appears to be one huge traffic-free maze of a bazaar. The tradition of 'donkey travel' has been preserved, more especially to transport tourists along the lanes, to the foot of the steps up to the Acropolis. It is difficult to nominate the most undesirable, unwholesome, unedifying outcome of this manifestation. Is it the spectacle of grossly overweight tourists sagging over the flanks of the tiny donkeys? Is it the possibility of being trampled underfoot by the selfsame, overloaded donkeys, skidding and teetering out of control? Or is it the chance of losing one's footing, by slipping on the donkey droppings, which are splattered all over the almost mirror-shiny, stone paved streets? One certainty, is that the hoarse encouragements of the donkey men and the clip-clop of the donkeys' hooves, are the only sounds that break through the ceaseless babble of human voices.

Around the periphery of the village, off the well signposted 'beaten track' to Acropolis steps, are some twisting streets that are still devoid of commercialism, with hardly a bar or taverna in sight.

Lindos was a superior holiday location for many years. John Ebdon, in his immensely amusing book *Ebdons Odyssey**, narrates the 'possibly' apocryphal story line, that, in the past, when the wind was in the right direction, the clinking of cocktail glasses could be heard as far away as Rhodes City. Would that he could see the place now! The cocktail has been nudged aside by more egalitarian quaffing, and the 'smart set' have ghosted away, in the face of an unstoppable tide of popular package holiday clients. That's progress.

*Published by Peter Davies Ltd. London.

The holiday villa companies have taken over most of the old houses and their plaques proudly declare the official villa name. Traditional food shop sand stalls have been displaced by a welter of cocktail and music bars, fast food establishments, 'pubs', and tourist shops.

One of the distinctive qualities of Lindos has been the settlements ability to survive, for so many years, in fact thousands of years. It is referred to in Dorian times, that is prior to 1000 BC, but a one-time   population of some 17,000 has now dropped to approximately 700. Goodness only knows what the summer months number reaches.

THE ACCOMMODATION & EATING OUT

The Accommodation There is not a lot, as most of the suitable houses have been taken over by holiday and villa companies. Package tourists should note that certain firms are now squeezing three persons into what was once regarded as a tight-fit for two, and pricing for three - even when only two book! Accommodation available to independents tends to be very expensive, and is usually full. It appears that the only time a bedroom 'comes on the market', is when an incumbent has to unexpectedly depart, or dies! Average double bedroom rates fluctuate between 5000-6500drs. Whow! Admittedly that may well take in the use of shared kitchen facilities, but at that price it should include a swimming pool, scooter, and... The weary Lindiot landladies are battle-hardened in 'room search repartee'. Enquirers foolish enough to own up to requiring a room for anything less than at least three nights, will discover there simply aren't any available. On one occasion, a 'worthy' soul suggested the beach, rather than let a room for one night, due to all the work that would involve! Travellers dismounting the bus may be offered a room, and a manifestation here is for foreign girls, operating on a commission basis, to bestride luggage, as it is unloaded, in an effort to secure clients - for accommodation, I hasten to add. The usual method, of wandering along the streets and making enquiries of likely looking women, may not be fruitful. The Tourist office will help locate a room, as will Lindos Suntours (*See* Tour and Travel offices). A number of visitors sleep on the beach.

An important factor for villa holiday-makers to bear in mind is the location of their villa, vis-a-vis the donkey route from the main square to the Acropolis. The donkey droppings along this well-worn alley result in an above normal number of mosquitoes in the vicinity. You have been warned.

The Eating Out The only relatively inexpensive eateries are the fast food stands. That which laughingly passes for service, at the best, borders on the brusque and rude. Restaurants range from the expensive to the extremely costly. An example of the general 'carry-on' is the *Lindos Taverna*, which has a seemingly attractive menu (stuffed chicken) and nice panoramic view, but oh dear! The Scottish voiced proprietor is gruff, the staff are Brits, the chicken was, in fact, a fillet (served not only with tinned peas, but tinned carrots & Colonel Ben's rice), added to which the overall quality and attitude were poor.

THE A TO Z OF USEFUL INFORMATION

BANKS The National and Commercial (Emboriki) **Banks** are close to the main square, off Acropolis St. Open Mon-Fri between 0830-1400hrs.

BEACHES The lovely sandy bay of the Grand Harbour, down to the left (*Fsw*). Round to the right is the much smaller St Pauls Bay.

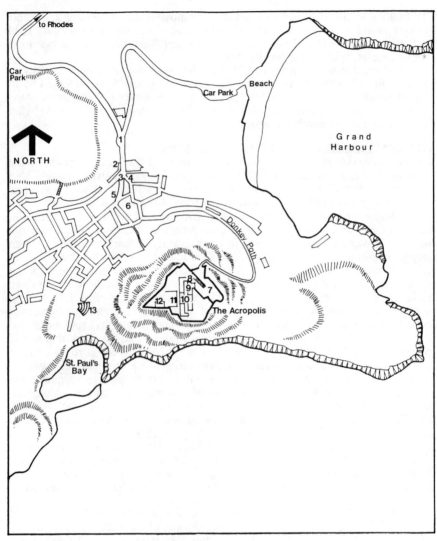

Key

1	Main Square	8	Knights' Castle
2	Donkey Corral	9	Byzantine Church
3	Commercial Bank	10	Temple entrance
4	Post Office	11	Temple
5	OTE	12	Temple of Athene Lindia
6	Byzantine Church	13	Ancient Theatre
7	Acropolis Entrance		

Illustration 7 Lindos & the Acropolis

BICYCLE, SCOOTER & CAR HIRE Lindos Suntours provides cars, but for cheaper prices **Lindos Rental** and **Pefkos Rent A Car** are still better choices. Prospects should wander round and compare rates, as individual firms make 'attractive, can't be bettered' offers for a particular day.

BOOK LENDER An expatriate American lady runs a lending library service from No 381. She charges between 100/700drs a day, depending on the popularity, size and state of a book, with 1000drs deposit.

BREAD SHOPS Next door to the National Bank.

BUSES The main square doubles up as the bus terminal. For timetables *See* Buses, Rhodes City.

DISCOS To preserve the old world milieu, every so often the 'worthy burghers' decree that all disco and bar music has to cease at midnight.

EXCURSION BOATS Craft daily set-out from Grand Harbour for Rhodes City at 1500hrs, the round-trip costing 3000drs.

LAUNDERETTE No 456. A load costs some 700drs. Closed on Sundays.

MEDICAL CARE
Chemists & Pharmacies Yes, up the hillside, first right beyond the donkey 'marshalling yard', and open Mon-Fri 0930-1400 & 1630-2000hrs, Sat-Sun 1000-1300hrs. The nice and helpful pharmacist is a trained doctor.
Clinic (Tel 31224). To the left of Acropolis St, down the hill opposite the donkey corral.

OTE No 156, behind *Alexis Bar*, on Acropolis St. Open Mon-Sat 0730-2100hrs, Sun 0800-1300 & 1700-2200hrs.

PLACES & EVENTS OF INTEREST
The Acropolis Open daily 0830-1500hrs, closed Mondays. Entrance 800drs, There are toilets on the left of the entrance. Early morning arrival ensures a relatively free-from-the-hordes amble round the site. It is possible to travel on a donkey, at a cost of about 500drs to ascend, and 350drs to descend!
    A splendid situation, but the Knights plonked down castle walls, over and around earlier Byzantine fortifications. The enthusiastic laudation and favourable comparisons with Delphi, that precedes a visit to the site, may well result in some disappointment. It is a muddle of a 4thC BC Acropolis, a 13thC Byzantine church, and medieval castle walls. It should be no surprise that the place was reconstructed by the once, ever-present and energetic Italian archaeologists and, even now, appears to be undergoing, year in, year out, even more renovation.
    The steep ascent on foot is by narrow, zig-zagging flights of steps. The route to the Acropolis cannot be mistaken, as all along the path are Lindiot women, with their weaving, linen and crochet work, spread out for sale over the wayside rocks. Once on the flat area, edged by cypress trees, immediately beneath the walls are some Byzantine cisterns. Then, swinging round, almost in a semi-circle, the rock wall on the left reveals the relief of part of a trireme, a 2ndC BC warship. Unless I am very much mistaken, this is very similar to the one carved into the rock beside the quay road of Simi island harbour.
    A ticket man sits in his hut, whilst the ticket collector lolls on a stool, alongside! After the climb to the walls, the entrance way is through a

dungeon, or more correctly, a vaulted hall. Whatever, this resembles a Second World War pill-box and, thus, should possess that distinctive, dank, animal smell, but does not. From the vaulted hall, beneath the Fort Commanders' rooms, the remains of the church are on the left. This is followed by a stairway to and through an entrance gate (propylaea) towards the forecourt of the temple, followed by the Temple of Athene Lindia, which dramatically terminates at the perimeter wall, edging the cliff, and overlooking both the:

Ancient Theatre Not a lot left, apart from some of the seating and gangways and:

St Pauls Bay A small, almost circular cove, surrounded by bare rock. This is supposedly the spot where, in days of yore, a bolt of lightning and a clap of thunder caused the rock to split asunder. The phenomena caused a lagoon to become a harbour - which enabled a storm-tossed boat, in danger of capsizing, to reach safety. A passenger in this fortunate craft was St Paul. Well, well! His unexpected arrival, in AD 51, is not unnaturally considered to be when Christianity reached the island, and has given rise to the annual festival of St Paul, on 28/29th June.

Lindos Churches These include the *Church of the Assumption of the Madonna* (St Mary, Panaghia), sited close to the middle of the main village and the junction of Acropolis and Apostolou Pavlou Sts. It is possibly older than the inscription of 1484-90, for these dates may refer to a period of rebuilding, by the Knights. The external appearance is pure, simple Byzantine, with the red tiled, domed, seven-sided cupola offsetting the white walls. It starkly contrasts with the dark gorgeousness of the interior, the excellent frescoes (painted in 1779, but restored in 1927), the wooden screen and the Byzantine icons.

Houses of Lindos The settlement is famous for the sheer number that have survived, relatively intact, to the modern-day. Some, medieval in age, are notable for the uppermost 'Captains Rooms', which allowed a clear view of the harbour. The interiors of these houses are often distinctive, possessing decorated, lofty wooden ceilings and mosaic floors. Later houses of the 16th and 17thC display an unusual family bed arrangement. In this, the bed is raised on a platform, set under an arch, in the main room and reached up a low flight of steps. One other architectural hallmark, worthy of note, are the individually decorated doors and their accompanying hand knockers. They are so distinctive that some of village shops retail a poster illustrating Lindiot doors. There are two other idiosyncracies: the ceiling suspended, angled mirrors (seen on Simi, as are some of the other features of Lindian houses); and the wall-hung decorated plates, some dating from the 16thC, which probably originated in Persia, but are now definitely of Rhodian manufacture.

Many of the villagers throw open their doors, but only to sell ceramics, plates, shawls and quilts.

Tomb of Kleoboulus A tentative connection to a 6thC BC tyrant leader of Lindos, who ruled for 40 years and was one of the Seven Sages of the ancient world. This circular tomb, made of large, cut square stones, is sited on the headland of the Grand Harbour. It possibly dates from the 5th or 4thC BC, and was used as a church, in medieval times.

A number of relics from Lindos now reside in Copenhagen Museum, as a result of excavations by the Danes, in the early 1900s.

POST OFFICE Close by the donkey yard on Acropolis St, just off the main square, and *en route* to the pharmacy. Open Mon-Fri 0730-1400hrs.

POLICE (Tel 31223) Beyond the Post Office, at No 521 Vas Pavlou. Manned Mon-Fri 0800-1500hrs. There is a 24hr telephone service.

TOILETS A reasonably clean public lavatory is by the main square.

TRAVEL AGENTS & TOUR OFFICES There are many firms. Some swear by **Lindos Suntours**, beside Acropolis St. But *See* Tourist office.

TOURIST OFFICE (Tel 31428) Situated alongside Plateia Eleftherios, open daily 0930-2200hrs, and answers the usual enquiries.

From Lindos the road to Pefka passes St Paul's Bay, scales the brow of a hill, to wind across a plain, edged by a glowering bay, on one side, and menacing cliffs, on the other. Surely this must have been a Minoan settlement, an impression reinforced if Gournia (Crete) is recalled. The evening brings about that same brooding atmosphere of anticipation, of ancient overlay and ghostly presence. Whatever, over the saddle of the the hillside edging the plain, on the far side, and into view hoves the burgeoning:

PEFKA (58km from Rhodes) This once quiet, unspoilt seaside village has become a busy tourist resort, complete with Chinese restaurant, moped rental firms and shops. The houses are widely spread out over a small, but broad headland, the low cliffs of which border a splendid, gently curving bay. The narrow, sandy beach is dotted with umbrellas, whilst a small *Cantina* backs up to the cliff-face. A number of sailing yachts lie at anchor.

Quite recently, there was little else but the beach. Nowadays, ever increasing development is inexorably infilling, with a vengeance. Most of the *Rooms* and the *Pension* are pre-booked by holiday companies. If price and availability is a problem, why not try nearby Lardos - above *Supermarket* 'George'? George, a charming man who speaks excellent English, has five rooms, all en suite, sharing a kitchen, costing 4000/5000drs per night.

Instead of forking off to Lindos, the main route passes through:
PILON (Pilona) (53km from Rhodes) It may well be worth considering giving Lindos the 'accommodation cold shoulder', to stay here, at the *Hotel Pylona* (Class D, tel 44247). Double rooms, sharing the bathroom, cost from 3500drs, and en suite from 4000drs. The hotel has a nice restaurant, in addition to which they operate a scooter hire business. There is another Pension and a taverna in the village.

Beyond Pilon the main road skirts:
LARDOS (57km from Rhodes) The 'jolly', touristy village is unremarkable, but the overall road layout is rather confusing, with the settlement inland of the highway. The Hotel Reno - 'Swimming pool everyone is welcome', is one of a number of hotels. The St George Campsite (Tel 44203) offers superb facilities, which include a swimming pool, various sports courts and grounds, a bar, restaurant, shop, disco and TV lounge, to name but a few. There is a camp bus to Lindos. They charge 500drs a head per night.

A filling station marks the Old Road, now a turning down to:
Lardos Beach Beyond Lardos Beach Apartments, is a long, fine pebble beach, sporting beds, umbrellas and pedaloes, stretching as far as the *Lardos Beach Restaurant*. The latter is sited at the end of the bay, and not only sports thatched umbrellas, but a car parking sign alongside the restaurant. Ugh!

Two side roads branch inland, the first to:
Thari Monastery (14km) The turning initially heads to **Laerma** village, which has its own delightful church. Then, selecting the Laerma to **Profilia** road, after some 2km a track winds towards the monastery. The ancient building, dating from as long ago as the 9thC AD, is famous for its outstanding, high quality, 13thC frescoes.

The second side road leads to:
Ipseni Monastery (4km) At the far end of Lardos village, a track advances in the direction of the monastery, in front of which a hill is set out with the Stations of the Cross. The shaded grounds have a drinking water fountain.

Also in the vicinity, back along the coastal road towards Pefka, is a pleasing location. This has beautiful sand set in a small circular bay, backed by shrub covered dunes, but some rubbish is present.

The main route, curves sharply around a small, hilly projection, the far side of which is a most unsightly factory and concrete jetty. Although the works seem deserted, there is the usual 'scrap' of abandoned machinery, and trucks. After this 'blot on the landscape', a splendid bay is passed on the left.

I prefer to keep to the Old Road. This skirts the coastline and a series of bays, of varying length, some sheltered and secluded, some with a fine shingle shore, or rock. These border the road, until the thoroughfare clatters into:
'A Seaside Shanty Town' (66km from Rhodes) Well, how would you describe this untidy, unnamed, ramshackle settlement of jerry-built chalets, with a couple of tavernas, and a small, signposted beach?

Still on the Old Road, about 1½km further on heralds the outset of a long, long, lovely, pebbly beach, which stretches besides the clear sea's edge, for some 11km. Beach umbrellas mark the backshore position of some side-by-side beach tavernas, and the seaward end of the concreted track down from:
GENNADION (70km from Rhodes) The New Road environs of this once-upon a-time, unpretentious village, are indicated by a couple of rather large tourist hotels. They are the *Rodi Maris* and the *Holiday Sun*, with more completed, and yet more under construction. In addition to the hotels, there are supermarkets, touristy tavernas, a church and a clinic.

Returning to the beach, for the moment it remains quiet and relatively unpopulated, even in the busier summer months. This state of affairs will change, dramatically, once all the new Gennadion holiday construction has reached its zenith, and come on stream. Certainly, the one, all-encompassing, ceaseless, daylight hours sound, that filters through to those on the beach, is that caused by the workers erecting the various apartments and pensions. As if to foreshadow the anticipated build-up of tourists, the beach already hosts a full panoply of water sports activities. These are now positioned alongside the sun beds and umbrellas, and beach showers. The clutch of backshore, tree shaded beach bar/taverna/restaurants now numbers four, and they stand in front of an area of beach where the sea-bed shelves quite steeply.

Incidentally, Gennadion marks the east coast watershed, the Rhodian divide, south of which is emptier, drier, and from whence some semblance of a Greek island ambiance commences. The point at which this demarcation rives the west coast is to the south of Monolithos.

From hereon, it is probably best to select the New Road, which is reasonably well metalled. That is, apart from spaced out, irregular and infuriatingly small sections, where the road surface has broken up. The metalling increasingly deteriorates beyond **Hohlakas** (83km). In this village, and from the main road, are signposts indicating the tarmacadamed road, to the left, down to:

Plimmiri Beach The tree shaded shack is the *Taverna Plimmiri*, the sole, but reasonably priced culinary establishment. Requests for a menu usually result in a client being directed to the kitchen - full of Greek women cooking.

To the right of where the access track bottoms out, is an extended   stretch of initially tree shaded, shingly sand shore, edging a pebble   sea-bed. The beach and the sea become cleaner, the further one walks to the right. To the left is a long, fishing boat finger quay, beyond which is a small caique bay. Unfortunately, the location is sometimes   included in the fun-loving, beach buggy 'Safari run'.

Continuing south, the landscape is expansive and dished. Prior to reaching Kattavia, the road rolls through the rather strange, almost deserted village of: **AG PAVLOS** (88km from Rhodes) My original notes, made many years ago, rambled on about 'the spot not seeming to have a *raison d'etre* ..., scattered farm buildings, one of a monastic appearance..., and a large, 1930s(?) Italianesque agglomeration of buildings, of a religious aspect, bordering the roadside, and partially filled with hay and farm equipment'.

A turning to the left shapes towards the isthmus of: **Cape Prassonissi** This is the southernmost point of the island, topped off with a lighthouse, 'manned' by a couple who look after the beacon. The access road peters out, after some 2km, degenerating into a track. Progress is made just that little bit more difficult, as the area is utilised by army tanks, occasionally carrying out manoeuvres. There is a huge expanse of shelterless sand, and, thankfully, two summer month tavernas.

Returning to the main route, three kilometres on, and the last village of this eastern route is attained. That is: **KATTAVIA** (91km from Rhodes) The final approach to this sleepy, rural farming community is along an unmetalled slip road. It passes by a Shell filling station, on the left, prior to juddering on to the irregular square, at the heart of Kattavia. To the fore are a pair of taverna/kafeneions, pleasantly shaded by large trees. The one on the left, with wooden tables and chairs, is the most frequented, and offers accommodation, as well as food. Herein a double, sharing the bathroom, costs 2400drs. Those considering eating here might reflect that, despite initial appearances, it is a 'greasy spoon'. Further-more, the proprietor is not such a simpleton as he might appear. He trades on the fact that most (midday) diners will be ravenous, and that they will assume, at this distance from all the tourist glitz, that the prices will be 'country reasonable'. Forget it. An ordinary, lunch, for two, of an omelette, a pork chop, 1 salad, a bottle of retsina & a Fanta, costs about 4000drs.

Other establishments offer *Rooms*, such as the *Kattavia Club* (?), as well as a couple of stores which are handy for provisions.

From Kattavia, a poorly surfaced road heads north, in the direction of inland **Mesanagros**, climbing up and on to the spine of a low mountain range. This vantage point allows some splendid views.

ROUTE TWO
To Kattavia via Kamiros Skala & Monolithos (108km from Rhodes) The west coast road to Paradissi is described under **Excursions to Rhodes City**

Surrounds. There can be no doubt that this side of the island is much less tourist exploited, and is thus much quieter. The reason is that there aren't any of the glorious east coast sweeps of sandy beach. Say no more.

The countryside 'over here' is rather a mix of lowland agriculture, dotted about which are villages and hamlets of a more traditional mien, with verdant mountain ranges dominating the inland aspect. The markets and stalls reflect the richness of the agriculture, with an abundance of inexpensive, fresh fruit and vegetables for sale.

At the turning off to **Theologos** (Tholos) there is a filling   station. Three kilometres further on, the main road passes through **Soroni** village, and on to: **FANES** (Fanai) (26km from Rhodes) At the far end of the settlement is a right-hand track, signposted 'Hotel Delfini' - Fish Restaurant, which traipses across a windswept stretch of open coastline, to a narrow, stony beach. This is attractive, in a rather unkempt fashion, has two precast concrete bench seats and is the proud possessor of a four-head shower unit - it's similar to spotting a two-seater loo. No, oh well... The hotel to the left (*Fsw*) runs a windsurfing school, so there are lots of enthusiasts here.

Returning to the village, a turning heads inland towards **Eleousa**. After some 4km, a tree lined track trails off, to the left, past a clearing, complete with a makeshift racecourse (yes, a racecourse...), to: **Ag Soulas Church** The sole purpose of this church appears to be to host the annual feast and celebrations, held on the 30th July. One of the unusual features of the day is a donkey derby, and thus the... It all reminds one a bit of Watford, doesn't it?

The road to **Dimilia** and Eleousa is a 12km uphill climb. The description of this is included with that of the inland incursion to the Eleousa, Platania, Apollona and Nani circuit. This circles Mt Profitis Ilias, from the direction of **Kalavarda** (30km), some 4km further along the main road. At the latter settlement, the side-road rises steeply, in a series of loops, to:

SALAKOS (38km from Rhodes) A delightful, large, spaced-out village, radiating out from a big, irregular, tree shaded main square, whereon a drinking water fountain, and surrounded by cafes and tavernas.

The road soldiers on for some 5km, through **Kapion**, to a junction at which the left turning makes a northern loop around: **Mt Profitis Ilias** The expert estimates of the height of this pine tree covered mountain vary, between 650 and 900m, which seems a rather wide spread to me. A wooded path from Salakos village 'huffs & puffs' to the mountain top. The track crosses the road close by the alpine style *Hotel Elafos-Elafina Mt* (Class A, tel 22225). This is set in thickly planted trees, in and out of which it is not unusual to spy the occasional mountain goat, 'a clambering'. Some deer are penned in large, wooded enclosures, and there is a childrens' playground. It would be strange if the views were not outstanding.

The descending 9km of road is unpaved and rough, in places, passing through heavily wooded countryside. At about half-distance is a solitary chapel. Beside the final approach to Eleousa is an inexplicably positioned, large, agreeable spa-type pool, in the middle of which is a stone 'funnel'. The waters host some fish and ducks, and this makes a secluded picnic spot.

ELEOUSA (59km from Rhodes) An unusual village, with a bewildering road layout. Dominating the centre of the settlement is a big 'Hacienda' style dwelling, complete with an extensive palm tree planted courtyard. This is an Army camp, rather reminiscent of some South American location.

The confusion in respect of the road directions is how on earth to get out of the place. Well, more to get to where you really want to go, a desire not helped by two signs 'stamped' 'Eleousa' - and pointing in opposite directions! Fairly close by is **Ebonas**, for details about which read on.

Between Eleousa and Platania, much of the landscape has suffered the ravages of out-of-control forest fires. These conflagrations are, unfortunately, almost an annual event, with much of the southern area of the island's hillside vegetation being lost to the resultant holocausts. On these occasions, the fierceness of the blaze is such that the smoke blots out the sky, with the daytime sun showing through as a diffused, red orb. The wind-blown air smells strongly of charred olive wood. Quite often, if the right vantage point can be found, it is possible to spend many a fascinating hour watching events. The truly riveting sight is that of the yellow coloured, 'fire engine' aircraft skidding on to the sea, collecting a 'hold-full' of briny, and, once water-laden, slowly, ever so slowly, shaking the fuselage free of the waves. Thereafter, they rumble on to the fire, drench the flames, and once their load is dumped, loop back, to scoop-up yet another cargo of the 'damp stuff'. This can go on for days at a time. **Platania** is an agreeable, unspoilt village, beyond which the hillsides roll on to **Apollona**. This is a 'so, so'. A not so nice, and oh so average village, which, for some inexplicable reason, is on the excursion coach ambit. Due to the latter quirk of tourism, there are lots of tavernas, bearing signs in English. There is a filling station, close by the junction with the road to **Laerma**.

Between here and the junction with the main road back to Salakos, the gentle farmland makes way to pine clad hills, a transition that takes place at a fountain bowery.

Back at Kalavarda, the main road fastens on to the coastline, close to sea-level, until adjacent to the archaeologists' delight of Kamiros. Proximity to the site is indicated by three taverna/restaurants, positioned on two small, adjacent headlands. Trees grow down to the water's edge and there is a satisfactorily sandy beach, on which are 'planted' some beach umbrellas. Two of the establishments are 'imaginatively' named. One is the *Old Kamiros*, the other the *New Kamiros*, beyond which an inland turning advances 1km, gently up a slope to:

Ancient Kamiros (34km from Rhodes) (Illus 8). Open daily, except Mondays, between 0830-1900hrs, closing at 1500hrs on Saturdays & Sundays, with entrance costing 400drs.

The beautiful site and excavations are hidden from view until a rise is breasted. The ancient city is revealed, to the left, lying in a large, shallow, saucer-shaped depression, hollowed out of a gentle hillside. The site, dating back in part to the 6thC BC, was discovered in 1860, and extensively excavated by the Italians, around 1929. Surprisingly, there is no evidence or sign of an acropolis, or other fortifications, and history does not record any invasion. The overwhelming impression of the presence of the Minoans, at one or two Rhodes' locations, is lent credence here. Both legend and conjecture suggest that the first inhabitants of Kamiros were from Crete. No concrete reason has been established for the final abandonment of the city, the remains of which include a very large, 6thC BC water cistern, a restored

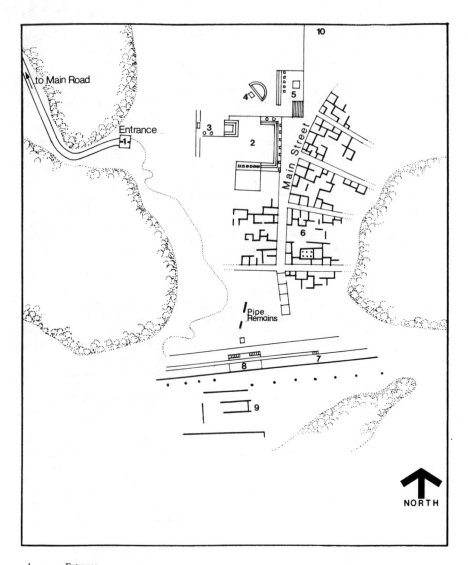

1	Entrance
2	Sanctuary
3	Doric Temple
4	Exedra
5	Sacrificial Area
6	Helenistic House
7	Stoa
8	Cistern 6thC BC
9	Temple to Athena
10	Public Baths

Illustration 8 Ancient Kamiros

Stoa, that has unfortunately experienced a collapse, a Temple to Athena, as well as drainage pipes and a main street, off which radiate various remains, including a Doric temple.

Back in the 20thC, the coastal road, is encroached upon by low, landward foothills, which advance inexorably towards the sea's edge. In the area of **Mandrikon**, the coastal strip widens out to a vaguely lunar, mucky plain. Another (modern) Cretan influence flaps into view, in the shape of plastic greenhouses. Eminent archaeologists assure me they are not Minoan!

The road climbs around a bluff, through a landscape green with vineyards, olive trees, and agricultural cultivation. It drops down again, to a large headland and inlet, in which nestles the village and port of:
KAMIROS SKALA (48km from Rhodes) (Tel 0246) On the left of the main road junction is a *Taverna/Pension*. This establishment is cheaper than the competition, and is where the ferry-boat captains while away their spare time. A simple, but clean double room, sharing, costs 3000drs, the fish meals are better and less expensive, than the rivals, and a Nes meh ghala costs 100drs. This pension also marks the spot where the Rhodes City buses stop.

The slip road for the harbour/ferry-boat quay tumbles past the *Taverna/ Pension Artemis*, where bedrooms cost 500drs more than the previously listed place, and the dishes are all about 100drs pricier. Down on the left, close by the small mole and the commercial harbour, is yet another reasonably priced taverna, opposite a newish building, serving breakfasts and meals, which is frequented by the locals. The quay is across the way, and is the prime *raison d'etre* for Kamiros Skala, as this is the main port for Chalki island.

Incidentally, the tavernas tend to allow the trade to simply wash over them, offering a leisurely service, and menus that show a distinct piscatorial bias.

Ferry-boats They depart daily (except Sundays) at 1430hrs, with a Rhodes City bus arriving, in time to allow supplies and passengers to embark. The craft return the following day, at about 0530hrs. The one-way fare is 800drs. On Sundays, the schedule is altered to allow a day's outing, departing at 0900hrs, and returning at about 1700hrs. *See* Chalki island.

Independents are best advised to avoid the smaller craft, the **FB Chalki**, and one other, which are primarily used by the clients of package holiday companies. They are slower and have to wait until the flight and connecting coach arrives. In any case, first off the mark is the alternative craft, the **FB Aphrodite**. This is a vessel of great character, an ancient ferry-boat, operating to a schedule, and with every appearance of being constructed from 'bits of driftwood and scrap metal'.

Beyond Kamiros Skala, the road commences to climb steeply, and where it dips, there is a sign to the right, pointing along a slip road. This almost immediately forks, with the first choice, an unsurfaced, dusty track, once again signposted in the direction of 'Jimmi's Taverna/Beach'. The track descends to a quiet, pebbled cove, sheltered by two pine and scrub covered limestone bluffs. Where these form the rock sides of the cove, they exhibit an interesting, granular rock structure, similar to that of ruined, dry stone walls. Drawn-up on the near backshore are about a dozen fishing boats. The farbackshore is a dusty affair, used as an *ad hoc* car park, and turning point

for the more inquisitive of the summer months rent-a-car hordes. To one side
is a shanty dwelling. Above this, tucked on to the pine tree covered hillside,
and overlooking the   beach, is the aforementioned *Jimmi's Taverna*. Best
avoided, if only due to a predilection to overcharge. A meal, for one, of a
small plate of shrimps (old & 4 in number), a Sprite soft drink, some patatas,
a Greek salad, a small bottle of Ilios wine & a plate of stewed octopus, cost
5420drs!!! Perhaps the fact that Jimmi's is popular with Germans explains the
blatant, rip-off charges. Best to use the beach, and the well maintained taverna
toilets, set below the building, should nature so dictate.

Back at the main road, the route winds inland, whilst to the right **Kamiros
Castle** hoves into view, way across a valley. If the detour is thought
worthwhile, the narrow road signed 'Kastelos' is in good   condition. The
ruined fortress, once restored by the Knights, makes a splendid location for a
view over the inshore islands dotted about offshore. They include **Strongili,
Makri, Tragoussia** and **Alimnia**, with **Chalki** in the distance.
　　The journey skirts the west side of Mt Attaviros (1215m). The flanks of the
mountain range are amply covered with vegetation and trees, whilst the
uppermost summit is singularly bare, almost in the style of a monk's tonsure.
　　Beyond **Kritinia**, is a junction, alongside which is a winery. Visits are
possible, and free samples may be sipped. How nice. The left-hand turning
takes an inland, circular route, via **Ebonas** village, famed for lusty and strong
women, and from whence, with the aid of a guide, the summit of Mt
Attaviros can be reached. The journey continues to wind on round to **Agios
Isidoros** village, and back to the main road. In this region tobacco and grapes
are the predominant crop.
　　Between Kritina and Sianna, an unmetalled track plummets to the right and
is grandly signposted:
Paradise Beach & 'Glyfada Restaurant & Rooms' The 5km dirt road loops
steeply down, through pine forested hills, to a small, remote settlement, on the
edge of the coast. There are two taverna/pensions, the remains of a lookout
tower, a strip of large pebble sea-shore and a small caique quay.
　　The *Glyfada Restaurant/Taverna* is set back some 50m from the foreshore,
and is run by Harry and his wife. Originally from Rhodes, they spent most of
their life in Australia, and consequently speak a marked 'Grine'. Their
hospitality is straightfoward and, despite the relative isolation, their company
is good. The rooms are simple, being lit by oil lamps, and the shower and
lavatories basic. You might be offered a 'special' ouzo, about which Harry
waxes lyrical, in flowery prose, singing the praises of the amber nectar... In
reality, I am fairly sure the potent brew is very similar to Cretan raki - a
refined ouzo, and a powerful 'little brew'. On a visit, some years ago, when
it was mentioned that the shower did not work, Harry's wife exhibited the
alternative. This was a standpipe, round the back of the building, to which was
attached a length of hosepipe. Mmmh! Simple, but effective, as long as a
guest has a companion handy, who will aim the hose. The lack of hot water is
a little annoying, and the flush of the toilets reverberates throughout the
building, especially in the middle of the night. Mind you, any sound is
magnified, as the bedroom walls are paper thin. If the generator is not swung
into life, at dusk, the paraffin pressure lamps are lit, which, due to the poor
quality of the fuel, often give out small explosions and plumes of flames, with
the resultant danger of conflagration. On these nights, guests are handed a
torch. The patio is shared with marauding cats, as well as the bees and wasps

that inhabit the trellis vegetation shading the terrace. The meals, like everything else here, are simple but wholesome, with many of the vegetables freshly picked from the garden. A double room costs 3000drs.

Harry is disposed to extol the virtues of 'the beach'. His directions must be followed, to the half-metre. If not, those who choose to wade about, in search of the much vaunted strip of sandy sea-bed, in amongst the enormous pebbles, may come to the same conclusion as I did, that it is yet another Greek myth.

Close by the shoreline is the other building, housing the *Paradissi Taverna*. Maybe it was this taverna's name that led me to believe that the shore might be a golden stretch of warm, yielding sand! For those who wish to escape the all-pervading tourist invasion of Rhodes, this locale is a possibility.

The main road continues high above the now distant coastline, through pine clad, *Rio Grande* type countryside, to:

SIANNA (75km from Rhodes) A pretty, working village, hanging on to the hillside, with many kafeneions and a glorious view down along the distant Apolakkia Bay. The church clock has a painted face, a characteristic to be observed on other, country church timepieces. A number of guide books refer to a path from here to **Cape Armenistis**, but the best way down to the headland is from beyond:

MONOLITHOS (80km from Rhodes) This village's *raison d'etre* might well be solely to indicate the upper road to 'Frourion'. I cannot understand this, and am not sure where Frourion is, but the so-signed track does lead to a large lay-by, overlooking the startingly sited:

Monolithos Castle (82km from Rhodes) Open daily, round the clock, with free admission. The fortress impossibly nestles, neatly on the top of a 250m high pillar of rock. The pinnacle rises, needle-like out of the plain, in the middle distance. There is a vast backcloth of incredibly blue sea, with, off the rocky headland of Armenistis, a small island. The scene is a heady, magic mix of 'Aegean Walt Disney' seascape and German Rhineland castle.

Access to the castle is gained by following the stony track down and round, to below the far side of the rock, on which it is perched. In the castle confines is the unremarkable Chapel of Ag Pantaleonos. Prior to reaching the viewpoint overlooking Monolithos Castle, a turning to the right is signposted to Kimisala, Kirameni and Pyrgos, but travellers should not bother unless they enjoy bumping over extremely rugged, rocky paths that clatter down through sylvan-clad hillsides. Close by Mt Armenistis are the vestiges of a long deserted village, some way above the sea, on the edge of a small ravine.

Back at Monolithos village, the wide, surfaced roadway gently descends through groves of olives to:

APOLAKKIA (91km from Rhodes) The plastic littered approach to the village is generally rather messy, with the final run-in over a summer-dry river-bed. An agricultural settlement, with few concessions to other than the locals' pursuits, and why not? But there is a periptero, the *Pension Manolis*, *Restaurant Manolis*, several tavernas, as well as (100m down the unmetalled Kattavia track) the *Hotel Restaurant Skoutas* (Class E) and the *Pension Kosta*. There is also a filling station, but the owner may well require rousing.

On Sunday mornings, during the grape season, a back-of-truck market turns up in the form of an agricultural rotavator pulling a trailer, from the back of which is suspended a huge pair of scales.

A metalled road traverses the island, all the way to the east coast road at Gennadion (*See* Route One), whilst the unsurfaced west coast road turns back towards the coastline. After some 3km, signposts indicate Furni, around a headland to the acute right, and Limni, but neither is more than a house or two. Additionally, a track wanders down to a long beach, which is made up of cleanish, large stones. There are sweet-water, if brackish pools close by the sea, and goat herds, rather incongruously, graze their sheep and goats right up to and across the stony foreshore.

The first stretch of the backshore coastal road is edged by rock dunes, which are followed by sand dunes, scrub trees and ravines, set in the wild countryside. There is some cultivation amongst the low, stumpy hills on the inland side. After 7km a track to the left sallies forth to:

Skiada Monastery (102km from Rhodes) An interesting diversion. The monastery, in the control of caretakers, is set in perfect island countryside, far from the madding crowds of tourist hordes (to only slightly misquote Gray's Elegy), and allowing magnificent, if distant sea views. Accommodation, but not food, may be available.

The last section of the main track rises into more substantial hills, curving away from the coastline. A further 9km leads to Kattavia (*See* Route One).

Another housing start? No, Lindos Acropolis being restored, yet again.

4 CHALKI (Chalkis, Khalkia, Khalki, Halki) * *

Dodecanese Islands

FIRST IMPRESSIONS Niche package tourists; no *Room* signs; Jackdaws.

SPECIALITIES Package tourists & their attendant publicity - stickers & decals; 'precious' yachties.

LOCAL RELIGIOUS HOLIDAYS & FESTIVITIES 2nd Aug - Festival Ag Ioannis; 15th Aug, one of THE National religious festivals is celebrated in a 'big' way here.

VITAL STATISTICS Tel prefix 0241. The island has an area of 28sqkm & a population of about 340 people.

HISTORY Unremarkably, followed the 'hemline' of Rhodes. The Knights of St John built the castle overlooking Horio, the old capital.
  In comparatively recent times, Chalki was a sponge fishing island. Unfortunately, the sponge beds disappeared, due to disease, leaving the inhabitants no other method of earning an equally lucrative living. It is only necessary to look around the arid barrenness of the countryside, combined with its relative hilly formation, to appreciate that agriculture, on any scale, was out of the question. Some reverted to fishing, but large numbers emigrated to - Tarpon Springs, Florida, in the good old US of A. This quirk of fate explains the incongruously named *Tarpon Springs Boulevard*, which was generously financed by Chalkian expatriates.

GENERAL Chalki may well be a slight disappointment, to the first-time visitor. There is something strange about this dry, almost lunar, quiet little island, though it is difficult to pinpoint the cause. A few day's nosing about suggests that many of the rather off-hand, disinterested inhabitants, gorged on a rich diet of the better-heeled British package tourist, are riddled with community ill-feeling, and are constantly feuding with each other. Chalki is a 'soap-opera' island, without the TV appeal. 'For-instances' are the two ferry-boat brothers who don't speak, and race each other to and from Kamiros, and the taverna owner who, having had a row with the baker, ships his bread over from Rhodes. So it's not the (welcome) lack of motor vehicles. Whatever the reason, the result is that the island appears to have been preserved, as if in some time-warp, almost like a laboratory specimen, in a museum exhibition case. There is an 'emptiness', with the usual cachopany and rhythm of Greek village life simply not present.
  Given the rave reviews, heralding its peace and seclusion, first-timers might be taken-aback to find the island's accommodation packed to capacity, with away-from-it-all package tourists. Even at either end of the summer season, their numbers are 'healthy'. On the other hand, to travellers stuck on Rhodes, and searching for an escape from the worst excesses of the down-market holiday industry, then Chalki must appear a very good bet. That is as long as the 'escapee' appreciates the cries and whoops of the 'greater Home Counties, gin and tonic set'. I have to advise, if I were seeking a quieter, nearby alternative to Rhodes, I would probably head for Kastellorizo, or Tilos.

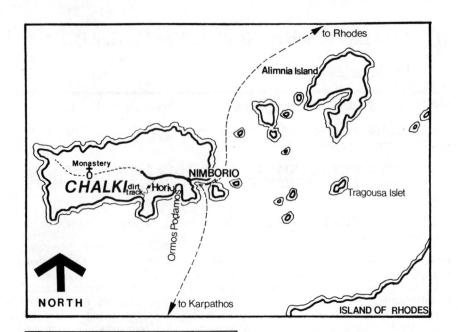

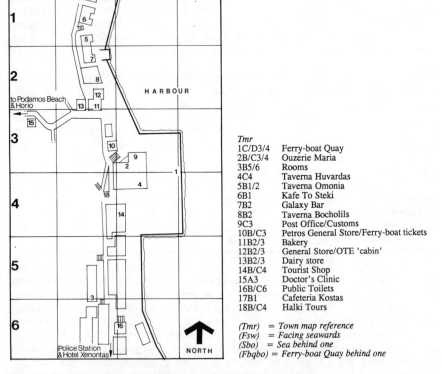

Tmr	
1C/D3/4	Ferry-boat Quay
2B/C3/4	Ouzerie Maria
3B5/6	Rooms
4C4	Taverna Huvardas
5B1/2	Taverna Omonia
6B1	Kafe To Steki
7B2	Galaxy Bar
8B2	Taverna Bocholils
9C3	Post Office/Customs
10B/C3	Petros General Store/Ferry-boat tickets
11B2/3	Bakery
12B2/3	General Store/OTE 'cabin'
13B2/3	Dairy store
14B/C4	Tourist Shop
15A3	Doctor's Clinic
16B/C6	Public Toilets
17B1	Cafeteria Kostas
18B/C4	Halki Tours

(Tmr) = *Town map reference*
(Fsw) = *Facing seawards*
(Sbo) = *Sea behind one*
(Fbqbo) = *Ferry-boat Quay behind one*

Illustration 9 Chalki island & Nimborio Port

The frantic rebuilding boom of some years past, has now petered out, if only for the time being. The conversion of the old houses was, thankfully, carried out with sensitivity. Much of the work was simply to accommodate even more *BPTs* . This points to one major, positive result of tourism, for, were it not for their influx, and the money they generate, the island would probably have become a moribund, crumbling wasteland. The careful renovation of the houses, similar to that to be seen on the island of Hydra, can be traced back to Chalki's nomination, by UNESCO, as an 'Island of Peace & Friendship of International Youth'. Oh dear me, the what...! This was some sort of international federation freebie, which resulted in boat loads of Greek bureaucrats luxuriating at the *Hotel Xenontas*, where they caroused the evenings away. When the locals finally twigged, that these activities did not actually improve their lot, they grasped the nettle. They contacted the Mayor of Rhodes, and had the freeloaders slung off the island. The ensuing release of hotel, pension and villa accommodation was then more productively and profitably made available to the niche holiday company clientele. Some might wonder why this clipped English accent, cocktail sipping, reasonably well mannered, 'house trained' invasion, imbuing Chalki port with a remarkable 'shire' ambiance, have not driven off the remaining inhabitants! It may be something to do with the underlying Chalkian character. A pointer to the latter may be deduced, when it is recalled they made Margaret Thatcher an honorary island citizen, in 1988, during the Rhodes based EC summit!

Independent travellers might find the milieu offputting. Apart from experiencing some difficulty with the twee holiday villa names, such as 'Villa Pink', the determination of tour operators to stamp their corporate identity on everything, as evidenced by the decals and stickers that 'brand mark' almost anything that doesn't move is decidedly unsettling.

The traditionally water-short island experiences severe problems in coping with the summer tourist invasion, and every effort is made to conserve the liquid. Isolated instances have been heard of pension guests being supplied with a bowl, in which to stand, whilst showering. The resultant, husbanded overflow to be used to flush the toilet! Most of the original houses have their own 'sterna', or cistern, in which to collect and store water, similar to Simi. Despite this, the majority of the island's needs are met by shipping it in, and pumping it up to the concrete reservoir, to be seen on the hillside, to the right (*Sbo*) of the port. To a great extent, this course of action has done away with the old complaint, that the tap water was so saline that it actually stung one's eyes. It used to be said that one might as well go for a dip in the sea, as shower in some pensions.

NIMBORIO (Emborio, Skala): capital & port (Illus 9). The port is charming, very picturesque, quiet and, mercifully, mopedless.

Locals relate that by the 1960s most people had departed inland Horio, for the sea-level delights of the port. Certainly the piping-in of the water supply and the installation of an electricity supply, via an under-sea cable from Rhodes, made everyday life much easier.

It might be appropriate to question the value of constructing the Tarpon Springs Boulevard, all the way through the centre of the island, past the castle, to end abruptly on a steep slope. Surely some of the money spent could have been invested in some other project? An idea would have been to 'regularise' the power supply, which can be 'indeterminate'. I'm sure the consequent, frequent interruptions to the power interfere with the ice-making (for gin and tonics, luvy). But, a far more important consequence is that the mosquito 'death-dealers' don't, without the 'fluence'. And that's just what the aerial dive bombers have been stalling around for - 'zoro-zoro'!

ARRIVAL BY FERRY Most visitors arrive on a Kamiros Skala boat, and some owners of accommodation wait for prospects. But, Chalkians do not regard 'single-nighters' with anything but a jaundiced eye. Those fancying a 'brief island encounter', may find themselves sleeping under the stars.

THE ACCOMMODATION & EATING OUT
The Accommodation There are few signs advertising accommodation, and almost all the possibilities are reserved by tour operators. What is available, is usually only so for several nights on the trot, and is relatively expensive.

Rooms (*Tmr* 3B5/6)
Directions: To the left (*Sbo*) of the Ferry-boat Quay, in a street one back and parallel to the Esplanade.

Iraklides, the sometimes difficult to locate owner, occasionally wanders down to meet the boats. The house overlooks the bay. The simple bedrooms are fitted with sparse, but modern furniture, are pleasant, and share the bathroom, at a cost of 3500drs a night. The two upstairs rooms open on to a balcony, with a lovely view of the port. On the other hand they are only separated by an ill-fitting, sliding door, so it is to be hoped that 'them next door' are quiet.

Pension Argyrenia
Directions: Take the Podamos Beach road, and the *Argyrenia* is a newish, single storey building. It is down an alley off to the right, immediately beyond the school, and some three terraces back. The rows of rooms are set by a vine trellis shaded terrace.

The old dear is one of those owner's who is reluctant to let a room, for less than a few nights at a time. In her efforts to ensure that this remains the case, she can appear rather rude. A double room, with modern bathroom and hot water shower, is charged 3500drs.

Also on the right-hand side of this road, one block further on, is possibly the best Chalki accommodation, namely the:

Hotel Kleanthe   Tel 37648/57334
Directions: As above, and more a pension than a hotel. The captain of the **FB Aphroditi** is a brother of the owner, and can be approached. Failing this, a nice little girl, who speaks some English, is usually dispatched to the Ferry-boat Quay, to ensnare clients.

Comprises three spacious double rooms, in a renovated captain's house, and, nearby, two very large apartments, which have two double bedrooms, as well as a kitchen and bathroom. Both buildings are newly converted, with extremely clean bedrooms fitted with pine furniture, supplied with clean sheets and towels, and the water is hot, all day long. The double rooms are charged at 3000/3500drs a night, and the apartments 4000drs.

Hotel Xenontas
Directions: From the Ferry-boat Quay, climb the steps and set out to walk to the left *Sbo*), round the bay, from the right of the Toilet block (*Tmr* 16B/C6). Continue past where the houses thin out.

Owned by Greco-Italian interests, and most agreeably situated, it being possible to swim from the terrace of this large (for Chalki) hotel. An en suite double costs 5500drs, including breakfast. Also owned by the hotel, and next door, is a disco, which might disturb a guest's slumbers.

Another possibility is the independent:
Captains House' Pension   Tel 57201
Pre-booking is essential, so telephone ahead.
The owners, Alex & Christine Sakellaridis, have attractively refurbished this old house, without losing any of its character. In the winter they can be contacted at 50 Aristippou St, Athens 10676 (tel 7231919). There are 4 double rooms, one which is small, with bunk beds. The shared, modern toilet facilities are some 3m distant, across the courtyard. Charges are 3500drs a night, including the use of a fridge and kettle, in a separate kitchen, but there aren't any cooking facilities.

At 10min distant Podamos Beach is:
Markaris Podamos Beach Restaurant & Rooms Toilet (*sic*).
Directions: As above.
Nikos' accommodation comprises some four en suite double rooms, priced at 3500drs. This is a very pleasant location, with views of the garden and the sea. Either side of the peak summer months, the restaurant is closed in the evenings, thus the nights are delightfully quiet.

The Eating Out There are some three to five port eateries, depending on the time of year, plus the *Podamos Beach Restaurant*. They are spread along the Esplanade, with their tables and chairs set out in front. The vociferous BPTs are very evident, more especially in the evenings. Their presence is not only the reason for a lack of caring accommodation owners, but is the prime cause for the lack of attentive service and the, at the best, mediocre food served at the various establishments.
Taverna Huvardas (*Tmr* 4C4).
Directions: This popular taverna is housed in the same block as the Post Office, right in front of the Ferry-boat Quay.
Serves variety, at reasonable prices. A meal for two of octopus (generous helpings), two plates of giant beans, chips, feta, two beers & bread, costs some 2200drs.

Ouzerie Maria (*Tmr* 2B/C3/4).
Directions: A quiet, shady corner of the promenade, tucked away round in the lee of the Post Office, opposite Petros Store.
Maria and her three daughters run a very nice establishment, serving good if possibly expensive dishes. A meal for two of moussaka (deliciously light & tasty), gigantes (jolly tasty) & 2 imported beers cost 3600drs.

Taverna Omonia (*Tmr* 5B1/2)
Directions: To the right (*Sbo*) of the Ferry-boat Quay.
The service can be slow, and surly. The rumour is that it is the owner of this taverna that has fallen-out with the island baker. It goes without saying that the taverna's bread is sometimes horrid. Another disconcerting habit is that listed prices only bear a limited, passing relationship to the actual bill, with each individual item being subject to an impost! A meal, for two, of 2 dips, 2 aubergine with garlic dressing & 2 large cans of Heineken cost 2400drs. Another of 2 moussakas, a green salad, 2 large cans of beer, bread & service, was charged 3950drs! Yes. 3950drs.

Kafe To Steki (*Tmr* 6B1)
Directions: Further north along the Esplanade.
A most congenial place around which the fisherman sit and mend their nets, 'of a morning'.

Cafeteria Kostas (*Tmr* 17B1).
Directions: The most 'northerly' of the Esplanade establishments, close by the church steps.
A reasonably priced cafeteria, serving coffee, drinks, pastries & toasts. The proprietor continues to give good service and keeps smiling.

Other 'offerings' include: *Yianni's* (brother of Nick of Podamos Beach), near the ice factory, serving good, simple Greek food, where the locals eat; and the *Taverna Bocholils* (*Tmr* 8B2), which has a well-to-do air and serves lobster. Not one of the tavernas appear to serve breakfast.

THE A TO Z OF USEFUL INFORMATION
BANKS None. *See* Post Office (*Tmr* 9C3), Petros General Store (*Tmr* 10B/C3), and Halki Tours (*Tmr* 18B/C4).

BEACHES It is possible to swim in front of the *Xenontas Hotel*, but the beach is some ten minutes walk from the port. Ascend the main, asphalt road (named Tarpon Springs Boulevard) from alongside the Bakery (*Tmr* 11B2/3). This climbs gently up the slope, past the school, and the *Hotel Kleanthe*. After three minutes, the road drops over the crest of the hill, with the small, sandy, usually overcrowded beach, busy with sun-beds & umbrellas, coming into view. The route descends past the corrugated metal clad generating station, on the left, and down a painfully dry, grey and rocky slope to the fine grey sand of Podamos Beach. Bathing is a pleasure, with the clear, clear aquamarine blue water allowing easy sight of the white sea-bed, which goes on, and on, and... *Nikos Taverna*, on the backshore, has already been mentioned under Accommodation. It is an excellent spot at which to have a snack or a meal.
For alternative beaches *See* Excursions to Nimborio Surrounds.

BICYCLE, SCOOTER & CAR HIRE None.

BREAD SHOPS The Bakery (*Tmr* 11B2/3) is alongside the outset of the Horio/Podamos beach road.

BUSES None.

COMMERCIAL SHOPPING AREA More a few shops and stores, with most supplies arriving daily from Kamiros Skala (Rhodes). There are two Esplanade General stores, selling a little of everything. **Petros Store** (*Tmr* 10B/C3) serves sliced meat, as well as canned foods, and many other supplies. The owner transacts foreign exchange and sells tickets for the **FB Kimolos**. The **Dairy** (*Tmr* 13B2/3) also sells a limited amount of fresh fruit and vegetables, and is to the right of the outset of the Horio/Podamos beach road. Callers should try their honey pancakes. Diamantis, the unsmiling owner of the other **General store** (*Tmr* 12B2/3), speaks English, stocks vegetables, as well as some tourist items, but most importantly houses the only island OTE 'cabin'. The **Shop** (*Tmr* 14B/C4) to the left (*Sbo*) of the Post Office block sells souvenirs, sun-tan oil, hats, tea towels (on which is depicted an island map), T-shirts and other 'vital forgetabilia'. Opening hours are the 'small island norm' - that is prospective customers must allow for a reasonable siesta.

DISCOS The *Hotel Xenontas* runs more of a disco-pub, the **Extasis Pub**, which is adjacent to the hotel.

FERRY-BOATS Chalki enjoys a weekly scheduled ferry-boat link with other Aegean islands, as well as a daily service to the Rhodes island, west coast hamlet port of Kamiros Skala. In respect of the 'Kamiros connection': this is a half-hour sea passage, and of the three craft that ply the route, the **FB Aphrodite** and the **FB Chalki** tend to slug it out for the prime Nimborio quayside berth. Woe betide any small boat that impedes their dash for the jetty. The third craft is tour company dedicated. Most independents will value the opportunity to travel on the Aphrodite (!), the young skipper of which belies his somewhat piratical appearance having a heart of gold. Passengers who lack the sea-legs can avoid the elements by sitting in the bridge, and watching the captain exercise command. Passengers, who board the 'package reserved' boat, must beware of a little sting, rumoured to be perpetrated by one or more of the less principled of the companies representatives. This involves their conning free-lance travellers into paying a 'surcharged' fare... otherwise the captain will get upset', or similar. Establish the cost of a ticket, prior to boarding the boat, and stick to it. You have been warned.

Scheduled Ferry-boat timetable (Mid-season)

Day	Departure time	Ferry-boat	Ports/Islands of Call
Tue	0830hrs	Kimolos	Simi, Rhodes.
	1600hrs	Kimolos	Diafani(Karpathos), Karpathos, Kasos, Sitia(Crete), Ag Nikolaos(Crete), Santorini, Sikinos, Folegandros, Milos, Siphnos, Piraeus(M).

For details of the Rhodes link *See* Kamiros Skala, Route Two.

FERRY-BOAT TICKET OFFICES Petros (*Tmr* 10B/C3), he of the General Store, sells tickets for the **FB Kimolos**, whilst those travelling on the Kamiros Skala boats pay on board.

MEDICAL CARE The combined **Clinic/Doctor's/Pharmacy** (*Tmr* 15A3) are to the left of the Horio/Podamos Beach road, opposite the school. The building is a low, white house, with dark brown painted shutters.

NTOG/TOURIST OFFICE None.

OTE A 'cabin' within the Store (*Tmr* 12B2/3), open daily 0800-2200hrs.

PLACES & EVENTS OF INTEREST Not a lot. A museum, or mosque, there is not. The pretty Ag Nikolaos Church, right (*Sbo*) along the Esplanade, displays a beautiful pebble mosaic floor. In addition, it claims to have the tallest campanile, in all of the Dodecanese.

POLICE
Town Five minutes walk round to the left (*Sbo*) from the quay, in the direction of the *Hotel Xenontas*. The building has no sign but is recognisable by its unusual, red painted, domed roof and peeling, cream painted walls. The

policeman is young, friendly, helpful and informal.
Port Housed in the same building as the Customs office (*Tmr* 9C3).

POST OFFICE (*Tmr* 9C3) Up the stairs from the quay. Transact currency exchange, and open weekdays 0730-1400hrs. Are the stickers meant to indicate that it is a holiday company sponsored facility?

TELEPHONE NUMBERS & ADDRESSES

Doctor (*Tmr* 15A3)	Tel 57206
Police Port (*Tmr* 9C3)	Tel 57255
Town	Tel 57213

TOILETS (*Tmr* 16B/C6) A fairly clean, white painted block.

EXCURSIONS TO NIMBORIO SURROUNDS Caiques run trips to various island beaches, including **Areta**, **Kania**, **Trachia** and **Giali**, but most can be reached on foot. Supposedly, the best beach is on the nearby islet of **Alimnia**, where there is also a ruined castle, but the caique cost, added to the one hour voyage, seem rather excessive. Enquiries should be made of Halki Tours (*Tmr* 18B/C4), or, best of all, directly to the fisherman/caique owners. Surprise, surprise, they are to be located at one or other of the Esplanade bar/tavernas.

Horio & on An enjoyable, if vigorous 2½hrs, each way hike. The actual journey time depends on the number of byways selected. The walk allows excellent views back down the valley, in the direction of Nimborio. To set off, follow 'Boulevard Tarpon Springs' out of the port.
    To attain **Kania Beach**, turn right, before reaching Podamos Beach, on to a track which climbs up on to the left-hand side of the large water catchment area. The wide path passes through a ramshackle gate, keeping a clump of pine trees on the left, to the small pebbly beach. It is about 35min, each way.
    Continuing beyond Podamos Beach, the concrete path leads to the dirt-track Horio turning. Following this is a trudge to the ruined and uninhabited mountaintop Chora of **Horio**. Here the Knights of St John built a castle, on the site of an ancient acropolis. The site provides   wonderful views over the sea and the island. The track continues on, with the castle and village to the left, to spiral down to the small, shingle, rather deserted **Giali Beach**.
    Back at, and continuing along the 'yellow brick...'. The still concrete roadway climbs past a small chapel. Eventually the route surface degenerates, becoming a rough track, leading to the **Monastery of Ag Eleftheriou**. Hard going, but worth it. Walkers must wear stout shoes, take some water, and start out early in the day.

5 KASTELLORIZO (Kastelorizo, Kastellorizon, Kastelloriso, Castelorizo, Megisti) * * * *
Dodecanese Islands

FIRST IMPRESSIONS Italians; crystal clear seas; dolphins; nesting swallows; attractive port; private yachts; bygone affluence; crumbling houses & ruins; fiercely Greek.

SPECIALITIES Seafood; the famed *Stravo* & *Katimari* pastry sweets, made with honey & nuts - but they are difficult to find "Yes, tomorrow we'll have them"; Italian spoken, by everyone.

LOCAL RELIGIOUS HOLIDAYS & FESTIVALS incl: 24th April - Feast of St George, at the two large churches in Megisti (both named Ag Georgios) & the Monastery of Ag Georgios, in the mountains; 21st May - Ag Konstantinos (the main Church on Horafia Sq); 20th July - Festival, Profitias Ilias.

VITAL STATISTICS Tel prefix 0241. The island is about 6km from top to toe, up to 3km from east to west, with a total area of 9sqkm. The population numbers about 250 souls. This is the most easterly of the Greek islands, being 120km from Rhodes & lies only 2km from the Turkish coastline.

HISTORY Mentioned by Homer. The island's first named settler was supposed to be a King Meges from Echinada, who may be responsible for its alternative name of Megisti. On the other hand, Megesti (or Megiste - the largest) probably relates to the fact that Kastellorizo is the biggest of a small archipelago of some ten or twelve other, uninhabited islands and islets.
   The islanders sent ships to Troy, and there are records of inhabitation since Neolithic times. The Dorians first built a fort, where the 'Red Castle' now stands, and they constructed an ancient acropolis at Paleokastro, the walls of which are still visible.
   The island came under the rule of Rhodes, for much of its history, with the Knights of St John reconstructing the castle, in the 1380s. The red rock used in the building of the fort's wall resulted in the island's current name, Kastellorizo (from the Italian Castello Rosso, or Red Fortress). In 1440, it was occupied, for the first time, by the Turks, followed by the King of Naples, in 1450. By 1523 the island was made part of the Ottoman empire, though the Venetians occupied it for two more periods, in 1570 and 1659. In 1821, the islanders took part in the War of Independence, being the first of the Dodecanese islands to revolt. Despite this brave action, in 1833 Kastellorizo was handed back to the Turks, in exchange for the island of Evia! After 1856, the French were nominally in charge. Even so, towards the end of the 19thC, the islanders prospered greatly from their involvement in shipping. This was Kastellorizo's period of supreme affluency, when there were between 15,000 and 17,000 inhabitants, and many of the big houses were built. The island's merchant navy numbered as many as three hundred ships but, unlike the Kasiots, the owners did not understand the revolution that steam was to bring to the world's fleets.
   However, it was the First World War that heralded the onset of the island's modern tragedy. During those hostilities, Kastellorizo was bombarded by both the Turks and Germans, which shell-fire destroyed much of the port's

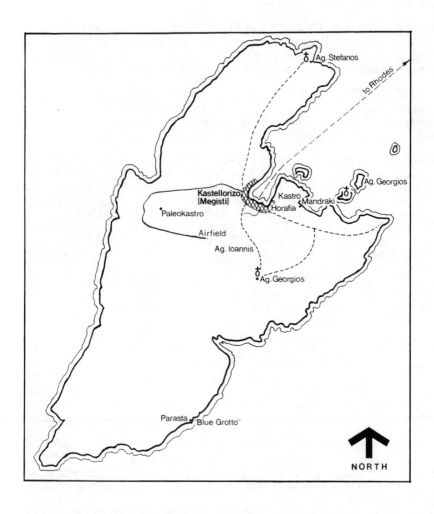

Illustration 10 Kastellorizo island

infrastructure. With the economic downturn that followed the Great War, 'serious' emigration began. In 1927 a huge earthquake destroyed many more buildings, despite which, during the 1930s, Kastellorizo enjoyed a short autumn of prosperity. In common with a number of other Greek islands, the coming of the sea-plane, combined with Italian suzerainty, resulted in daily flights to the island, from a number of Western European capital cities.

But, it was the events of the Second World War which really finished off the island. At the outset of the fighting, the remaining population, already lowered by many thousands, were evacuated to Egypt, by the Allies, who then occupied the island. Prior to the residents return, the island had been almost completely destroyed - though there are different 'stories' about how this occurred. One version maintains that the destruction was caused by enemy bombardment. Another account broadcasts that the British carried out the despoliation, either to cover the massive amount of looting their troops had wrought, or on the 'scorched earth' policy - if we can't have it, it will be no use to any one else, so there! Whatever the reasons, the town and port had been fired and ruined, beyond recognition. If that were not enough, the few islanders who chose to return, at the end of the war, had to survive the transport ship sinking. It is said that the expatriate islanders (most of whom emigrated to Australia, some to America, whilst others spread-out throughout Greece) always consider themselves as Kastellorizons, first and foremost, and natives of their adopted country, second. Furthermore, the two hundred and fifty permanent inhabitants are regarded as preserving the island, in the manner of custodians, for all those temporarily absent, who have left, and are scattered throughout the world!

GENERAL Kastellorizo, tucked away some 120km to the east of Rhodes island, beneath the southern coastline of Turkey, is a geopolitical absurdity. The restricted, but heavily subsidised ferry-boat connection does not strictly reflect the island's requirements. It is more a manifestation of the pressing need to keep the resident population intact and happy, as well as ensure a steady flow of tourists. This, 'goes the perceived government thinking', will discourage the Turks from any territorial ambitions! Have I got news for the civil servant who dreamt-up that line of thinking. A squadron of Turkish air force F15s would have a quite dramatic effect on both the islanders resolve, and their 'motions'!

Despite the historical disasters, tourism, such a despoiler elsewhere, has proved to be the one saving grace for Kastellorizo. Until very recently, the tourist industry was in its infancy, but nonetheless had brought about a revival of interest in the place. However, the island's prime position in the 'this is a find' category, has been seriously affected by a number of events. The first was the comparatively recent construction of an airport, with reasonably frequent summer connections to Rhodes, and a second was the increase in the number of international yachties wandering about the Mediterranean. But the third occurrence, the greatest 'happening', by far, was the decision of an Italian film company to make a motion picture about a group of Second World War Italian troops stranded on Kastellorizo. If that were not enough, the 'icing on the cake of island fame', was that the producer selected the island as the location, on which to shoot the film. That is not so absurd an aside, as might seem to be the case, when it is considered how many movies are filmed anywhere else, but the original place at which the original story was written or scripted. If all that were not enough, the film *Mediterraneo*, by Gabriel

Salvatore, was nominated for an Oscar, as the best foreign film - and won! The understandable determination of an increasing number of Italians to holiday anywhere, but in their own crime-ridden country, combined with their national herd instinct, and the fame which the film imparted to Kastellorizo, had the inevitable result. Hordes of Italians added the island to their list of holiday destinations. Additionally, the story-line had a lot to do with the resultant popularity. The plot was based on parodying the overall Italian wartime occupation of Greece. It centred around the exploits of a boatload of troops, who landed after the Germans had withdrawn. Instead of re-embarking and getting on with the war effort, the squaddies went native, succumbing to the island's charms, and more particularly those of a Greek 'lady of the night', whom the Germans had carelessly abandoned on retreating. Much of the film's action takes place in and around the 'good-time' lady's house cum brothel. The building pressed into service was actually the *Blue & White Pension*. Apparently 'film fever' possessed the islanders during the filming, and the whole motion picture circus brought with it untold opportunities and abilities for the natives to earn 'big drachmae'.

To illustrate the effectiveness of the film, nowadays any **FB Nissos Kalymnos** head-count will reveal some one hundred and thirty 'pasta people', out of a total of one hundred and fifty passengers. The balance is usually made up of Brit's and Germans. This explains the resultant Italian tourist 'imbalance', why the 'lingua-franca' is Italian, and that the call for *Rooms/domatia* has been replaced with requests for 'Stanza'!

It is not too late for dedicated 'islandophiles' to visit, but it is to be hoped that this most recent 'specialist bubble' of interest dies back, just a little, so as to reinstate some balance. The enlarging population, combined with increasing tourism, results in big problems with height of season accommodation. To help cope with this state of affairs, a couple of years ago, the Government decided to fund the building of some fifty new houses, at Mandraki, as an islander's 'overspill'. The idea was that the out-of-town 'council' houses would leave more bedrooms available at the port. Unfortunately..., the recently started scheme has only proceeded to the initial groundworks being constructed. Work has had to stop, for the time being, because the builders added sea water to the cement! Oh, dearie me. To help with the overworked, and slightly noisy electricity generator, a new plant is being constructed to the south of Mandraki. There are also consistent rumours regarding the possibility of the installation of a 'proper' desalination plant. The present solar powered plant, overlooked by the castle, is described in some books as supplying the whole island. In fact, it is a fairly inefficient affair, to which the *Hotel Megisti* has a direct line, and reportedly takes the lion's share. It is best to be cautious with the   drinking water, for, despite the positioning of large cisterns and wells, overlooking the town, there isn't any piping to the houses. Thus, the island relies on water boats for supply. In operation, this is a rather comical system, with an ex-Japanese oil tanker mooring in the middle of the bay, and directing the water down very long hose pipes, to the individual houses. This method of supply also applies to all the dwellings in Mandraki. What would normally be an extremely expensive operation, is very heavily subsidised by the Government, aided by the employment of National Service troops. In effect, the islanders only have to pay for the wages of the crew.

Despite the lack of any beaches, there are plenty of quiet, rocky coves suitable for bathing, with the fish-filled seas amazingly clear. The people, though reportedly 'odd', do not appear so peculiar, although there are a few, obvious cases of inbreeding. They certainly are most friendly and helpful.

Kastellorizo remains a 'find', a great little island full of character, excellent for exploration, with reasonable facilities for food and accommodation, except in July and August.

KASTELLORIZO (Kastellorizon, Megisti): only town & port (Illus 11)   The initially attractive appearance of the port and town belies the   fact that most of it has been ruined. A wander through the back   streets of the areas known as Horafia and Mandraki reveals the true   picture. To appreciate the real decline that has taken place, over   the decades, it is only necessary to purchase one or two of the old   postcards, for sale in the tavernas.

ARRIVAL BY AIR The small, but efficient airfield is situated on top   of the island, about ten minutes drive from the port. Its size   precludes all but Dorniers landing, thank goodness. There is a   waiting room, and not much else - apart from the Greek flag. Now the   field has been completely fenced off, there is no need for the goats   and sheep to be chased off the runway, prior to an aircraft landing   or taking off. The town bus attends arrivals and departures, at a fee   of 250drs, a fare that must seem eminently reasonable to those who   select to make the very hot, long descent, on foot.

ARRIVAL BY FERRY The ferry-boats dock at the Quay (*Tmr* 1E4), to the left (*Sbo*) of the deep bay, around which the port and town   circles. As the ferry calls only twice a week, it is met by most of   the population, and general chaos ensues. Owners of accommodation have developed the habit of lounging at the Esplanade bars, from   whence they shout 'Stanza', picking off clients as they wander past.   It is best to locate a *Room* fairly quickly, because the patron's   only tend to be on the premises, at around about the time of the ferry's arrival. Outside of these periods, enquirers may well have to   scour the cafes, bars and tavernas.

THE ACCOMMODATION & EATING OUT
The Accommodation Although locating accommodation is usually no problem, the months of July and August can be difficult. From the Ferry-boat Quay (*Tmr* 1E4), arrivals should set out along the Esplanade. A narrow side-street off to the left, prior to the *Cafe/Restaurant Sampsakos* (*Tmr* 12D6), is signed *Horafia,   Mandraki*, and leads down a twisting street, between crumbling mansions. After about 150m, at a right bend in the street, is the:
Rooms Kastraki   Tel 29074
Directions: As above, and on the left in a tall, angular building.

It is best to book in advance, as the owner can be hard to locate. Quite well kept, if rather dark bedrooms, sharing, with a   double priced from 3500drs.

Twenty metres further along, the same narrow street widens out into a dilapidated square, to the right of which is:
Pension Barbara   Tel 29295
Directions: As above, and situated in a three storey building, with   the name painted in blue and yellow on the outside wall.

This colour scheme continues indoors, where a rickety blue and yellow staircase connects the wooden landings. The shared bathrooms have a   sign *The water is not to be drunk*. The top storey rooms open on to   a pleasant, flower-laden, wooden balcony, and there is a communal   fridge on each floor. Some of the rooms are cell-like and dank, some are unclean, some have a

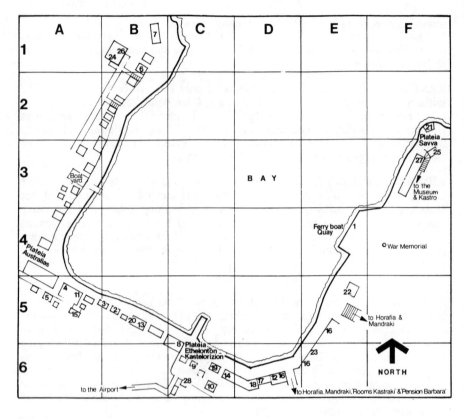

Tmr

1E4	Ferry-boat Quay	18D6	Supermarket
2B5	Rooms	19C6	'Periptero'
3A/B5	Taverna Apolavsis	20B5	Tourist Shop
4A4/5	Rooms/General Store	21F2/3	Disco
5A5	Rooms Paradisos	22E5	Clinic/Doctor
6B1/2	'Blue & White' Pension	23D/E5/6	Dizi Tours/Olympic
7B1	Hotel Megisti	24B1	Post Office/OTE
8B/C5/6	Taverna Lazarakis	25F3	The Mosque
9C6	Restaurant Mavrou	26B1	Town Police
10C6	Restaurant Oraia Megisti	27F3	Port Police
11A5	Taverna International	28C6	Public Toilets
12D6	Cafe Restaurant Sampsakos		
13B5	Taverna Parisi	(Tmr)	= Town map reference
14C/D6	Snackbar Meltemi	(Fsw)	= Facing seawards
15A5	Baker	(Sbo)	= Sea behind one
16	Food Stores	(Fbqbo)	= Ferry-boat Quay behind one
17D6	Fruit & Vegetable 'Market' Shop		

Illustration 11 Kastellorizo Port

lavatorial odour, whilst some possess all three 'attributes'. The pension is distinctly a bit quirky, and it is difficult to shake-off the impression that the place is about to collapse around one's ears! 'Barbara' and her husband have a free market pricing system, it being best to 'firm-up' on the 'starter' offer. For instance, a double sharing may well kick off at about 3000drs. Subsequent to'ing and fro'ing can find this figure escalating through 3500drs, even to scale the dizzily unrealistic heights of 5000drs. It has to be admitted that the latter price is more often than not reserved for those who have 'earlier in the day' turned down the opening overtures, but return later, head bowed, to make further enquiries.

Rooms 'No Name'
Directions: Opposite and just to the left of *Pension Barbara*, in a whitewashed, single storey building.
   The accommodation comprises two small, new and clean apartments, complete with bathroom and kitchen. To unearth details, enquire at the *Taverna Lazarakis* (*Tmr* 8B/C5/6).

Returning to the Esplanade, and continuing on round to the west, past the quayside square, Plateia Ethelonton Kastelorizion, leads to *Rooms* (*Tmr* 2B5, tel 29292). In the next block, the *Taverna Apolavsis* (*Tmr* 3A/B5) advertises *Rooms*, but this refers to *Pension Barbara*. Beside the Plateia Australias is a General store (*Tmr* 4A4/5) advertising *Rooms*. This relates to:
O Paradisos (*Tmr* 5A5)   Tel 29074
Directions: Turning left down the narrow side-street, beside the church, leads to a three storey, blue and white, rather palatial looking building at the end.
   The proprietor is to be found 'in attendance' at the General store (*Tmr* 4A4/5). Double rooms, sharing, are priced from 3500drs.

'Blue & White' Pension (*Tmr* 6B1/2)
Directions: Facing the Esplanade, on the far side of the 'U' shaped bay from the Ferry-boat Quay. This pension has no sign, but enquiries should be made at the *International* (*Tmr* 11A5), which is 'under the same ownership'.
   Paul Zervos and his wife, Peggy, run the pension. A very agreeably situated place, in front of which it is possible to swim. Being painted in pale blue and white, it clearly stands out. Smallish double rooms, sharing the bathroom, cost 5000drs. There is constant hot water, a shared fridge and kitchen, with cooking facilities, and a 'back yard' complete with washing lines and pegs. As with many other Kastellorizo possibilities, it is best to book in advance, thus contact Jack Benitsis, at the *Taverna International* - tel 28263/29348. One correspondent, who stayed here, related the charming story that... "our stay of five nights was enhanced by the fact that two expatriate Australian brothers, who were guests at the same time, had been born in 'our' room some sixty years ago, and that the house had been built by their grandparents". A recent German rumour alluded to fleas in the beds, but I stress that is not a personal observation, and was probably the result of some of our EC allies being denied the first, second, third, and... place, alongside the quayside - there being no swimming pool! Because of the shape of the bay, late night music tends to echo about. This is fine as long as the auditory assault is gentle Greek music from the Esplanade tavernas, but not so good if it emanates from the disco opposite! Guests who consider they might be kept awake by the rock music sound waves, might consider requesting a room at

the back. This is a shame, as the front rooms have such super views.

The latter advice also applies to the modern, but tasteful:
Hotel Megisti (*Tmr* 7B1) (Class C)
Directions: Beyond the *Blue & White Pension*.
Very clean and comfortable, with a double room en suite priced at
10000drs, yes... On other islands the cost would be about 5000drs, but here,
at Kastellorizo, there isn't very much competition. The once unchallenged
expatriates from Australia now have to scramble and compete with the
overwhelm of Italians. The hotel has a broad patio and is a lovely place for an
evening drink. Breakfast is an extra, and is self-service, buffet style choice.

One other accommodation opportunity is to visit **Dizi Tours** (*Tmr* 23D/E5/6,
See Travel Agents).

The Eating Out There are some excellent tavernas, but generally they are not
inexpensive. This is not only because both Italians and yachties are competing
for the available seats, but that all supplies have to come all the way from
Rhodes, as distinct from Turkey. Perversely, seafood is comparatively cheap.

In the Esplanade area of the 'Market' shop (*Tmr* 17D6) are a number of
opportunities, which take in:
Kafeneion/Restaurant Sampsakos (*Tmr* 12D6)
Directions: As above, and on the left (*Sbo*).
Popular with both aspiring and retired sea captains, which patronage should
be noted. They sell Amstel beer, in the bottle, and Beck cans, only when the
former has run out. There are very acceptable plates of mezes, as well as
chicken, giros, souvlakia and salads. Two cans of Beck cost 530drs.
And the:
Kafeneion Tis Iromonis
Directions: Also close to the 'Market' shop (*Tmr* 17D6).
A locals 'snack-stop' offering alfresco, quayside grilled octopus. An ouzo
with ample mezes, and a Sprite cost 250drs.

Plateia Ethelonton Kastelorizion (*Tmr* C5/6) is the 'taverna' square. One of
the best here, and in the port, for that matter, and no less expensive than most
of the others, is:
Taverna Lazarakis (*Tmr* 8B/C5/6)
Directions: As above.
Candlelit dinners for yachtsmen, at tables and chairs spread out on the
square and small boat jetty. The taverna is run by a 'papa', and his two young
and extremely pleasant sons. The latter are among the few youthful islanders
who continue to live all the year round on Kastellorizo. They are delighted to
discuss, at length, the future of the island (or lack thereof). The taverna
usually displays a big 'fish of the day', ready for 'the carving'.
Restaurant Mavrou (*Tmr* 9C6)
Directions: Another Ethelonton Kastelorizion Sq establishment.
This restaurant exhibits one of the cardinal eating out 'no, no's' - a glass
case displaying various menu alternatives, contents which will   include
swordfish kebabs and octopus. Generally, the food is standard fare. This is
yet another yachties' taverna, and is hosted by the initially agreeable Angelo.
It does not take too long to realise that Angelo's enthusiasm is, in fact, a very
well polished act, one that begins to grate after inumerable obeisances, and

offers of free drinks. He is particularly attentive to the yachties, of course! However, it is to admitted that he can prove helpful, in a number of areas. He has a metered phone (the Post Office phone, only extending as far as Rhodes), and will cash travellers cheques.

Meltemi Cocktail Bar
Directions: Close to the *Restaurant Mavrou*.
Owned by Angelo's brother, here are served exotic cocktails and ice creams, to a background of pop music. Clients tend to be those who have come-up on the pools, or who been fortunate enough to be a beneficiary of a stash of 'ash cash', left in a wealthy relatives will. Despite advertising lots of 'stickies', the *Meltemi* can run-out. Its opening hours nobly cater for the early morning airport bus departure (0800hrs), and defy the siesta. A Nes meh ghala, with a plate of bread, butter & honey, costs 550drs.
Also 'on the square' is the *Restaurant Oraia Megisti* (*Tmr* 10C6).

Taverna Parisi (*Tmr* 13B5)
Directions: 'West, young man (or woman)', and bordering the Esplanade. I hope readers note this socially 'correct speak', and my feeble efforts not to upset the ladies. This stems back to a spat I had with a lady librarian, from Sheffield, who advised me my books would be banned, if I did not promise to cease, forthwith, asides such as... 'the little woman'. Whow!
The old, weather-beaten, gap-toothed fisherman is very friendly, as long as prospects can speak Greek, and (even then) understand him. One is not the same as the other. He serves simple, 'Kastellorizo inexpensive', but excellent meals. A 'bill of fare', for one, might be a whole, grilled baby octopus (delicious), a Greek salad with chillies, a plate of kalamares, a bottle of retsina, and a large bottle of water, all for a cost of 2150drs. Incidentally, his caique is moored to the quayside, hard by the taverna, and he arranges boat trips to, for instance, the Blue Grotto (*See* Excursions). He only sets forth in calm seas, and thus is probably a better bet than 'Pension Barbara's' husband.

Taverna I Apolavsis (*Tmr* 3A/B5)
Directions: *En route* to Plateia Australias.
Apparently out of action as a taverna, but is 'strong on' big boned, languid, smoking, drinking youths, who parade at the pool table. It continues to double-up as the 'front room' for Barbara (she of *Pension Barbara*) and her henpecked, intimidated husband, a 'room with a view' from which to watch the world go by. 'Hubbie' has his caique berthed across the Esplanade. Accompanied by a seemingly witless, geriatric sea captain chum, he also runs boat trips to the Blue Grotto. In comparison to his *Taverna Parisi* competition, he is less discerning about the sea-state, and thus whether the swell will preclude entrance to the cave.

Taverna International (*Tmr* 11A5)
Directions: This taverna is on the way round towards Plateia Australias, with its tables and chairs on the quayside, and beneath a cool, shady, vine trellis covered terrace/garden. Prominent are photographs of two worthies, who have 'made it big' in the outside world, and originate from Kastellorizo families. Despite the fine display of international flags flying, there isn't an Italian one.
The agreeable host is Jack Benitsis, with an Australian background. Although in the past praised for its excellent dishes, serving perhaps the most ambitious meals available, our last research means that 'little Jack's' report must be downgraded to 'rather slick, tourist style, often slow service'. A meal

for two, of 1 plate of roast potatoes (a welcome change to chips), a courgette & mushroom pie (tasty, if stone cold at the centre), a pork chop (uninspiring and served on 2 lettuce leaves, with 3 slices of saute potato, frozen peas, carrots & rice), a Sprite, and a bottle of beer, cost 2040drs. The slowness of delivery was not ameliorated by the continuous solicitations. A bowl of plastic flowers on the table, canned Italian music, as well as green and red garden lamps, ensure this taverna has the least atmosphere and Hellenic ambiance, of any Kastellorizo establishment. The locals don't appear to patronise here, and the television, that is often constantly turned on, tends to divert customers attention. If an Italian film is being shown, the premises becomes inaccessible. The *International* is a very pleasant, if pricey, morning spot, serving a filling breakfast. This might include cornflakes (with hot milk), toast, butter, marmalade, orange juice, a boiled egg, and Nes meh gala. Money and cheques can be changed (in fact might have to be changed!), and the published commission rate is often more competitive than that at the Post Office.

For a change from the busy waterfront scenario why not try the:

Taverna Platania
Directions: This little taverna is up on the hill, at Horafia. The location is a peaceful and quiet, if not desolate townscape, beside the wide, grand, ruined Horafia Square. All the 'main roads' from the left (*Sbo*) of the waterfront lead here, as this was once the centre of the town, prior to the Second World War 'blitz'. The square is bordered by two churches, the school, the village hall and several ruined buildings, as well as a larger than life-sized bust of the old lady of Ro (who also has a picture in the museum - is a new myth developing in front of our very eyes?)

The clientele are usually a few old locals. A tasty, if small meal, for two, of a Greek salad, chicken & boiled potatoes, a green bean stew with potatoes, and 2 Cokes, cost 1950drs.

THE A TO Z OF USEFUL INFORMATION
AIRLINE OFFICE & TERMINUS *See* Dizi Tours, Travel Agents.
Aircraft timetable (Mid-season)
Kastellorizo to Rhodes
Mon/Wed/Fri/Sun   0915hrs
Return
Mon/Wed/Fri/Sun   0810hrs
One-way fare: 7900drs, duration 45mins.
Note those passengers flying on to Athens can benefit from a 25% discount.

BANKS There isn't a bank, but the owner of the *Taverna International* (*Tmr* 11A5) is the representative for the **National Bank**. Dizi Tours (*Tmr* 23D/E5/6) and the Post Office (*Tmr* 24B1) conduct foreign currency exchange.

BEACHES There are no beaches, not 'nowhere'. In July and August fishermen ferry tourists across to the islet of **Ag Georgios**, whereon a chapel, a house, and a few shingle slopes, which nearly qualify as beaches, but not quite. It is a 'must' to ensure that sea urchins are not infesting a bathing spot. It is ironic that such a pretty island, with such beautiful seas, should be plagued with such a multitude of the spiny horrors. The areas in front of *Pension Blue & White/Hotel Megisti*, and below the castle are the best for swimming and sunbathing. It is suggested that the developer of a now, long mooted hotel, rumoured to be built in the barren little bay of Ag Stefanos, is going to 'build a beach', as well ... Good luck to him!

BREAD SHOPS The **Baker** (*Tmr* 15A5) is south of the *Taverna International*, along a narrow alley, opening and baking every second day. It is run by two young, Vietnamese refugees, picked up by a Greek ship, in the South China sea, and granted asylum here.

BUSES The sole bus only travels to and from the airport, at a fare of 250drs. It departs at 0800hrs, on the due days, from behind the *Restaurant Mavrou* (*Tmr* 9C6). There is no Olympic bus.

COMMERCIAL SHOPPING AREA There are adequate **Food** shops (*Tmr* 16), spaced out all the way around the Esplanade, a **Fruit & Vegetable Market** shop (*Tmr* 17D6), as well as a **Supermarket** (*Tmr* 18D6). The 'Periptero' (not a kiosk here - *Tmr* 19C6) is run by a blind man, who sells cigarettes, postcards, island maps, when available, and old photos of Kastellorizo, as does the 'Tourist Shop' (*Tmr* 20B5). Fresh fruit and vegetables are only for sale when the ferry-boat docks, and all will have retailed by the next morning. The same applies to yoghurt, which is sold at the the referred-to Periptero (*Tmr* 19C6). Despite strictly observing the siesta, most shops open on Sundays.

DISCO (*Tmr* 21F2/3) At the very right-hand end (*Fsw*) of the bay, near the mosque. Opens sporadically, but when it does, the intrusive noise blasts around the harbour, causing a nuisance to the owners of accommodation, across the water. Usually closes by 2330hrs.

FERRY-BOATS The only ferry is the clean and comfortable, four year old **FB Nissos Kalymnos**, which also runs up the Dodecanese islands. The money for the craft's construction was raised by the islanders of Kalimnos. Travellers should keep an eye open for dolphins, which are plentiful as the boat closes on Kastellorizo. A reader pointed out that island-hoppers should not leave Kastellorizo to the end of their trip. If the weather turns nasty, it is nail-bitingly possible that the ferry won't materialise on time. On such occasions, a seat on an aircraft is usually impossible, and it must be borne in mind that their schedules can also be subject to disruption, in bad weather.

Ferry-boat timetable (Mid-season)

Day	Departure time	Ferry-boat	Ports/Islands of Call
Tue/Sat	0330hrs	N. Kalymnos	Rhodes, Simi, Tilos, Nisiros, Kos, Kalimnos.

One-way fare 2200drs; duration 5hrs.

FERRY-BOAT TICKET OFFICES *See* Dizi Tours, Travel Agents.

MEDICAL CARE
Doctor/Pharmacy (*Tmr* 22E5) The Doctor's clinic cum pharmacy is housed in a white building. The doors open daily, morning and afternoon. When shut, ask around. Serious cases have to helicoptered or shipped to Rhodes.

NTOG/TOURIST OFFICE The shell of an Esplanade office has, as far as I can ascertain, never seen any action.

OTE (*Tmr* 24B1) There are a couple of metered telephones in the same building as the Post Office. *See* Post Office.

PLACES & EVENTS OF INTEREST

The Castle To get to the fortress follow the path marked 'Museum' from behind the Mosque (*Tmr* 25F3), watching out for snakes, until immediately prior to the museum. Then track along a broad, walled, ruined street to the right, which climbs up the hill to the Castle, and the old windmill. Alternatively take the narrow street from the left of Horafia Square (*Facing Mandraki*), which advances through ruined houses to the hilltop.

The fort was originally built in Doric times. The 'Red Castle', which is believed to have given the island its name, was rebuilt by the Knights of St John, around 1380. A very large Greek flag continues to fly proudly from the hilltop tower. In addition to the national 'flutter-flutter', there is an EC flag, no doubt to indicate to the 'Brusselcrats' the eastern limit of their fiefdom.

A now white-painted section of the castle has been renovated, and accommodates the:

Museum To find the building follow the signs behind the Mosque (*Tmr* 25F3). A delightful building, and well worth a visit, if only for the views from the ramparts. The interior is agreeably laid out, and way above the average, 'small island' museum - but then Kastellorizo has a 'way above average' history. Interesting exhibits include clay pottery from a 13thC shipwreck, a one hundred year old sponge diver's suit, with iron shoes and compressor, as well as vintage photographs and drawings of the port, town and island, in its heyday. The museum is open daily, except Mondays, 0730-1430hrs. Entrance is free.

The Lycian Tomb Instead of bearing right outside the museum, up to the castle, continue straight on beyond the museum. Proceed down the hill, amid ruined dwellings, to a very steep, uneven staircase cut into the rock face, where it is necessary to watch one's footing. The Tomb is at the top, and to the right, distinguished by a heavy stone entrance, beyond which can be seen the burial chamber. There are others on the island of Kos, as well as Lycea (Turkey). The site features on a current EOT poster, and is a popular place at which to carve one's name.

The Mosque (*Tmr* 25F3) The 200 year old, quayside Turkish Mosque is attractive from the outside, but remains firmly closed.

POLICE

Port (*Tmr* 27F3) A large building, close to the quay.

Town (*Tmr* 26B1) The friendly, informal 'shop' is to the front of the Post Office block. A few soldiers from the castle 'hang out' here.

POST OFFICE (*Tmr* 24B1) Located behind the *Blue & White Pension*. Transacts foreign currency exchange, and open weekdays 0730-1400hrs.

SPORTS FACILITIES Fishermen equipped with lightweight, freshwater tackle and some decent bait (dried shrimp) should hit the jackpot. The harbour is a prime spot.

TAXIS None.

TELEPHONE NUMBERS & ADDRESSES

Doctor (*Tmr* 22E5)	Tel 29067
Olympic Airways *See* Dizi Tours.	
Police, town (*Tmr* 26B1)	Tel 29068
Town Hall	Tel 29069

TOILETS Beside E. Kastellorizion Sq is a fairly clean block (*Tmr* 28C6), with another on Horafia Sq, near *Platania Taverna*.

TRAVEL AGENTS & TOUR OFFICES Dizi Tours (*Tmr* 23D/E5/6, tel 29239) is beside the eastern Esplanade. The distinguished proprietor is 'West European efficient'. This is THE office at which to carry out currency transactions, and book all or any tickets, be it for air or ferry-boat travel, for which he accepts credit card settlement. This is the Olympic ticket office, representative, terminal, and check-in base. If advised elsewhere, that there aren't any return flights from Kastellorizo, do not despair. It appears the office goes 'long' on plane tickets, and reserves numbers of them, 'on spec'. Those departing by plane should ensure they catch the bus (*See* Buses), as there aren't alternative means of transport.

EXCURSIONS TO KASTELLORIZO PORT SURROUNDS
Caique Trips These are available around the island, to other nearby islets, and, most commonly, to the 'Blue Grotto', on the east coast. For details look out for the signs at the various waterfront shops and cafes (*See Tavernas Parisi* (*Tmr* 13B5) & *Apolavsis* (*Tmr* 3A/B5)). A rough sea can preclude entrance to the Grotto. Out of the height of season months, boat trips are less frequent, because the fishermen require at least four passengers, if not five or six, to make the journey worthwhile.

The **Blue Grotto** is certainly not to be missed, if at all possible. The caiques take about forty minutes to reach the cave, which is almost invisible from outside, as the entrance is very low indeed. Inside however, the cave opens out into a vast cavern in which the sunlight reflects off the surface of the sea, making everything a fluorescent blue. There are stalactites in the cave and a 'resident' pair of seals, who come here to breed. If they are 'at home', their presence can be distinguished by loud splashing noises. Some of the boatmen allow their passengers a swim inside the cave. The trip costs between 500-1000drs per person, depending on the number of 'punters'.

'Non-Excursion' to Turkey An official day-trip to Turkey used to be on the tourist agenda, and may be still mentioned in older guides. In fact, this practice was stopped in 1985, by the Port police, presumably on Government orders. Even the islanders' own sorties were halted, which is to be regretted because Turkish foodstuffs and other goods are much cheaper, and more convenient than those shipped in from Rhodes. There is a wild, unsupported rumour that discreet enquiries may 'unlock' a boat owners irresolution. The rumour goes on to maintain that 'illegals' are smuggled aboard a craft, for the crossing, at a cost of 5000drs, for a three hour trip to Turkey.

ROUTE ONE
To Horafia & Mandraki Taking this short walk, over the hill to the left (*Sbo*) from the port, illustrates the full extent of the area's demise. Previously the hill on which the castle stands was covered with houses, all destroyed during the Second World War. However, the wide roads, paths, archways and squares still remain.

Taking either the broad, white painted flight of steps from the nameless plateia (*Alongside the Doctor* (*Tmr* 22E5), or the side-street close to the Fruit Market (*Tmr* 17D6), leads to a broad square bearing the sign **Horafia**. On one side is the huge and impressive Church of Ag Georgios, to another side the

Church of Ag Constantinos, the lower and more modern of the two churches. Next to Ag Constantinos is the school - much too large for the island's present-day head-count of some thirty-five pupils. Behind the   childrens' swings is the Town Hall. All these buildings are in a good state of repair, but there are ruins to all sides.

Continuing past the *Platania Taverna*, down the main road sloping towards the sea on the other side, heads for the seaside area known   as **Mandraki**. Here, all that now remains are huge, crumbling mansions, some of which are in good repair, but most of which have fallen down. The road continues beside the shore to the left, towards the cemetery, which is set down on a promontory. Apart from the abortive 'council housing' estate, beyond this is another possible site for a new hotel, but the promising-looking continuation of the road merely leads to the town's rubbish tip.

ROUTE TWO The only other paved island road is that to the airport. The adventurous can make a two hour trek across the island, starting out from the end of the airport runway, and finishing by descending steps cut into the rock face, above the port. Why not take advantage of the bus to the first base camp - the airport? Here ask the personnel to   point out the start of the path. A rejoinder to those who must hike   about the countryside, without consideration to a body's long term good - turn left at the French-looking farmhouse.

6 KARPATHOS (Scarpanto)
Dodecanese Islands

South island   *
Mountains   ***

FIRST IMPRESSIONS Tourist infested; locals speaking German, notices in German, as well as English; wind tortured trees; stunning views; BMWs; appalling roads; wealthy villages & returned expatriates; many white chapels.

SPECIALITIES Women's costumes (Olympos).

LOCAL RELIGIOUS HOLIDAYS & FESTIVALS incl: 28-29th Aug - St John the Headless, Avlona.

VITAL STATISTICS Tel prefix 0245. Nearly 50km long, up to 12km wide & down to 4km narrow, with an area almost as large as the island of Kos, but a population of only some 5,500 (compared to the 18,000 of Kos), of which about 1,500 live in the capital, Karpathos (Pighadia).

HISTORY Findings of antiquity are few and far between, and even then only fragmentary, though there is evidence of a number of important, ancient sites. An idiosyncrasy was that the Knights only stayed two years, handing the island back to the previous overlords, the Venetian Cornaros family. The Turks, in the shape of the pirate Barbarossa, took over in 1538.

GENERAL The charms and attractions of the island have become only too well-known, to a wide number and variety of European holiday-makers. This has resulted in the capital port having a strong, a very strong reek of the Kosta Brava, with numbers of costly hotels and international restaurants. Even the time-warped, ancient village of Olympos is undergoing a to-be-regretted tourist transformation.
    The natives advise that travellers should visit the island - in the month of May, for the flowers, and September, for the fruit and to swim, but that between the 15th June and the 15th September, the wind blows, and blows....
    A curious inheritance law, shared with the Dodecanese islands of Leros and Simi, is that the eldest daughter, not the eldest son, is the rightful heir. This anomaly led to hardship, not only for the sons of a family, but for the mother and the other daughters. Reputably this quirk encouraged the males to emigrate, in order to make their fortune, but most islands lost their young men, due to a lack of work, added to the glitter of golden opportunities, in the New World. Without doubt, Karpathos is an island where the returning expatriates resulted in 'North American' being the second language, that was until German climbed the linguistic charts. Another manifestation of these 'home-comers' is the seeding of some unusual and unexpected cultural pursuits, such as Video Clubs and a disproportionate number of ladies' salons.

KARPATHOS (Pighadia): capital town & main port (Illus 13) The town is set down on the edge of a large, lovely bay, flanked by mountainsides to the north, with a small islet plonked down in the middle of the sea inlet.
    The rapidly changing skyscape of hastily constructed apartment blocks gives an impression of the town being comparatively new. The layout is a little muddling, and much larger than at first appears to be the case.
    The night-time activities of the town's stray cats can keep even a heavy sleeper awake.

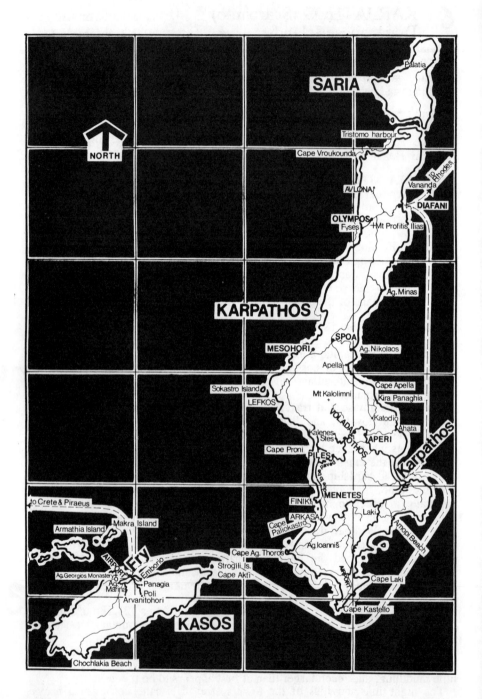

Illustration 12 Karpathos & Kasos islands

ARRIVAL BY AIR The windy airfield transformation enables both the tiny, inter-island Dorniers and their larger, international equivalents to land. The enormous expanse of runway totally dwarfs the smaller aircraft, which only require one hundred metres or so of the seemingly endless swathe of concrete.

A brand new, two storey terminal building is in the last knockings of being completed. Until it is, the old block has to cope with domestic and international flight arrivals and departures. The authorities cope with this dilemma and 'chaos possibility' by the simple expedient of locking the existing facility, when domestic flights are turned round. Thus, instead of a baggage carousel, passengers mill about to extract their luggage from the trolleys, having manhandled aside the usual overlay of bundled Greek newspapers.

Local flights and independent travellers do not benefit from an Olympic coach or an island bus service. Apart from setting out on the 15km hike to Karpathos town (or possibly the some 7km distant main road junction, for Amopi Beach, where one of the twice daily buses might be connected with), the only choice is a taxi. This virtual monopoly must be 'drachma from heaven for our Hellenic hackney-cab fraternity', and they charge a 'miserly' 1700drs a head, for a shared ride. Those prone to travel illness, and who were not air sick, even on the steeply banked landing approach, quite possibly with the plane being banged about by a gusting Meltemi gale, should not prematurely congratulate themselves. Oh, no! Travel sickness is a generic description, also covering transit in a vehicle..., and a number of the taxi drivers regard themselves as skilled rally drivers! That might be acceptable, if it were not for the wind blown, poorly surfaced route to the capital.

ARRIVAL BY FERRY The neat, substantial quay (*Tmr* 1C/D1) allows ferries to dock on all three sides, but they usually berth on the far wall. The short Esplanade to the centre of the town is often littered with the large packing cases shipped from the USA or Canada, the worldly goods of the aforementioned islanders, returning home, once and for all. After disembarking, passengers should turn right (*Sbo*) along the waterfront, and follow the road round to the Clock Tower (*Tmr* 2C/D2) - about five minutes at a brisk pace. Night-time arrivals will find many Esplanade bars open, until the early morning hours, and owners of accommodation meet the ferry-boats.

Note, passengers wishing to disembark at the northern Karpathos port of Diafani must check that any particular ferry is scheduled to dock there, and not just at Pighadia (or vice versa).

THE ACCOMMODATION & EATING OUT
The Accommodation Probably the best 'ferry-boat arrival pickings' are to be located by turning left up the main street, Odhos Dimokratias, and then right on to 28th Octovriou St. At the height of the season, accommodation can be difficult to find, and it is advisable to act quickly, to secure a bed at one of the very good places available.

The first (bum-steer) possibility, from the quay, and on the right, is the:
Hotel Coral (*Tmr* 3D2) Apod Karpathion
Directions: As above, and above the *Rendezvous Restaurant*, with which it has no connection, at all. Understood, none!

Block-booked, noisy, and owned by an extremely surly man, who is also proprietor of the High St Pharmacy (*Tmr* 27D2).

Odhos Dimokratias connects the Esplanade and Odhos 28th Octovriou.

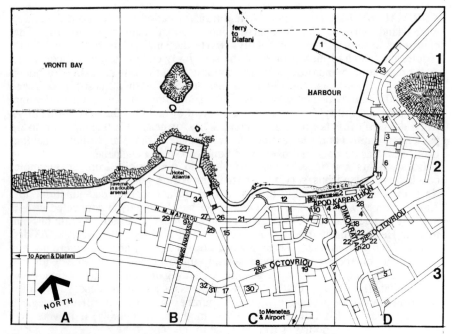

(Tmr) = *Town map reference*
(Fsw) = *Facing seawards*
(Sbo) = *Sea behind one*
(Fbqbo) = *Ferry-boat Quay behind one*

Illustration 13 Karpathos Port

Pension   Artemis   (Tmr   4D2/3)   Tel   22724
Directions: Turn left (*Sbo*) on to 28th Octovriou, left again, and the building
is on the left of a quiet cul-de-sac.

These clean and new apartments are a 'best buy', each comprising a
bedroom, bathroom, kitchenette, entrance hall and balcony, costing a mid
season 3000drs per night. Golly gosh! And this with: a shower head
delivering hot water, and capable of being positioned, where you will; clean
sheets and towels; as well as a fridge and cooker, in the kitchenette. And
there isn't a sudden change of attitude if a prospect admits to only being
interested in a 'one night stand'. But why anyone should turn down the chance
of staying for at least a few nights, I cannot conceive. This accommodation is
only available due to a tour operator's poisoned chalice, which, just for once,
became an independents joy. The relaxed landlady was left in the 'goat
droppings' by a holiday company going to the wall. The top floor rooms allow
clear views of the rapidly changing Pighadia skyscape. Those who wish to
leave in a hurry, should be aware that Thanasis Antoniou, the landlady, lives
in the ground floor, with her front door on the right (*Facing the building*).

Almost opposite the junction of Dimokratias St with 28th Octovriou, and to
the left, south across a 'bombed vehicle lot', is the:
Karpathos   Hotel   (Tmr   5D3)   (Class D)   25   Vass.   Konstantinou   Tel 22347
Directions: As above.

Clean rooms, but the dangerous looking, teeth snapping, 'Lassie' style
sheep dog, tethered to the outside of the hotel, could be considered a 'bit of' a
hazard. An en suite single is charged 2800drs & an en suite double 3800drs.

Opposite the *Karpathos* is the *Hotel Titania* (Class C, tel   22188), which is
usually block-booked. West along Odhos 28th Octovriou, and a 'pant or two'
up the now steeply climbing street, and on the left is:
'Harry's Rooms to Rent'   (Tmr   7C/D3)   28th Octovriou   Tel 22188
Directions: As above.

A very pleasant, inexpensive choice with well decorated rooms, fitted with
solid, wooden furniture. Each room has a section of a balcony. The shared,
spotless, modern bathrooms, don't have any of the oft present, 'evil
shortcomings'. The water is hot all day, with soap and towels supplied. The
helpful owners are Harry, who directs operations, and his wife, who spends
most of her time cleaning the pension. A single room costs 1800drs per night,
a single person, in a double room, is 2000drs, and a double room 2550drs.

Rooms To Kanaki   (Tmr   8C3)   28th Octovriou   Tel 22908
Directions: Continue west along Odhos 28th Octovriou, beyond the main road
turning off to Menetes, and the accommodation is on the right.

En suite double rooms are expensive, with a ground floor option priced at
3850drs, whilst first floor rooms, which have a balcony, are charged at
4500drs. The rooms are small, not very clean, and rather smelly.

Rooms 'Menetes Road'   Tel 22477
Directions: From 28th Octovriou, turn up the Menetes road for a hard ten
minutes climb out of town. The hilltop building is on the left.
Apart from the views over Vronti Bay, the inconvenience of the position is
well balanced by the low, double room price of 2000drs.

Whilst in this neck of the suburbs, a seeker after accommodation, may be
accosted by Fotoula Hristodoulaki, who drives about in a yellow, 'jeep' type

Citroen (with no exhaust or silencer). This very helpful lady will advise that she has rooms "...for a special price - you can look - no obligation". They prove to be basic but clean, with excellent views over the town, if only from the roof! Prospects may well be advised to ignore the sign stating 'Hot showers - 150drs', with the aside that this instruction is "...for the others, not for you"! She might ply guests with orange juice, whilst relating that she lived in New York, for 12 years, and then came home. The directions are unclear, other than to proceed up the hill, heading for the Menetes road, turn left (by the dead yellow truck with the flat tyres), follow the alley, climb the steps, cross the road, and ascend more steps, beside a post box. There is a yellow sign *Rooms to Rent Neochori* Tel 22519.

Hotel Anessis (*Tmr* 9B2/3) (Class D) 2 E. Anastasis/Matheou Tel 22100
Directions: Keeping along Apod Karpathion from the Esplanade leads, switchback style, to a square, beside which is the OTE (*Tmr* 25B/C2/3). Straight across the 'OTE square', and the hotel is sited on the far corner, of the first turning to the left. This was the first hotel in Karpathos.
    Singles sharing cost 1600drs, doubles sharing 2600/2800drs & en suite doubles 2800/3000drs.

Rooms, pensions and hotels are also sited along the road to Aperi, which skirts Vronti Bay. The recommended *Hotel Panorama* (Class C, tel 22739), with en suite singles priced at 3100/3800drs & doubles 3800/4400drs.

The Eating Out The swamp of tourism has downgraded the essential Greek quality of almost all the establishments. The inevitable result is an overlay of bland, entirely forgettable eateries. Breakfasts, where and when advertised, betray strong Germanic and Scandinavian tourist influences - everything with cake. The port is a desert for lovers of that essential of eating, in Greece, namely the souvlaki. It is essential to 'forage' early, for the evening 'troughing', as the restaurants and tavernas fill up quickly.

Kafeneion Halikas (*Tmr* 12C2)
Directions: On beyond the *Acropolis* (*Tmr* 10C/D2/3), to the right, on a rise in the road with the seafront in sight, and alongside the roof on an unfinished, unidentifiable community building.
    Now, the only 'proper' taverna left in the town. It is a pity that the owner and waiter are disinterested, the portions are 'starter' (mezes) sized, and the toilets require a strong constitution. On the other hand, the atmosphere is decidedly Greek, and almost all the locals drop in for an ouzo, but they are quite possibly charged a 'native' rate. Open breakfast to night-time. A small meal, for one, of tzatziki, green beans, a Greek salad, bread & a soda water, costs 1600drs. The most enjoyable time to visit, is in the evening when the locals settle down to the serious drinking. If you are lucky, you will come across Manolis Kritikos, the local philosopher and a twinkling eyed professor (well, more the local schoolmaster). Conversation is sometimes sketchy, but if his attention can be kept, his self-taught English is excellent.

Mike's Taverna (*Tmr* 13C/D2/3)
Directions: In the lane connecting Apod Karpathion and 28th Octovriou.
    The proprietor, Mike, speaks perfect American, as would be expected of any man who spent 22 years in Baltimore and New York. The place opens evenings, with the tables and chairs scattered along the roadside, across the

way from the large establishment. It used to be known as *Restaurant Pizza*, but the service, food and value remain good, even if the taverna mainly targets tourists. It is nice to report that dishes are varied, and retsina is on the list. A filling meal, for two, with wine, costs around 2500/3500drs. An enjoyable, traditional repast, for two, of 2 fried fish in batter with skordalia (500drs each, served as starter), 1 pork chop & chips (970drs), 1 prawns served with a risotto (1100drs), 2 crown cork retsinas (300drs each), a basket of bread, 2 Greek coffees & 2 ouzos, cost some 4200drs. Mike can be extremely helpful with, for instance, information about walking trips.

Taverna To Kyma (*Tmr* 14D1/2)
Directions: Almost on the quay square.
Probably the cheapest of the Esplanade choices, and 'cooking' equal quality, even if the inspired menu of years ago has disappeared. This is probably because the need to produce a 'trayful' of inexpensive, tasty and varied dishes has been eroded, by a constant stream of undemanding tourists. Diners with little or no appreciation of Greek food, who eat whatever is served, without comment - and just keep coming back. So, thinks the taverna owner, why not simply dish-up any old collation, and as little of it as possible, and hang everybody - or thoughts to that effect. The menu may still appear varied, but a lot of that listed is often 'orf'. A meal, for two, of 1 bread slice each, on a plate, a Greek salad (400drs) & 1 gigantes, 1 stifado (the only stew available, and not a stifado - more a veal stew - nice though and served with peas and rice), 1 lamb chop, served with chips & peas, 2 crown cork retsinas and a tin of soda, cost some 3900drs.

Georgios Taverna (*Tmr* 16C2)
Directions: Beneath the National Bank, beside Odhos Apos Karpathion.
Often, Georgios, the owner is both chef and waiter, and on those days the service is extremely slow, but cheerful. When his waiter is tooled-up and ready for the off, the service accelerates to simply being slow, very slow, and cheerful. The food is fine, but expensive. A meal, for two, of 1 gigantes (600drs), (followed some time later by) onion rings fried in batter (600drs), (a long pause and then) a fish stew (800drs), a plate of lamb and potato (900drs), 2 crown cork retsinas (400 each), 1 tin of soda (200drs), bread in a basket (100drs) & service, totalled some 4000drs.

Zorbas Taverna (*Tmr* 6D2)
Directions: Alongside the Esplanade, at the Ferry-boat Quay end.
Under 'new'ish' management, in the last few years, and continues to be recommended. Although the meals are satisfactory, they are not cheap. A breakfast of yoghurt & honey cost 400drs. A meal, for two, of a slice of bread, on a plate, with a wrapped pat of butter, a plate of chips, 1 gigantes (served as first course), 1 stifado (in a clay bowl, a good portion - and it was stifado - onions, vinegar, cinnamon), 1 moussaka (very nice, freshly made, but not a lot of meat), and a 750ml bottle of retsina (no crown cork available), cost 4050drs. The main dishes were served with chips and vegetables.

Karpathos Cafe Bar
Directions: Alongside *Zorba's* (*Tmr* 6D2), beside the Esplanade.
Lined up outside are two plastic tables and a wooden bench. This joint is a popular locals' haunt. The apparent wolf-whistles do not emanate from the clientele, but an African grey parrot, perched on the first floor balcony. When

the wind is blowing from the 'wrong' direction, it carries with it the fumes of *Zorba's* kitchen. A breakfast of bread, butter & jam, and orange juice costs 350drs, whilst a small yoghurt, with honey & fruit, and a strong Greek style expresso coffee is priced at 500drs. There is a metered telephone.

To the town side of *Zorba's* is:
Ouzeri Snackbar (*Tmr* 11D2)
Directions: As above.
The usual offerings and prices. Between 8pm and midnight a duo, 'armed' with a lyre and a lauto, play traditional music. Sample drinks, plates and prices are: an ouzo 250drs; a small can of Heineken 220drs; a Greek salad 500drs; pork chop 1000drs; chicken 800drs; and kalamares 600drs.

Restaurant Rendezvous (*Tmr* 3D2)
Directions: In the ground floor of the *Hotel Coral*.
Appears to be run by a group of hunky young men, at least one of whom speaks excellent American, but expensive. A round of 4 ouzos and 2 cans of Sprite cost 1400drs!

Taverna Kassos (*Tmr* 34B2)
Directions: Round towards the 'Municipal offices' promontory, and popular with tourists and some locals.
The atmosphere is 'manufactured' by the provision of piped musak, possibly Karpathian in origin. Some is a heavy duty wail, whilst on other occasions it is a 'mangle of a tape', the latter being particularly awful. This taverna's 'forgettable' offer is '...a free Greek salad for two persons ordering a set meal, of starters (orektika), main course and a drink each'. A dinner, for one, of a plate of gigantes (tasty), roast chicken with rice & chips, a tomato & cucumber salad, and 2 cans of soda cost 2160drs.

Down the steps from the *Kassos*, towards the seafront, is an:
Italian Restaurant
Directions: As above.
Unsurprisingly, Italian in style. Certainly a change, but, as the dishes and drinks are of other than Greek origin, the prices are just that much more expensive. A 'for instance' is that the Italian bottle of 'house red' costs in excess of 1000drs.

THE A TO Z OF USEFUL INFORMATION
AIRLINE OFFICE & TERMINUS (*Tmr* 15B/C2/3) A large office of modern appearance, located close to the Matheou/Karpathion Sts crossroads. The office is open Mon-Sat between 0800-1600hrs.

Aircraft timetable (Mid-season)
Karpathos to Athens (direct flights)*
Tue/Thur/Sat   1400hrs.
Return
Tue/Thur/Sat   1210hrs.
One-way fare 19200drs; duration 1hr 25mins.

*Karpathos to Athens can also be arranged via Rhodes.

Karpathos to Kasos
Mon/Wed/Fri/Sun   1340hrs
Return

Tue/Thur/Sat   0800hrs
One-way fare 2400drs; duration 15mins.
Karpathos to Rhodes
Mon/Wed/Fri/Sun   1630, 1840hrs.
Tue/Thur/Sat   0835, 1045hrs.
Return
Mon/Wed/Fri/Sun   1530, 1740hrs.
Tue/Thur/Sat   0945hrs.
One-way fare 8200drs; duration 40 mins.
Karpathos to Sitia (Crete)
Tue   1625hrs
Return
Tue   1500hrs
One-way fare 8200drs; duration 35mins

BANKS There are three, the: **National** (*Tmr* 16C2); the **Commercial**, close to the National; and the **Agricultural** (*Tmr* 6D2). The latter, in contrast to most other Agricultural Banks, carries out foreign exchange transactions.

BEACHES The town has a small, rather rubbish littered strip of sandy shore, close by the town clock. The domestic ducks, whose land base is beneath the tables of an adjacent taverna, often disport themselves on this particular bit of sand. The main beach is a dusty 15min trudge, to the west, in the direction of Aperi. The first, smaller, people, beds and umbrella overcrowded bay, allows a pleasant bathe. It has a sandy shore which climbs steeply up the backshore, the crest of which is topped off by the ruins of a couple of old houses. To the left (*Fsw*), alongside the outset of some small boulders, is a grove of trees affording welcome shade. Where the north horn curves round, bamboo groves screen an extremely expensive taverna, that caps the mini-headland. The inshore area hereabouts is swampy. Beyond the taverna, is a much larger, crescent of sandy foreshore encircling the cleaner waters of the adjoining bay. It peters out alongside a distant refinery plant. This more northerly beach is usually almost empty of people, and benefits from a backshore taverna, just beyond the ruins of an early Christian basilica. The taverna tends to only open for the height of season months.

A memorable day might be enjoyed by walking to the beach at **Forokli**, with every chance of not seeing another soul, from dawn to dusk. Select the the first track, off to the left of the Menetes main road, south of the town. At the right time of the year it may be necessary to wade through wild flowers. The path suddenly ends, about a mile from the sea. From here head left downhill, until a dry river-bed is reached, which must be followed. This is quite heavy going, for a short distance, but the reward is a fine shale beach. As a reader put it rather nicely '...the fish were so surprised, they jumped out of the water, when we jumped in'. Those who do venture forth, should commit the last section of the route to memory, to help retrace their footsteps, with as little difficulty as possible.

BICYCLE, SCOOTER & CAR HIRE When hiring transport it is essential to consider the island's mountainous terrain, the general state of the roads in the south, and the lack of almost any metalled roads in the north. *See* Petrol.
Scooter & Car Hire Circle (*Tmr* 17B/C3)   Tel 22690
   Directions: Close to the top end of 28th Octovriou St.
   A small selection of two seat, 50cc scooters, costing 2700drs a day, with no fuel allowance. Car hire prices start off from 7500drs.

Karpathos Travel/Maloftis Rent A Car (*Tmr* 18D2/3)   Tel 22285
Directions: Beside Dimokratias St, and also trading as **Twin Eagle**.
A Fiat Panda costs from 7500drs a day.
Gatoulis Hire   Tel 22747/22958/22088
Directions: Out of town, in new premises beside the Aperi road, and
displaying the flags of the EC, but not the UK 'duster'.
A good selection of scooters and mopeds, as well as some cars, but this
establishment is more expensive than its competitors. Francesca, a large,
cuddly, friendly lady is unfailingly helpful.

BOOKSELLERS A small Supermarket (*Tmr* 26B/C2/3) has a counter from
which are sold the usual two or three day old newspapers, amongst which are
some British editions. In front of the National Bank (*Tmr* 16C2) is a
Newspaper shop, selling some interesting old books and dictionaries, and
which is agent for the **FB Kimolos**. A local has written a yellow covered,
photocopied booklet, in respect of the history of Karpathos and Kasos.
Unfortunately this is a 700drs, rambling, incoherent, poorly produced, badly
written product - and I promise that's not professional jealousy.

BREAD SHOPS (*Tmr* 19C3) At No 76, beside 28th Octovriou St, up the hill
and beyond *Harry's Pension*.

BUSES The buses 'terminus' at the *ad hoc* depot (*Tmr* 20D3), on the far
corner of the crossroads formed by Odhos Dimokratias and 28th Octovriou.
Buses also park behind a 'church prominent' (*Tmr* 30C3).

Bus timetable (except Sun & hols)
Karpathos Town to Finiki, via Menetses, Arkasa.
Daily0700hrs
Return journey
Mon/Wed/Fri   1430hrs
Tue/Thur/Sat   1145hrs
Karpathos Town to Piles via Aperi, Volada, Othos.
Daily   0700, 1100, 1245hrs.
Return journey
Daily   0800, 1140, 1345hrs
Karpathos Town to Amopi Beach
Daily   0930, 1430hrs.
Return journey
Daily   0930, 1630hrs
Karpathos Town to Lefkos via Arkasa, Finiki (one-way fare 1000drs)
Mon/Wed   0930hrs
Return journey
Mon/Wed   1700hrs

Due to the infrequency of the buses, the taxis are very active.

COMMERCIAL SHOPPING AREA No market, but the usual mix of
specialist shops and a number of good value **Supermarkets**. The latter include
a large unit (*Tmr* 22C/D3) on the corner of Dimokratias and 28th Octovriou,
and another alongside the Bus terminal (*Tmr* 20D3). Fish are sold most days,
from boxes laid out on the pavement, opposite the Town clock (*Tmr* 2C/D2),
and there is a **Butcher** (*Tmr* 21B/C2/3). Almost all the shops close by 1930hrs.

DISCOS Many, too many.

FERRY-BOATS Pull in at the eastern Esplanade Quay (*Tmr* 1C/D1).

Ferry-boat timetable (Mid-season)

Day	Departure time	Ferry-boat	Ports/Islands of Call
Wed	0700hrs	Kimolos	Diafani(Karpathos), Chalki, Simi, Rhodes.
	2030hrs	Dialana	Iraklion(Crete), Santorini, Paros, Piraeus(M).
	2100hrs	Kimolos	Kasos, Sitia(Crete), Ag Nikolaos(Crete), Santorini, Sikinos, Folegandros, Milos, Siphnos, Piraeus(M).
Thur	1000hrs	Rodanthi	Rhodes, Iraklion(Crete), Santorini, Paros, Piraeus(M).
	2330	Romilda	Rhodes.
Sat	1000hrs	Rodanthi	Rhodes.
	2400hrs	Rodanthi	Iraklion(Crete), Santorini, Paros, Piraeus(M).

During the height of season months at least one additional ferry-boat a week 'noses' into the schedules.

FERRY-BOAT TICKET OFFICES Beside Dimokratias St are: **Panorama Travel**, at No 8 (Tel 22916); and **Karpathos Travel** (*Tmr* 18D2/3, tel 22754). They both represent the **FB Daliana & Rodanthi**. Another agent for the Daliana & Rodanthi is **Possi Travel** (*Tmr* 24C/D2, tel 22235), Apod Karpathion. The Bookshop in front of the National Bank (*Tmr* 16C2) is the representative for the **FB Kimolos**.

The prices of the various excursions at friendly **Karpathos Travel** (*Tmr* 18D2/3), who do not represent any of the package tour companies, are slightly cheaper, than are those offered at rival **Possi Travel**. The latter establishment is staffed by a bevy of helpful, slick, 'Karpatho-American' girls. This business represents countless tour operators and holiday companies, and 'windows' numerous excursions, in various languages. There are at least four other travel agents throughout the town,acting for this or that operator, and offering (the same) excursions and trips.

Coach excursion destinations include: Kira Panaghia; Spoa; Mesohori; Lefkos Beach; Arkasa; as well as a round-trip to Aperi, Othos, Piles, Finiki, Arkasa, Menetes and back to Karpathos Town. Not to be forgotten, as if you could, is the 'Karpathian Night'.

Boat and caique trip boat destinations include: Diafani/Olympos (3000drs); Kira Panaghia/Apella/Ag Minas; and Kasos (but I would prefer to catch the scheduled ferry, for such a crossing as this). Note these craft are often very crowded and latecomers can miss the return voyage, due to lack of space and or an earlier than scheduled departure! Passengers booked for a late afternoon or evening return trip should pack a cardigan or sweater. This is because the sun dips below the mountain range, running the length of the island, earlier than might be expected, and it can become rather cold at sea. Bearing in mind the generally bad state of the roads, for once, trip boat excursions are a meritorious possibility.

HAIRDRESSERS Unusually, more ladies salons than mens, a favoured street being 28th Octovriou.

MEDICAL CARE
Chemists & Pharmacies (*Tmr* 27) There are two beside the Esplanade, and another alongside 'OTE' Square.
Dentist A Surgeon's clinic (*Tmr* 28D2) is beside the Esplanade.

Hospital (*Tmr* 29B2/3) Situated alongside Odhos N & M Matheou.

MUNICIPAL OFFICES (*Tmr* 23B2) Another Italian inspired building.

OTE (*Tmr* 25B/C2/3) Beside a dusty square, and a pleasantly disorganised office, the staff of which are helpful, cheerful and speak good English. Of the four booths, only one (No 4) is for international calls, but queues remain relatively small. Open weekdays 0730-1510hrs. Outside is a periptero with a metered phone, waiting for which are lengthy queues, whilst across the street is a bar which also has a metered phone.

PETROL There is a filling station along the Aperi road, and another beside the Airport road. Unfortunately there isn't one in the north of the island, so scooter forays to north Karpathos must be planned with great care - after which abandon the idea! Not only does the up-island road above Spoa remain in very bad condition (*See* the relevant Route description), but a scooter tankful is unlikely to suffice. This is a shame because the north has the most spectacular mountain scenery, and the famed village of Olympos. Those still intending to venture forth, must not mention any such thoughts to a hire company. They become not a little disturbed at the prospect of one of their machines being involved in such a trip! A more positive answer is to negotiate with one of the excursion boat 'chappies' to bring you, and the scooter back from the port of Diafani.

PLACES & EVENTS OF INTEREST Due to the lack of archaeological remains, not a lot. Even the Church (*Tmr* 30C3) is modern.
Fly Zappers These antiseptic blue neon killers have been attached to lamp posts spread out along the Esplanade. If the nightlife is dull, sit out and wait for the hapless, winged insects and wildlife to go up in flames, and be grilled.
Wind Karpathos must be one of the windiest locations in the Mediterranean. Apart from windsurfers, the phenomenon is spawning a row of modern windmill electricity generators along the ridge overlooking Arkasa.

POLICE
Town/Tourist (*Tmr* 32B3) Proceed up Odhos 28th Octovriou, and the office is a few buildings along from the Post Office.

POST OFFICE (*Tmr* 31B/C3) Open weekdays between 0730-1400hrs.

TAXIS (*Tmr* C/D2) The rank is along Odhos Dimokratias, close to the junction with the Esplanade. A recognised method of island travel and sharing is order of the day. For journeys to Olympos or Diafani a taxi is the only (extremely expensive) alternative to the trip boats. Sample fares are: to the airport 1700drs; to Lefkos 5000drs; to Amopi Beach 1000drs; and to Olympos/Diafani 20000drs - why not buy a taxi and hire yourself, and it out?

TELEPHONE NUMBERS & ADDRESSES
Hospital (*Tmr* 29B2/3)	Tel 22228
Police, town (*Tmr* 32B3)	Tel 22222
tourist (*Tmr* 32B3)	Tel 22218
Taxis	Tel 22705

TOILETS At the bottom of the Ferry-boat Quay (*Tmr* 33D1),but they are extremely ethnic,being 'squatties', and unbearably odorous.

TRAVEL AGENTS & TOUR OFFICES *See* Ferry-boat Ticket offices.

ROUTE ONE
To Amopi & Laki Beaches, and on to the Airport (15km) The road out of
Karpathos Town is a fairly steep, steady climb.
  The turning to Amopi is signposted. The road loops down, with *Laki
Beach* to one side of the small headland and Amopi to the left. *Rooms* are
advertised on both beaches.

AMOPI BEACH (8km from Karpathos) Probably the largest island resort.
The road peters out on the edge of the lovely, clean and sandy beach,
bordering a small bay. A number of small, neat holiday flats, built on the edge
of the foreshore, have been overrun by hotels, all of which are package tourist
pre-booked, with an overwhelm of German companies involved. The
expensive restaurants outnumber the tavernas, and Amopi is more costly than
Pighadia. To landward are the sun-beds and umbrellas, to seaward are water
sport activities. At the *Golden Beach Taverna* end, to the right of the bus
pull-up, a couple of sun-beds and an umbrella cost about 800drs, for the day.
  One of, if not the original building here is that occupied by the fore-
mentioned *Golden Beach Taverna*, splendidly situated on the edge of the
backshore. The service is cheerful, 'interesting' and quite good, when the
place is quiet. When it is busy, clients may well observe the four or so staff
'almost running'. Officially opens midday, but Manolis can become perturbed
if prospective clients 'hammer' at the doors, prior to the official time. A meal,
for two, of 2 small bottles of Carlsberg, 2 bread buns, each on a plate (no
butter), 1 stuffed peppers, a Greek salad, a bottle of boutari retsina ("I don't
keep the cheap crown cork stuff, it gives you a headache"!), 1 tin of soda, 2
Greek coffees, and 2 ouzos, cost some 4000drs. Incidentally on another
occasion, later in the same period, kortaki retsina was available.
  The coastline to the south, in the direction of the airport, is some of the
most unattractive of the island, being flat, desolate and short of any
vegetation. Despite which, it would appear the shore is going to be filled in
with even more hotels. Oh dear me!

Houses, and the occasional chapel, are to be found dotted around the
landscape, either side of the route to the airport. The other noticeable feature
is the almost horizontally snake-blown, stunted trees scattered about the
barren countryside. Once the road commences to wind down through the
unforgiving, granite stone littered plain, towards the southernmost headland,
the view is quite dramatic with curving beaches to the east of **Cape Liki**.

ROUTE TWO
To Finiki via Menetes & Arkasa (20km) The overall condition of the road to
Finiki are generally good. The main road junction for Laki marks the start of
a very steep, twisting and turning climb up to the hilltop settlement of:

MENETES (8km from Karpathos) Beside the last hairpin approach to the
village is what appears to be a 'dancing man'. Two steep flights of steps lead
to the monument, which is in memory of an event of 8th October 1944. A
statue in the village square of Finiki explains all.
Built on and over the crest of the hillside, Menetes is unspoilt and quiet, with
some 1930s Italian influenced architecture and marvellous views. Close to the
centre is a sign to the right, indicating a museum. The path leads, through a
small playground, to what must be one of the smallest of its genre in Greece,
but it is invariably closed. Enquiries will no doubt bring forth a key.

There are some *Rooms*, and a few of the more intrepid independent travellers have become aware of this settlement's charms.

The road west of Menetes is similar to driving over a moorland of granite, speckled with green.

ARKASA (17km from Karpathos) The old town, across a ravine and celebrated for the remains of a 5thC church, is agreeable, if scruffy. The 'wedding cake' church spire dominates the tavernas spread around the square. Old Arkasa has spawned a rather unpleasant suburb, more correctly a resort, and not a very lovely one at that. The golden sand beach has resulted in Cretan style, concrete block, holiday condominiums, and a villa complex being built, close by the seashore. Oh goody! There are sufficient signs for *Rooms* and apartments, with package tourists in evidence.

Facing out to sea looks over the headland of **Cape Paliokastro**. There is a classical and mystical ambience about the setting, which is not surprising as it was the site of Ancient Arkesia.

To the left of the main road into Arkasa, a green painted sign, proclaiming *Rooms For Rent*, points down an unmade track. About 200m along this, and the tree shaded, dirt road is straddled by a pension and taverna. To the right, a path leads to a sandy beach, on which 'Nudism Prohibited'. Proceeding further along the track, and the landscape opens out into a beautiful, if barren countryside. The shoreline is mostly rocky, and broken-up by the occasional, plastic littered cove of shingly beach. The map indicates an unmetalled track, connecting with the main airport road, but the profusion of odd paths, interspersed with deep ravines, will probably defy any but the most determined explorer. A very wide track has been driven through to **Cape Ag Thoros**. On this stands, in solitary isolation, a chapel, set in a surround of blue sea, with the island of rocky Kasos in the middle distance.

Returning to Arkasa, to the right (*Fsw*) is a well surfaced road which heads north, to run parallel to the coastline. After some 1½km, the route passes by a rubbish dump, alongside a cemetery, on the way to a minor 'parting of the ways'. Here is a backward angled road, to the left, tracking along to:

FINIKI (20km from Karpathos) A quiet, if uninspiring, rather desolate, dusty, unattractive fishing hamlet. It would appear to have been the recipient of a 'face-lift', in an effort to appeal to tourists. Around the core of the settlement, some new, square buildings have been erected.

Finiki hosts three tavernas, which cater for 'the passing carriage trade'. They offer seafood dishes, and specialise in lobster preparations, all caught by the well-buffeted village fishing fleet. An example of that on offer can be sampled at the *Taverna Kentron Finikis*, owned by the family Houvardas. Judging from a proudly displayed magazine cutting, they 'have made it big in the USA'. This enrichment came about as a result of 'infiltrating' an American fast food chain, and most of the family now reside, 'over the pond'. I bet they do. The ambiance is somewhat 'plastic flowers and plastic tablecloth'. A meal, for two, of tzatziki, gigantes beans, a Greek salad, kalamares, chips, a small bottle of foreign beer, and a Coke, cost 2200drs. Bus timetables are pinned to the taverna wall.

The village square monument, in which is set a water tap, is a statue inscribed *To Plio tis Sotir*. It commemorates seven Second World War heroes, who set off, on 2nd October 1944, from Finiki to Alexandria, carrying a message to the King of Greece. Delightful *Rooms* are available. To the left is a small, dirty, if sandy beach. To the right is a concrete quay, to which moor the village's medium-sized fishing vessels, all overlooked by a chapel, mounted on a hillock.

From Finiki, the Old Road is a wide track, which crabs its way along the coast for an attractive, 7km journey, to the village of Piles.   The alternative New Road runs all the way to **Cape Proni**, it being necessary to turn right, after 5km, to reach Piles (*See* Route Three).

ROUTE THREE
To Piles via Aperi, Volada & Othos (15km) The road is, in places, in a terrible state. It runs parallel to the foreshore of Karpathos Town bay, nearly all the way round to a refinery, from whence it commences to climb and wind its way up to:

APERI (8km from Karpathos) This clean, shaded and tidy hill village positively reeks of wealth. The opulence is due to money remitted   from abroad, and the return of well-heeled expatriates. The houses   even display name plates and dates, proclaiming which family funded the building - similar to personalised car number plates? There are a few shops, as well as a couple of roadside bars and tavernas, but no road signs.
Aperi was once the island's capital, in the days when the inhabitants had to constantly flee from marauding pirates - instead of intrusive tourists?

Prior to the steep turning off for the eastern route north, signposted to Ag Nikolaos (*See* Route Five), is a roadside, Cycladean style chapel. Still climbing, the road advances to **Volada** (10km), a 'dead-ringer' for Aperi, and from whence, looking upwards, allows a sighting of **Othos** (12km). The main road (*sic*) narrows through the crescent shaped mountain village, edging the curved hillside. The situation, high above and looking down over Vronti Bay, allows magnificent vistas. The village taverna is traditional, and none to clean, but serves good value food, from a restricted choice of dishes.

Immediately beyond Othos, the route breasts a mountain saddle, to slope down to Piles, with, in the distance, the island of Kasos sliding into view. Further on, by a cemetery, the route allows beautiful panoramas over the coastal plain, stretched out between Arkasa and Cape Ag Thoros.
PILES (15km from Karpathos) A small, lovely, quintessential island village. The local cheese is scrumptious and can be purchased in the first general store, to the right, on entering the settlement.
Before Piles, a road runs off to the south, to join up with Finiki (*See* Route Two), whilst through Piles, the New Road   continues on to the western coastway, which heads to the north (*See* Route Four).

ROUTE FOUR
To Diafani via Lefkos, Mesohori, Spoa & Olympos (48km) Select Route One or Three, and proceed along either the Old or New Road. The two merge just to the north of **Cape Proni**, from whence it is a stunningly beautiful, but poorly surfaced journey, alternately crossing open, sun-scorched countryside and plunging through fir tree bowers, all the while skirting Mt Kalolimni. Some 3km north of Piles, a turning to the left angles back, southwards. This choice of track advances to a lovely, crescent shaped bay, with large slab rock set in a deserted, small, shingle foreshore, with only one homestead in view.

Beyond Cape Proni, the wide track falls away to the west, with distant views of Lefkos flanked by a captivating and small, curving bay. After some 24km, a signpost indicates the 2km turning to Lefkos. The absolutely magnificent vista takes in a small chapel built alongside a natural, encircling cove, within the larger bay, south of **Sokastro island**.

LEFKOS (26km from Karpathos) Once a deserted paradise, with a few, white, square homesteads scattered about, and known to very few. The stunningly beautiful, long, clean, sandy beach, bordering a deep bay, stopped off by a headland chapel, has ensured a steady build-up of *Rooms*, tavernas, apartments, and stores, in, on, and around the surrounding countryside. It is said that German tour operators are responsible for much of the exploitation of Lefkos. Even the wild plant life is being uprooted and replanted in the gardens of the new villas. Incidentally, the shops only stock the basics, and often run out of those. Double room prices 'kick off' at 3500drs a night.

The access road is paved and, where it enters the village, bends to the right. A path to the left leads to a beach, alongside which is a small, red domed church. The road curves to the left, revealing the full glory of the fantastic sweep of sand, which runs out on a grassy headland, all sides of which are sandy beaches, and rocky, sea-washed islets. For reasons of tidal flow and currents, if there is an oil spillage at sea, these shores attract more than their fair share of the resultant tar. On the other hand, the selfsame elements that cause the filthy stuff to be deposited hereabouts, ensure it is soon   dispersed. The locals have renamed the various beaches, which now have nomenclatures such as 'Town Beach', 'English Beach' and 'German Beach'. Another (stonier) beach, alongside the *Small Paradise Taverna*, is where the flocks of sheep and goats are still watered, around midday.

There are now at least seven tavernas within a couple of miles of the harbour. The two overlooking the harbour are relatively expensive, whilst the *Pension/Taverna O Mikhalis* is not too costly. Mine host at the latter is 'very relaxed', and 'on the surly side of dour'. Why I cannot say, as his young, friendly German wife, who speaks excellent English and carries their baby everywhere, appears to do most of the work, while he goes fishing, day and night! An en suite   double room costs 4000/4500drs a night. The *Sunlight Pension/Taverna*, run by Kali and Steve, who spent 21 years in Brooklyn, have similar rooms, at a cost of 4000drs, but their fare is rather expensive. A meal, for two, of 2 cheese omelettes, 1 chips, a salad, 1 Amstel beer, a small bottle of retsina, bread & service, cost 3700drs.

One of the best, and cheapest taverna's is *Small Paradise*, about a mile from the harbour. This is run by obliging and welcoming Nikos and Irini (Sofia?) Horokpos (House Census No 33, tel 71220). Their daughters Sophia and Maria help at table, in the evenings, after school, whilst Irini's father, plays the lyre and speaks good, if basic English, which he taught himself from a book. He is a joy to listen to, whilst he waxes eloquent, relating one of a remarkable fund of stories, many of them concerning the Second World War, during which period he was a partisan. When the German clients are close by,   he relates the tales *sotto voce*. Irini prepares a 'mean' briam. A sample meal, for two, of a Greek salad, 1 briam, 1 stifado, 2 plates of chips, 2 beers, a bottle of wine, bread & service, cost 3900drs. The family also have a block of new Studio Apartments, looking out to sea.

Nearly two miles from the harbour, and on the right, is a *Taverna* run by George and Potheti, where the food is good and cheap. If George likes a client, he has been known to accompany them on a couple of walks into the nearby mountains, a journey of about 5 miles   each. During these hikes he displays catacombs and cave dwellings, which are several thousand years old, the caves being occupied until some forty or fifty years ago.

At the top of the concrete road out of Lefkos, at the junction with the road from Arkasa to Mesohori, is a typical kafeneion, serving a limited menu of excellent, inexpensive food.

Back on the 'main road', after another 4km the wide track rises through the same mix of stunningly beautiful countryside, to a   junction signposted: **MESOHORI** (29km from Karpathos) It is inconceivable that a visitor will not be enchanted by Mesohori, which clings on to the steeply   sloping mountainside, high above the coastline.

On the edge of the village is a large building, complete with a swimming pool, and overlooking the 'ocean'. Years ago, I thought this had the makings of a pension, but, seemingly, not so. The track to the settlement ends abruptly by a warehouse of sorts, alongside which is the flight of steps. These descend into the maze of narrow, whitewashed lanes and alleyways, that wind up and down, and in and around the huddle of white cubic buildings, which make up the core of the settlement. Deep within is a simple 'upstairs taverna', the directions to which defy description. I only found my way there by asking and being handed on from one inhabitant to another. Once located, you can rely on a simple, filling and satisfying meal.   Communication with the few card playing locals is difficult, but a knowledge of Italian is a help. There is also a 'bottom-left' kafeneion. Many of the women wear traditional dress, as a matter of course, and not 'tourist driven', and appear to do all the work.

Returning to the 'main track', after some 3km, immediately past a ridge, on which stand five ruined windmills, the route runs into a   spacious, dusty, totally unsignposted junction. It has to be admitted that there are new signs, if approaching this junction from either   the eastern coast route, or from the direction of Diafani. The track to the right is the eastern coast route back to Karpathos Town   (*See* Route Five), whilst the left fork leads to another, narrow   junction immediately above **Spoa** (33km - western route, or 24km - eastern route). The path to the right leads to this unexceptional, mountain village, beyond which a track descends to the tiny harbour of **Ag Nikolaos**.

Before and above Spoa, a track climbing the hillside, to the left, appears to be a minor donkey path, but persevere, for this is the Diafani road. Well, not so much a road, more one of the worst, spine-juddering rides it is possible to experience. In places, the amazing landscape is lunar, the area having suffered severe forest   fires, with round-topped hills shouldering aside ravines and fjord-like sea indents. The track undulates violently, fording small spring-like streams, as the rock face 'leaks' water. In places, the route runs along the top of the narrow, mountainous spine of the island, with steepling drops to either side, then plunges down to the bottom of the sheer-sided mountain, only to limb steeply out again.   After 8km, a turning to the right tumbles down to the beach at **Ag Minas**. Ignore the left-hand branch track, another 1½km further on along the route.

Prior to attaining the celebrated Olympos and rounding the slopes of **Mt Profitis Ilias**, on which the village is built, there is what can only be described as a 'Deserted Medieval Village'. This Greek version is a hauntingly terraced, abandoned habitation, that is, apart from one stone built house, around which are signs of cultivation. Once observed were a person, a donkey and a truck.

OLYMPOS (45km - eastern route, from Karpathos) The approach is marked by more, very neat terracing, a number of now disused windmills, many small and beautifully painted chapels, sundry round, stone threshing floors, and the occasional woman spinning on the threshold of the family house, complete with distaff and spindle. A dead bus 'lurks' to the right, whilst the village lies to the left, around and surmounting a mountainside hill-top.

The pre-publicity suggests a riot of tradition, with the village women attired in their distinctive head-dress and costumes, many churches, rich soil and a general air of neatness. This latter virtue used to be encouraged by a number of orange bins, which now litter the mountain slopes, either side of the settlement! Unfortunately, the mass-transportation of tourists has resulted in Olympos achieving the status of a Hellenic Disneyland theme park village. Until recent years, its inaccessibility preserved an ancient way of life, in a kind of time-warp. Reputedly, the houses retain an affinity with those of Homer's day, the give-away indicators being the sectioning into three, the striking, solid timber doors, with wooden keys and locks, and the colourfully painted verandas. The house interiors are singular, more especially the front rooms, dominated by a balcony bed or furniture, including carved dressers, more often than not laden with gilt framed photographs, plates, glass and trinkets, standing on embroidered, woven coverings and or lacework.

The women bake the village's bread in outdoor, community ovens, which are sited up a stony path to the left. A batch is prepared whenever the village runs out - about once a week. This baking had almost religious overtones. The inhabitants are said to retain a dialect dating back to the Dorians. The womens' unique dress consists of a black headscarf, often embroidered, a white ruffled and buttoned shirt, black waistcoat, a black or grey skirt overlaid with a large apron, thick stockings, and boots or sandals, depending on the weather, in addition to which ample jewellery is worn.

Before whining on about how things used to be, it should be reiterated that this mountain village is still very beautiful, the houses and paths that divide them winding up the slopes, reaching out towards more derelict windmills. A definite photographer's paradise. Nowadays, a constant stream of tourists 'drops in', every day, carried here by excursion boats from Pighadia port to Diafani, and then by bus, up the valley to the outskirts of the settlement. These invasions have somewhat lessened the 'hidden valley' ambiance, once the hallmark of the village!

There are many simple *Rooms*, small pensions, cafe-bars, tavernas, and tiny shops. The average double room rate, sharing a bathroom, is 3000/4000drs per night. The most recommended establishment is the *Pension/Restaurant Olympos* (Tel 51252). From the bus stop proceed up into the village, and the *Olympos* is on the right, after a few flights of steps. The remarkably nice owners are the mid-thirties couple, Anna and Mikail Lentaki, who speak English, and have received glowing commendations. The bedrooms are basic, but clean, and share the bathroom, at a mid-season cost of 2000drs. Hot water is plentiful. The restaurant is popular with locals, who use it as a kafeneion. Anna makes her own bread, and cooks scrumptious, local flavoured meals. Pension guests may be encouraged to help themselves to food and drink, totting-up as they go. Further into the village is the *Pension Posidon*. A combined pension/taverna is run by one of the partners in the trip boat that runs between Karpathos Town and Diafani, whilst the *Hotel Astra* is beside the 'main road'. There is a clinic (tel 51201), close to the aforementioned *Olympos*. For bus connections *See* Diafani.

A westward path drops steeply towards the tiny port and beach of **Fyses**. From Olympos to Diafani, the carriageway resembles a wide, dry river-bed, a downward tumbling, snaking swathe, which cuts through the surrounding pine forests. It is still rumoured that this length of the route is to be surfaced, after which the road from Spoa will be treated. Oh yes!

A turning off to the left, on a broad, sweeping bend in the track, proceeds to the small, abandoned settlement of **Avlona** (50km) The area is spring watered, and possesses a rich soil. From Avlona, paths lead left to **Cape Vroukounda** and a beach, whereon are littered remains and ruins of an ancient civilisation, with chambers cut into the cliff-face. At the site of **Ag Ionnis** a festival is held every year, on 28/29th August, in remembrance of St John the Headless, around which dates the tracks and byways become crowded, with locals and expatriates.

A path to the right leads to the ancient harbour of **Tristomo**, almost at the very north end of the island, the sea entrance to which is difficult, except in calm weather. The now deserted, waterless island of **Saria**, tops off Karpathos, from which it is separated by a narrow, fairly shallow channel. Saria island was the site of a Byzantine, east coast settlement of **Palatia**.

Back at the route from Olympos, the boulderous track tumbles down a wide, rocky causeway edging the desirable port and village of:
DIAFANI (49km from Karpathos) Originally constructed as the harbour for Olympos, the name means 'transparent', or 'clear'. Unfortunately, the seas hereabouts do not now particularly back up this interpretation.
Arrival by road The entrance to the settlement almost has to be divined, but pick the largest (short) lane, which is the High St, and runs down to the seafront. The village is built on a grid layout, and the flavour is similar to that of Olympos, but rather more Turkish. The women, of gypsy appearance, dress in a traditional costume, woollen leggings, leather boots and jewellery, including large, gold, dangly ear-rings.
Arrival by boat The pint-sized finger quay, to the right (*Sbo*) of the *Mayflower Hotel*, is usually draped with fishing nets, and, apart from the to-be-expected caiques and excursion craft, can only accommodate the smaller inter-island ferries, such as the **FB Kimolos** - as long as the sea state is calm. For excursion and ferry-boat connections *See* Karpathos Town.

The small, pleasant *Mayflower Hotel* (Class B pension) is run by Nick Vasiliadis and his wife. The six rooms have thirteen beds and the rates for a double room start at 3500drs. Nick's American is excellent and was learnt in Baltimore. Other accommodation is available at the *Hrisi Akti Hotel* (Class E), the *Golden Beach Hotel & Restaurant*, the *Pensions Diafani Palace* and the *Claros*. The proprietor of the *Golden Beach* is a partner in the trip boat business, and is agent for the ferry-boat company. In addition, there are plenty of *Rooms*. The numerous tavernas usually display and proclaim their offerings, in English, but those beside the Esplanade are rather expensive.

The pebble and sand beach stretches to the right of the quay (*Fsw*). Camping is organised at the far end of the cove, which is edged by low cliffs, topped off by a church. There is another, agreeable beach at **Vananda**, about ½hr to the north of Diafani.

Diafani does not possess a bank, OTE (but there are a couple of metered telephones), Post Office, or filling station.

The oft-mentioned trip boat owners and crew are surly and generally rather unhelpful, which is rather significant as they make up a fair percentage of the local population. This attitude may be because they tend to be lionised by the Scandinavians and German tourists.

Probably the best way to visit Olympos is to stay at Diafani, for a day or two, and make use of the local bus, a taxi or walk - well, perhaps not. For those who must, it is a two hour trek, some of it alongside a 'stream accompanied path' through the forest. Close by Olympos this trail criss-crosses the vehicle track, but the route indicators can be difficult to spot. The Diafani bus connects with Olympos, weekdays at 0800hrs (for children who attend the Olympos school), 1100hrs (for ferry-boaters), and 1700hrs.

ROUTE FIVE

To Diafani via the east coast The spectacular, coast-hugging route, from south to north of the island, may be shorter, but is in an appalling condition. Believe me, it is much worse than the alternatives. Furthermore, when the wind is blowing a 'hooligan', it can be a dangerous choice, with great views!

Initially follow Route Three. The necessary track branches off above the village of Aperi, to advance via the lower flanks of **Mt Kalolimni**. There are side turnings down to **Kira Panaghia**, as well as the lovely and sandy beach of **Apella**, crowded in by towering cliffs, and boat-loads of tourists. This route joins the western route (*See* Route Four), immediately prior to Spoa, at a rather 'lunar' junction.

KASOS (Scarpanto)
Dodecanese Islands

FIRST IMPRESSIONS Rocks, stones, boulders and more rocks; barren, with nary a tree to be seen; very welcoming inhabitants; chickens everywhere.

SPECIALITIES Inexpensive fish; Suez Canal pilots; the Holocaust.

LOCAL RELIGIOUS HOLIDAYS & FESTIVALS incl: 6/7th June - Celebrations in memory of the 'Holocaust', Kasos Town.

VITAL STATISTICS Tel prefix 0245. Length 18km, up to 7km wide & a population of about 1,200.

HISTORY Kasos experienced are 'island notable' exceptions to the usual course of historical events. The inhabitants once numbered about twenty thousand. The depredation of the population was 'helped along' by the Egyptians, then allies of the Turks. They razed the island to the ground (well, more to the stone) during a savage assault, in 1824, still referred to as the 'Holocaust'. Apart from killing the menfolk and firing the villages, the Egyptians carried off two thousand women and children to slavery.
Such are the vagaries of history, that only thirty five years later some five thousand Kasiot men 'upped and off' to Egypt, to assist in the construction of the Suez Canal. This act of navvying, added to the renowned skill of the island sailors, had an interesting spin-off. Many of them became Suez pilots, resulting in the once sizeable Greek community at Port Said. Not many years later, and acting with a perspicacity to be displayed by subsequent generations of Greek shipowners, the Kasiots, realising the possibilities of the newfangled steam engine, legged it back to their island. Here they presumably hocked the goats, and granny, to commission and be amongst the first Greeks to opt for, and operate steamships, in preference to the then universal sail.
There are now few tangible remains of the resultant family fortunes (*See* Panaghia, Route Two), because they also had the foresight to emigrate, yet again. There is a local saying that if all the shipowners, with family ties to the island, were to return, they would circle the coastline, three times.

GENERAL Nowadays, many of the inhabitants commute to North America, for months at a time. It is wise to voice any adverse comments, quietly, as most of the locals have an excellent understanding of the 'American' language.
It is interesting that subsequent follow-up research confirms my original impression that the island has few redeeming physical features. Bonus points are the unfailing friendliness of the inhabitants, in addition to which Kasos is free of package holiday-makers, crowds, high prices, discos, rock bars, pubs, foreign food and drink, schlepping, and swimming pools - tourist induced manifestations that infest so very many locations. The conundrum is that countless of these selfsame tourists are most desirous to find the 'real' Greece. The Greece represented by the glorious disorganisation of ethnic squalor, studied inefficiency and indifference, slow, laid-back relaxation (to the point of torper), quiet, lethargic serenity, the riotous, colourful shambles of flower planted, whitewashed houses, unidentifiable shops, dark interior, mysterious, 'locals only' kafeneions, and villages 'announced' by the presence of a... rubbish dump! That is, everything that helps to form the

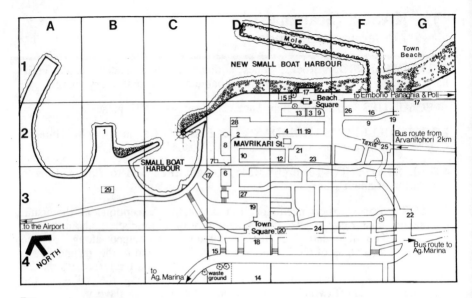

Tmr
1B2   Ferry-boat Quay
2D2   Rooms
3E2   Hotel Anagennisis
4E2   Hotel Anessis
5E1/2   Taverna Milos
6D3   Kafeneion
7C/D2/3   Clock Tower
8D2   Church
9E/F2   Airline Office
10D2/3   Store
11E2   National Bank Agent/Store
12D/E2/3   Bread Shop
13E2   Kassos Travel Agency
14D4   OTE
15C/D4   Fine old building
16F2   Post Office
17   Public Toilets
18D/E4   Town Hall
19   General Stores
20D/E3/4   Restaurant H. Kassos
21E2   Dentist
22G3/4   Hospital
23D/E2   Customs
24E3/4   Museum
25F/G2   'Bus terminus' Sq
26F2   Bar
27D3   Fast food
28D2   O' Mathias Ouzerie
29B3   Taverna

(Tmr)   = Town map reference
(Fsw)   = Facing seawards
(Sbo)   = Sea behind one
(Fbqbo) = Ferry-boat Quay behind one

Illustration 14 Fry Port

rounded whole that is Hellenic reality..., as is to be found   at Kasos! Thus, travellers wishing to see 'Greece in the raw' can do no better than drop in (and possibly quickly 'drop out' again) in order to be observe an island that is wholly representative of the old way of life.

FRY (Phry, Fri, Ophrys): capital town & port (Illus 14) In keeping with the already extolled, traditional qualities of the island, Fry is almost frenetically busy in the early morning. Then the informal fish market roars into life (on the square beside the *O Mathias Ouzerie* (*Tmr* 28D2), and the Kasiots go about their daily business. Apart from the activity generated by the fish market, locals are all out shopping, and the bakery is crammed with customers purchasing   their day's supply of fresh 'horiatiko' bread. After this early flurry, the hustle and bustle slows down, in preparation for siesta time. But not before a reflective ouzo or two, for the men, in one of the ouzeries.

A visit to this minuscule, open-air market is a must, the sightseeing highlight of a visit to Kasos. Fishing is now the island's major activity, and it would appear that at least half the town's population turns up to look over the previous night's catch, which is displayed on polythene sacks, laid down on the square. The duration of the market 'opening' is accompanied by the hubbub of fishermen discussing, shouting, swearing and cajoling, whilst the fish are bought and sold. As the trading draws to a close, the borrowed taverna chairs are replaced in their correct location, and the men retire for an ouzo and a hand or two of cards. During the ensuing games, judging from the theatrical gestures and the cacophony of sound, the previous night's fishing gains are won and lost, all over again. Once mentally and physically refreshed, the fisherfolk disperse, and the town drowsily, but inevitably slides into the long afternoon siesta.

At about 1800hrs, the citizens shoulder aside their inertia, and life floods back again. The fishermen make ready for the night's activity, repairing the nets, and baiting the hooks, whilst the taverna owners flash up their charcoal grills, in readiness to cook the evening's fish diners.

The ferry-boat service and provision of an airport tends to disproves the constant contention, the almost obsessional grizzle by Mr Manousos (a local worthy of whom more, much more later), that the Government simply refuses to promote the tourist 'delights' of Kasos. What delights?

ARRIVAL BY AIR A diminutive, neat, earth airfield, some 10min walk from Fry. The airport is graced with a simple 'terminal' building, in which are the waiting room, baggage handling and check-in, as well as the control room. Outside toilets and a do-it-yourself 'canteen shelf', complete with the necessary ingredients, are lumped together, in a 'lean-to', alongside the main block. There is also a 'local-call' telephone box.

There isn't a bus service, so arrivals are expected to walk into town, or hire one of the two or three taxis which run relays to the centre of Fry.

ARRIVAL BY FERRY All the ferries dock at the new'ish Ferry-boat Quay (*Tmr* 1B2), close to the centre of the capital and port. Those disembarking will probably be greeted with the universal cry "Welcome to Kasos, a rock"! Well, they said it. The boats are welcomed by the traditional scrum of passengers, vehicles, dogs and chickens, all fighting to get off the island, and on to the ferry. Independent travellers may be met by the possibly simple-witted Kasiot, representing his limpet-like, ferocious, black-clothed mother, who has accommodation. As the hotels are adjacent, and a known quantity, this offer can be turned down. But 'our landlady' is not easily put-off, and, a game of hide-and-seek develops, during the time it takes the old harpy to get it firmly into her head, that her 'wares' are not to be sampled.

THE ACCOMMODATION & EATING OUT
The Accommodation Almost all the 'in town' possibilities are within   one block of each other.

Rooms (*Tmr* 2D2) Mavrikari St   Tel 41218
Directions: From the Ferry-boat Quay wander round to the left   (*Sbo*), 'hugging' the 'Esplanade' past the first small boat   harbour. At the Clock Tower (*Tmr* 7C/D2/3), it is necessary to cut   south past and turn left along the far side of the Church (*Tmr* 8D2), follow the street round to the right, and the house is on the left.

The lady owner runs the shop next door, and double rooms sharing cost about 3000drs.

Hotel Anessis (*Tmr* 4E2) (Class C) 9 G Mavrikaki   Tel 41201
Directions: Further along, and on the same side of the street as the   already detailed **Rooms**. As there is no sign, it might be necessary to make a final check. It is not unknown for 'prospects' to have to commandeer a key, from the (inevitably) empty, first floor reception desk, enter the bedroom, and check the rate card pinned to the back of the door. The owner is, more often than not, holed-up in his ground floor General Store.

A standard D class style establishment, whereat an en suite double bedroom, boasting a balcony, and with clean linen sheets, is priced   at 3750drs. Late arrivals should grab a key from one of the nails driven into a sawn-off tree stump, decoratively adorning the   reception desk, and sort matters out in the morning.

Hotel Anagenissis (*Tmr* 3E2) (Class C)   Tel 41323
Directions: Instead of cutting south of the church, keep it on the   right (*Fsw*), and rounding its northern end, turn right along the   street leading towards the 'Beach Square', which edges the sea.

At some stage visitors are bound to meet the 'Mr Big' of Kasos, Emmanuel S. Manoussos, if only because this hard-working zealot owns both this hotel, and, in the same block, a travel agency cum large store. In this case I do not use the description 'Mr Big' in a pejorative way, for he is a most courteous, slim, quietly dressed man, with thinning hair, and a passionate, all-consuming belief in   the tourist future of Kasos. He speaks excellent English, having lived in America and been a merchant navy ship's captain.

Unfortunately, the earnest Mr Manousos is 'up against it', for not   only are the 'out-and-out tourist delights' of Kasos questionable, but local politics and politicians are not four-square behind him. It is rumoured, for instance, that the average 'town elder', rather than   endorse Mr Manousos praises of the 'golden sands' of the mysterious Chochlakia Beach (*See* Beaches), would prefer to use the selfsame sand, for the purposes of the construction industry. Oh dear! Mr Manousos and his like-minded colleagues, eagerly, nay fanatically, banging the drum of tourism, are not amused. Now down to the nitty-gritty. Singles sharing are charged at 1860/2700drs, singles en   suite 2290/3550drs, doubles   sharing   2390/3465drs &   doubles   en   suite 3370/5225drs. The best rooms face out over a square and the sea,   whilst the others face the back street. The beds are reasonably comfortable, with nice, fat pillows, as well as clean, ironed bedsheets. The shared showers are of the two-position variety - cold and 'oh, my goodness, that's hot!' The lavatories, which are cleaned daily, tend to smell.

Rooms
Directions: Some half-way between Fry and Emborio (*See* Excursion to Emborio Port), beyond the police station, and about a 10mins walk. A nicely kept, white and blue building, on the left.

Owned by the rather persistent matron, referred to in the preamble about ferry-boat arrival. Average rates, and popular with Greek holiday-makers.

The Eating Out To experience the cheapest, and worst breakfast, 'in all of Greece', simply patronise the 'no name' *Kafeneion*, next door to Kassos Travel Agency (*Tmr* 13E2). Here a breakfast, for two, of stale bread (but no jam or butter), tea, but no lemon, coffee, but no milk, costs a mere 270drs.

Taverna Milos (*Tmr* 5E1/2)
Directions: On the left (*Fsw*) flank of 'Beach Square', with views of the new small boat harbour, town beach, a windmill and, on the horizon, a smouldering rubbish dump. The barn-like building has a large terrace, the wall of which edges sea-lapped boulders, a few metres below. To counter the prevailing winds, the north-west side of the patio is shielded by matting.

The proprietor's father, a Suez pilot for 25 years, helps his son out when necessary. The owner is also assisted by a motley collection of young lads, and a fellow of piratical appearance. The father's second language is French, but the son speaks acceptable English. Reasonably priced offerings are enjoyed, with the sound of the sea in one ear, and bouzouki music in the other ear. When the proprietor is present, the more traditional strains are likely to be interspersed with the discordancy of heavy metal. An ouzo & mezes, and a Coke, cost 300drs. A meal, for two, of smallish red mullet, a tomato & cucumber salad, chips, a large bottle of water & extremely fresh bread cost 2400drs. The taverna's lavatories are adequate.

Restaurant H Kassos (*Tmr* 20D/E3/4)
Directions: A pleasant aspect, looking out on to the Town Square.

Two friendly women provide excellent, freshly cooked and prepared meals, from a clean kitchen. Popular with the locals, but, then there isn't exactly an overwhelm of tourists. All the meals are served with plenty of delicious, fresh bread. A meal, for two, of cucumber & tomato salad, 'vlita' (an up-market version of horta, or wild greens), tzatziki, stewed green beans & 2 cans of soda, cost 2160drs.

Taverna (*Tmr* 29B3)
Directions: The first bar/taverna encountered, on the way into town, from both the airport and the Ferry-boat Quay.

Serves drinks during the day, apart from siesta, and breaks into a 'cooking mode' in the evenings, dishing-up tasty, fresh fish meals.

Ouzerie O Mathias (*Tmr* 28D2)
Directions: To the front of the church.

A very lively, men-only meeting place, where the early morning fish market traders, and the village elders gather. The card games have every appearance of getting out of control, at times. For some obscure reason, the *Mathias* is the sole vendor of ice-creams.

Behind the town beach is the *Ouzerie Meltemi* (*Tmr* G1), a new, whitewashed establishment, with fine furniture. In addition, there are four, popular tavernas at Emborio, which do not close during the siesta, the first one of which is the:
Taverna Emborio
Directions: As above.
   The friendly owner chats-away in 'American', and is assisted by all his family. A meal, for two, of a Greek salad (very large), 1 big, charcoal grilled 'soupias' (cuttlefish, and reminiscent of kalamares), a souvlaki (2 sticks, with chips), skordalia (garlic   sauce flavoured aubergines), 2 bottles of Heineken, and bread, cost 1850drs. Beat that!

THE A TO Z OF USEFUL INFORMATION
AIRLINE OFFICE & TERMINUS (*Tmr* 9E/F2) The wind and rain weathered building appears to be derelict, but is not. Supposedly open Mon-Fri between 0700-1400hrs, but...! Anyone with a flight booked to depart Kasos, would be advised to   reconfirm the arrangement, on arrival. All transactions are 'handraulic' tasks, as there isn't a computer terminal in this office. Oh, no!

Aircraft timetable (Mid-season)
Kasos to Rhodes
Mon/Wed/Fri/Sun   1415hrs
Tue/Thur/Sat   0800hrs
Return
Mon/Wed/Fri/Sun   1240hrs
Tue/Thur/Sat   0700hrs
One-way fare 8220drs; duration 40mins.
Kasos to Karpathos
Tue   0800, 1550hrs
Thur/Sa   0800hrs.
Return
Mon/Wed/Fri/Sun   1340hrs.
One-way fare 2400drs; duration 15mins.
Note connections can be made at Karpathos with Rhodes bound flights.
Kasos to Sitia(Crete)
Tue   1005hrs
Return
Tue   1500hrs
One-way fare 6300drs; duration 30mins.

BANKS None, only an agency for the **National Bank** (*Tmr* 11E2), run by the owner of the *Hotel Anessis*.

BEACHES Mmmh! The Town Beach nestles between two heaps of rubble, the right-hand (*Sbo*) one being the mole of the new, small, boat harbour. The backshore is a dirt road, edged by derelict buildings. The steeply shelving shingle shore is popular with locals, despite the water being a bit murky and green. Neither are the waters of the   harbour of the sparkling clarity to be found in, say, Nimborio, Chalki. No, the Fry harbour solution is of a similar consistency to that of Piraeus.

The Airport Beach, or shore, is solid sandstone sculpted into sharp edges, and is liked by island families, and sea urchins. Noisy children spend their time jumping into sea-sculpted potholes. So, apart from the children and the sea urchins, and I am not sure in which order of repugnance I would place them, to ensure a truly memorable bathe, there is plenty of congealed tar.

There is chatter about a sandy beach, set in pleasant surroundings, on nearby **Armathia island**. But, this sandy Shangri-La is only accessible by caique. Assuming a fisherman can be located, who will undertake to deliver and, more importantly, collect his fare, the voyage takes some 15mins, and costs about 1000drs.

Mr Manousos continues to ramble on about the three hour distant **Chochlakia Beach**, way down at the south-west end of the island. This would be a very desirable and much needed facility for Kasos. Unfortunately, there aren't any buses, or hire vehicles, so the ephemeral delights of this distant possibility, must remain a myth.

BICYCLE, SCOOTER & CAR HIRE None.

BREAD SHOPS (*Tmr* 12D/E2/3) The **Baker** is busy, and sells delicious tasting produce.

BUSES The conveyance is a 'mini-bus', and the terminus (*Tmr* 25F/G2) is a square to the east of the town. The 15 seater mini-bus describes a circular route, via the villages of Ag Marina and Arvanitohori. The bus schedule refers to a 'Kathistres', which is a 'suburb' of Ag Marina.

The surly driver, who speaks English, deserves a medal, as the route through the two settlements is, in some places, extremely narrow and winding. He makes 'on request' sallies for passengers who, say, want to go to Panaghia. Apart from these unscheduled diversions to the timetable, further disruptions, to the smooth running of the service, are caused when a funeral is encountered. As all the islanders not only know each other, but were probably classmates, some 60 or 70 years ago, a cortege involves most, if not all of the passengers. The driver may well pull-up the bus, and join in the procession and formalities, along with the fare-payers. The antecedents, history and age of the deceased can come close to causing running fights to break out, between the living pensioners.

Bus timetable
Kasos Town to Ag Marina & Arvanitohori
Daily   0900, 1000, 1100, 1200, 1430, 1530 1700, 1800hrs.
(But do check).

The round trip fare is 200drs, with a 'destination stop' costing 100drs, and takes about 45 mins. This represents a very cheap 'tour' of the island.

COMMERCIAL SHOPPING AREA None, but a surprising number of **Stores** (*Tmrs* 10D2/3, 11E2 & 19) are distributed throughout the lanes and streets of the Fry town.

DISCOS There is one beside the road to Emborio, beyond the school, and its basketball ground.

FERRY-BOATS *See* Arrival By Ferry.

Ferry-boat timetable (Mid-season)

Day	Departure time	Ferry-boat	Ports/Islands of Call
Tue	0530hrs	Kimolos	Karpathos, Chalki, Simi, Rhodes.
	2330hrs	Kimolos	Sitia(Crete), Ag Nikolaos(Crete), Piraeus(M).
Thur	2330hrs	Romilda	Karpathos, Rhodes.
Fri	1200hrs	Romilda	Piraeus(M).

FERRY-BOAT TICKET OFFICE

Kassos Maritime & Tourist Agency (*Tmr* 13E2) In an effort to bump-up the number of tourists, Mr Manoussos wages a constant battle to increase the number of inter-island ferries docking at Kasos. The office opens Mon-Sat, closing between 1300-1630hrs. He has a map of the island, with the enigmatic Chochlakia Beach etched in place. When questioned about transport to these Elysian sands, Mr Manoussos has to own up that the buses do not go there, the taxis won't, and there isn't any motorised transport to hire! His explanation, vis-a-vis the lack of rental facilities, is that the island espouses a policy of restricting the number of vehicles, in order that Kasos can remain a haven of tranquillity. Ho, hum! A booklet of excruciating poetry is for sale, penned by an Irish nurse, with fond memories of Kasos.

MEDICAL CARE

Chemists & Pharmacies None, but the stores stock this-and-that. An official information leaflet advises that the town possesses '...surgery with oxygen, a sterilisation unit and a doctor'.
Doctor *See* Telephone Numbers & Addresses.
Hospital (*Tmr* 22G3/4). Housed in a largish, yellow painted, rather pleasant looking building.

OTE (*Tmr* 14D4) The new'ish office is south'ish of the Town Hall, and opens weekdays between 0730-1510hrs.

PLACES & EVENTS OF INTEREST The Church (*Tmr* 8D2) has a seriously leaking roof, with the result that the internal paint and plaster is peeling off. The inhabitants have some idea that the EC is about to leap into the breach, with an enormous grant, to facilitate repairs. I have my doubts that Athens will let too much of the 'old gravy' funds seep this far.

The Town Hall (*Tmr* 18D/E4) is from whence the museum key may be obtained. In amongst the portraits of past worthies, is a wall-hung photograph, of 1955, which portrays the 'Kassian Benevolent Society of America', meeting at the Hotel New Yorker. Evidence of their benevolence is rather hard to discern, whilst casting about the island, but the chaps look as if they are having a great time.

The Museum (*Tmr* 24E3/4) is, in reality, more a rapidly decaying house, with a peeling and rotting entrance door, and shutters, surrounded by an unattended garden, in which are deposited a haphazard jumble of artefacts. The building can be identified by the blocks of carved marble, lurking in the front garden. Not to one's entire surprise, admission is free. The Greek speaking, pebble-bespectacled curator, of the motley collection of dust-covered and soil-caked collection, spread across the floor of a small room, admits that there isn't a significant archaeological site, on Kasos. The neatly tagged exhibits include a collection of rifles, various revolvers, some shotguns, all in various states of advanced decay, shards of pottery, a rusty coffee roaster, ships winches, and other deck gear, a pipe, and a number of historic flags and pennants. Of this perfectly forgettable archaeological backwater, it was said "...there is a museum, but we are unfortunate in Kasos that most of our ruins are underground". Well, they would be, wouldn't they?

One other centre of pilgrimage might be the abject Beach Square (*Tmr* E1/2), where a desultory effort has been made to create a focal point. A cloth draped stone urn, flanked by four small cannons, is the central monument.

At No 5 (*Tmr* 15C/D4), opposite a waste ground lot, beside the Ag Marina road, is a reminder of the ship-owning wealth, of the days of the yore, namely a fine, but rapidly dilapidating house.

POLICE
Town Located in a refurbished building, decorated in blue and white, and sporting the national flag, on the right-hand side of the Emborio road (*See* Excursion to Emborio Port).

POST OFFICE (*Tmr* 16F2) Open weekdays between 0730-1400hrs, and almost opposite a general store, the latter owned by islander's who regularly commute between Kasos and the USA.

TAXIS At least two, which are to be found ranked close to the 'Bus Sq' (*Tmr* 25F/G2), or in the front of the Olympic office (*Tmr* 9F2).

TELEPHONE NUMBERS & ADDRESSES

Doctor	Tel 41333
Hospital (*Tmr* 22G3/4)	Tel 41333
Town police	Tel 41222

TOILETS The original public toilet block (*Tmr* 17E1/2) is now derelict, and will probably have to be blown-up. There are replacement facilities, with one (*Tmr* 17G1/2) behind the new, small boat harbour, one (*Tmr* 17C/D2/3) behind the 'not so new' small boat harbour, with yet another planned for the Ferry-boat Quay.

TRAVEL AGENTS & TOUR OFFICES *See* Ferry-boat Ticket Offices.

EXCURSIONS TO FRY SURROUNDS
Excursion to Emborio Port Once the ferry-boat port, Emborio is a 10/15 minutes walk round the curving coastline, to the east of town. The road passes through a scattering of houses, past the old and new schools, a column-fronted building, of grandiose proportions, and uncertain antecedents, the town police station, a windmill and, a fairly modern block with *Roo*ms. Next door to the school, and basketball ground, is a *Disco/drinks Bar*.

That the locals have a heart is nowhere better illustrated than beside this walk. Amongst the dusty, rubbish and general roadside sleaze, young saplings are planted, albeit inside rusting, forty gallon oil drums. The latter encasement is an effort to deter the depredations of stray donkeys and goats, which animals eat anything. There certainly is little enough plant life on Kasos, without further   pillaging. Unfortunately, these well-intentioned efforts are sparsely rewarded, as many of the saplings appear to die.

The harbour is now a rather squalid and untidy fisherman's 'play-place'. The larger fishing boats berth in the crook of the harbour wall. A thin stretch of 'beach' runs down to the other angle, where the smaller craft are slipped over smooth, flat rocks. Sea-urchins abound in the shallows. Long abandoned pretensions to grandeur remain in the shape of a small, still projected public garden, a municipal toilet block, which is 'kept' in an indescribable condition, and a rather avant-garde, but unused, column-mounted port office. Four tavernas vie for business (*See* The Eating Out). Close to one is a large church, which is worthy of more than a passing glance. An old lady, who lives close by, is the phylax, or custodian of the key, and, with pride, shows visitors the interior of the church, which is suffering from a serious attack of 'the damp'. The grandiose, pebble mosaic floor is interesting, and harks back to the days of the affluent, long departed ship owners and sea captains. If the municipal toilet block offends, which it will, an area in which to carry out one's ablutions is reached by climbing the steep bank, behind the taverna, and stumbling into a ruin bestrewn hayfield. Hey ho! I have been chided for this gratuitous piece of information, it having been pointed out that there is a "...perfectly adequate and inoffensive lavatory, a few steps beyond the entrance to the church courtyard". Smacked hand Geoffrey!

ROUTE ONE
To Arvanitohori via Ag Marina (4km) From the Bus Square (*Tmr* 25F/G2), the narrow, badly surfaced tarmacadam road winds through the back streets of Fry. This drive calls for unbelievable judgement by the bus driver, who is, understandably, fond of using his horn. The road emerges at the west of town, curving up the heavily terraced, but painfully dry foothills. Incidentally, there are no bus stops, the driver simply pulls-up outside individual's homes.

AG MARINA (1km from Fry) An attractive settlement, straddling a hill overlooking Fry. The village is dominated by a pleasantly constructed, cobalt-blue and white painted, red domed church, with a separate, wedding cake tiered bell tower.

From Ag Marina, the road descends, gradually at first, but increasingly steeply, towards Arvanitohori, demanding more valiant efforts on the part of the driver. At one point, the route crosses a dry river-bed, full of stones and scorched-looking, dead trees - which rather seems to sum up Kasos!

ARVANITOHORI (2km from Fry) A straggling village, with quite a lot of new building taking place, amongst the ruins of the old. The name Arvanitohori refers to the fact that this was where a nucleus of Albanians settled, in a 16thC migration. There are a few *Rooms*. It is here that the bus driver makes a ten-point turn, to rejoin the circular route, back to Fry.

ROUTE TWO
To Poli via Panaghia (4km) The climb up the ever-ascending foothills, takes off from the Fry to Emborio road. After about a kilometre, a narrow road, to the left, branches off to what, at first sight, looks like a new housing estate, but is actually the village of:

PANAGHIA (1 km from Fry) A closer look is well worthwhile, because beyond the newer houses leads to an 'Old Quarter'. Here is where many of the large houses, constructed by sea captains and ship owners, were built, and are now almost all fallen, or falling down. It must have been a substantial and prosperous community, once upon a time, but the wealthy emigrated, when the Italians appeared on the scene. They first moved to Syros island, and then on to London, never to return. A certain amount of bulldozing appears to be taking place and the locals, have utilised the wooden doors and window shutters, of the old mansions, to assist in the construction of jerry-built chicken and turkey pens.

To one side of a surprisingly large church and clock tower, are   public toilets, constructed after the fashion of Cycladean chapels. I wonder about the thought-process that conjured-up that particular architectural style.

The villagers are particularly friendly, striking up conversation with passers-by, and sometimes proffering a hospitable drink.

The main road, if it rates such a descriptive word, twistingly   ascends towards:

POLI (3km from Fry) The hike to this neat village takes about one hour. To the left, a wide track advances in the direction of a well kept church and clock tower, set down on thehillsides.   Centuries old   terracing climbs up, and up, and up the flanks of a massive mountain range, to the right.

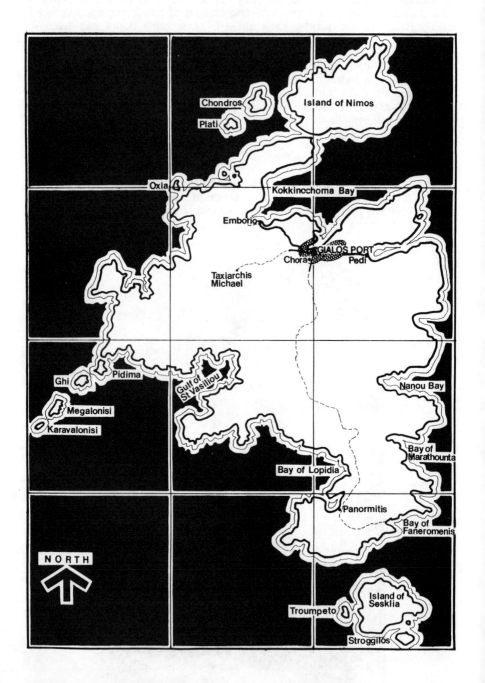

Illustration 15 Simi island

8 SIMI (Symi, Syme)
Dodecanese Islands

* * *

FIRST IMPRESSIONS Breathtakingly beautiful island port; expensive, tourist & trip-boat trap; shortage of accommodation & water.

SPECIALITIES Day-trips; herbs; sponge stalls; down-market day-trippers & up-market package holiday-makers.

LOCAL RELIGIOUS HOLIDAYS & FESTIVALS incl: 7th-9th Nov - Panormitis Monastery.

VITAL STATISTICS Tel prefix 0241. About 12km long & 10km wide, with a population of 2,500, most of whom live in or around the main town (Chora) & the port (Gialos).

HISTORY Much of Simi's history has centred around the inhabitants' ability as builders of sea-going vessels. The islanders were purported to have supplied battleships, as long ago as the Trojan wars, when they constructed and crewed three of the legendary triremes. The Knights of St John and the Turks, during their respective occupations, used the skill of the Symiot boatbuilders. Incidentally, here, as was the case for many other Aegean islands, the constant felling of trees, with which to construct ships, was not accompanied by a programme of forestry management. Inevitably, this deforestation altered the climate conditions, resulting in the dry, treeless, barren state of the island, as is to be seen today.

The worthy citizens represent yet another collective, rumoured to have been the first of the Dodecanese islanders to rise up against their Turkish overlords. This was at the outset of what was to become the War of Independence. Another war related curiosity, is that the official German surrender of the Dodecanese, to the Allies, was signed on Simi, on 8th May 1945. This ceremony took place in the building half-way along the north side of Gialos harbour, now the *Pension (& Restaurant) Les Katerinettes (Tmr* 5B1/2).

Apart from boatbuilding, another lost skill is that of sponge diving, now almost entirely the preserve of the islanders of Kalimnos. Despite absence of a sponge boat fleet, the prized marine organisms are sold, by the stall-full (*See* Commercial Shopping...

The deserted, empty and derelict houses, seen on many Greek islands, are a constant source of bewilderment to overseas visitors. Much of the cause lies in the Greek inheritance laws, and the complications that ensue when the beneficiaries of a will are a number of offspring, who fail to agree on the best course of action, in respect of a property. This problem is exacerbated, in respect of Simi, where, in common with one or two other Aegean islands, legacies pass through the female line. In the past, this quirk was responsible for an even greater migration of young males, than was usual.

GIALOS/SIMI: the port (as opposed to Chora, the old town) (Illus 16) The stunning, 'film set' harbour is, quite simply, one of the most strikingly attractive, Greek island port's. The first visit will remain indelibly engraved on any seaborne caller's memory. But not all that 'glistens is gold...' The lack of many of the usual social graces forcibly strikes most visitors, as must the inordinate amount of rubbish littering the back streets, that climb the

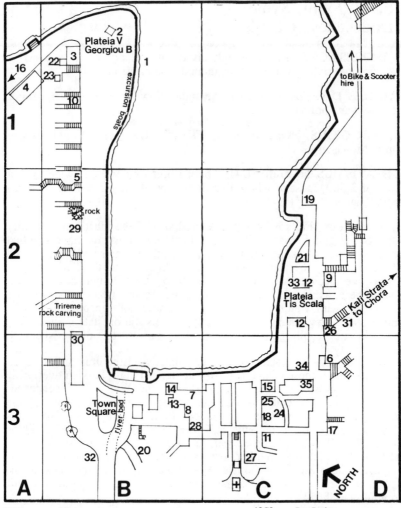

(Tmr) = Town map reference
(Fsw) = Facing seawards
(Sbo) = Sea behind one
(Fbqbo) = Ferry-boat Quay behind one

Illustration 16 Gialos Port

surrounding hillsides. It has been suggested that the location is no more than an elaborate stage-set, with a neat and tidy facade, to keep the day-trippers enthralled. Behind the scenes is the reality of 20thC Simi, with everyday life, and the rubbish, blown-out of sight, into the back streets. It's a thought.

The inter-island ferries and excursion boats steam into the horseshoe bay of Gialos, hemmed-in by steep hillsides. The slopes are piled-up with the port's buildings, which rise, amphitheatre-like, in the fashion of a Doric set of playing cards. It seems as if each house is stacked-up, one on top of the other. This proximity has resulted in a modern-day, social engineering problem, with which the authorities and citizenry have to struggle. The difficulty is that, often, the cellar and septic tank of one dwelling, is the upper bedroom wall of the next one down!

This feature and the chronic shortage of drinking water have combined to channel the tourist development of Simi into a day-trippers 'paradise'. It was but a few years ago that the port shops only really kick-started into operation, immediately prior to the onset of the excursion boats' arrival, shutting their doors immediately they departed. The short-term nature of most visitors sojourn, tended to result in a general attitude of 'take a profit, while it's there'. It can be no coincidence, that it was of Simi, that a possibly apocryphal story was related. This concerned the police being forced, on several occasions, to close down every restaurant and taverna, in the place, for excessive profiteering. There is no doubt that the normal, leisurely Greek nature has been supplemented by a rather disagreeable, graceless, 'take it or leave it' attitude. The locals tend to dismiss these suggestions, expostulating "No, who...?" When advised of a particular instance, the cry goes up "Ah, yes, we know all about him!" In defence of the islanders, they are subjected to a daily invasion, of up to six or seven excursion boats, from nearby Rhodes and Kos, day in, day out, week in, week out, for some six months - which would be quite enough to try the patience of any saint.

Gialos, and its surrounds, become extremely hot, during the day, as the windless bay acts almost like an oven. This is just one more reason for the wise to abandon the area, between the trip boat hours of about 10am to 4pm.

ARRIVAL BY FERRY (*Tmr* 1B1) The ferry-boats berth close to the Clock Tower (*Tmr* 2B1), at the right-hand (*Sbo*) harbour promontory. Across the quayside is the Greco-Italianesque police headquarters (*Tmr* 3B1). From the docking point, it is a 'bit-of-a-trudge' to the centre of activity, at the bottom of the 'U' of the harbour bay. This is along an unmade and, at night, poorly lit Esplanade. The outstanding skills of the Greek ferry skippers is as well illustrated here, at Simi, as anywhere else. That floating ferry-boat phenomenon, the **FB Nissos** Kalymnos, skirts the island, on its approach from Tilos island, nips through the channel, formed by the main island and **Nimos** island, as a short-cut to Kokkinchoma Bay, and thence to Gialos port. This passage can only be selected, on 'a calm' day, as the clearance between the sea-bed and the keel is no more than a metre - as evidenced by the beautifully clear, aquamarine blue of the waters hereabouts. After that bit of shallow-channel-crawling, the ferry zips into the constricted mouth of the port and makes a sharp, left-hand-down turn. The captain pushes the boat's bow out, towards the far bank, and, whilst still turning, drops anchor and, simultaneously, throws the boat into reverse. The stern moment is such that the aft ramp is still clanking down towards the horizontal, as the stern of the craft 'kisses' the quay. At this point the anchor winch takes the strain, creating an acceptable gap between the boat and the wall. Magic! The excursion boats from Rhodes and Kos dock close to the Ferry-boat Quay.

THE ACCOMMODATION & EATING OUT For other options than those detailed here, *See* Chora.
The Accommodation Finding a bed is not easy, and when located, it will be one of the most expensive, in the Dodecanese. Furthermore, owners of *Rooms* often insist on a minimum of two or three days occupation. The situation is exacerbated due to a steady flow of devoted Simi visitors, who stop-over for the duration of their vacation, and tend to stay put. In the old days, the standard of private house accommodation varied between 'simple to primitive'. A cautionary tale, told to us, by a Greek lady friend, graphically illustrates that which used to occur, in years gone by. She disembarked at Simi, and on asking the landlady the location of the bathroom, was directed, to a very large rain-water butt! Enough to say, she beat a hasty retreat.
Now, to return to the present. The Travel firms of Simi Tours, Simian Holidays and Sunny Land can assist in placing enquirers in accommodation (*See* Travel Agents &...). The suggestion that the overall situation would be relieved, by the long-awaited completion of the refurbishment of the **Hotel Nireus** (*Tmr* 4A1), must remain a distant hope. This topping-out process has now been promised, for in excess of eight years, and the delay will, no doubt, be extended by a similar amount of time, now that the building is starting to fall-down again!

Hotel Aliki (Class A)   Tel 71655
Directions: Beyond the shell of the *Nireus* (*Tmr* 4A1).
Unquestionably a lovely set-up, but probably rather too 'rich' at about 12000drs, for a double room en suite. The adjacent quayside is not really wide enough for the hotel's waterfront tables and chairs, to be anything but part of the 'ramblas'. A regular flow of 'human traffic' is assured, as this bit of the Esplanade is the outset of the path to the local beach. One other drawback is that the waters hereabouts can be rather murky and smelly.

Proceeding down the Esplanade, the next accommodation is the:
Pension Les Katerinettes (*Tmr* 5B1/2)   Tel 71671
Directions: As above.
This establishment was closed for refurbishment, but is now reopen, and probably represents the best combination of quality and price in town.

If dropping-in does not 'bring forth' a room, try the Sunny Land agency (*Tmr* 29B2). If there is 'room at the inn', they will arrange a double bedroom for 4000drs, or 4900drs, with a balcony. Guests can breakfast downstairs, in the restaurant, which also serves Greek and French flavoured dinners.

Behind the river bed, and on the left, is the:
Hotel Kokona (*Tmr* B2)   Tel 71549/71451
Directions: As above.
A new'ish hotel, offering en suite doubles at a price of 6000drs, which includes breakfast.

About middle of the bottom of the bay are a number of *Rooms* (*Tmr* 7B/C3), whilst around the back of the selfsame block, on the corner of which is *Pizza Simi* (*Tmr* 14B3), is:

Rooms Titika (*Tmr* 8B/C3)   Tel 71501
Directions: As above, and advertised over a close-by *Giro stall* (*Tmr* 13B3).
A double room with en suite bathroom costs 5000drs.

Hotel Albatros (*Tmr* 11C3) (Class B pension)   Tel 71707
Directions: From the Esplanade, turn down the lane, to the nearside of the
Ionian Bank (*Tmr* 15C3), as far as the crossroads, alongside which is the
pension and *Taverna O Meraklis*. The blue painted building is to the right
(*Sbo*) of the taverna.
      The taverna window stickers advertise that the hotel's information and
booking office is in... Paris! Do not worry, it isn't necessary to catch a plane,
to France. All rooms have an en suite bathroom, with singles priced at
3650/4820drs & doubles 4400/5300drs.

Further on round the Esplanade, the other side of the quay, and behind the
Trawler Taverna (*Tmr* 12C2/3), or, more correctly, at the rear of the Plateia
Tis Skala, is:
Rooms Agli (*Tmr* 9C2)
Directions: As above. Maria is the mama who runs this clean pension with
the help (or more accurately, the hindrance) of her disenchanting (*sic*)
daughters. She does not live on the premises, but in a house up the steep steps,
to the left of this accommodation.
      The bedrooms are cleaned every day. Maria even remakes the beds, if they
do not meet her standards. Clients should attempt to claim an upstairs room,
if possible. The ground floor ones can be rather 'aromatic', and the slumbers
of light sleepers disturbed, as the water pump cuts in and out during the night
hours. A double room sharing costs 3500drs, but she may well insist on a
minimum stay of three days. There is a communal fridge on the landing.
      Maria has a number of *Rooms*, scattered about the vicinity, with another
pension to one side of, and beyond the main Town Sq. This latter house is
quieter, has good views, and is priced at 4000drs for a double. The building
is quite interesting as it is, in the main, unspoiled by the conversion work
necessary to create the accommodation. That is apart from the modern
bathroom built on to the back of the house. Architecturally of note are the
wooden shutters, old wooden stairs, the ceiling-hinged mirror (reminiscent of
those to be seen in Lindos homes, Rhodes island), and the old-fashioned
kitchen dresser. The water continues to be drawn from a well, but nowadays
with the aid of a modern, Japanese pump unit.
      Maria would appear to be onside to become the 'Mrs Big' of Simi island.
Her son runs one of the waterside tavernas, and she is rumoured to be having
a hotel constructed.

The Eating Out The various establishments are on the expensive side, in
addition to which much 'schlepping' takes place. Beer is often only obtainable
in cans (a pet hate of mine) or, worse still, 'on draught'.

The Pastry Shop (*Tmr* 10B1)
Directions: The first waterfront cafe, down from the clock tower.
      Rather touristy in style, and prices. Without doubt, it is the best cafe from
which to watch the ferry-boat activity.

There are any number of eating places, but I have chosen to list just a few,
including the:

Taverna O Meraklis (*Tmr* 11C3)
Directions: Close to a crossroads, on a lane leading down from alongside the Esplanade bordering Ionian Bank.

As the establishment is set back from the main (tourist) thoroughfare, it is less frenetic than its Esplanade-side competitors. No doubt, to compensate for this lack of prime site position, and with the perspicacity to realise on which side his bread is oiled, the proprietor maintains an efficient, friendly service, dishing-up good, freshly cooked food, at reasonable prices. A lunch, for two, of 2 Greek salads (generous sized & 400drs each, compared to 500drs elsewhere), 1 moussaka (delicious & 600drs, instead of the 'going' Simi rate of 700/750drs), a large bottle of water & very tasty bread, cost 1620drs.

Next door is the even less expensive *Restaurant Obelitirio*.

Back at the Esplanade, alongside the Ionian Bank, and continuing straight on, instead of following the Esplanade round to the left, on the far side of a junction, and on the left, is the:
Taverna Vrachos (*Tmr* 6C3)
Directions: As above, opposite the *Bar Vapori* (run by an English woman).

A traditional taverna, not opening until the evening. It is a totally scurrilous to suggest that this, and other Simi tavernas do not open midday, in order to avoid the daytime crowds, which spill out of the excursion boats. Comes well recommended, and is patronised by the owner of the *Hotel Aliki*, and his wife. The food has been praised as the best to be found on Simi, and no more expensive than anywhere else. The one very friendly waiter/owner seems to have to do the work of four, despite which the service is satisfactorily speedy.

Bar Vapori (*Tmr* 34C3)
Directions: As for *Taverna Vrachos*.

Overseas newspapers are draped over the chairs and tables, no doubt to tempt event-hungry passers-by. This does not come cheap. An exotic bottle of (Mexican) beer and a glass of Coke costs 550drs. I think I'll buy a paper.

Taverna Trawler (*Tmr* 12C2/3) Plateia Tis Skala.
Directions: Beside the 'east' Esplanade.

The chairs and tables of this excellent establishment occupy most of the square, and only open in the evenings. The owners employ a rather peculiar system of displaying their fish and other wares, in a bar, on the right-hand (*Sbo*) side of the plateia, whilst cooking the meals, in a cellar kitchen and outside grill, on the opposite side. The prices are reasonable, for Simi, and they sell a small bottle of retsina. The service becomes a 'little hectic' as the evening wears on.

There is a *Giro stall* (*Tmr* 13B3), behind the Esplanade edging *Pizza Simi* (*Tmr* 14B3). The latter employs schleppers to advertise the place's offerings, and to convert passers-by into customers. Pies are still available here. On the right of the Main Square is the tree shaded *Taverna O Yannis,* serving run-of-the-mill Greek dishes. Despite being somewhat off the well-beaten track, the prices are relatively expensive.

Prior to departing this subject, a reader recommendation is the:
Restaurant O Tholos
Directions: Back at the Ferry-boat Quay (*Tmr* 1B1), and round past the Clock Tower (*Tmr* 2B1), along the Esplanade to the beach.

Run by a young Athenian couple, Fotis (Simian grandfather) and Hasoula Arthela. I am advised this young lady can 'really' cook, and she speaks perfect English. The menu includes local shrimps, gigantes beans, chicken with potatoes, melitzanes (aubergines) with feta, the last two both oven cooked - class food, fairly priced. And her father brews the ouzo, back at the family distillery, in the Plaka, Athens. There have plans to build new toilets, round the back of the restaurant - in old lime kilns. Makes sense!

THE A TO Z OF USEFUL INFORMATION
BANKS The **Ionian & Popular** (*Tmr* 15C3) and **National Bank** (*Tmr* 28B/C3) have branches. For some reason a Store (*Tmr* 35C3) is agent for the National Bank, whilst the **Telegraph & Exchange office** (*Tmr* 30B2/3) conducts foreign currency transactions.

BEACHES The minuscule and over populated Town Beach involves a walk round past the Police office (*Tmr* 3B1) and the *Hotel Aliki*. The track skirts a small caique repair yard, and the slopes on which stand's a splendid, large, cobalt domed church. The latter was built in 1948, to celebrate the reunion with Greece, and is reached up a steep flight of steps. Beyond a small bluff, beneath the church, the path leads to a beach bar discotheque. It is necessary to wander through this establishment to gain access to the extremely small, fine pebble beach. Crowded it may be, but it is located in a lovely setting. Nude sunbathing takes place on the rocks beyond.

BICYCLE, SCOOTER & CAR HIRE The official island maps optimistically detail roads, that are simply nothing more than rough paths and tracks. The roads to the Chora, Pedi, and Emborio are large and asphalt surfaced, but these are the only few kilometres of thoroughfare. Despite this, there is a rental firm, the:
Scooter & Bike Hire
Directions: A 'waterfront warehouse', located beyond the Bus park (*Tmr* 19C2), on the right-hand (*Fsw*) side of Gialos Bay.
    The rates are extremely expensive, a scooter being priced at 4000drs a day, with a tank of fuel. There isn't an island filling station. For car hire *See* Travel Agents & Tour Offices.

BREAD SHOPS There are two bakehouses. One **Baker** (*Tmr* 17C3) is run by a splendid, moustachioed man, with every appearance of being a comic opera bandit. The other **Baker** (*Tmr* 18C3) is owned by a rather ungracious family, whom, on occasions, exhibit a pecuniary peculiarity - any change due might be slow to cross the palm of a shopper. Nod, nod, wink, wink!

BOOKSELLERS More a newspaper shop (*Tmr* 33C2), which sells some foreign language books. *See* Bar Vapori, The Eating Out.

BUSES There is a 14 seater mini-bus, which circulates along the route from Gialos, up to Chora, and then down to Pedi. The vehicle has to be small, to wriggle through the winding, narrow streets of Chora. Rather than a strict timetable, the vehicle simply continues up, round, down, and back, all day long. As the journey takes about quarter an hour, it should pass a specific spot, every half an hour, as long as there are passengers. If they run short of custom, there is definitely an hourly service. The single Gialos to Pedi fare is 100drs. It must be one of the cheapest purchases on the island. In strict

contrast to the *laissez faire* attitude of the past, there are now designated bus stops which the driver respects. What a pity.
The buses park (*Tmr* 19C2), on the right-hand (*Fsw*) side of the bay.

COMMERCIAL SHOPPING AREA None. Spaced out throughout the lanes and streets are a variety of shops, stores, and peripteros. A Kava (liquor store), opposite the Baker (*Tmr* 18C3), sells bulk ouzo, and there is a **Butcher** close to the Town Square. Generally the opening hours are those of most small islands, with an afternoon siesta.

Beside the Esplanade, in the area where the excursion boats berth (*Tmr* B1/2), is a Sponge shop. The owner is Nikos, a young marine biologist. He gathers together crowds of day-trippers, to deliver a short lecture in respect of the history of the island, as well as an evironmental talk vis-a-vis the life cycle of sponges and loofahs. He will only sell unbleached sponges, and encourages 'his' audience to purchase this type of product - from him. Nikos is quite a character, and intersperses his delivery with risque jokes and remarks. Usually the audience are left spellbound, and anxious to part with their money. Couriers, desperate to have something, anything, with which to keep their 'charges' busy, and occupied, herd them in his direction.

DISCOS One is located in the old market building 'AKTAION', beyond the Bus park (*Tmr* 19C2), and is aptly named **Waves**.

FERRY-BOATS & HYDROFOILS The inter-island ferries dock (*Tmr* 1B1) close to the top end of the north-east horn of the bay. Stern-too berthing can well prove to be a tricky manoeuvre, in a strong wind. The quay wall is scattered with vertically mounted, old gun barrels, positioned to provide mooring bollards. Being spaced rather close together, the ferry ramp may, in adverse conditions, catch on one of these stout obstacles. The adjacent quayside is often used for the bulk storage of building materials. Hydrofoils pull up alongside the quay, half-way down from the Ferry-boat Quay (*Tmr* 1B1), but they only run if there are sufficient passengers who wish to visit Simi from Rhodes.

Ferry-boat timetable (Mid-season)

Day	Departure time	Ferry-boat	Ports/Islands of Call
Mon	1300hrs	Nissos Kalymnos	Rhodes, Kastellorizo.
Tue	1200hrs	N. Kalymnos	Tilos, Nisiros, Kos, Kalimnos.
Fri	1300hrs	N. Kalymnos	Rhodes, Kastellorizo.
Sat	1200hrs	N. Kalymnos	Tilos, Nisiros, Kos, Kalimnos.

In addition to the above, local excursion boats, which include the **Simi I &** **Simi II**, ply to and from Rhodes. Tickets for these trips are purchased on board and the return fare costs 2500/3500drs.

Hydrofoil timetable (Mid-season)
They only run if there are sufficient passengers, and the sea state is calm'ish.

Day	Departure time	Ports/Islands of Call
Daily	1600hrs	Rhodes.

One-way fare 2000drs.

FERRY-BOAT & HYDROFOIL TICKET OFFICES Ferry and excursion boat tickets can be purchased on board.

LAUNDRY (*Tmr* 31C2) A Dry Cleaners open weekdays 0800-1400hrs.

MEDICAL CARE
Chemists & Pharmacies (*Tmr* 21C3) Beside the Esplanade, beyond Plateia Tis Scala. They will call the doctor or dentist, if necessary.

OTE (*Tmr* 20B3) Located in a pleasant, old, stone building to the left (*Sbo*) of the river-bed. The office opens daily between 0730-1400hrs. There are a pair of metered telephones at the **Telegraph & Exchange** office (*Tmr* 30B2/3).

NTOG None, nor a Municipal office. *See* Travel Agents &...

PLACES & EVENTS OF INTEREST Gialos has scraped the barrel and lashed together a **Nautical Museum** (*Tmr* 32B3), in a building next door to the Town Hall. At a 100drs a head, it is difficult to award this exhibition the museum world's equivalent of the sandy beach pinnacle of achievement, namely the accolade of a 'Golden Starfish'! The museum houses a paucity of sponge trade related items, such as modern replicas of sponge boats, an ancient diver's 'clobber', and various other bits and pieces. Sadly, the old craftsman, who constructed the boats, died in 1992.
   The very interesting Chora (the Old Town) has a small museum and, overlooking the houses, a castle built by the Knights (well, well), within the walls of which is a church.The ridge overlooking the harbour bay, to the left of the Chora castle, is ringed with 'dead' windmills.
   The large, carved portion of rocky hillside, located half-way down the right-hand (*Sbo*) side of the bay's Esplanade, close by the Telegraph & Exchange office (*Tmr* 30B2/3), portrays a *trireme*. This is similar (at least to my eyes) to the famous sculpture at the entrance to the Lindos (Rhodes) Acropolis, but I can find no mention of it in official literature.

POST OFFICE (*Tmr* 22B1) Up steps to the side of the Police station.

POLICE
Port (*Tmr* 23B1) Almost opposite the Post Office.
Town (*Tmr* 3B1).

TAXIS They rank close to the Bus 'terminus' (*Tmr* 19C2), and the drivers include a lady. The fare to both Chora and Pedi is 300drs.

TOILETS (*Tmr* 24C3) Yes, in the block behind, and to one side of the Ionian Bank. They are extremely dirty and smelly.

TRAVEL AGENTS & TOUR OFFICES The firms advise, arrange and assist regarding all and everything, and are open daily, at least until siesta time. Businesses include:
Simi Tours (*Tmr* 25C3, tel 71307). Also operate a book-swop scheme;
Simian Holidays (*Tmr* 26C2/3, tel 71077). Laskarina agent;
and
Sunny Land (*Tmr* 29B2, tel 71413/71320). Book-swop, trip boats, free luggage storage, and a safe deposit box.
   Their services encompass a selection of boat trips, with fares costing about

2500drs per head. Another exponent in this field is **Katerina** (*Tmr* 35C3). Incidentally, destinations take in: Emborio; Nimos island; Nanou Beach; St Marina; St Nikolaos; St George; Marathounta Bay; and Sesklia island. A beach barbecue is held daily, at one of these venues. Despite the apparently exorbitant cost of the BBQ, when added to the caique 'fare', reports indicate that participants consider the food to be acceptable, and good value.

An example of that on offer is:

Nanou Beach Set in a deeply indented bay, the beach is only accessible by a 40min caique voyage. There is a height of season, backshore taverna, and a donkey. The beach comprises large round white rocks, with a few areas suitable for sunbathing. Tar can be a problem. If the daily 'beach barbecue' is not arranged for this location, then it will probably remain fairly deserted. The bay is frequented by lobster/crab fishermen, in small boats, using glass-bottomed buckets to spot their catch on the sea-bed.

CHORA: the old town The mini-bus makes the trip up to Chora, high on the hillside above Gialos Port, on the way to Pedi village. Chora may also be reached by climbing, if not scaling, the wide, broad, flagstone staircase which ascends from Plateia Tis Scala (*Tmr* C2). The flight of steps is lined with bars and tavernas (such as *Jean & Tonic* - oh dear).

First on the left (*Sbo*) is the *Restaurant Dallara*, which has a vine trellis shaded terrace, overlooking the adjacent rooftops, and the sea. A meal of 1 tomato & cucumber salad, 1 Greek style lasagne, 1 green bean stew, and a small bottle of water, cost 1380drs. The friendly, bearded owner is a fanatical PASOK supporter (the 'for-the-moment' opposition, socialist party), as testified by the banners pinned to the walls. His wife's embroidery also graces the inside of this pleasant, family-run establishment.

The ascent finally decants on to Chora Main Square, whereon the *Rainbow Hotel*, to the right of some old windmills. Chora and Gialos are as different as a quiet old town and a bustling, frenetic port could be. Chora is a very large village, which has evolved in a maze of garishly coloured houses, lanes and alleys, that jig up and down, and round and about. The chaos of the layout is such that the museum and castle, so thoughtfully signposted at the outset, are 'left to their own devices' and have to be hunted down. Why not spend a day or three in this peaceful, high altitude backwater, well away from the madding crowds?

The *Village Hotel* (Class A, tel 71800) has en suite singles priced at 3000/4000drs & doubles at 4300/5500drs, whilst the much more peaceful *Fiona Hotel* is a newly constructed, but 'in traditional style' alternative. The latter is reached by following the road curving round to the right, from the *Village Hotel* cum bus stop. Immediately thereafter, prior to the road making a tight left-hand turn, there is a side-street, beside which is the hotel, on the right, and set back from the main thoroughfare. The double bedrooms are kitted out with traditional furniture, and have en suite bathrooms, for which is charged 5500drs per night, including breakfast. The excellent location allows fine views out over the harbour, and the owner is very pleasant. It's a thought.

ROUTE ONE
To Pedi via Chora (2km) It does seem further than two kilometres, when walking up to Chora, and down to Pedi. The mini-bus takes to the long, uphill track, that streaks out of the harbour, from the right-hand (*Fsw*) side of the bay, before winding and 'narrowing' tortuously back into Old Town.

PEDI The straight, steeply angled, metalled road down to the port and small hamlet, that makes up the settlement, is hemmed in by hills that are almost painfully dry. I do not state 'small' port, as the concrete jetty stretching into the bottle-necked bay is surprisingly large. Quite often, fairly big ships berth alongside for running repairs and painting. There are unheralded *Rooms* in the village, as long as a prospect wants to stay several nights. Enquiries at the few travel offices or of locals will elicit directions.

Painted wall signs, pointing to the left (*Fsw*), indicate the direction of 'New Beach'. Keep walking, until the road runs out, and then cut upwards and over the hill. Sun-beds and umbrellas.

The access road from the village makes a T-junction with the waterfront, opposite the main jetty. The 'Esplanade', hugging the edge of the curving bay to the right (*Fsw*), is simply a track edging the backshore, with very small, stone jetties projecting, here and there, into the water. Prior to the bus pulling up on an unmade square, it charges along the narrow but sandy shore, on a track which is indistinguishable from the beach. It certainly makes the sunbathers sit up..., and this happens every hour or so. Much of the water's edge is composed of large pebbles, whilst the shallow, shelving sea-bed is slimy, algae covered round stones. Half-way round the semi-circle of the bay is the curious, acropolis-style upper storey architecture of a *Bar Restaurant*, which tends to pull one up, with a start. This establishment is followed by another, more expensive taverna, close by which is a bus stop. Continuing on around the bay leads to a church, followed by the pleasing, and new *Rooms Lancaster*, the sign for which is tiny, and almost illegible. Close by is a gate, on which is written 'Open'. Through this, and following the 'red paint' marked path up and over two hills, for a 'bit of a scramble', leads to the attractively situated, delightful:

Ag Nikolaos Beach There is a small church, as would be expected from the location's name. The beach is lined with tamarisk trees and is mostly sharp rocks and pebbles, with a small sandy area in front of the backshore hut of a taverna. The taverna opens, when the owner thinks there will be sufficient customers. The menu is very limited, and there are only two tables and four chairs, so don't all feel hungry, at once. As it is, clients may well have to defend their food from the attentions of some resident goats, who have become rather tame. Ablutions have to be carried out in 'the wild', as there aren't any formal facilities. The proprietor hires out sun-beds, and appears to be almost fanatical about keeping the beach clean and tidy. He has actually been observed to clear the weed from the shoreline rocks, and remove sea urchins!

Back at the bay, the *Pedi Beach Hotel & Restaurant* requests 7900drs per night for an en suite double room, which charge includes breakfast. Meals here are also expensive. The bay possesses a scattering of spindly trees and a couple of palm trees, growing close by the centrally located church.

To the left (*Fsw*), the foreshore curves away, without even the semblance of a track. The wide, raised concrete patios and steps of the equally spaced houses are connected in a series of small jetties. This frontage finally runs out on a disorganised, flat, scrubbly plain at the far left-hand end of the bay.

ROUTE TWO
Panormitis Monastery The location lies at the south end of the island, and the best method of making the excursion is to 'catch' a caique. Anyone of the

Gialos travel agents will arrange the necessary. For instance, the **Simi II** departs Gialos at 1400hrs, dropping in at the Monastery, prior to continuing on to Rhodes, and if it is operating, the hydrofoil, from Rhodes, also calls in, *en route* to Gialos.

The substantial, unattractively overblown, rather municipal-like, 18thC Monastery Archangel Michael, and associated buildings, which incorporate a museum, stretch along the edge of a bay and a small beach. Entrance to the monastery is free, but note the 'clothing rules' are strictly applied, although there is a pile of 'jumble' for those who do not arrive decorously attired. Immediately on the right is a shop selling holy relics and religious paraphernalia. Entrance to the museum costs 100drs. This entitles a browser to look over the to-be-expected items. In addition there is a fascinating jumble of Hellenic 'car-boot' memorabilia, which takes in: old sponges; an ancient monastic dinner service; a letter from Mr Kapodistria, the first Prime Minister of Greece, immediately after the War of Independence; as well as a bizzare collection of stuffed crocodiles, carved elephant tusks, and some old, threadbare koala teddy bears - some what?

It is possible to stay overnight at the monastery, at the following room rates: with 3 beds & bathroom - 1500drs; 6 beds, bathroom & fridge - 2700drs; 6 beds, bathroom, kitchen & fridge - 4000drs; and 8-10 beds, with no other facilities - 1400drs! I stress, these are per bed, not per head prices.

To the left (*Sbo*) of the monastery entrance, there are: an ice-cream shop, with metered telephone; a sign for a bread shop, inside the colonnaded arcade; and a toilet block. There are a couple of expensive tavernas, many fishing caiques, and a small beach, on the right (*Sbo*). At the end of the settlement is a path that leads to a windmill.

The site is probably more organised than would be expected and is the venue for the 'extravaganza of a religious festival', held between 7-9th November. To sum-up, the monastery, and surrounds, are probably the least attractive of all the island locations.

ROUTE THREE Emborio (Nimporios) About two kilometres to the west of Gialos. Emborio, historically a commercial port, is now a summer package tourist resort, with a beach. There are some Byzantine mosaics still visible.

9 TILOS (Telos, Episkopi)   * * * *
Dodecanese Islands

FIRST IMPRESSIONS Peace & quiet; off the outright tourist track (just); varied & exotic bird life - hooded crows & bright blue rollers; friendly islanders; wind, on occasions.

SPECIALITIES Honey; water - an underground source was discovered in 1989, and the Tiliots are very proud of this fact. "Why go to Simi when WE have water here?".

LOCAL RELIGIOUS HOLIDAYS & FESTIVALS incl: 15th Aug - Festival, Panaghia Church, Mikro Chorio; 23rd Aug - Festival, Panaghia Monastery, Nr Livadia; 27th Aug - Festival, Ag Panteleimonos Monastery.

VITAL STATISTICS Tel prefix 0241. The island is some 17½km, north-west to south-east, & 'waists' down to 3km, at the narrowest point, with a population of approximately 300.

HISTORY A specific claim to fame originated in the discovery of some mastadon skeletons, in hill caves, some fifteen years ago.

GENERAL The island was almost ignored for many years, most ferry-boat voyagers steaming on past, to other, more inviting prospects in the Dodecanese island chain. Not so now, for Tilos has become a target for both thoughtful independents and clients of at least one of the more selective package tour operator's. One of the factor's allowing an increase in tourism has been the comparatively recent discovery of underground water.
    The increased tourist activity only required a nudge, as Tilos has always possessed a number of indigenous attractions. These encompass: a pleasant port, with sufficient accommodation and dining establishments; an old town, Megalo Chorio; a ruined castle; many beaches, some of very good quality; and reasonably frequent ferry-boat connections. One misdirected manifestation of the increased tourist thrust must be the excursion trips, organised from Rhodes, on the **EB Mistral**. Presumably this 'jolly wheeze' has been dreamt-up by the couriers, scraping the barrel in order to keep their flock of package holiday-makers happy, and travel agents, to earn any, let alone a fast drachma. This excursion allows a total of one and a half hours stop. Yes, one and...! The islanders have, quite rightly, decided to ignore these totally unnecessary occurrences, thus no one meets, schleps, or even welcomes the sad boatloads of forlorn passengers, who fleetingly, and aimlessly wander through the few streets, and around the sparse diversions, presented by the port. Almost as if to reinforce this disinterest, in the more transient of the visitors, the Ferry-boat Quay is used as a builders yard, on which are dumped any amount of construction materials. All this sand and gravel results in rather gritty dining, in the vicinity of the quay, on windy days.
    I can only fervently hope and pray that the rash of package company stickers is not a precursor that Tilos will go the way of Chalki.

LIVADIA (Levadhia): port (Illus 18) Set in a large, broad, hill-surrounded inlet, with the development to the right-hand side *(Sbo)*, and a clean, narrow, almost white, pebble and shingle seashore sweeping away round the bay, to

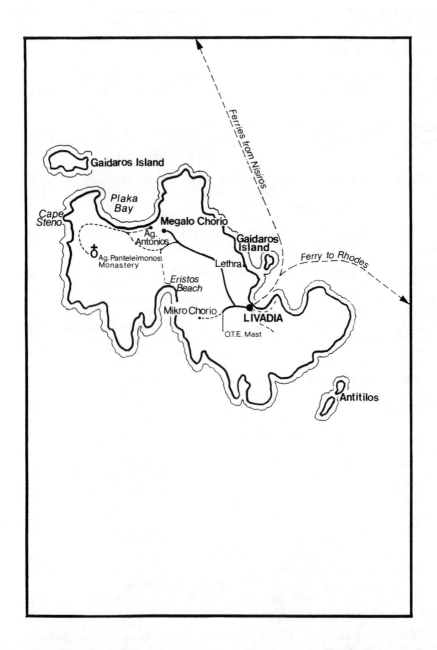

Illustration 17 Tilos island

the left. From a distance the whiteness of the sea's edge gives the appearance of waves breaking on the foreshore. There is plenty of space still available, for even more construction, despite the gradual, but steady infilling that continues to take place.

Life in the port focuses on the small but adequate Ferry-boat Quay (*Tmr* 1A/B1). Conveniently sited on the edge of this quay, and behind which is a small terraced hillside, is *La Luna Bar* (*Tmr* 2A2), where many of the locals 'hang-out', watching the comings and goings of the boat passengers.

The seafront and port is prettily planted with tamarisk and cypress trees, whilst there is a grove of fruit trees to the east of the attractive, 'standard', Italian municipal building (*Tmr* 3B3), housing the police and customs offices.

ARRIVAL BY FERRY As would be expected, there is acted out, at each and every docking, the usual, small island chaos that greets the arrival of a ferry-boat. The locals attending the event to (collect provisions, mail, relatives, and anything else which may have been unloaded) are churning around the disembarking passengers, with yet another frantic thrust of all those attempting to embark, prior to anybody getting off. This frenzy is 'enhanced' by the need of the boat, passengers and goods to avoid the building materials haphazardly stacked in piles of this, and that. To add to the comic opera milieu, ferries that dock early in the day have to mix-it with the informal, morning fish market that takes place after the catch has been landed. Room owners, including Stamata of *Alex & Stamata* fame, meet the ferries, though they can be missed amid the general confusion.

THE ACCOMMODATION & EATING OUT
The Accommodation For years there have been rumours, in respect of the imminent construction of a vast hotel. The name has varied, but not the project. The site (*Tmr* * E4) is selected, the title is (now) the *Tilos Oasis*, a photograph of the maquette is pinned to the wall of the Tilos Travel agency, but fortunately work has not yet started. Sighs of relief, all round.

The closest accommodation to the Ferry-boat Quay is:
Casa Italiana
Directions: Immediately behind/above *La Luna Bar* (*Tmr* 2A/2).

These are nice rooms, with a view over the jetty, and quiet, except when ferries or cargo boats dock. If Demetri is not present, a shy Greek lady asks callers to await his return. He is very friendly, speaking mixed Greek and Italian, with a bit of English thrown in. The most agreeable, airy, cool, double rooms cost some 3500drs a night. In each room is a fridge, stocked with drinks, at slightly above the supermarket prices. Demetri is at great pains to confirm that guests do not have to buy them, and can stock the machine with their own provisions.

Hotel Livadia (*Tmr* 6B/C4) (Class E)   Tel 53202
Directions: South of and up the slope from the Main Square, and run by the nephew of the owner of the nearby general store.

Inexpensive rates, but then so they should be, as the place is rather run-down. The adequate double bedrooms are charged 2200/2600drs, sharing, and 2600/3000drs en suite. Rooms at the front have good views. The snackbar in the basement is rather expensive. There is an advertisement in respect of boat trips to distant beaches, though, on enquiring, the fisherman concerned takes some finding.

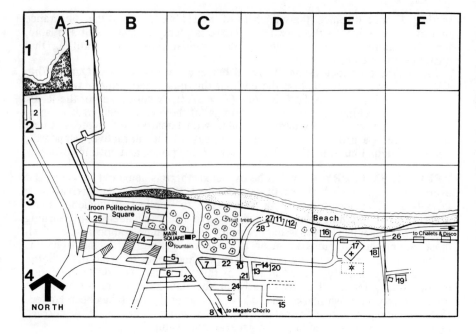

Illustration 18 Livadia Port

Tmr
1A/B1   Ferry-boat Quay
2A2   La Luna Bar/Tilos Travel
3B3   Police/Customs Office
4B3/4   Post Office
5B/C4   General Store/Moped Hire
6B/C4   Hotel/·Snackbar Livadia
7C4   Pizza Tilos
8C4   Fish Restaurant Trata
9C/D4   Rooms
10C/D4   Public Toilets
11 & 12 Rooms Alex & Stamata
13D4   Souvlaki Snackbar
14D4   Supermarket
15D4   Pension Castelli
16D/E3/4 Taverna Irina
17E3/4   Ag Nikolaos Church
18E/F4   Doctor
19E/F4   Hotel Irini
20D4   Fruit & Veg Shop
21C/D4   Bakery
22C4   Pension/Snackbar Souvlaki
23C4   George's Apartments
24C/D4   E. Stefanaki Rooms
25A/B3   Kostas Taverna/Stefanakis Travel
26F3/4   Taverna Sophia
27D3   Stelios Rooms
28D3   Aleco Rooms
*E4   Site of projected Tilos Oasis Hotel
P = Periptero

(Tmr)   = Town map reference
(Fsw)   = Facing seawards
(Sbo)   = Sea behind one
(Fbqbo) = Ferry-boat Quay behind one

Illustration 18 Livadia Port

George's Apartments (*Tmr* 23C4)   Tel 53243
Directions: Near the *Livadia*, prior to a bend in the street, on the right (*Sbo*).
   New, spacious, very clean, with sparkling furniture, the double rooms, with
bathroom and kitchen en suite, cost 5000drs a night.

   From *George's*, a few metres further to the south, and on the left are:
overpriced *Rooms* (*Tmr* 9C/D4), with the double room being the family living
room, rather shabbily disguised; and *Rooms Zimmer* (*Tmr* 24C/D4), owned
by Evangela Stefanaki. Still further east, and then right and left, is the
modern, reasonably priced *Pension Castelli* (*Tmr* 15D4), with bedrooms
sharing the bathroom.
   From the south-east corner of the Main Square, the street to the east,
leaving the orchard on the left (*Main Square behind one*), passes by a
Pension/Snackbar (*Tmr* 22C4), on the right. Left again doubles back towards
the shoreline, and a veritable 'clutch' of accommodation possibilities, such as:
NTOG approved *Aleco Rooms* (*Tmr* 28D3), in a well maintained, two storey
building, charging 3000drs for a double room, sharing; and *Stelios Rooms*
(*Tmr* 27D3), only offering triple bedded rooms, sharing the clean toilet and
shower. In respect of *Stelios*, the first floor room is the best choice, being
fairly clean and cool, whilst the ground floor room is rather dark and dingy.
It is probably best not to purchase anything from 'mine host', as it is
rumoured that charges are 'seriously' more expensive, than the same goods,
elsewhere. For prices *See Rooms Alex & Stamata*.

An'old' favourite, in a wonderful situation, is the aforementioned:
Rooms Alex & Stamata (*Tmr* 11 & 12D3)
Directions: As above, close to the beach backshore.
   Not only a great location, but 'typical' island accommodation, of a type and
style that is becoming increasingly difficult to find, with the passing of the
years. Both buildings have patios built out over the sea's edge and there is the
provision of a shared fridge, as well as a washing line. Stamata speaks little
English, and her husband's only linguistic pretension is a smattering of Italian.
Stamata is decidedly reluctant to countenance 'one-nighters', and not ecstatic
about two night bookings, muttering on about the laundry, despite the presence
of a new'ish washing machine. A congenial double room, sharing the clean
bathroom, costs 2700drs. Quoted rates are not negotiable, even if the 'room'
appears to form part of the corridor, to an adjoining bedroom! Breakfast of,
say, Nes meh ghala, bread, butter and jam, costs 500drs, and is expected to
be taken, at whatever time guests rise. If the tasty, speciality omelette is
scoffed, then the cost of the *dejeuner* increases. Thus, over-indulgence or,
more probably, unthinking acceptance of a 'landlady bearing gifts', can result
in a hefty tab, on the day of reckoning. The latter event takes place by
retreating to the back of the establishment, the family-living quarters. Here
Stamata calculates the bill, with the use of a complicated broadsheet, of railway timetable proportions. On the occasions when it occurs, it is not always
clear if 'change shortages', from a 1000drs note, are human error, or simply
unidentified penalty clauses, 'written small' in the unpublished house rules.
Certainly the use of hot water, for laundry, may be charged as an 'extra'.

   Following the road on, beyond the lane down to *Rooms Alex*, advances past
the Church (*Tmr* 17E3/4), and then back down to the shore. Immediately
beyond the church, a lane to the right is signposted to the:

Hotel Irini (*Tmr* 19E/F4) (Class C)   Tel 53293
Directions: As above, and on the left, along a short track.
    Extremely pretty, tasteful and attractive accommodation..., at a price. These
superb en suite double rooms, with balcony, and inclusive of breakfast, are
simply the 'best in town', but cost between 5000/7500drs a night. Elias, the
hotel owner, aided and abetted by his wife Dikea and the rest of his family, is
either entrepreneurial, or rather 'pushy', depending on an observer's
standpoint. Without doubt, he is a very efficient young man, who is extremely
enthusiastic about tourism on Tilos. The modern, spotless hotel has many
thoughtful and useful 'little extras', including a metered telephone, island
maps, as well as a book and magazine-swop scheme. Elias is happy to give
detailed advice about the various places of interest. The lovely garden is
devotedly kept in trim by his father. The hotel caters for package tourists, but,
apart from the height of season months, there is usually 'room at the inn'.

The Eating Out For such a small location, the selection is indeed   diverse.
Apart from people-watching the locals, Tilos has an almost equally diverting
pastime, namely eavesdropping the BPTs (British package tourists). I am
aware that it is not chappish to make fun of one's own, but... And I am ever
reminded of myself and fellow chums when we infest the local pub! As the
social strata is definitely Home Counties and the Shires, there is an almost
unbelievably Wodehouse quality to the entertainment. Parties of friends
reserve tables, and   talk in very loud voices about public schools, pension
funds, and the unbelievable difficulties in finding a domestic 'treasure'. They
chatter-on, in that timeless style of the committed commuter, about the most
cost-effective way in which the islanders could maximise their profits from
tourism. Unfortunately the Greeks tend to select an easier 'profit route', they
bung up the prices of accommodation, drink and food. Oh dear!
    The quayside sited Blue Sky, of many years fame, has been 'rehashed' and
renamed *La Luna Bar* (*Tmr* 2A2). Rumour has it that this change-over was
due to the Rhodes based landlord continually raising the rent. It is now simply
a local-popular cafe-bar, at which the Saturday night village hops are held.

Taverna Kostas (*Tmr* 25A/B3)
Directions: From the base of the Ferry-boat Quay, round to the left, and on
the right of Plateia Iroon Politechniou, in the ground floor of a building, the
upper floor of which is occupied by Stefanakis Travel & Shipping Agency.
    An excellent location from which to distantly observe the harbour activities.
On calm evenings, the situation is idyllic, even if the interior could be said to
lack atmosphere. The local Papa is a frequent visitor. A very jolly man, he is
often accompanied by his daughter and small, noisy grandson. The chef
attempts, with success, to add imaginative touches to standard Greek dishes.
Try the mezes, and his garlic sauce with zucchini is delicious. The Cretan dry
white wines are excellent. It is not uncommon, if understandable, that some
of the tastier dishes are 'orf', quite early in the evening. Closed lunch times.
A meal, for two, of 1 plate of white beans (terrific), 1 Greek salad, a plate of
stuffed tomatoes & courgettes, a bottle of water, a Fanta, and bread, cost
1700drs. Popular with TV watching locals, when a football match is in play.

Taverna Irina (*Tmr* 16D/E3/4)
Directions: Proceed towards the church, at which swing down in the direction
of the beach backshore.

Run by Georgi, a very friendly and affable man, who has good, if self-taught English. Despite once occupying the 'taverna top spot', Irina's is suffering badly from the runaway success of *Sophia's*. Perhaps this is why the atmosphere reflects a less hectic, more laid-back level of activity? The competition has resulted in the friendly staff schlepping, in an effort to stem the flow of dinners, on their way past, and the quality of the food falling away. A meal, for two, of 1 kalamares, a bean soup, 1 Greek salad, 1 crown top retsina, and fresh bread, cost 2250drs.

Taverna Sophia (*Tmr* 26F3/4)
Directions: Beyond the church, the turning down to *Irini*, and on the left.
Sophia's is the in-place, and although everything is exactly as it should be, in order to create the perfect taverna ambiance, a slight niggle might intrude, suggesting that something is not quite right. I put this down to the fact that the referred to BPTs predominate, with the 'greater yah-yah' call noticeable, over and above the usual hubble-bubble of taverna conversation and background noise. The food is inexpensive and good, even if it is more international than traditional, and the menu has been subtly modified to suit 'PTs' (that is all and every nationality, rather than picking on the Brits) - starters first, main course next..., and etcetera. The internal decor is dominated by walls covered with photographs of the ever-smiling Sophia family, and various clients. The service is friendly, efficient, prompt and solicitous. But this is not the true, timeless, indolent, easy-going, lackadaisical Hellenic quality, that one yearns for, especially when at the receiving end of this type of remorseless, manufactured environment. Mind you, when patronising one of those isolated, deep in the heart of the country, ethnic taverna's, waiting for an eternity to be served, by an insolent waiter, with anything but the order uppermost in his mind, when it is necessary to put-up with ill-assorted, messily dished-up plates languidly sloshing across a plastic covered table top, then a   strong yearning develops for an establishment where meals are served speedily, on time, and in some sort of sequence - such as Sophia's!
The taverna becomes well and truly packed, a popularity testified to, and by, a plate, affixed to the wall, awarded for 'Outstanding Services to Greek Tourism'. Oh, really! Sophia is a kindly, smiley lady, whilst her most helpful, friendly son Vassilis, who speaks excellent English, waits at table, and her husband Kiryakos (Ikonomou) 'chef's', very well. They work hard to produce daily changes to the menu, and there is often a 'Sophia Special'. Vegetarian dishes are prepared, as long as some notice is given. A meal, for two, of 1 bean soup, 1 aubergine dish baked with parmesan (an Italian dish - melanzane alla parmigiana), 1   tzatziki, 1 moussaka, 1 souvlakia, Ilios wine, and 2 Greek coffees, cost 2300drs.

The *Kafenion Ominion* is alongside the Post Office (*Tmr* 4B3/4). The patron is smiley, the prices are inexpensive, with a bottle of retsina costing 320drs, ensuring the *Ominion* is a good selection for a pre, or post prandial drink. An enjoyable breakfast is conjured-up. This is where the locals hunker down for a game of cards, but when the wind whistles through the square, the ouzo, cards, and money end up on the floor. Another *Kafenion*, claiming to be traditional, bizarrely serves cocktails and long drinks. Very traditional! There are a number of *Souvlaki* pita places (*Tmr* 22C4 & 13D4), the first listed also running a *Pension*. These 'snack shops' are understandably popular with the locals, so there is usually something going on.

Trata Fish Restaurant (*Tmr* 8C4)
Directions: From the Main Square, south past the *Livadia*, and on the right.
The *Trata* continues to hold the nomination as the most expensive of the Tilos eateries. But, in Greece, it is usual to have to pay 'deeply' for freshly caught fish, in general, and lobsters, in particular. The owner, a fisherman, and a 'bit-of-a-charmer', falls over backwards to please guests, and often honours first-time customers by serving their meals on his prized, glass, fish-shaped plates. Clients are encouraged to view the catch, during which the proprietor, whose English is just about up to it, entertains with a commentary about that on offer, from his personal knowledge of the particular crustaceans and fish. Daughter Maria serves at table, and they are 'kind' to their cat population. Closed lunch times.

THE A TO Z OF USEFUL INFORMATION
AIRLINE OFFICE Despite Tilos not having an airport, **Stefanakis Travel** (*Tmr* 25A/B3) represent Olympic. The office is run by the 'not-so-quick-on-the-uptake' son of the owner of the *Kostas Taverna*, above which eatery the firm is located. When in receipt of questions concerning domestic flights, 'our man' has an engaging little habit of advising enquirers to telephone the Olympic office, at Rhodes!

BANKS None. *See* Post Office.

BEACHES The white pebble beach, and sea-bed, of Livadia Port stretches for about 2km along the long bay, with beautifully clear waters for bathing. This is the best beach in the area, but the steady increase in the numbers of tourists has ensured that one is not always alone. Those who wish to try another location should take the cliff path north from Livadia port, which leads, after an hour's walk, to **Lethra**, a narrow, white pebble beach.

BICYCLE, SCOOTER & CAR HIRE Bicycles are hired from *Kostas Taverna* (*Tmr* 25A/B3) at a fee of 800drs a day.
    All the island's main roads and tracks can comfortably be covered in a day, using less than a half-tank of fuel. Mopeds are available from the **General store** (*Tmr* 5B/C4), beside the Main Square. The 50cc, two seater machines are new'ish, and thus in excellent condition, as well as 'coming' with a wide range of normally missing accessories. As the years go by, these machines will doubtless deteriorate into that state of disrepair only too familiar to dedicated hirers of Greek scooters. For the time being, customers should luxuriate in their splendid state, and the daily hire fee of 3000drs, which includes a full tank of petrol. Incidentally, the owner, in an effort, no doubt to ensure that his steeds remain in a continuingly acceptable condition, advises clients that the Ag Panteleimonos Monastery track is 'tiger country'.
    Motorbikes are for hire from Tilos Travel (*Tmr* 2A2), incorporated in the *La Luna* building. This establishment's machines are in a terrible state, and depending on the engine capacity, cost between 2500-5000drs a day, with a tank of fuel. These machines usually require much kick-starting to even tick-over. There isn't any car hire.

BOOKSELLERS None. The *Hotel Irini* (*Tmr* 19E/F4) operates book-swap.

BREAD SHOPS (*Tmr* 21C/D4) The friendly, perspiring baker also sells biscuits, delicious cakes, croissants, pies, and drinks. A couple of tables and chairs outside allow customers to 'buy and sit'. He opens twice daily, but not necessarily at the same time, each day!

BUSES A 14 seater, orange mini-bus operates a whimsical, highly erratic service. Due to the surly manner of Nikos, the driver, this is impossible to refine down to a timetable. The driver usually parks on the Main Square, awaiting the docking of the various craft, and 'goes' where passengers request. I bet! Yorgos, he of the *Pizza Tilos* (*Tmr* 7C4), beside the Main Sq bus stop, can shed some light on the day's plans. Notes, in respect of the service, reveal the difficulties of being definite, and read: 'except to collect from Eristos, dead on time - no waiting for stragglers, the arrangements appeared fluid'. In theory, the route is Livadia/Megalo Chorio/Ag Antonios/Eristou, but out of a number of journeys, the driver sometimes proceeds directly to Eristos, sometimes diverts to Megalo Chorio, and occasionally proceeds to Ag Antonios! A 'tracer' is that the bus goes to Eristos at 1500, 1700 & 1800hrs. In between, or even at scheduled times, he appears to take parties, here and there. Livadia to Megalo Chorio costs 150drs; to Eristou 250drs; and to Ag Antonios/Megalo Chorio 100drs.

COMMERCIAL SHOPPING AREA Apart from the **Supermarket** (*Tmr* 14D4), there are one or three shops/stores. The Main Sq **General store** (*Tmr* 5B/C4) is cheaper than the Supermarket. Next door to the latter is a **Fruit & Veg shop** (*Tmr* 20D4). Opening hours are the small island 'norm'. The **FB N. Kalymnos** dumps the usual pile of provisions on the quayside, including frozen chickens, which steadily defrost, until collected.

DISCOS Yanni's (ex Live Sound) is 500m east along the beach road.

FERRY-BOATS During inclement weather, Tilos is a difficult 'port of call'. In stormy conditions, especially at either end of the summer, the island can be cut off, for several days at a time. During these periods, foodstuffs run down, as little is 'home-grown'.

Ferry-boat timetable (Mid-season)

Day	Departure time	Ferry-boat	Ports/Islands of Call
Mon	1100hrs	Nissos Kalymnos	Simi, Rhodes.
Tue	1400hrs	Nissos Kalymnos	Nisiros, Kos, Kalimnos.
Thur	0415hrs	Ionian Sun	Rhodes.
	1500hrs	Ionian Sun	Nisiros, Kos, Andros, Mykonos, Rafina(M).
Fri	1100hrs	Nissos Kalymnos	Simi, Rhodes.
Sat	1400hrs	Nissos Kalymnos	Nisiros, Kos, Kalimnos.

There isn't an 'official' hydrofoil service, and no 'home-based' excursion craft, although visiting vessels irregularly drop-in.

FERRY-BOAT TICKET OFFICES Stefanakis Travel (*Tmr* 25A/B3) acts for the **Nissos Kalymnos**, setting up his table, inside *La Luna Cafe-bar* (*Tmr* 2A2), on the quay, about two hours before the ship docks. **Tilos Travel** (*Tmr* 2A2) represents the **FB Ionian Sun**.

MEDICAL CARE
Pharmacist/Clinic/Doctor (*Tmr* 18E/F4). The Livadia surgery displays the consulting hours and days. The doctor, an Athenian exile (what did he do?),

spends much of his time circulating around the island, visiting patients and friends. But there need be no cause for concern, should an illness develop, whilst he is absent. Oh, no. There are a number of methods of 'attracting' his attention. The sick can: look-out for his bright orange Opel saloon; slump down, close to the surgery, until he returns; or advise one's landlord/landlady of the illness. The latter results in 'all of Livadia' being aware of the dilemma, within a remarkably short space of time. From then on, almost everybody picks up their telephone, to phone around, until he is located - wherever. There is another clinic in Megalo Chorio.

NTOG None.

OTE There is an OTE booth inside the Supermarket (*Tmr* 14D4), as well as a metered telephone at *Kostas Taverna* (*Tmr* 25A/B3).

PETROL The filling station is at Ag Antonios.

POLICE
Port & Town (*Tmr* 3B3) The Customs officers double up as Port policemen, and all three services are located in the blue and white, castellated building, on the edge of the seafront square, Plateia Iroon Politechniou.

POST OFFICE (*Tmr* 4B3/4) Beside the Main Square and open weekdays between 0730-1400hrs. The Post Office man changes money and travellers cheques, but... And it is a big but, as certain ordinary events throw a spanner into the well oiled machinery. For instance, the impending arrival of a ferry-boat is quite sufficient to bring all statutory functions to a dead halt. It appears this Post Master General leaves completion of the documentation, that must be handed over to the ship's purser, until the last moment. With the office counter elbow deep in scattered papers, he has no time to fiddle about with the footling requirements of any customers. And that includes those desperate to change sufficient money, so as to be able to purchase ferry-boat tickets! At moments such as this, it becomes a battle of wills, or the moment to express disgust, turn on one's heel, and hare over to Tilos Travel, fast.
    The other 'happening', that can cause the gears to creak to a dead-stop, is the departure of the bus. For some obscure reason, this vehicle has to have 'slipped' the Main Square, for about half-an-hour, before currency exchange can be transacted.
    And that's another quirk of the 'Tilos wheel' of bureaucracy - once engaged in money matters, the Post Office chappie telephones Rhodes, to check the rates. More often than not, an argument ensues with the 'Treasury', the other end of the line, during which the Tilos man slams down the phone, presumably cutting short the high-powered, financial negotiations. He then hurls the money across the counter. Ho, hum.

TAXIS None.

TELEPHONE NUMBERS & ADDRESSES
Doctor (*Tmr* 18E/F4)   Tel 53214
Megalo Chorio   Tel 53210
Police, town (*Tmr* 3B3)   Tel 53222

TOILETS (*Tmr* 10C/D4) A new'ish block, but not very 'invitingly' maintained. This toilet and the Police station 'sport' large, ultraviolet fly zappers. There is another public toilet to the east, close to the holiday chalets.

TRAVEL AGENTS & TOUR OFFICES *See* Ferry-boat Ticket Offices.

EXCURSIONS TO LIVADIA PORT SURROUNDS More walks, really.
Walk 1. Follow the beach road, east along the seafront backshore, and then the path up and over the hill, following some indistinct red paint blobs. Turn right on the hilltop, from whence an amazing view over Livadia. Continue down the zig-zag path, to the road behind the *Hotel Irini*.
Walk 2. Turn left (*Sbo*) and select the path behind *La Luna*, to **Lethra**. It is then possible to walk up a summer-dry river-bed, to join the paved road, close to the turning for Mikro Chorio. Here, turn left and follow the road back down to Livadia.

One walk that is definitely not worth the effort, is that in search of the 'Elephants Cave'. The cavern is extremely difficult to locate, across a difficult chasm beside the road to Megalo Chorio. Once discovered, the only tangible evidence is a rope hanging down, in the direction of a mangy bag of broken bones, of dubious provenance.

ROUTE ONE
To Megalo Chorio (9km) & the beaches of Eristos & Ag Antonios via Mikro Chorio The concrete road linking Livadia with Megalo Chorio, climbs steeply, in a series of hairpin bends, up the hillside behind the port.

After 1km, the road levels out and another concrete track heads-off, to the left. This is signed *OTE*, and leads either to the transmitter/receiver, on top of the mountain, or, more interestingly, after a few hundred metres, along a rough, narrow track, signed 'Mikpo Xopio' (on a hand-painted board), to the hillside settlement of:

MIKRO CHORIO A rather weird, quiet, deserted village. The pink, red and white, 'edible-looking' church is the only building kept in a good state of repair. The key is no longer stashed-away in a convenient hidy-hole, due to thievery. But, if the key-holder can be tracked down, the lovely icons still remaining, are well worth seeing. Above and to the right of this church, is another, also with frescoes, and a red roof. The door is open but, unfortunately, the building is not maintained, so is falling to bits, despite which, whilst hereabouts, it is worth having a gander. There is yet a third church, slightly beyond and below the second, which has even better frescoes.

The main road continues on, along a gentle downward slope, past quarry workings, on the right, and a narrow valley to the left. After 9km, above the road, on the hillside, hoves into view:

MEGALO CHORIO (9km from Livadia) The island's biggest and only other inhabited settlement, with a population of some two hundred and ten inhabitants. It is a pretty, quiet, whitewashed village, with narrow streets and steps twisting among the houses. A path leads up to a ruined Venetian fortress, on a rock-top above the centre. This castle, as in the case of other Dodecanese strongholds, was built on and over much earlier fortifications, and incorporates some noticeable features from the previous buildings. Details of the main gateway, as well as a marble flight of steps, inside the gates, are particular hallmarks for which to look-out.

There are an almost disproportionate number of churches, as well as a small, single story museum. Naively, the islanders hoped that the various local archaeological finds, in addition to the Mastadon bones, to which previous reference has been made, would be displayed in an island gallery. But no such luck, as all bits and pieces, of any value were long ago trucked-off to Athens, or Rhodes. A familiar story. The museum is closed on Sundays.

Megalo Chorio has accommodation *Rooms* at the modern-looking *Rooms/ Bar-Restaurant*, to the left, at the outset to the village. This establishment enjoys fine views over the plain spread out below. They charge 2500drs for a clean and pleasant double room, with en suite bathroom. Not only is this a handy pit-stop, whilst *en route*, but they serve enjoyable, freshly cooked food. A 'for instance', a most enjoyable meal, for two, of freshly caught, tasty fish - gopas & maridhas, a Greek salad, 1 crown cork retsina, a large bottle of water, 2 coffees & 2 ouzos, cost about 2500drs.

A supermarket, a main square post box, and a clinic, beyond which is a toilet block, complete Megalo Chorio's facilities, all except for one other cafe. It is all too easy to become lost in the maze of streets, but, in amongst this labyrinth, is the *Kafeneion*. It is close to a church - one of the churches! An indicator is the word 'Restaurant', painted on a nearby wall. Despite the location and comparative lack of local business, let alone passing trade, the prices tend to be anything but cheap. Inside is a wall-mounted picture of two handsome young men, with headgear that looks suspiciously like turbans, one of the figures being the owner, taken in Rhodes, in 1943.

Those who do not mind walking, might consider the village to make a good base-camp, from which to explore the north of the island - but a couple of aspirins should dispel any such notions. Without doubt, unless a committed 'mad dog...', do not attempt to hike here, from the port.

Beyond Megalo Chorio, the paved road divides. The left-hand fork is surfaced, and leads, after about 3km, to:
Eristos Beach This is a vast sweep of coarse sand, shingle and pebble beach. A few caiques may be drawn-up on the shore, but there isn't a beach umbrella or sun-bed in sight. In places, the pebble sea bed can be bothersome, to those bathers with tender feet, but the swimming is lovely. Eristos is usually an extremely quiet location, but even on a busy day, there will only be a handful of couples, with the whole shore over which to spread-out.

Where the concrete access road makes a T-junction with the backshore, it splits into two dirt tracks, edging the beach, to run behind a row of tamarisk trees. About ½km prior to the referred-to junction, is the tree shaded and quiet *Rooms/Taverna Tropicana*. This establishment provides good, basic fare 'from the pages' of a limited menu, and offers NTOG approved double rooms, sharing the bathroom, at a price of 2000drs a night. A meal, for two, of 1 Greek salad, 1 dolmades, 1 kalamares (fresh), a large bottle of water, an Amstel, and bread (well past any sell-by-date), cost 1750drs.

Immediately before the T-junction, is a dirt road which swings round to the left, in the direction of the *Nausica Rooms/Restaurant*, surrounded by a garden-cum-campsite. The peaceful *Nausica* is an ideal, 'get-away-from-it-all' location. A row of ethnic looking bedrooms, sharing a bathroom, are set down on one side of the garden, and a double costs 2000drs a night. A two-person tent, pitched in the garden, cost 500drs, use of the shower included. Basic, simple meals and drinks are available, as well as 'home-made' lemonade, in season. Not much English is spoken.

Taking the right fork beyond Megalo Chorio, the concrete road eventually divides around the beach at:
Ag Antonios. A deserted, peaceful, remote, small, very windy bay, with a filling station (alongside which is a liquid gas installation), a large hotel, and a taverna. The harbour contains many fishing caiques, and the messy, pebbly, weedy beach is rather dirty. Some building is underway.

To the right, the road leads to a small harbour backed by a taverna, and behind that, the *Hotel Australia* (Tel 53297), where a double room, with en suite bathroom, costs 5200drs. It must remain a constant source of amazement that the hard-working, enthusiastic, congenial Georgaras brothers chose to build their extremely agreeable, relaxed, serene hotel here, instead of at Eristos. They woefully lamant that the beach used to be sandy, but that the sand was used-up for building works. Every so often, working parties of soldiers are detailed off, to clear the place up, but even they can't manage to widen the shore! It is also a very breezy situation, which one of the Mr Georgaras insists is an advantage, because it never gets too hot... Mmmh! On one visit, a gale was blowing, and the breakers were fairly crashing about.

The aforementioned taverna edges the beach backshore, fronting a house. The omelettes and fish served here are tasty, and inexpensive.

Apart from visits on the orange bus, a trip boat from Nisiros island occasionally calls in.

Instead of turning right, towards the *Hotel Australia*, to the left advances past a ruined windmill. The dusty, unmetalled track, which can easily be negotiated on a scooter, proceeds beyond a track off to the left, in the direction of the monastery, to the empty **Plaka Bay**, where the occasional yacht moors, the sea is clear, and the beach is clean and sandy. There isn't a bar, taverna or hotel in sight, yet. An about-to-be-completed construction might become a 'place of business'. Maybe the total of six or eight people has encouraged someone to see the tourist potential!

From the bay, a fork on the way-in, at the top of the first rise, gives access to a wide, part concreted surface. This choice of route allows wonderful views, all the way to the:
Monastery Ag Panteleimonos An impressive, well-maintained but uninhabited mountainside monastery, with stupendous panoramas, a spring, and plentiful shade, provided by cypress and plane trees. The chapel guest book indicates that the location is extremely popular with visitors to Tilos. Locals pop in, at weekends, to look after the building and grounds.

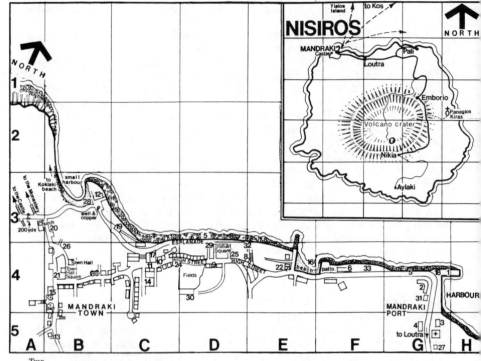

Illustration 19 Nisiros island & Mandraki Port

10 NISIROS (Nisyros, Nissiros) & Yialos Dodecanese Islands   * * * *

FIRST IMPRESSIONS Extremely green, considering the island's volcanic nature; crumbling, Italian conceived municipal buildings; peaceful - out of excursion boat hours; old, very friendly inhabitants.

SPECIALITIES Sumada, an almond cordial diluted with water, and available in shops, cafes & tavernas.

LOCAL RELIGIOUS HOLIDAYS & FESTIVALS incl: 20-21st June - Festival of Ag Nikitas, a Church close to the harbour; 15th Aug - Festival of Panaghia, Monastery of the Lady Virgin of the Rocks.

VITAL STATISTICS Tel prefix 0242. The island is almost circular, being 10km wide & 8km long. Of the 1300 inhabitants, 800 live in Mandraki. The island's central core is a sulphurous, bubbling volcano recessed in a large, crater, approximately 4km across.

HISTORY As for other islands in the group.

GENERAL Due to a general lack of facilities, Nisiros has largely remained a day-trip island. Despite the general lack of places and events to encourage a regular flow of tourists, at least three or four craft a day call at this 'bargain basement Simi'.
    The inquisitive embark excursion boats, at nearby Kos island, in order to view the volcano. On landing, they are jammed into one of three or four buses, marshalled on the harbour quay. These vehicles crawl and steeply wind up the extensively terraced, very green mountain slopes. Deciduous trees are quite 'thick on the ground' of the countryside bounding the road. The route breasts the rim of the large, cultivated, but parched looking, sunken plain edging the core of the volcano. The still paved roadway descends into the huge crater, to one side of which is the epicentre of the sulphuric activity. Once down there, one of the most noticeable details is the total lack of 'touristabilia', a complete absence of T-shirts and postcards. Good! Having sniffed the pungent air; viewed the yellow, fissure-riven land; watched the sulphurous fumes; listened to the boiling morass, below the earth's crust; taken a short, expensive respite at the shack-like cafe-bar; perhaps used the curiously sited, small garden-shed-of-a-toilet (spaced some 5m to one side of the cafe); then it's back to Mandraki. Here the inquisitive (and not so inquisitive) loiter away the rest of the day, in a lacklustre, rather bored, 'why am I here' fashion.
    As the maze-like town only slowly offers up and reveals its charms and secrets, the committed traveller would do well to spend at least several days here, as Nisiros is a Dodecanese jewel.
    The islanders have a surfeit of civic pride, as evinced by the numerous signs, soliciting locals and visitors, alike, to 'Please Keep Nisiros Tidy'. In addition, there are any number of rubbish bins and park benches, all contributing towards the overall impression that the island is cared for, and about, by the island worthies. Countless notices forbid hunting, despite which

wild life appears to be thin on the ground. That is not so surprising considering the evidence of a dedicated, island 'shooting, fishing & killing' fraternity. For instance, there are an unusual number of dog owners (not 'stray owners'), and most of them are hunting breeds. In contrast, the owner of the *Enalax Bar* leads the 'Hellenic Monk Seal Preservation Society', with all his mopeds sporting 'Save the Monk Seal' stickers. These state what action should be taken on encountering an ill, sick or injured seal. In recent years, these lovely creatures have been frequently sighted, off Mandraki, in the winter months, and a family has taken up residence at Koklaki Beach.

It is possible that a new desalination plant is now 'on stream', the cash coming from the Yialos island pumice mining profits.

MANDRAKI capital town & port (Illus 19). A strange, many-faceted, strung-out locale, with almost all the older buildings constructed of volcanic rock. The immediate approach, from the direction of the harbour, is shabby, unprepossessing, and dusty. This is followed by a narrow-lane, toy-town milieu. A disproportionate amount of building work is usually under way, the 'crumbling old' being pulled down, rebuilt or modernised. Round the back of the 'fields', an air of affluence pervades.

At the far, south-west, right-hand side of the settlement is a Mandraki 'suburb', which climbs the hillside, and possesses a rather Welsh mountain village quality. The terraced houses, and their small flights of steps, edge very narrow alleys. The women sit on the doorsteps, dressed in traditional costumes, knitting and gossiping.

In direct contrast, by keeping round to the left, to the south end of the town, and the character is more that of a pedestrian only, French Dordogne village. The grand Town Hall is followed by a tree shaded square, edged with kafeneions and cafe-bars, whilst a little further on, beyond more ouzeries, tavernas, a butcher, and the library, is a French style restaurant.

Without doubt, out of trip boat times, Mandraki is a lovely, seemingly deserted and desolate location. For a comparatively short number of midday hours, the town teems with aimless visitors, wandering about, looking for things to do, goods to buy, and diversions to keep everyone occupied. Fortunately, the Kos based craft depart early in the afternoon, and the streets return to calm normality, with only the gentle lapping and wash of the waves breaking the silence.

A day with a difference is Saturday. Then Nisiriotes reverse the excursion boat flow, by taking an 'away day' to Kos. The purpose of the mass visitation is to stock-up with provisions, clothes and consumer durables, for the week. On their return, at about 6pm, the islanders are to be observed trooping back along the High St, laden down with bulging plastic carrier bags.

ARRIVAL BY FERRY All craft berth at the 'town-distant' Ferry-boat Quay (*Tmr* 1G/H4). The island's three buses, in addition to the Polyvotis Tours mini-bus, park close to, and on the quay. The 'corporation' buses have a dual role. They operate a scheduled service, as well as fulfil the demands of the volcano day-trippers. Polyvotis Tours has a prime position, quayside office, as does a   'Moped for Hire' business, operating from a shed (*See* Hotel/Bar Enallax - *Tmr* 27G/H5).

The Ferry-boat Quay is on a bend in a road, connecting Mandraki Town to Loutra and Pali, as well as the crater-edge villages of Emborio and Nikia. To one side of the road is a board on which is a picturesque outline of the island layout, indicating the position of Mandraki town, the other villages and the distances between them, as well as a lurid depiction of the volcano - exploding. Opposite the quay, beside the same bend in the road, is a crumbling, curved, Italian-Greco, neo-municipal administration block (*Tmr* 2G4), 'home' to the Customs, Port police, Post Office, Town police (in that order), and a Tourist office. Next door, and facing the quayside often taken up by private craft, is a new, as yet unamed *Harbour Cafe-bar* (*Tmr* 31G4).

THE ACCOMMODATION & EATING OUT
The Accommodation To the left (*Fbqbo*), up a slight rise, both 'bed and victuals' are catered for by the:
Three Brothers Hotel & Restaurant (*Tmr* 3G5)   Tel 31344
Directions: On the left, alongside a church.
   A double room cost 3000drs a night.

Opposite, on the right, is the:
Romantzo Motel (*sic*) **& Restaurant** (*Tmr* 4G5)   Tel 31340
Directions: As above.
   Double rooms en suite cost 3000drs. Nico Mousas, the owner, is praised for his friendly help and willingness to defer to clients' wishes.
   Both hotels have large terraces and are, in reality, pensions.

Beyond the church, and on the left (*Fbqbo*), is the:
Hotel Enallax (*Tmr* 27G/H5)
Directions: As above.
   The hotel is brand new, and has been constructed above the 'up and running' *Bar Enallax*.

There is a more distant possibility *en route* to Loutra, for details of which *See* Route One. For other options it is necessary to set off on the 5/10min walk, towards the heart of Mandraki. The sea edging road leaves one of the town's public lavatories on the right. After some 100m, and also on the right, is:
Pension/Taverna Karava (*Tmr* 6F4)
Directions: Recognizable by the awning covered taverna tables and chairs.
   Now one of the cheaper alternatives in town. The quality has deteriorated over the years, which is probably why it is one of the least expensive. The per night, per head charge is 1000drs, for an en suite bedroom. Incidentally the owner is the captain of the *Nisiros Express*, a trip boat that sails daily between Mandraki Port and Kardamena (Kos). As distinct from the accommodation, the taverna is possibly the most expensive - in town.

Continuing on, the road skirts a dirty, sandy beach, edged by a small quay. A few swings have been erected and a children's playground created, on the sandy backshore. A handful of small caiques are beached. Beyond a Kava drink shop (*Tmr* 7E4), the road divides. The High St proceeds to the right-hand, past a statue mounted square (edging the sea below). Opposite the plateia is a lane to the left, leading to the:

Hotel Porfyris (*Tmr* 30C/D4) (Class C)   Tel 31376
Directions: As above, and on the edge of the fields.
   Built with package tourists in mind, and complete with a swimming pool. Assuming there are vacancies, an en suite single is priced at   4500drs & a double 5500drs.

Returning to the High St, and continuing towards the centre of the town, passes by the *Coffee-bar Tassos* (*Tmr* 9D4), a general store and shop, the fields, and a few metal shuttered store fronts, on the right. The High St then narrows down and is hemmed in by buildings, in amongst which is the *Pension Anna* (*Tmr* 10C4). This is on the right, but only opens, if at all, in the height of season months. A few shops, and a side turning further on, and, to the left, is 'Mama Annea's' Butchers Shop (*Tmr* 11C4). It is easily identified by a vivid painting, depicting a cow's head, and a sign on the wall for *Rooms*. The accommodation is the:

Pension Drosia (*Tmr* 12B/C3)
Directions: Mama Annea, a very nice and helpful lady, owns the pension and often walks prospects to her 'digs'. From the shop it is necessary to turn right, down the next shallow flight of steps, and keep close to the sea wall, as far as a small, crowded square. The crowding is due to most of the area being taken up by a large, old-fashioned, fire-heated copper, combined with a well. This is a communal, Hellenic 'twin-tub', and is still used, on some washdays. On the far side is the pension.

The *Drosia* is clean, if a touch cramped and spartan. The shower water of the shared bathroom is hot, all and every day, and the location is excellent. The narrow balcony, circling the building, allows guests views out over the adjacent sea wall. The bedroom furniture is solid, even if there aren't any lampshades. The room rates include use of a kitchen, complete with cooker and fridge, as well as a clothes line and pegs. What's the catch? None, the double room rate being 1500drs, yes 1500drs. It must remain one of the best value offers in the Greek islands. By the way, there are six bedrooms, but avoid No 6, if at all possible, as it is next to the automatic water pump/heater, which is rather noisy. A word to the wise, is that the motor can be switched off, for a peaceful night.

Hotel Nissiros (*Tmr* 28B3)
Directions: To one side of, and a little more up-market than the *Drosia*, but lacking a comparable view.
Whitewashed, concrete walled double bedrooms, with en suite bathroom, tiled floors, wooden fittings and beds, and a balcony, cost 3500drs a night.

The Eating Out A fairly wide variety of good food, at inexpensive prices, with BBQs and charcoal grills a common feature.
Taverna Manolis (*Tmr* 32D/E3/4)
Directions: To the right (*Fbqbo*), and prior to 'Statue Sq'.
A waterfront setting, with the taverna fronting on to a sea wall edging patio. The outside of the building is adorned with local, 'native' paintings, whilst the patio is shaded with a tarpaulin, and illuminated by a street lamp. The rather garish, plastic-topped patio tables are decorated with basil planted pots. A charcoal grill is set hard by the sea wall, ready for the octopus. The meals are served on a variety of patterned china plates, by a couple of friendly old ladies, from what would appear to be their own, private kitchen. A snack, for two, of 2 Greek salads, 1 omelette, a large bottle of water, fresh bread & service, cost 970drs.

Following the 'Esplanade' from 'Statue Sq', and proceeding in a south-west direction (away from the Ferry-boat Quay), passes by three establishments - taverna, bar, taverna. The last of the trio is:

Mike's Taverna
Directions: As above, and on the right, fronting the sea.
   Mike's most friendly wife serves the usual snacks, drinks, and taverna fare. Thi is to the accompaniment of 'piped' bouzouki and rembetika music, emanating from twin speakers hooked on to the outside wall of the building. Opposite the establishment is a 'spare niche', alongside the sea. Mike, who whiles away much of his time reading a paper, outside, has here created a 'tourist corner' (a what?), as a welcome relaxation point for visitors.

My favourite establishment remains the:
Taverna Nisiros (*Tmr* 14C4)
Directions: In a fly-popular side-alley, to the left (*Fbqbo*) of the High St, beyond Mama Annea's shop (*Tmr* 11C4).
   Still one of, if not the most popular place in town. It is run by an extremely pleasant mama and daughter, and is frequented by locals and tourists alike. The local custom of serving meals on the family crockery is practised here, where some of the patterned plates have a rose motif, and others are gold edged. The prices are very reasonable and, each day, a speciality of the day is freshly prepared. A meal, for two, of a fish soup, a Greek salad, 1 gigantes beans, 1 plate of fish, a Pepsi, a crown top retsina, and bread, cost 2000drs. This is one of those islands, and this is one of those tavernas, where a bottle may mysteriously appear at a diner's elbow. Super, but a word of warning. If you can identify the benefactor, and attempt to return the favour, you will only be bought another bottle, and so it goes on... Here's to you, blue eyes!

The *Taverna Delfini* (*Tmr* 19B/C3/4), beside the last seafront 'square' heading towards the *Pension Drosia*, from *Mike's*, may well be permanently closed, but then again, it may not be! I hope not, as the owners were a most affable old couple, who charged extremely reasonable prices.

Restaurant Spesial Franzis (*sic*) (*Tmr* 13B5)
Directions: From the 'Town Hall' Sq (*Tmr* B4), turn left (*Fbqbo*) and walk across the next square, passing by various establishments. The flag festooned restaurant is on the right.
   The restaurant's target clientele are day-trippers, to which end the proprietor/cook 'goes the whole hog', kitting himself out with a striped pinafore and a tall chef's hat.

Heading towards the harbour, passes by the:
Taverna Karava (*Tmr* 6F4)
Directions: As above.
   The *Karava* lacks a patio, terrace or garden, but can prove to be very popular, especially when it is cold and or the wind blows - hard. The sign outside, indicating seats at the rear 'with ocean views', points to a large area, inside! The food is nice, but pricey.

Round past the Ferry-boat Quay, beside the Loutra road, and opposite the *Hotel/Bar Enallax* (*Tmr* 27G/H5), is the:
Ouzerie Paradeisos
Directions: As above.
   The ouzerie, housed in a single story building, with a large garden and solid concrete tables, provides an extremly congenial place at which to enjoy a drink. It is open midday and in the evenings. The amiable, aged proprietor

proudly displays a yellowed, framed cutting. This is cut out from an American newspaper, and features his cousin - a millionaire, who owns a string of some eighty supermarkets, and a private jet. Quite a contrast! Be that as it may, an ouzo, 2 mezes, and a large can of Amstel cost 350drs. Whow! No wonder the *Paradeisos* is local-popular.

THE A TO Z OF USEFUL INFORMATION
BANKS (*Tmr* 24C/D4). Actually an agent for the **National Bank**, who has a small shop from whence can be purchased books, newspapers, and excursions to Yialos island (for 700drs, on the Alexandros' boat).

BEACHES There is a small Town Beach (*Tmr* 16E/F4), two-thirds of the way to the harbour, as mentioned in the preamble. It is messy, kelp covered and rather cluttered with 'this and that', the locals treating it as yet another 'town square'. Every so often a bulldozer loads the kelp on to lorries.
  To the left of Mandraki Town (*Fsw*) is the unusual **Koklaki Beach**, which is not so much a beach, more a small bay of very large pebbles and stones. To pursue the 5min walk, it is necessary to climb round the tiny harbour, close by *Pension Drosia* (*Tmr* 12B/C3), and follow the rocky path, scrambling over the volcanic boulders beneath the cliffs. A farmer has been known to corral his pigs in the undercut of the rock face. The sea is clear and warm, but the black/brown stones are uncomfortably large. As the bay curves away, the large, round, rocks gradually reduce in size, until they are more pebble-like, at the far side. There are few, if any spots convenient to sunbathe, but there are few, if any visitors, so it has enormous attractions.
  Some 200m east of the Ferry-boat Quay (*Tmr* 1G/H4), is a wisp of narrow beach with some sand, and a lot of pebbles.

BICYCLE, SCOOTER & CAR HIRE The *Romantzo Motel* (*Tmr* 4G5) hires scooters and the proprietor of the *Bar Enallax* (*Tmr* 27G/H5) maintains a moped hire shed on the Ferry-boat Quay. The latter rents relatively new, and 'in good working order' Peugeot mopeds, at a fee of 2000drs a day, with a full tank of fuel. There are at least two more firms, one (*Tmr* 22E4 - rumoured to have the worst kept machines, ever seen, on any island!) is situated close to the Town Beach, whilst the other (*Tmr* 25D/E3/4) is beside 'Statue Sq'.

BREAD SHOPS The town's **Baker** (*Tmr* 29D4) is beside 'Statue Sq', in a white and blue painted building. Open Mon-Sat, from 0830hrs.

BOOKSELLER (*Tmr* 24C/D4) Beside the High St. Sells some foreign language newspapers and books, and is the National Bank agent.

BUSES The three island buses, numbered 1, 2 & 3, vary in age. They termini close to the Ferry-boat Quay (*Tmr* 1G/H4), but do not operate to a strict timetable, more a 'when there are sufficient customers' routine. The route is quite simple, namely Mandraki to the volcano, and back. Those who wish to visit Pali or Nikia, will probably have to walk, or avail themselves of a taxi. The return volcano fare is fairly expensive, costing 300drs.
  The green painted mini-bus of Polyvotis Tours parks adjacent to the other buses. A large sign outside their quayside office goes into some detail, no doubt to convince passengers that there is a formal schedule. Forget it, for their vehicle also only flashes into life, when there are sufficient people to ensure all the seats are filled.

COMMERCIAL SHOPPING AREA There isn't a central market, but there are a large number of shops, selling a surprisingly diverse range of items, including electrical goods, as well as at least two shoe repairers. Shopper's should remember that almost all supplies have to be freighted in, on the ferries, so the freshest fruit and vegetables are on sale, after that day's boat has docked. Opening hours are the usual, small island 'norm'.

A most unusual feature is the practice of 'announcing' a particular shop's presence, by displaying an oil painting of the particular activity in which the retailer is engaged.

DISCO More music bars. The **Bar Enallax** (*Tmr* 27G/H5) is close to the harbour, and the **Miramare Restaurant Night Club**, about 1km distant. The latter's forte is bouzouki, accompanying Greek dancing.

FERRY-BOATS An excellent daily service, especially so if the Kos connections are included into the timetable.

Ferry-boat timetable

Day	Departure time	Ferry-boat	Ports/Islands of Call
Mon	0900hrs	Nissos Kalymnos	Tilos, Simi, Rhodes.
	1530hrs	Excursion boat	Kardamena & Kefalos(Kos).
	1600hrs	Excursion boat	Kos Town.
Tue	1400hrs	Caique	Kefalos(Kos).
	1530hrs	Excursion boat	Kardamena(Kos).
	1545hrs	N. Kalymnos	Kos, Kalimnos.
Wed	1530hrs	Excursion boat	Kefalos & Kardamena(Kos).
	1545hrs	Excursion boat	Kos Town.
Thur	0800hrs	Caique	Kardamena(Kos).
	1430hrs	Ionian Sun	Tilos, Rhodes.
	1530hrs	Excursion boat	Kardamena(Kos).
	1545hrs	Excursion boat	Kos Town.
	1645hrs	Ionian Sun	Kos, Tinos, Mykonos, Andros, Rafina(M).
Fri	0900hrs	N. Kalymnos	Tilos, Simi, Rhodes.
	1530hrs	Excursion boat	Kardamena(Kos).
	1600hrs	Excursion boat	Kos Town.
Sat	1530hrs	Excursion boat	Kardamena(Kos).
	1545hrs	N. Kalymnos	Kos, Kalimnos.
Sun	Excursion boats.		

Mandraki is also an occasional port of call for **Mistral II**, a cruise ship based at Rhodes, and owned by Epirotiki Lines.

FERRY-BOAT TICKET OFFICES The owner of the *Three Brothers* (*Tmr* 3G5) is an agent for the **FB Nissos Kalymnos**, and sets-up a table on the Ferry-boat Quay (*Tmr* 1G/H4), more accurately at the quay bar, a few hours prior to the ship's arrival. The High St firm of **Enetikon Travel** (*Tmr* 33F4, tel 31465) is an agent for both the **FB Ionian Sun & Nissos Kalymnos**.

MEDICAL CARE One or two shops sell pharmaceutical products, but anyone in need of medical care should get themselves to Kos, quickly.

NTOG (*Tmr* 2G4) More a municipal tourist office, located in the same building as the Police and Post Office. When and if open, and it is a very big if..., the pleasant and helpful staff distribute a Nisiros leaflet and answer timetable enquiries.

OTE None. A small shop (*Tmr* 25D/E3/4), selling camera film, refreshments, and much more, possesses a metered telephone. The ancient, pebble-spectacled owner is extremely short-sighted, so much so that he can lose out to the unscrupulous, as he is prone to misprice articles. Fortunately, for his till sales, he is occasionally aided and assisted by his son or friends.

PLACES & EVENTS OF INTEREST

The Monastery of the Lady Virgin of the Rocks* Perched on the cliff-edge hemming-in the town, at the west side, and reached via a steep, narrow flight of steps that ascend from the 'Welsh Quarter'. A signpost points the way. Unusually the door is often left open. An extremely lovely, if 'standard', rich and dark Byzantine monastery interior, with marvellous rooftop views.

The cliff has been stabilised, underpinned and faced with concrete, which, for some obscure reason, has been striped with yellow paint. Perhaps the authorities are worried about low-flying aircraft?

*Variously and also named Panaghia Spiliani or Virgin of the Cave.

The Castle Dominates the hillside headland to the west of the town, and is accessed by the next flight of steps up from those to the monastery. The signs label the direction 'To the Castle' and 'To the Ancient Wall'. Where the steps run out, a medieval, uphill, stone path takes over until a broad swathe cuts across the track. Here, it is necessary to turn right, up the hill to the ruined, large, hewn-block fort walls, which are up to three metres thick in places. The views are magnificent.

A local farmer has taken advantage of the fortification, utilising a section of the wall to form one side of his smallholding and animal enclosures. Perhaps it is the same chap who keeps the pigs penned in, way down at the bottom of the cliff-face of Koklaki Bay?

The castle can also be reached along the concrete surfaced road that spurs off the coastal road to Loutra, beyond the harbour.

Museums

Town (*Tmr* 20A/B3/4) Situated in a quaint corner, opposite an extensively restored Byzantine church which possesses splendid wall paintings. The tiny, two-storey Dickensian house contains items of local interest and is open daily 1000-1500hrs. Admission is free, and it is well worth a visit.

Private (*Tmr* 21A/B4) This collection is in the home of a local historian and archaeologist. He has made some very interesting finds, but is losing his sight, and has had to curtail his activities. A knowledge of Greek is necessary to have any conversation with him.

POLICE

Port & Town (*Tmr* 2G4) Both are located in the 'municipal' building, close by the harbour, with the doors 'wide open' for 'business' weekdays between 0700-1400hrs. The town police can be raised, at any hour, if the matter is sufficiently serious.

POST OFFICE (*Tmr* 2G4) In the same block as the Police, and open weekdays between 0730-1400hrs.

TAXIS Two firms, **Bobby's** (Tel 31460) and **Irene's** (Tel 31474). Sample fares to: Pali 600drs; Emborio 1500drs; Nikia 2000drs; the volcano 4000drs; and an island tour 6000drs.

TELEPHONE NUMBERS & ADDRESSES

Doctor Tel 31217
Police, town (*Tmr* 2G4) Tel 31201

TOILETS There are two public toilets. One (*Tmr* 5G4), close to the Ferry-boat Quay, beside the road into town, is rather dirty, smelly and often lacks toilet paper. The other (*Tmr* 5D3/4), close by 'Statue Sq', might be shut. Before finishing this discourse, in respect of 'matters sanitary', it is noteworthy that the environs are well equipped with pedal-operated bins, which (of course) rarely appear to be emptied. The town's rubbish is collected by a small, three-wheeled cab, which can only just squeeze between the buildings edging some of the narrow lanes.

TRAVEL AGENTS & TOUR OFFICES The Polyvotis Tours office (*Tmr* 1G/H4) is conveniently based on the Ferry-boat Quay, and the notice board, just inside the entrance, is very informative. Eliciting more detail from the taciturn owner is a 'winkling job'. **Enetikon Travel** (*Tmr* 33F4), alongside the road into town, offers an extremely helpful service, and a day-trip to Yialos island, at a cost of 1000drs. Note, this compares poorly 'to our' National Bank agent (*Tmr* 24C/D4), who has the same excursion 'on his books' at a fee of 700drs. For further details *See* Ferry-boat Ticket offices. For some reason, there is an Olympic representative (*Tmr* 26B3/4), who also acts for the **FB Ionian Sun** and the **Nissos Kalymnos**.

ROUTE ONE (and only one)

To Nikia (about 10km) via Loutra, Pali & Emborio From Mandraki Town, the road turns past the Ferry-boat Quay, and east along the backshore of a mainly rocky coastline.

The route passes by, on the right, the (to-date) two storey *Hotel Harikos* (or Haristo, a Class B pension, tel 31322). This is owned by a Greek, who worked in Canada, for years, to pay for the building's construction costs. Some up-market, package holiday-makers utilise the hotel, and it is block-booked, by a German firm, for the height of summer. Assuming there is 'room at the pension', a clean, double, with en suite bathroom and sea-view balcony, cost 5000drs a night, including a simple continental breakfast. The carpets would 'appreciate' a once-over with a vacuum cleaner.

Benches border the roadside, pleasantly sited and convenient for weary walkers. After a long trudge, one chances upon the rather strange hamlet of:

LOUTRA (2km from Mandraki) A large, seafront building, partly in ruins, houses a small and rather incongruous taverna. Next door is a big warehouse, which is actually a government sponsored thermal spa. Problem specialities take in gynaecology, eczema, rheumatism and arthritis. Rooms are available for patients, who enjoy the hot mineral waters, collected in tanks, on the inland side of the building. The thermae opens morning and afternoon, with a break between 1300-1700hrs, whilst the staff run the next-door taverna!

From Loutra, the road climbs and winds up an amply vegetated, if dusty hillside, past the town rubbish dump, and old olive groves. Half-way towards the Pali turning, some deserted workings overhang the sea, accompanied by the usual scattering of abandoned vehicles. A quay and associated buildings, that once belonged to the now 'dead' quarry, sprawl over a bluff. Beneath this is a delightful, silver sand beach that benefits from the sea-water somehow being warmed by the volcano. The large *White Beach Hotel* (Tel 31396/31437), erected at the top of this beach, is package company booked, but either side of the busiest summer months, can offer an en suite double, with a balcony, at a price of 5000drs per night. The arrival of this accommodation has removed the appellation 'deserted' from the island's only sandy shore, once the nudist beach (what a barefaced cheek).

High on the hillside, close by a chapel, is a turning that branches off to the left, down to:

PALI (4km from Mandraki) Rather than follow the extravagant loops of the road, it is possible to scramble down the slopes, recross the road and wander into the nearside of Pali, close by a church.

A roundabout opens a traveller's account of this pleasing, widespread fishing settlement, the inhabitants of which are busy getting on with their lives. To the left is a rocky breakwater, forming a large caique harbour. Beyond the roundabout and the onset (yes onset - how else, but as a disease, could one detail this abomination?) of a one-way system, is a central, open space. There are two supermarkets. The one behind the rather too touristic *Restaurant Aphrodite*, is run by a 'big' girl, with a penchant for filling her spare-time cycling about, scattering unsuspecting pedestrians. It has a metered telephone. The other supermarket, along the street backing the Esplanade, is more a garden shed.

To the right of the aforementioned roundabout, is the congenial terrace of the *Captain's House Snackbar*, where can be consumed breakfast, tost, drinks, and snacks. Beside the open space 'square' are a store, post box, periptero, and the *Hotel/Restaurant Hellenis*, where an en suite double costs about 3000drs. The hotel restaurant is patronised by some locals, but does not deserve more than a passing mention.

From the roundabout, left along the Esplanade to the end leads to *Rooms*, at No 5. The amiable landlady charges 3000/4000drs a night for a double bedroom. In the winter months she returns to Athens.

The right-hand road, which bends round east out of the village, from the entrance on the way in, passes by a baker, in front of which is a sea facing bar/taverna. The concrete road continues on, now skirting a long, volcanic sand, but rather debris littered beach backshore. To the inland side spreads out a ramshackle sprawl of dwellings and scattered backyards. The road edges by a still-to-be topped-off, local rock faced spa building, which is reminiscent of a Victorian prison. Alongside a Tyrolean caravan (yes, a Tyrolean...), of hideously bad taste, possibly the property of an expatriate North American, and inscribed *Halcyon Days* (*sic*), the surface of the thoroughfare deteriorates, to become nothing more than a dusty track.

Should a traveller wish to get away from it all, then it is only necessary to keep on along the increasingly badly surfaced path, until it peters out at a volcanic, goat infested beach, set in lovely, wild and deserted countryside.

Returning to the main road, the route snakes on up the beautiful mountainsides to a junction. Here the right-hand turning leads to the volcano, and the left-hand choice to the crater-edge villages of:

EMBORIO What an amazing location for a settlement, looking down into the volcano, whilst to seawards is Kos island, hunkered down on the horizon. Sadly, Emborio is almost deserted, but... The other side of the village square, beside which is a post box, and to the right, just around the corner - is a kafeneion, an inexpensive 'little watering hole'.

And
NIKIA This 'wrong side of the crater' settlement, is more alive, populated, attractive, and closer to the rim of the volcano's sunken plain, than Emborio. The roofs of the dwellings are, unusually, angled towards the sea, maybe in an effort to defeat the depredations of the prevailing winds.

There is a to-be-recommended, peaceful, and welcoming taverna, with Kos panoramas. This is (unsurprisingly) the *Taverna Nikia*, run by a father and his three sons. Customers can sit beneath a vine covered veranda opposite, from which are views down the hillside. A lunch of 2 large salads, a tzatziki, and a bottle of water, cost 1200drs.

Despite these obvious attractions, Nikia has failed to capture the capricious attentions of the excursion trip organisers, thank goodness!

The Volcano The 'delights' of the volcano trip have been discoursed about in the Introduction, but a few more words will not go amiss. Most visitors head for the obvious blow-hole crater, in the ground near to the taverna shack. But the more interesting, less obvious, and thus less gawped-at crater is to be found by wandering off to the right (*Taverna in front of one*), along a narrow path. Breasting the rubble of the mini-caldera reveals a deep crater from which emanates a stream of grey, sulphurous-yellow fumes. Further to the right is another, smaller, satellite crater containing blow holes, from which pour forth steam, and circled by crystallised sulphur.

EXCURSION TO YIALOS ISLAND (Giali) The excursion boats take about twenty minutes to cross over to Yialos, at a round trip cost of 700/1000drs per head. The least expensive craft departs at about 0930hrs, the other a little later, and tickets can be purchased on board.

The odd appearance of the island is due to extensive surface mining, for building materials and pumice. The excavations are slowly chewing away at the island's 'superstructure', rather similar to one of those 'pack man', pub-video games, or, in this case, 'island champing man'. Workers commute daily from Nisiros. Despite the drawback of the noise caused by the quarrying machinery, and the uninviting appearance of the place, there is a long, volcanic sand beach, and some backshore 'support facilities'.

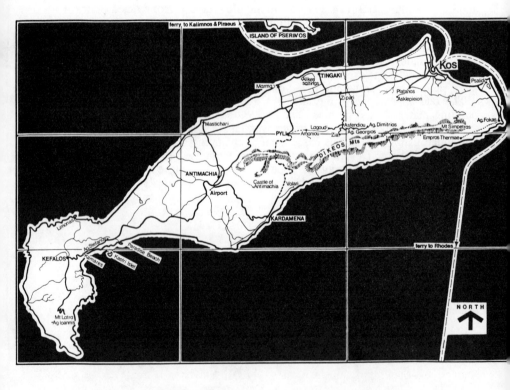

Illustration 20 Kos island

11 KOS (Cos)   **
Dodecanese Islands

FIRST IMPRESSIONS Mass tourism; Scandinavians; the 'Kosta Brava' of the Greek islands; splendid ruins; expensive; palm trees, oleanders & bougainvillea; plastic signs; photo-developing shops; verdant countryside; cows; wildlife.

SPECIALITIES Alcoholic spirits & perfumes.

LOCAL RELIGIOUS HOLIDAYS & FESTIVALS incl: 24th June - Fire of St John; 30th July - Festival of St Apostle, Antimachia; Aug - Festival of the Oath of Hippocrates, Asklepieion; 6th Aug - Saviours Metamorphosis, Kos Town; 7th Sept - Festival of St Virgin of Tsukanon, Kardamena.

VITAL STATISTICS Tel prefix 0242. The second largest of the Dodecanese islands, being 45km from tip to toe & up to 10½km at the widest point. Due to the irregular outline, these figures are subject to diverse interpretation. Despite being second in size, Kos is only about one fifth the area, so it is a poor second. Out of the overall population of some 18,000, about 8,000 live in the capital.

HISTORY Naturally, much of the island's history paralleled that of Rhodes. Alexander the Great occupied Kos, in 336 BC. On his death, the Egyptians took over and their rulers, the Ptolemies, visited, as did Cleopatra. She is rumoured, to have kept some of the family jewels stashed on Kos, for safe-keeping. The Romans held sway until the Byzantine Empire took over, only for the Saracens to sack the place, in the 11thC. It took the Knights six more years to conquer Kos, than it did for them to overrun Rhodes. No matter, they lost it to the Turks, in the same year as Rhodes.
   Earthquakes wrought havoc during the last century BC and in the early centuries *anno Domini*. As recently as 1933, Kos Port and Town were badly damaged by tremors. Interestingly, this last, devastating seismic disturbance revealed hitherto unsuspected archaeological finds.

GENERAL For an age Kos was raved about by the travel writers. Even as recently as ten to twelve years ago, it was feasible to escape from the all-pervading hordes of summer visitors. Nowadays, that is impossible, as the holiday centres are equally spread throughout this green and pleasant land. From Kos to Kefalos and from Kardamena to Mastichari. In fact, the only areas that the developers have left unsullied are the eastern flank of the Mt Dikeos range and the land to the west of Mt Latra, and then only because both are almost inaccessible!
   The peasant women of one or two villages continue to wear the native work-a-day clothes of head-dress, white shawl, black skirt and coarse stockings.
   The north and south sides of the island have distinct and different weather characteristics. The northern coast enjoys a constant cooling breeze, resulting in small waves breaking on the sea-shore. The windless, southern shores tend to be hotter and the sea calmer.
   Kos is a duty-free port and alcoholic spirits are cheaper than some other Dodecanese islands. Incidentally, despite the name Kos, there is not a lettuce in sight!

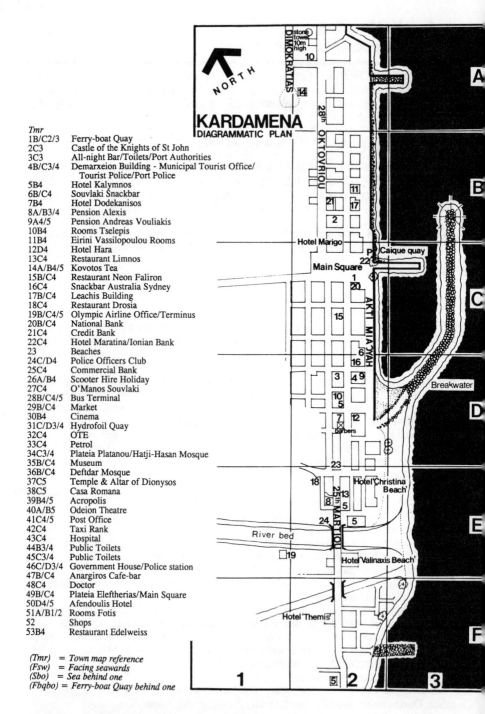

Tmr

Tmr	
1B/C2/3	Ferry-boat Quay
2C3	Castle of the Knights of St John
3C3	All-night Bar/Toilets/Port Authorities
4B/C3/4	Demarxeion Building - Municipal Tourist Office/ Tourist Police/Port Police
5B4	Hotel Kalymnos
6B/C4	Souvlaki Snackbar
7B4	Hotel Dodekanisos
8A/B3/4	Pension Alexis
9A4/5	Pension Andreas Vouliakis
10B4	Rooms Tselepis
11B4	Eirini Vassilopoulou Rooms
12D4	Hotel Hara
13C4	Restaurant Limnos
14A/B4/5	Kovotos Tea
15B/C4	Restaurant Neon Faliron
16C4	Snackbar Australia Sydney
17B/C4	Leachis Building
18C4	Restaurant Drosia
19B/C4/5	Olympic Airline Office/Terminus
20B/C4	National Bank
21C4	Credit Bank
22C4	Hotel Maratina/Ionian Bank
23	Beaches
24C/D4	Police Officers Club
25C4	Commercial Bank
26A/B4	Scooter Hire Holiday
27C4	O'Manos Souvlaki
28B/C4/5	Bus Terminal
29B/C4	Market
30B4	Cinema
31C/D3/4	Hydrofoil Quay
32C4	OTE
33C4	Petrol
34C3/4	Plateia Platanou/Hatji-Hasan Mosque
35B/C4	Museum
36B/C4	Deftdar Mosque
37C5	Temple & Altar of Dionysos
38C5	Casa Romana
39B4/5	Acropolis
40A/B5	Odeion Theatre
41C4/5	Post Office
42C4	Taxi Rank
43C4	Hospital
44B3/4	Public Toilets
45C3/4	Public Toilets
46C/D3/4	Government House/Police station
47B/C4	Anargiros Cafe-bar
48C4	Doctor
49B/C4	Plateia Eleftherias/Main Square
50D4/5	Afendoulis Hotel
51A/B1/2	Rooms Fotis
52	Shops
53B4	Restaurant Edelweiss

(Tmr) = Town map reference
(Fsw) = Facing seawards
(Sbo) = Sea behind one
(Fbqbo) = Ferry-boat Quay behind one

Illustration 21 Kos Port & Town

ARRIVAL BY AIR The airport is situated about the centre of the island. Arrivals by Olympic Airways have the advantage of an airline bus, and tour-operators lay-on transport, for their clients. Independent travellers are at the mercy of taxis, or must walk some 1½km to the nearby village of Antimachia, where a scheduled bus service stops (*See* Buses).

KOS: main port & capital town (Illus 21). The small harbour is almost wholly and attractively enveloped by the town, with a fort romantically bordering one edge of the port. The quayside, and its immediate surrounds, are a gathering place for the marina jet-set, whilst the inner town, abounding with archaeological ruins, has an almost tropical milieu. This latter impression is heightened by the huge palm trees that line some of the streets. In addition, there are giant, colourful, luxuriant bougainvillea, oleander and jasmin. When they blossom, the profusion of flowers and herbs makes the air heavy with an almost pungent, aromatic, sweet smelling odour. The outer town has a quiet, prosperous, suburban ambience.

The town burghers, in their infinite wisdom, have replaced most of the blue background, stencilled street signs, which bore both Greek and Roman scripted names. The smart replacements are made of marble, but only 'carry' a carved, Greek version of the particular street name. These are extremely difficult to read, that is to other than those who are Greek, or the minority gifted enough to be able to read Greek. At the same time, a number of the street names have been altered, probably to make them 'politically correct'! Hey, ho. Some of the streets form part of this or that one-way system, in order to cope with the demands of the traffic. Sounds unpleasantly familiar.

It must remain a mystery how any holiday-maker can capture the essentials and true spirit of Greece, and its people, in a town festooned with cocktail and music bars, fast food joints, instant print shops, and chain stores, such as Benetton and Body shop. Surely, visitors would like, even fleetingly, to feel, see and touch that quintessential Hellenic quality of life and living? It is unfortunate that the authorities of a city yielding up so many archaeological treasures as Kos, have surrendered to the tidal wave of anti-culture, descending to the lowest common aspirations. A for-example is the manner in which the worthy, but misguided burghers decided to pedestrianise and renovate certain streets and one or two of the squares. This has not been achieved tastefully, with *simpatico* local stone, with old-fashioned lamp standards, and park benches. No, the areas concerned have been proletarianised by installing glitzy, post-modernistic, high-tech lamp posts, street furniture, fountains, and paving stones. Oh dear me!

ARRIVAL BY FERRY The ferry-boats dock (*Tmr* 1B/C2/3) alongside the narrow necked access of the almost circular harbour, close to the Castle of the Knights of St John (*Tmr* 2C3). Once disembarked, it is necessary to walk down the quay, past a large single storey building (*Tmr* 3C3). This ensconces the Port authorities, and, at the far end, a rather expensive *Bar*, which stays open all night. This facility provides an extremely useful refuge for passengers who have endured an exhausting ferry-boat voyage, and land at some unearthly, early morning hour. The convenience has to be weighed against the behaviour of some of the late-night revellers, and a few of the travellers who find the availability of all-night drinking rather 'tiring'... It is a strange place, the duty-free liquor shelves rubbing shoulders with a cafe-bar, snacks and hot food counter. At least the lavatories are fairly clean. The staff occasionally 'bed down' behind the drinks counter, for a rest. Beyond this establishment, the narrow quay walk, with the castle walls to the left and the harbour to the right, follows the waterfront around to the right. Fortunately, it is only 500/600m from the point of disembarkation to the Esplanade.

The ferry-boats are met by the owners of accommodation, but it is   at this point that many a weary traveller has to make a choice that could, in part, further blight a stay on Kos. Further blight! Oh dear, Geoffrey, your inherent prejudices are showing. It is the habit of landlords, meeting the early morning boats, and blagging dead-on-their-feet prospects, to insist that " ...the cards are placed on the table" (or phrases to that effect). This is an effort to extract a promise that their accommodation will be accepted, unseen, and for the duration...! Don't imagine these chaps haul themselves out of bed, at ungodly hours, simply to enjoy a dawn   stroll, and be the bearer of good tidings. Oh, no! They have it in   mind to hog-tie travellers, to extract a commitment to their pension,   whilst a visitor stays on Kos. And at 4am in the morning, when the   brain and mouth may not be connected, little slips and promises can   be made. You have been warned. My best advice is that arrivals see   the rest of the night out, on a handy Esplanade bench, or beneath the castle walls. Then launch into a measured search, without pressure, in the mid-morning, perhaps fortified with a breakfast of coffee, yoghurt and honey. To those who simply must find a bed, there and then, the best course of action is to promise to stay one night, with the option to extend the 'contract'.

THE ACCOMMODATION & EATING OUT

The Accommodation There are at least a couple of possibilities close to the waterfront, namely the:
Hotel Kalymnos (*Tmr* 5B4) (Class E) 9 Riga Fereou   Tel 22336
Directions: Standing back, where Riga Fereou St runs into the Esplanade, Akti Kountouriotou.

This solid establishment was built by the Italians, immediately after the 1936 earthquake - and the genial, stout, old landlady retains fond memories of Il Duce (I bet she does). She regards him as the personage responsible for "...turning a mosquito infested swamp into the pleasant harbour we find today". In 1992, the hotel was undergoing a floor by floor renovation, possibly the first since it was constructed! The *Kalymnos* is situated in a noisy location, as   the marine cafe society does not quieten down, until the early hours. A particular nuisance is a nearby music bar, belting out non-stop   pop. In an effort to minimise the inconvenience of the entrance being cluttered-up, day and night (the landlady's words), with a rag-bag of tired and emotional drinkers, the doors have been repositioned, in the lane behind the building. Depending when the reconstruction is finally completed, ground floor doubles, with en suite bathroom and a kitchenette, are charged at 4000drs. Upper storey bedrooms may well still retain a period charm, of yesteryear, and a variety of prices. A dank single, sharing, costs 2500drs, a dingy double, also sharing, is priced at 3500drs, whilst a tatty triple, with en suite bathroom, is charged 3000drs. Some of the 'old' rooms retain an early Italian, bedsit ambiance - it would come as no surprise to find that Mussolini had slept in one or three of the sheets/blankets. The newly installed solar system ensures plentiful hot water, all day and early evening. Late arrivals may find the showers only lukewarm - it rather depends upon the capacity of the installation, and how many bodies have previously enjoyed a hose down.

Hotel Dodekanisos (*Tmr* 7B4) (Class D) 2 Alex Ipsilantou   Tel 28460
Directions: As above, and just around the corner from Riga Fereou St.
   Grubby, and no less noisy than the *Kalymnos*. Singles sharing cost
1600/2100drs & en suite 2400/2850drs, whilst doubles sharing are
2300/3000drs & en suite 3100/4400drs.

Hotel Helena (*Tmr* B3/4) (Class D) 5 Megalou Alexandrou   Tel 22740
Directions: To the right (*Sbo*) along the Esplanade, for some three blocks, as
far as the blue barrel, that substitutes as a roundabout. Here, Megalou
Alexandrou St 'avenues' off, at a right-angle.
   Well recommended, with vine covered balconies overlooking the clamorous
street. Prices for a single room, sharing, are 2500drs, a   double sharing
3500drs & en suite 4200drs.

From Megalou Alexandrou St, to the right (*Sbo*) along Irodotou St, leads to
Omirou St, the first turning left. On the far corner is:
Pension Alexis (*Tmr* 8A/B3/4) (Class E) 9 Irodotou/Omirou   Tel 28798
Directions: As above.
   A very pleasant, 'provincial digs', wherein all rooms share the respective
floor's bathroom. The pension is not inexpensive, despite the ambiance of
easy-going, devil-may-care, what's money between friends? Mine host Alexis
knows 'what's money'! The dark, ground floor double bedrooms cost about
3500drs a night. The first floor doubles, benefiting from easy access to the
pleasant, large terrace, cost 4000drs. Breakfast, served on the patio, can be a
coffee, or a full-blown 'English' affair and, although an extra, the cost
represents reasonably good value. As with similar pensions, there is a 'rare'
scramble for the bathroom. The neatly bearded Alexis   masterminds the
operation, and has a very smooth line of patter (especially with the ladies),
whilst his wife does the work, and father helps out. The atmosphere is
pleasantly cosmopolitan and off-beat, the international guests coming from
wide and varied backgrounds. Alexis can be extremely helpful, if a little
patronising. If there is no room at the inn, he is just as likely to   pop the
'disappointed' in his vehicle, and run them round to an   alternative, most
acceptable establishment. This is the *Hotel Afendoulis* (read on), owned by his
wife!   Taxi drivers appear to be related to the family, as they often
recommend the pension.

On the corner, opposite *Alexis*, is a less high-profile pension, with well
appointed, slightly more expensive rooms. The middle-aged owners, do not
possess Alexis' command of English (nor his polished, urbane approach) and
seem absolutely bewildered by his success in filling his rooms. They may
well be worth approaching, if *Pension Alexis* is full, or prospects do not wish
to be a 'bit-part' player in the daily 'production'.

Pension Andreas Vouliakis (*Tmr* 9A4/5) 2 Argirocastro   Tel 28740
Directions: Proceed 'sort of' westwards, along Megalou Alexandrou St, over
the crossroads with El Venizelou St, to an open roundabout. Here turn right
(*Sbo*) along Argirocastro St, the second exit to the   right. Possibly rather
distant from the centre of the town, being   almost on the outskirts, but
commensurately quieter.
   A clean, neat, calm place at which to stay, and comes very well
recommended, by me and others. The placid, unobtrusive, extremely nice

owner, Andreas, and his wife, live on the premises of their good value accommodation. There is a communal refrigerator on each floor. The toilets and showers are shared and, as the water is solar heated, it is prudent to 'take an early bath'. I am not sure, but I think the building is redecorated, at least once every two years. Doubles are charged 2000/2500drs per night.

Rooms Eirini (*Tmr* 11B4) 11 Kolokotroni   Tel 28298
Directions: Possibly the best route to select is to proceed to Megalou Alexandrou St, turning off left (*Sbo*) at the crossroads with 31st Martiou St, which runs into 25th Martiou St, and then right on to Kolokotroni St.
    Eirini Vassilopoulou's husband (with his car) is one of those who solicit 'small-hour ferry-boat arrivals'. They run a clean digs, even if the shared bathroom is somewhat cramped. Whilst 'procuring' at the quay, prospects are advised that a single room costs 2000drs a night, and doubles 1500drs per head. If the offer is taken-up, guests will learn that use of the shared bathroom costs an extra 500drs a night! Naughty, very naughty. Eirini's is popular with student backpackers, who don't mind sleeping three to a room. Long stay guests wishing to negotiate, should be able to remove the bathroom impost.

Rooms Tselepis (*Tmr* 10B4) 29 Venizelou/Metsovou Sts Tel 28892/23925
Directions: From Eirini's Rooms/Kolc`.otroni St, turn right at the next crossroads to the south-west, that is on to El Venizelou St, and the *Tselepsis* is on the right corner of the second crossroads, with Metsovou St.
    The gum-chewing proprietor is usually to be found slouching about on the street corner, watching the world go by, if he's not in the kafeneion next door. Failing all else, check his apartment on the first floor. The en suite bedrooms are spacious, clean, fitted with pine furniture, and a large wardrobe, and have a small balcony. The water is solar heated. The price is 2500drs low season and 4000drs in the height of summer. A nice touch is that guests may leave their bags behind, after checking out, and collect them later-on.

For more distant pastures, in the quieter, smarter eastern suburbs, from the Esplanade, turn left (*Sbo*) to follow the very pretty, curving, palm-tree-lined Finikon Avenue beneath the castle access bridge, out on to Akti Miaouli.

Hotel Hara (*Tmr* 12D4) (Class D) 6 Halkonos/2 Arseniou   Tel 22500
Directions: Proceed south-east along Akti Miaouli, turn right on to Arseniou St, after which, at right-angles, is Halkonos St.
    No singles, the double rooms are en suite, and cost 3600/4200drs. Guests wishing to 'graze' in the vicinity have the 'across the street' option of a clean and reasonably priced pizzeria, or a Chinese restaurant with sufficient red facade to double-up as the background scenery for a rendition of the Mikado.

Pension Afendoulis (*Tmr* 50D4/5) (Class B) 1 Evripilou   Tel 25321/25797
Directions: A couple of blocks further south-east of the *Hara*, and close to the junction of Evripilou and Artemesia Sts.
Owned by of the redoubtable Mrs Alexis, she of the *Pension Alexis* (*Tmr* 8A/B3/4). This new establishment is nicely furnished. All bedrooms have en suite bathrooms, with singles priced at 4000/5000drs & doubles 4800/6300drs.

Unusually, the 'East End' of Kos Town is actually the north end! This suburb was once reserved for industry and the homes of working families. Having the benefit of a long, sandy beach, it was only a matter of time before the entrepreneurial fringes of the holiday industry took an interest in the area. Some years ago the markers had been thrown down, and now the development and reconstruction is steadily engulfing this end of town. A haphazard welter of bars, clubs, discos, music bars, pubs, hotels, guest houses, tavernas and restaurants have been thrown together, much with the haste and charm of a post-war housing estate. This is not a quarter to interest the traveller, wishing to soak-up the finer points of Hellenic culture. This is more a downtown locality, catering for the transient masses engrossed in the holiday triangle of 'beach-bar-bedroom'. In amongst this 'deep-joy' are some possibilities. To head in the correct direction, proceed right (*Sbo*) round the Esplanade, almost to the far, north side of the harbour. Turn along the lateral, extremely night-noisy street of Odhos Averof, beside which are the: *Xenon Australia* (*Tmr* B2, tel 23650), at No 39, where the accommodation lacks finesse, with doubles priced at 4000drs & triples 4500drs, all sharing the bathroom; and, next door, *Pension Poppi* (*Tmr* B2, tel 23475), at No 37, all as for the *Australia*.

Hotel Fotis (*Tmr* 51A/B1/2) 23 Porfirou   Tel 23889
Directions: Continue along Averof St, as far as the crossroads with Porfirou St, at which turn right, and the hotel is on the left.
   The swept back haired, Australian speaking owner has double rooms priced between 3000-4000drs.

Don't forget the Tourist office (*Tmr* 4B/C3/4) has extensive lists of accommodation, their class and charges (*See* Municipal Tourist office).

Camping Set out from the south-east end of town, and keep to the coastal roads of V. Georgios B and G. Papandreou. This is the direction of the eastern headland. After some 2¼ km is:

Kos Camping (Class C) PO Box 48, Psalidi   Tel 23275
Directions: As above, and a fair walk. Open April-Oct.
   This site is well recommended, even if it is on the inland side of the road. The setting is congenial, with the tents spaced out beneath olive trees and bushes. The facilities are excellent and include a washroom, kitchen, clean toilets and showers (with hot water), a metered international phone, a well stocked supermarket, a small bar and a kiddies playground. Next door to the campsite is a taverna, and the pebble beach is just across the road. The friendly staff speak English and the owners prudently hire mopeds and bicycles. Daily fees are 500/700drs per person and 200/300drs for a tent.

The Eating Out The town is singularly bereft of even good, let alone outstanding, eating places. Banality and mediocrity are the 'rule of the stomach'. Fast food and tourist driven establishments have finally usurped almost all the traditional kafeneions and tavernas, wherein crusty old Greeks, in everyday clothes, eat *au naturel*. Despite, or, more correctly, in spite of these thoughts, beside Konitsas Sq is a typical, local popular souvlaki bar, the: **O Manos** (*Tmr* 27C4)
Directions: As above.
   Frequented by working men and harassed mothers, wanting a between-meals snack, and billowing with blue smoke. There are three tables inside and one outside, although most customers 'devour on the hoof'. A souvlaki costs 130drs, chips 150drs, and a beer 230drs.
   The majority of the dining places are lined up, 'table by cloth', along the

castle end of the waterfront Esplanade, Akti Kountouriotiou. If I had to select one of these run-of-the-mill offerings, it continues to be:

Restaurant Limnos (*Tmr* 13C4) Akti Kountouriotiou
Directions: Situated at the quieter end of the harbour front.
   Clean, quick, polite, unpretentious, and reasonably priced. An average meal, for two, of 1 fassolakia freska beans (450drs), a Greek salad (530drs), pork chops (880drs), 1 moussaka (660drs), bread & service, cost 2585drs. Retsina is sold by the bottle.

A traditional eaterie is the:
Restaurant Neon Faliron (*Tmr* 15B/C4)
Directions: At the top, or more literally the upper Main Sq end, of Odhos Riga Fereou (which angles down to the Esplanade).
   Only insomniacs need consider this establishment, as Michalis does not open until midnight. Known for a good line in soups.

Proceeding south'ish along Vassileos Pavlou St, from the Main Sq, and on the right, beyond the Market (*Tmr* 29B/C4), is the very pleasant, fig tree shaded (well, almost tree obliterated), raised square, or terrace, in the centre of Plateia Xanthou. Along the street edge of this terrace are the tables and chairs of some cafe-bars on the opposite side of the road. My nomination is:

Anargiros (The Pancake Cafe) (*Tmr* 47B/C4)
Directions: As above.
   The coffee drinking locals keep to the cafe side of the street, whilst the more adventurous, intrepid tourists, 'on safari' from the waterfront, lounge on the terrace. Bearing in mind the separation of kitchen from these latter clients, overdue delivery of an order (even by Greek standards) may indicate that the waiter has been run over! A likable spot, with a pretentious bill-board announcing 'The best breakfast in town'. Without doubt the maple syrup filled pancakes (500drs) do 'set one up for the day'. Yoghurt & honey costs 300drs, tea 180drs, a frappe 200drs, toast, butter & marmalade 190drs, and the service is reasonable.

Further along Vassileos Pavlou St, on the left (*Sbo*), in the block immediately prior to a waste ground fun-fair area, is the:
Snackbar Australia Sydney (*Tmr* 16C4) 29 Vassileos Pavlou
Directions: As above.
   The lady owner lived in Australia, as a young girl, returned to Greece, married and set up this establishment. The advice that here was a good value and variety snackbar, may have to be modified. This somewhat down-at-the-heel place is now well patronised by komboloe-flicking, philosophising locals, who have annexed the inside as a sort of kafeneion. Unexpected custom may come as a surprise, although they rustle-up a not inexpensive, so-so meal. Nero, the large white and tan Labrador (?) remains on guard to wolf any unwanted bits and pieces.

Off Vassileos Pavlou St, to the left along El Venizelou St and in the second block, opposite the Post Office (*Tmr* 41C4/5), is a 'tasty' *Pie & Sandwich Snackbar*. This is run by a French speaking, Greek lady and her husband.
   Further eastwards, El Venizelou St runs into a small square. Turning left along Korai St leads on to the Esplanade, Vassileos Georgiou B. Incidentally,

this seafront road could also have been reached by proceeding along the palm tree lined Finikon Avenue, on to the dual carriageway of Akti Miaouli, which runs into Vassileos Georgiou B. The junction of Korai St and Vas Georgiou B is opposite a sea bordering, Greco-Italianesque pile of architecture (*Tmr* 24C/D4). Part of this houses the Police officers' mess with, to one side, a public, paved seaside patio, complete with a beach shower and sun umbrellas. Vassileos Georgiou B, the tree lined highway heading towards Ag Fokas, borders a pebbly, narrow beach to the left, and some smart hotels, restaurants and cafe-bars to the right.

Under The Accommodation and the *Hotel Hara* (*Tmr* 12D4) mention is made of a couple of establishments. Whilst out this way, further to the east, close to the junction of the streets of Artemesias and Harmilou, is *The Follia* (*Tmr* E5). This is kept by a villainous looking native, who prides himself on remaining open all year, maintaining this is evidence enough that the *Follia* is no tourist trap. Reputed to serve good food.

Back at Plateia Eleftherias (*Tmr* 49B/C4), two restaurants occupy the ground floor of the distinctive, 1930s Leachis' building (*Tmr* 17B/C4). Their blind covered, pavement based tables and chairs face out over the square and the Mosque of Deftedar (*Tmr* 36B/C4). The restaurant beneath the tower is 'expensive value', but clients can while away an hour or so here, in more peaceful surrounds than the waterfront frenzy. One of the theatrical waiters may well reward a client's custom with a 'matinee' performance.

The opposite side of the same square, beyond the mosque and across the road from the eastern side of the Museum (*Tmr* 35B/C4), is the bougainvillea covered, medieval gateway, the Portal Forou or 'Gate of the Taxes'. Through this stone arch is a very attractive, flowering, tree and oleander edged terrace, Navklirou St, which curves down to Platanou Square. The vine trellis sheltered and shaded pavement, bordering the Ancient Agora on the right, has row upon row of prettily laid out tables and chairs. These belong to the restaurants which share the left-hand side of the crescent with a string of late-night, music hot-spots. Close to the arch is the *Restaurant Drosia* (*Tmr* 18C4), where the menu offers a list of varied, but, by any standards, expensive, very expensive dishes.

At the bottom of Odhos Navklirou, beyond the Hatji-Hasan Mosque, is the delightful Plantanou Square (*Tmr* 34C3/4). The plateia is edged by a variety of buildings. These include the mosque, an Italianesque municipal block, the approach works and stone walkway (that bridges Finikon Ave) to the castle, and the fabled plane tree, beneath which Hippocrates is 'legended' to have taught. Beyond the central building, to one side of the plane tree, is a small *Cafe-bar*, run by a mama, in shaded and quiet surroundings.

Wandering round to the west, to Megalou Alexandrou St, and on the right (*Sbo*), close to the 31st Martiou junction is:
Restaurant Edelweiss (*Tmr* 53B4)
Directions: As above.

At first glance, the clean, bright interior, fresh cotton tablecloths (that's a give-away), with a warm splash of clients spread around the patio/terrace, that runs along two sides of the building, look extremely promising. Unfortunately, the Edelweiss is no more than a nicely presented, tourist 'Greek experience' - the name should have been another surefire indicator. The menu and prices are written on a notice board, displayed outside, in English and other foreign tongues - Giro special 800drs, moussaka special

800drs, stuffed tomatoes special 700drs, and so on. A meal of a potato salad, a Greek salad (more, half a bowl of some strong, raw, green onions, tomatoes, & a slither of feta), 1 pork chop (thin, anaemic & served with defrozen chips), warm bread (with 'Tafel margarine') & service, cost 2660drs.

Whilst hereabouts, in the region of the *Pension Alexis* (*Tmr* 8A/B3/4), are the: *Restaurant Hellas* (two blocks further down the same street), and fairly costly, but serving a hot, tasty moussaka; and the *Barba George Taverna*. Further west, beside Odhos Averoff, is the *Restaurant Tropicana*, at No 66, which is recommended as a good place to eat, serving most edible English food. South a touch, close to the ancient Odeion, beside Odhos V Ipirou, close to Odhos Grigoriou E, is the:
Kovotos Tea House (*Tmr* 14A/B4/5)
Directions: As above.
    'The aroma of dreams' is a herbal tea house, in a clean, gaily painted house, with a front garden/patio, on which are small marble tables and wooden chairs. Inside are a pair of small rooms, and the owners are a young Greek couple. The ambiance is hippy'ish, but the piped music is Latin American guitar. Nes coffee/herbal tea is priced at 300drs, home-made cakes 200drs, and crepes cost from 400drs.

THE A TO Z OF USEFUL INFORMATION
AIRLINE OFFICE & TERMINUS (*Tmr* 19B/C4/5) Situated on the right-hand side, and nearly at the far end of Vassileos Pavlou St. The office ticks over with the usual Greek mixture of studied indifference and chaos. When the airline bus operates, it is with a nail-biting disregard for aircraft departure times. A notice advises 'Bus every day 0630 & 2110hrs, cost 700drs'.

Aircraft timetable (Mid-season)
Kos to Athens
Daily   0825, 2310hrs
Return
Daily   0655, 2140hrs
One-way fare 13700drs; duration 45mins
Kos to Rhodes
Tues/Thurs/Sat   1245hrs
Return
Tues/Thurs/Sat   1155hrs.
One-way fare 7500drs; duration 30mins.

BANKS The National Bank (*Tmr* 20B/C4) is located in a large building, on the corner of Ant Ioannidi and Riga Fereou Sts. Next door, down the street towards the harbour, is the Bank's foreign exchange office. Despite the amazingly sensible separation of the two disparate functions of the usual, local banking activities, and the frenzy of currency transactions, the office is usually easily identifiable by the long queues that develop. Two English speaking, laconic and nonchalant young Greeks efficiently marshal the desk. Personal cheques are changed when backed by a Eurocheque card. This facility opens weekdays between 0845-1330hrs & 1800-2000hrs. At the height of the summer frenzy, it also opens Sat 0900-1200hrs. The **Credit Bank** (*Tmr* 21C4) is towards the castle end of Akti Kountouriotou, and has a 'Visa-in-the-wall'. The **Ionian Bank** is in the ground floor of the *Hotel Maratina* (*Tmr* 22C4), close to El Venizelou and Vironos Sts. The exchange desk works weekdays between 0800-1400hrs & 1800-2000hrs. East along El

Venizelou St, to where it   crosses Korai St, leads to an **Agricultural Bank**. Closer to the centre of the town, near to Eleftherias Sq, beside Vas Pavlou St, is the **Commercial Bank** (*Tmr* 25C4). Do not forget that the Post Office (*Tmr* 41 C4/5) conducts exchange transactions.

BEACHES The nearest beach to the harbour is a narrow, small pebble and sand, rather grubby strip in the shadow of the castle walls (*Tmr*   23C3). At least it is convenient for a quick dip. Another convenient spot is the Mini-Lido to the left (*Fsw*) of the seafront building, in which is situated the Police officers' club (*Tmr* 24C/D4). Beach umbrellas, beds and a shower.
  The town is flanked by narrow beaches. To the northern, or left-hand side (*Fsw*), is a long, clean, shelving beach of coarse grained sand edging clear seas. Naturally, crowded with people, sun-beds and parasols. *See* The Accommodation for a description of the area's infrastructure. To the south of Kos Town, the tree lined Esplanade edges a narrow pebble beach that stretches all the way to Plateia 7th Martiou (*See* Excursion to Ag Fokas).

BICYCLE, SCOOTER & CAR HIRE Due to the suitability of the north coast of the island for cycling, moped hire remains inexpensive, compared to most other Greek islands. There are any number of hire firms, with some based on El Venizelou St (*Tmr* B/C4), between the junction with Megalou Alexandrou and Vas. Pavlou Sts. It is pleasing to report, after some ten years or so, that **Holiday** (*Tmr* 26A/B4) remains a   favourite recommendation. Located on the left of Megalou Alexandrou St. The per day rates for a bicycle start off at 300drs, whilst those for a moped kick off at 1500drs.
  Some writers advocate hiring bicycles. It is suggested that, apart from the spine of mountains to the south, the comparatively flat nature of the countryside is conducive to 'pedal power'. I hate to   act as devil's advocate, but must point out that this is a relative statement, for even the road to the Asklepieion is an uphill climb. And in the heat of the midday sun... Well, it's up to you. German package companies organise conducted 'cycle tours'. Just surveying the lie of the land, you know!
  Car hire is plentiful, and expensive, as elsewhere in Greece. Apart from local firms, such as **Stamatis Hire** (*Tmr* C3/4), at the bottom end of Navklirou St, there are the international outfits of: **Hertz** (*Tmr* B/C4), 12 A. Ioannidi St, off the Main Sq; **Avis** (*Tmr* B4), 3 Tsaldari St, which is east and parallel to Megalou Alexandrou St; and **Interrent** (*Tmr* B4), 28 El. Venizelou St.

BOOKSELLERS There are a number of foreign language newspaper shops, stocking best-seller paperbacks, ranged up the right-hand (*Sbo*), colonnaded side of Odhos Vas. Pavlou (*Tmr* B/C4). But, for a 'real' **Book shop** (*Tmr* B4), stocking Greek and English, as well as a number of other language books and dictionaries, proceed to the junction of Tsaldari St with 31st Martiou St.

BREAD SHOPS There is a **Baker** (*Tmr* B4) beside Kolokotroni St (follow your nose). Close to the *Hotel Dodekanisos* (*Tmr* 7B4) is a **Bread shop**, whilst the **Store** (*Tmr* C4) on the left-hand side of Vas. Pavlou St, opposite the large, tree shaded terrace of Xanthou Sq, south of the Main Sq, is now a patisserie.

BUSES The main terminal (*Tmr* 28B/C4/5) is located on Plateia Pissandrou, an open square beside Pissandrou St. This is to the south side of the Olympic office and adjacent to large areas of archaeological remains (which include

'The House of the Abduction of Europe'... sounds risque!). The ticket office is a small shack sited down a gentle slope from Plateia Pissandrou, but tickets are purchased on the bus, for some routes.

There is a city Bus terminus beside Akti Kountouriotou, in front of the Municipal Tourist office (*Tmr* 4B/C3/4). Buses to the Asklepieion (*See* Excursions to Kos Town Surrounds), and other destinations.

Bus timetable (Mid season)
Kos Town to Asfendiou
Mon-Sat   0700, 1300hrs
Return journey
Mon-Sat   0750, 1600hrs
Kos to Kardamena
Daily   0920, 1300, 1630, 2030hrs
Return journey
Daily   0800, 1000, 1520, 1700hrs
One-way fare 310drs; duration 45mins; distance 32km.
Kos Town to Pyli
Daily   0700, 1300hrs
Mon-Sat   1030, 2050hrs
Return journey
Daily   0730, 1600hrs
Mon-Sat   1030, 2050hrs
One-way fare 170drs; duration 30mins; distance 18km.
Kos Town to Tingaki
Daily   0930, 1030, 1300, 1630, 2030hrs
Return journey
Daily   0945, 1115, 1340, 1615hrs
One-way fare 140drs; duration 20mins; distance 12½km.
Kos Town to Kefalos via Paradise Beach, Ag Stefanos, Kamares
Daily   0900, 1300, 2030hrs (Sun 1700hrs)
Return journey
Daily   0715, 1015, 1500drs (Sun 1530hrs)
One-way fare 440drs; duration 60mins; distance 43½km.
Kos Town to Antimachia
Daily   1300, 2030hrs (Sun 1700hrs)
Return journey
Daily   0745, 1530hrs (Sun 1600hrs)
One-way fare 250drs; duration 40mins; distance 25km.
Kos Town to Mastichari
Daily   1300hrs
Return journey
Daily   0800hrs
One-way fare 250drs; duration 40mins; distance 24km.

Please note these timetables are subject to alteration from day to day, let alone year to year, even if it is only fine tuning. They only relate to the summer schedules between about May and September.

CINEMAS The **Orfeas** (*Tmr* 30B4) is behind the restaurants that edge Plateia Eleftherias (*Tmr* 17B/C4). There is another, the **Kentrikon**   (*Tmr* B/C4/5), alongside Pisandrou St.

COMMERCIAL SHOPPING AREA The central **Market** (*Tmr* 29B/C4) is a fanciful, castellated, square building, positioned on the edge of Plateia Eleftherias. Ranged around the periphery, inside a colonnaded passageway, are small shops selling meat, vegetables and groceries. The building opens early morning to siesta time weekdays, and Saturday mornings.

Fish is sold from crates on the harbour quay wall, and fruit and   vegetables from the back of small trucks half-way round the Esplanade.

Ifestou St snakes off from the west of Plateia Eleftherias (*Tmr* 49B/C4) and houses a 'Plaka-like' mix of tinsmiths and antique shops, which half-heartedly extends across El Venizelou St on to Apelou St.

DISCOS The greatest concentrations are behind the northern beach area (*Tmr* B2), and beside Navklirou St, edging the Ancient Agora.

FERRY-BOATS & HYDROFOILS Ferry-boats 'pull in' at the quay (*Tmr* 1B/C2/3). A very comprehensive service but, due to some of the distances travelled, and number of islands included in the schedules, timetables tend to slip, by up to several hours.

Hydrofoils dock at the Quay (*Tmr* 31C/D3/4), between 'County Hall' (*Tmr* 46C/D3/4) and the Police officers' club (*Tmr* 24C/D4).

Ferry-boat timetable (Mid-season)

Day	Departure time	Ferry-boat	Ports/Islands of Call
Mon	0230hrs	Ialissos/Kamiros	Rhodes.
	0800hrs	Nissos Kalymnos	Nisiros, Tilos, Simi, Rhodes, Kastellorizo, Rhodes.
	2430hrs	Ag Rafail	Rhodes.
Tue	0140hrs	Ialissos/Kamiros	Rhodes.
	0230hrs	Ionian Sun	Rhodes.
	1015hrs	Ag Rafail	Kalimnos,Leros,Patmos, Vathi(Samos),Chios, Mitilini(Lesbos), Limnos, Kavala(M).
	1530hrs	Ialissos/Kamiros	Kalimnos, Leros, Patmos, Piraeus(M).
	1655hrs	Ionian Sun	Mykonos, Tinos, Andros, Rafina(M).
Wed	0230hrs	Ialissos/Kamiros	Rhodes.
	1530hrs	Ialissos/Kamiros	Kalimnos, Leros, Patmos, Piraeus(M).
	2230hrs	N. Kalymnos	Kalimnos.
Thur	0140hrs	Ionian Sun	Nisiros, Tilos, Rhodes.
	0210hrs	Alkeos	Rhodes.
	0230hrs	Ialissos/Kamiros	Rhodes.
	0825hrs	N. Kalymnos	Nisiros, Tilos, Simi, Rhodes.
Thur	1530hrs	Ialissos/Kamiros	Kalimnos, Leros, Patmos, Piraeus(M).
	1720hrs	N. Kalymnos	Kalimnos.
	1820hrs	Ionian Sun	Mykonos, Tinos, Andros, Rafina(M).
Fri	0230hrs	Ialissos/Kamiros	Rhodes.
	0800hrs	N. Kalymnos	Nisiros, Tilos, Simi, Rhodes, Kastellorizo, Rhodes.
	1530hrs	Ialissos/Kamiros	Kalimnos, Leros, Patmos, Piraeus(M).
Sat	0230hrs	Ialissos/Kamiros	Rhodes.
	0415hrs	Ionian Sun	Rhodes.
	1530hrs	Ialissos/Kamiros	Kalimnos, Leros, Patmos, Piraeus(M).
	1630hrs	Ionian Sun	Kalimnos, Astipalaia, Mykonos, Tinos, Andros, Rafina(M).
Sun	1530hrs	Ialissos/Kamiros	Kalimnos, Leros, Patmos, Piraeus(M).

In addition to the above, there are the more costly, scheduled excursion craft. They 'voyage' to, for instance, the nearby islands of Pserimos, Kalimnos, Patmos and Nisiros. *See* Mastichari, for a Kalimnos connection, and Kardamena, for Nisiros boats. For details of the respective schedules, refer to the particular island chapters.

Hydrofoil timetable (Mid-season)

Day	Departure time	Ports/Islands of Call
Mon-Sat	0800hrs	Rhodes.
	2015hrs	Kalimnos.
Sun	Excursions - various!	

One-way fare 3800drs.

FERRY-BOAT & HYDROFOIL TICKET OFFICES Mainly centred on the Esplanade, Akti Kountouriotou, and 'shoulder to shop front' with the Municipal Tourist office (*Tmr* 4B/C3/4). A prime office in this line-up is that of **Dane Sea Lines**.

HAIRDRESSERS Too many to detail, with the greatest concentration beside El Venizelou St, Vas. Pavlou St, Plateia Eleftherias and Hippocratous St, with a 'mega one' close to Argircastro St (*Tmr* A4/5). But surely no traditional island would have this number?

LAUNDRY There are two coin-op launderettes. The older one is at the outset of Themistokleous St (*Tmr* B3), at No 3, where a wash costs 500drs and the drier 300drs. The other is **Speed Clean** (*Tmr* A/B3), at No 124 Alikarnassou, where a combined 'wash-n-dry' costs 700drs. Open Mon-Sat 0830-2030hrs & Sun 0830-1830hrs. There are some four **Dry Cleaners**, one (*Tmr* A/B2/3) beside the junction of Kanari and El Venizelou Sts.

MEDICAL CARE
Chemists & Pharmacies Very 'thick underfoot', as are doctors and dentists. I suppose this is natural for the island that nurtured our 'old friend' Hippocrates, but there must be more medical supernumaries, per head of population, than anywhere else in Greece. At least one pharmacy is open every day, with a rota operating.
Dentists There is a Surgery (*Tmr* B4) at No 38 El Venizelou St, alongside the junction with Metsovou St, whilst another is beside Metsovou St, next door to *Maxime's Cafe*, at No 14. 'Mouth opening' hours are 0900-1300 & 1700-2000hrs Mon-Fri.
Doctors Plentiful, including a Dr Perdis (*Tmr* 48C4) beside Hippocratous St. His surgery is open daily 0830-1330 & 1700-2100hrs. Conveniently, there is a large pharmacy next door.
Hospital (*Tmr* 43C4). Appropriately, alongside Hippocratous St.

MUNICIPAL TOURIST OFFICE (*Tmr* 4B/C3/4) The Demarxeion building also houses the Tourist police and, upstairs, the Port police. The Tourist staff offer an excellent service, proffering lists of accommodation, transport timetables, and more, including personal opinions. During the summer months, opening hours are Mon-Sat 0730-1630hrs & Sun 0800-1500hrs.

OTE (*Tmr* 32C4) 6 Vironos St. A tatty office, with a sign requesting 'Please queue'. Despite this straightforward request, certain tourists persevere in barging through, but I deny that they are all of teutonic background, even if tortured... Even the most 'lager'ish' of the 'Brits' form a queue, at the drop of a 'sleeve glass'. Open Mon-Fri 0730-2150hrs. During July/August add in weekends 0730-1500hrs. There are a number of places with metered telephones around the OTE, but the official organisation is where a caller can rely on being charged the correct rate. A nod is as good as a...!

PETROL Apart from the out of town filling stations, there is a pair of pumps (*Tmr* 33C4) beside Odhos Hippocratous.

PLACES & EVENTS OF INTEREST Kos, more than perhaps any other Greek   city or town, has remains littered all over the place. In fact, it is impossible not to fall over a Roman this, or ancient Greek that...
Ancient Agora & Port Quarter (*Tmr* C4) Open daily, entrance is free. The most convenient way on to this very large, sprawling site is from   Akti Miaouli, opposite the Hydrofoil Quay (*Tmr* 31C/D3/4). A number of interesting exhibits, dating as far back as the 4thC BC, lurk in the weed and boulder bestrewn landscape. Interestingly enough, it was the 1933 earthquake that destroyed many medieval buildings and enabled the eager Italian architects to get to work. Close by the north end of this site is the:
Square of The Hippocratic Plane Tree (*Tmr* 34C3/4) The lovely Plateia Platanou is dominated by an extremely old and arthritic tree, the branches of which are supported, at every possible point, by forked crucks (no, no crucks!). Old as the tree may be, and estimates vary widely, from 400 to 1000 years, it cannot possibly be 2,400 to 2,500 years old. And that is the age it would have to be for Hippocrates to have taught beneath its foliage. A delightful fountain bubbles into an old sarcophagus, beneath the spreading boughs. The buildings, which are spread about in and around the square, are of a most   diverse and dissimilar architectural milieu. Amongst these is the *Mosque of the Loggia/Hatji-Hasan*, built in the late 1700s by, surprise, surprise, the Turk, Hasan (Hadji-Hatji) Pasha. A pleasing flight of marble steps, a splendid minaret, as well as the many coloured stones used in the construction, make an impressive sight. The Italians, not to be left out, in the 1930s constructed an ambitious Town Hall (*Tmr* 46C/D3/4), to house judiciary and administration offices.

From the square, a flight of steps leads to a stone bridge spanning Finikon St, more poetically the Avenue of the Palms, which gives access to:
The Castle of the Knights (*Tmr* 2C3) This site, as are the museums and Roman Villa, is open Tue-Sun 0900-1500hrs, and entrance costs 300drs, which it does to each place. An imposing Crusader castle, the walls of which are in a surprisingly good state of repair. The Knights of the Order of St John built it on the ruins of a previous fortification, close by the entrance to the harbour. The overpoweringly beautiful Avenue of Palms/Finikon St was originally a moat. To complete the construction, the Knights 'borrowed' a great deal of the materials from other, older Greek and Roman remains, especially the Asklepeion. The castle is now appropriately used to store recently excavated archaeological finds, awaiting a final resting place.

The Main Square (*Tmr* 49B/C4) has a number of interesting features including the:
Museum (*Tmr* 35B/C4) A rather bland, small, yellow building of Italian construction, with an interesting collection of statues.

Deftedar Mosque (*Tmr* 36B/C4) Makes an island site towards one corner of the square. Various tourist shops are let into the base of the building.
Behind the mosque is the very pretty, if isolated, flower covered 'Gate of the Forum', or 'The Taxes', dating from medieval times.

From Eleftherias Square, westwards along Odhos 25th Martiou, is only a pace or twenty to a small archaeological site famed for its mosaics. An interesting way to gain access is to walk along the cul-de-sac extension to Riga Fereou St, and turn left between two houses. The building on the right contains a restaurant bar, the *Flamingo Pub*, in front of which stands a very large, re-rooting tree, but I digress. On the site, the path is a length of ancient road, with the occasional ruin here and there, beset by weeds.

Further along 25th Martiou St, which becomes 31st Martiou St, gives access to a larger archaeological site, bounded by Odhos Megalou Alexandrou and known as the *Old Stadium*.

Returning to Eleftherias Square (*Tmr* 49B/C4), Vas. Pavlou St runs south to a junction with Grigoriou E. St, around which are a lot of   interesting, archaeological 'goodies'. To the left (*Harbour behind one*) is the:
Temple & Altar of Dionysos (*Tmr* 37C5) Dated 3rdC BC, opposite which is:
Casa Romana (*Tmr* 38C5) The 3rdC AD remains of a Roman house, superimposed on the ruins of a larger Greek mansion, dated between   50-30 BC. The splendidly reconstructed house contains remnants and mosaic floors which are 'column by pediment' with the ruins of some Roman baths. Hours and fees are as for the castle, and the restored exhibit is well worth a visit.

West on Odhos Grigoriou E. leads past a very large 'L' shaped site on the right (*Tmr* B4/5). This includes an:
Acropolis (*Tmr* 39B4/5) With a minaret added.
Roman Road A paved way, with the remains of Roman houses here and there.
House of Europe Further west, and famous for its mosaics. Hereabouts, the site takes a turn to the north, which advances to more Roman roadways, or Via Cardo, followed by the ancient remains of: The Nymphaeum, The Xystos (gymnasium), baths, (once) sumptuous latrines, taverns and more mosaics.

Across Odhos Grigoriou E. is one of my favourite Kos ruins, the:
Ancient Odeion (*Tmr* 40A/B5) The theatre is approached through, and framed by, a deliciously cool avenue of stately cypresses. Despite being extensively restored, the Odeion evokes the centuries of tradition, and is a thing of great beauty, in a lovely setting. It is occasionally used for modern-day productions.

Two other sites deserve a mention, namely some Thermae or Baths at the harbour end of Megalou Alexandrou St, bounded by Odhos Irodotou and Iroon Politchniou Sq (*Tmr* B3/4). The other is, or more accurately was, a car park off El Venizelou St. It looks suspiciously like one of the British National Car Parks - yellow luminous signs with a hut and other familiar trappings. Here a leisurely archaeological excavation appears to be underway.

POST OFFICE (*Tmr* 41C4/5) Eastwards on Odhos El Venizelou, beyond the junction with Meropidos St. The doors are open Mon-Fri between 0730-1415hrs. In the busy summer months they also open Sat 0800-1415hrs & Sun 0900-1330hrs. Postage stamps are available from some of the Esplanade peripteros.

POLICE
Port & Tourist (*Tmr* 4B/C3/4) In the Demarxeion building, alongside the Municipal Tourist office.
Town (*Tmr* 46C/D3/4) Located in the large municipal block, alongside the quadrangle containing the old Hippocratic plane tree.

SPORTS FACILITIES Apart from an overwhelm of water sports, not a lot, unless a reader wishes to play football or basket ball. Why not?

TAXIS (*Tmr* 42C4) There is a main rank alongside the conjunction of   Akti Kountouriotou and Platanou Sq.

TELEPHONE NUMBERS & ADDRESSES

Hospital (*Tmr* 43C4) 21 Hippocratous	Tel 23000/22300
Olympic Airways (*Tmr* 19B/C4/5) 22 Vas Pavlou	Tel 28330/28332
Police (*Tmr* 46C/D3/4)	Tel 22100/28227
Taxi rank (*Tmr* 42C4)	Tel 22777/23333
Tourist office (*Tmr* 4B/C3/4) 7 Akti Kountouriotou	Tel 28724/24460

TOILETS Not as 'potty' conscious as Rhodes. There is one, set in the reverse side of the Market building (*Tmr* 29B/C4), one 'snuggled' away on the junction of Megalou Alexandra St with Akti Kountouriotou (*Tmr* 44B3/4), and yet another alongside Finikon Avenue (*Tmr* 45C3/4) - almost beneath the bridge between Platanou Sq and the castle.

TRAVEL AGENTS & TOUR OFFICES There are some beside Vas. Pavlou St and Akti Kountiouriotou, as well as 25th Martiou and El Venizelou Sts.

EXCURSIONS TO KOS TOWN SURROUNDS
Excursion to Cape Skandari (circa 3km) Due north of Kos Town, at the topmost tip of the island, by **Cape Skandari**, is a quite beautiful beach. The shore is only metres away from the coastal road.
    From the Cape, it is 14km to Tingaki (*See* Route One). The road edges the coastline to the west, for some 3km, after which the route is no more than a track, through agreeable farming countryside.

Excursion to Asklepieion via Platanos (4km) Leave Kos Town along Odhos Megalou Alexandrou and turn right at the junction with Koritsas   and Grigoriou E. Sts. About 1km out of town, the road forks right for Kefalos and left to Platanos. Select the left turning. Half-way along the gently ascending road to Platanos, and on the left is a long, white wall with red stone capping concealing a:
Turkish Cemetery Possibly rivals the one in Rhodes City, but rather tatty. The wrought iron gate is fastened with a chain and padlock, but it is easy enough to slip these over the top of the ironwork. The gravestones are in excellent condition, and stacked together, in piles. The distinctive, carved headpieces show up well.

PLATANOS (2km from Kos) A rather scruffy village, prior to the Asklepieion, with a number of tourist orientated tavernas 'slugging it' out for the available trade.
    The final approach, all uphill, is along a narrow avenue, lined with stately cypress trees. Along this metalled lane continually flows a tidal stream of air-conditioned tour buses, and a slower flood of cyclists. The Asklepieion is very much a part of the tourist merry-go-round, if not the major constituent of the 'circus', no circuit (a natural slip of the pen).
The Asklepieion (4km from Kos) The Sanctuary is named after the God of healing. It was probably constructed, after the death of Hippocrates, in the 4thC BC, on the site of sacred ground. The situation of the first medical school in the world is certainly impressive, if not breathtaking, the various terraces or levels rising up the pine tree clad hillside.

A 6thC AD earthquake 'rubbled' the site, the lazy Knights borrowed much of the stonework, to build their castle at Kos Town, but the Italians carried out extensive restoration - where did they not?

From the top level, gained by ascending the large and grand stone staircase, the views are truly magnificent.

Lawrence Durrell in his book *The Greek Islands** wrote that to camp hereabouts may result in a very disturbed night's sleep, hinting that the ghosts of the ancients still haunt the location.

**Published by Faber & Faber Ltd.*

Excursion to Ag Fokas (7km) Leoforos Akti Miaouli proceeds eastwards past the various grand Italianesque buildings into Vas. Georgiou B. This avenue is bordered by the sea and a very narrow, pebbly beach on the left. On the right is a mishmash of hotels, restaurants, housing and flats. These slowly degenerate in quality, as the avenue proceeds towards Plateia 7th Martiou, and then Odhos G Papandreou, in the direction of the hamlets of Psalidi, Ag Fokas and Empros Thermae. On the way, about 400m beyond the *Continental Palace Hotel* and just past the turning down to the *Ramira Beach Hotel*, are the *Restaurant Nea Syntrivani* and the *Restaurant Antonis*. Both establishments are recommended for inexpensive, well cooked, excellent value food, pleasantly served in an atmosphere approaching the 'real' Greek ambience. Can one say more?

The coast road skirts the town's rubbish dump, the headland of **Psalidi**, and heads to **Ag Fokas**. Here, at a cleft in the road, a turning winds down to a snackbar. From this point, another 4km of unmade track leads to the hot sulphurous spring at **Empros Thermae**, the waters of which dribble across the cliff edged, blackish beach into the sea.

ROUTE ONE
To Kefalos via Zipari, Antimachia & Kamares (43km) This is really the one and only route, with a number of forays off to north and south coasts. The main Kefalos road from Kos Town, on past the **Platanos** side turning, is the subject of ribbon development with a number of Spanish style villas, set in Spanish style, urban sprawl. Thankfully this messy state of affairs gradually peters out. It is replaced by the occasional taverna and more widely scattered buildings, surrounded by a broad plain bounded, on the left, by the Dikeos mountain range.

ZIPARI (8km from Kos) An unattractive village with many facilities, such as bakers, vegetable shops, a supermarket, and tavernas. Petrol is available beyond the village.

In Zipari is a side turning to the left, which winds up the mountainside, through lovely, varied tree clad hillsides. The large eucalyptus trees that used to line the road were cut back to stumps, following the cold winter of 1987. One wonders if this 'butchery' was to keep the home fires burning?

At a junction in **Asfendiou** village, roads lead off to the right, centre and left. The left turning proceeds to the very pretty, leisurely settlement of **Ag Georgios** (14km), where are a number of derelict houses. Next along is **Ag Dimitrios** (15km), similar to Ag Georgios, if more so. Apart from the commonplace nature of these untidy, but attractive, crumbling villages, their noteworthiness lies in the fact that they are very nearly the only quintessential Greek island communities left on Kos. Need I say more! It is certainly rewarding to walk through and round them.

Straight on at Asfendiou village heads south, via a captivating, almost alpine hill road, with stream water running all the year round. Below the roadway, on a sharp right-hand bend, is the old communal bath and washing area, immediately prior to:

ZIA (14km from Kos) Billed as a 'typical Greek mountain village', that is the one thing it certainly is not. There are two clean, spruce tavernas, the *Cafe Olympia*, a trim tourist shop and some very smart houses. So what's Greek? There used to be a clean, public toilet block, but it has been closed, much to the chagrin of the owner of the *Cafe Olympia*. He claims his outside toilet is now used by " ...eight or nine" coach loads of people, everyday. Of course they don't always leave the place clean - so he rushes in, the moment someone comes out! If he finds they have left it in an unsatisfactory state, he hauls the offender back and makes them clean up... Not a pretty sight! Despite these, no doubt hectic moments, the cafe is quite pleasant. The proprietor brews an 'interesting' red coloured cinnamon drink (*kanela*), as well as a fruity type of ouzo made from grape skins. A Nes meh ghala costs 150drs. The 'excursion machine' has resulted in Zia becoming a 'plastic replica'. So, why not pop round to Ag Georgios and or Dimitrios, before they are dusted down, smartened up and become commuter villages for Kos Town business people?

From Asfendiou, a now paved road winds across the countryside to **Lagoudi** village, from whence a dusty, unmade, flinty track forks right, and then left for **Amaniou** village. The route emerges close by a small, rather mean church, on the right-hand side. Left at this T-junction, a surprisingly broad, impressive, metalled road climbs steeply to... , nowhere really. In fact, this thoroughfare peters out in a very attractive cleft, high up on the side of Mt Dikeos. To say nowhere is not strictly true, as the track continues to climb to **Old Pyli**. Once a deserted settlement, it is now more a pile of rubble, overlooked by the remains of a Byzantine castle.

The track from Amaniou to Pyli is practically impassable, not because of the appalling surface, or lack of track, but because a sentry-guarded, ramshackle military base straddles the road. If an intrepid traveller does get through to Pyli, a left turn at the village advances along a wide, unmetalled, flinty donkey track, over and round the mountainside, through a rather green but lunar landscape (if that is not a contradiction in terms), and back down to a coastal plain. Here this route proceeds along a straight, tree lined avenue to Kardamena. Ignore those maps that detail the route as being a major or even a minor road, but it is exciting!

Pyli is more usually reached from a turning off the main road, some 4km on from Zipari. For the more conventional route to Kardamena follow the route description from Antimachia village.

Returning to the main route, at Zipari, one kilometre further west is a side turning to right. This arrows past discos, several large, smart, Spanish style restaurants (the type of barn-like places that seem empty most of the time), and houses with *Rooms*, to:

TINGAKI (Tigaki) (11km from Kos) A very smart, reasonably pleasant, if tourist crowded, seaside resort. To the right of a central grove of trees, are some up-market hotels. These edge a broad, sandy beach, from which projects a metal framed quay. There is some kelp in evidence at the water's edge. On the far horizon, is Pserimos island which, at its closest, is about 3km distant.

There are eleven hotels, and assorted pensions. Representative of the affordable hotels are the: *Constantinos Ilios* (Class C, tel 29411), where en suite singles are priced at 2600/3500drs & doubles 3370/4500drs; and the *Paxinos* (Class C, tel 29306), weighing in with en suite singles at 3000/3500drs & doubles 3500/4500drs.

A newspaper shop, postcards, beach bars, and restaurants, in addition to a Cantina, beach showers, sun-beds and umbrellas, complement the   natural qualities of sand and sea. Once upon a time, Kos Town 'residents' were wont to power their way out here, for a day out. Nowadays similarly adventurous souls are just as likely to pass-by Tingaki 'residents' - going the other way. There are mopeds and bicycles for hire, one old favourite being 'Mikes For Bikes' - 'If you don't like to hike, see Mike for a bike'. The resort's coming of size is amply substantiated by the provision of a backshore OTE caravan.

A coast-hugging track stretches both east and west from Tingaki. To the east stretches along the coast to Cape Skandari (*See   Excursions to Kos Town Surrounds*). To the west edges a large area of saltings (Alikes), a few metres from the seashore, and a natural sanctuary for a variety of wildlife. Ornithologists will be delighted with the diversity of bird life, which takes in storks, rollers, bee-eaters, owls, kingfishers, falcons, bitterns, and more, much more, in addition to the turtles. It would be appreciated if only those interested in the survival of the species were to stroll along this way. The wildlife hereabouts is practically all that is left on the island, after the Greek hunters have finished blasting away! After a 4km hike, and beyond the Alikes, is the seaside village of:

MARMARI (15km from Kos) Here is the *Hotel Caravia* (Class A, tel 41291), to which independent travellers probably won't apply, as the en suite room rates are 4520/9050drs for a single & 7000/11010drs for a double. The burgeoning resort is usually reached from the Kos Town to Kefalos road.

Back at the main route, prior to reaching the side turning to Marmari, there is a 'division of the ways', alongside a cement works and pond. The left-hand choice leads to:

PYLI (15km from Kos) This small, mountain village is not to be mixed-up with Old Pyli which, confusingly, is some 4km away, through   Amaniou village. It is not an outstanding place, even if there is a   Byzantine church, built over an ancient tomb. Beyond the large, airy, 'middle of the settlement' square, surrounded by tourist shops and taverna bars, is a fork in the road. Straight on advances to a public toilet, as well as a freshwater spring, beside which is a bar/taverna. The latter establishment appears to be patronised by demented locals. The other choice at the fork leads to a part of the village, wherein the old houses were damaged by the 1930s earthquake. Continuingon leads to the outskirts of Kardamena. At first this is a pleasing country ramble, but it degenerates into something akin to a tank assault course. Apart from the effects of wind, rain and scorching sun, the deep fissures in the track are due to its continual use by heavy lorries, carting loads from a mountain quarry, to other points of the island. Breasting the crest of a rise, reveals   the 'delights' of the metropolis of Kardamena, and a large blob of a tourist complex. Despite the impossibilities of this 'highway', moped mounted

Germans and Scandinavians enjoy the bone-breaking, spine-juddering ride.

The main route soldiers on, past a small concentration of plastic (greenhouses) and fields containing a noticeable number of grazing cows. After 2km, a cross country road, to the right, cuts off a large corner to join the Antimachia to Mastichari road. The countryside, hereabouts, resembles a cross between moorland heath and army firing range, with the occasional windmill dotted about. A kilometre before Antimachia, a narrow, flinty path to the left, switchbacks up and down, by a military camp to:
The Castle of Antimachia Sometimes labelled *Soroko*. The second-rate donkey track does not quite make the fort's walls. The castle is a large, impressive structure, with sound battlements, dating back to the era of the Knights. The main gates are around to the left, but the fortress can be entered almost directly, by a flight of steps giving access through a small, doorless gateway. The interior is rather messy, but there is a small church in the centre of the edifice. Scattered about are remnants of dwellings. These possibly housed local inhabitants, when they had to flee from the death and destruction wrought by marauding pirates. The isolation and views are splendid.

ANTIMACHIA (25km from Kos) The village is almost at the centre of the island, and without doubt is the epicentre of a convoluted road system, with two large roundabouts, a bypass, and the airport close by. Almost sounds like home, doesn't it? Tourist maps are often rather inaccurate in this area, but the signposting is not too bad around the village.
Within Antimachia there are no signs, at all. The village is dusty and sprawling, with a large, working windmill still prominent, and was once famed for its melons. There is a filling station beside the bypass. The *Snackbar Fotis* serves inexpensive meals, and overlooks the airfield runway.

The first, large roundabout gives access to Antimachia and the road to the coastal port and resort of:
MASTICHARI (30km from Kos) Sections of the road are in a bad state, as they have been for many years. The rate of rather haphazard development is absolutely staggering, with even more massed apartment blocks waiting to be topped off. It is obvious that Mastichari will continue to grow, and grow, and grow (as has Kardamena). The village has already spread, and backed-up the approach road, along which are spaced any number of holiday company villas. Not only the 'High St', but the whole settlement is festooned with signs for *Rooms*. In fact, almost every other building appears to be advertising accommodation, and there are at least three not-so-costly hotels. These are the: *Arent* (Class C, tel 51167), where en suite singles cost 3500/4000drs & doubles 5300/5800drs; *Faenareti* (Class D, tel 51395) with double rooms en suite costing 3750drs: and *Zevgas* (Class E, tel 22577), where the en suite double room rate for one night is 2500/4000drs.
No self-respecting tourist resort would be able to hold its head-up, without a disco, or two, a few travel offices, a number of Rent A Car and scooter hire firms, some souvenir shops, and some mini-markets - and Mastichari does not let us down!
Where the access road bottoms-out, at the waterfront, it does so on the edge of a comparatively massive port quayside. To the right-hand is the *Mastihari Beach Hotel* (Class B pension, tel 51371). There are also a couple of busy, good value, quayside tavernas. To the right is the *Sunset*, whilst to the left is

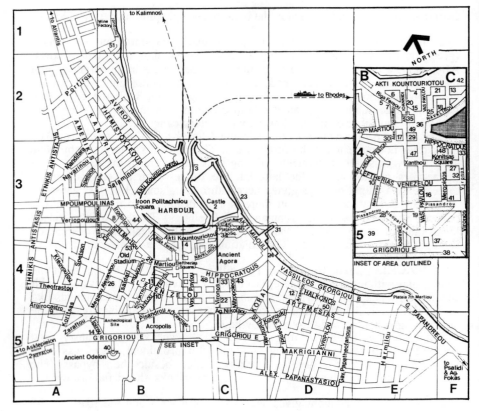

Tmr

1C2	Buses & Main Square	(Tmr)	= Town map reference
2B2	'V' Tours	(Fsw)	= Facing seawards
3C/D2	Kardamena Travel	(Sbo)	= Sea behind one
4D2	Maria Danelaki Rooms	(Fbqbo)	= Ferry-boat Quay behind one
5	Rooms To Let		
6C/D2/3	Restaurant Andreas		
7D2	Zacharoplasteion Silvia		
8E2	'Mammis House' Pub		
9D2/3	National Bank		
10A2	Scooter Hire Ilias		
11B2	Rent-A-Car Katerina		
12D2	Boutique		
13E2	Bread Shop		
14A2	Baker		
15C2	Butcher		
16C/D2	Supermarket		
17B2	Fruit Market		
18D/E2	Grocery Store Manolis		
19E1/2	George's Disco		
20C2	Municipal Tourist Office/OTE		
21B2	International Phone Shop		
22B/C2/3	Taxi Rank		
23D/E2	Aranghi Travel		
24E2	Post Office Van		

P = Periptero

Illustration 22 Kardamena

the *Kalia Kardia*. The latter's patio used to almost dip into the sea, but is now on the edge of the large, barrack-like square, adjacent to the port. The *Kalia Kardia* is constantly the recipient of praise in respect of its well-prepared, generously portioned food, and friendly, attentive staff. Another 'mega-plus' has to be the separate, clean toilets, complete with loo paper, soap, water and working hand drier.

Across the way, alongside the *Sunset* is the *Pizza Taverna*, followed by a scattering of bars, the port breakwater, and rows of apartment blocks. Beyond them, the seafront runs out on a boulderous foreshore, edged by a small, scrub and stunted-tree headland.

Around the 'corner', to the left (*Fsw*) is a beguiling, extremely broad, sandy beach, with a backshore shower, close to a scattered grove of trees. A number of restaurants edge the distant backshore and parasols 'march' across the beach. Some seaborne kelp dries out on the water's edge.

During the season, excursion boats run to Kalimnos and Pserimos islands. The **Apollo** connects three times a day to Kalimnos, the journey taking 30mins, at a cost of 500drs. The departure times are 0630, 1600, 1900hrs. The boat returns at 0900, 1800, 2300hrs. One of the purposes of this schedule is to ferry package holiday-makers, who have flown into Kos airport, over to their Kalimnos accommodation. The boat office telephone number is 51407.

From Mastichari, a donkey track can be attempted, which proceeds westwards along the coast, past the ruins of Ag Ioannis Church, to an interesting area of rather plastic-littered dunes and a sandy beach. This is absolutely deserted, with not even a beach-bar in sight, but may well be a prime site for the next Kos holiday hotel complex! The donkey track supposedly links round back to Antimachia, but...!

Returning to the main route, at Antimachia, the 1¼km bypass progresses to the second, large roundabout, around which are turnings to Antimachia village, the main Kefalos road, a spur off to the airport, and the road to:

KARDAMENA (27km from Kos) (Illus 22) The 5km drive to the village is unexceptional. Holiday-makers must not expect to unearth a small, attractive, fishing community and village, a quiet backwater steeped in a centuries-old way of life, pursuing country crafts, travelling by donkey and caique, each leisurely, rustic day extending into the next, as fisher-folk mend their nets and while away their spare time in the local kafeneion, their wives cleaning out sponges and gutting fish - as described in various brochures. If they do, they will be in for an extremely big shock. Even a trawl of the back streets fails to reveal the original core of the village. 'Kosta del Greco' has overlaid the place, which is no more than a lattice work of cocktail and music bars, gelateria ice-cream and soda pop counters, snackbars, pubs and clubs, interspersed by the occasional souvenir and tourist shop.

At Kardamena, the hardships of Aegean life have been reduced to deciding which 'happy-hour bar' to frequent, at which 'chips with everything' taverna to 'trough', or in which old English pub to drown one's sorrows. Even the pension accommodation has tiled bathrooms! Forgettable bar 'graffiti' recently recorded included 'Avoid a hangover, stay drunk' and 'I drink, I get drunk, I fall down, no problem'! The Brits rule. Okay?

As if this package demolition job were not sufficient, to the far left (*Fsw*) of the bay is a 'ginormous' complex, the *Norida Beach*, whilst not-so-far to the right is a holiday villa development - with street lights. Yes, street lights!

Arrival will normally be by road, and the buses decant their passengers on the Main Square (*Tmr* 1C2).

THE ACCOMMODATION & EATING OUT

The Accommodation Most of the hotels and pensions are block-booked, with wall-to-wall package tourists, but the buses are still met by owners of accommodation. There are some very pleasant, private rooms including:

Maria Danelaki (*Tmr* 4D2)   Tel 91474
Directions: To the right (*Fsw*) of the Main Square, in the street one back and parallel to the Esplanade.
   This is a nicely decorated, well-appointed house with en suite double rooms costing 4000drs. Maria does not arrive from Athens, until mid-June.

The *Pension Milos*, at the very end of the village, offers doubles for 4000drs. There are also **Rooms** at those locations marked *Tmr* 5 - *Tmr* 5D2 & 5E2.

The Eating Out There are a couple of reasonably priced snackbars and tavernas/restaurants including:
Andreas Restaurant (*Tmr* 6C/D2/3)
Directions: To the right (*Fsw*) off the Main Square, one block before the National Bank.
   Possibly the only establishment having any Greek atmosphere, the owners eschewing pandering to the overwhelm of tourists. Three 'Ya sou's' for them. Average prices for meals and drinks.

For breakfast, why not try:
Zacharoplasteion Silvia (*Tmr* 7D2)
Directions: One street back from the Esplanade, just beyond and the other side of the road to a boutique.
   Mama Silvia speaks some English and she and her husband, who doubles up as a barber next door, run a very friendly place with breakfast being served until late in the night. The 'breakfast bit' is because that is all their licence category allows. As they are in deadly rivalry with the establishment next door, they cannot stray from the culinary 'straight and narrow'.

THE A TO Z OF USEFUL INFORMATION

BANKS Apart from the **National Bank** (*Tmr* 9C/D2/3), a number of travel companies carry out exchange transactions.

BEACHES The beautiful, sandy beach is almost totally covered by sun umbrellas and beds, as well as every colour, hue, shade, size and state of the human body.

BICYCLE, SCOOTER & CAR HIRE Two wheels are well provided, including **Scooter Hire Ilias** (*Tmr* 10A2), and another firm at *Tmr* 10D2, whilst cars are available from **Rent-A-Car Katerina** (*Tmr* 11B2).

BOUTIQUE (*Tmr* 12D2) No resort would be complete without one.

BREAD SHOP The **Bread shop** (*Tmr* 13E2) is rather more central than the **Baker** (*Tmr* 14A2), at the north end of town, beside a scruffy little square.

BUSES Terminus on the Main Sq (*Tmr* 1C2). For timetables *See* Kos Town.

CHILD CARE Just to thrust home the point that this is no traditional Greek village fishing port, it is worth noting the presence of a baby-sitting agency, charging some 500drs per hour.

COMMERCIAL SHOPPING AREA A plentiful number of shops, of all shapes and sizes, including **Manolis Grocery store** (*Tmr* 18D/E2), **Angy's store** (next to Kardamena Travel - *Tmr* 3C/D2), which stocks drink, cigarettes and stamps, a **Butcher's** (*Tmr* 15C2), a **Supermarket** (*Tmr* 16C/D2), and a **Fruit Market** (*Tmr* 17B2).

DISCOS Include **George's** (*Tmr* 19E1/2), alongside the summer-dry river-bed.

FERRY-BOATS No ferry-boats. Excursion craft operate during the 'height of frenzy' summer months, voyaging to Nisiros island, subject to the sea state and weather conditions. *See* Nisiros island for details.

MEDICAL CARE Chemists & Pharmacies Only the basics are available from the supermarket (*Tmr* 16C/D2).

MUNICIPAL TOURIST OFFICE (*Tmr* 20C2) Conveniently sited beside the Main Sq. In business, during the summer months, Mon-Fri between 0800-1430hrs, and help in the search for accommodation.

OTE (*Tmr* 20C2) Open weekdays, at least for the same hours as the Municipal Tourist office, with which operation it shares the building. There is a metered international telephone in a Store (*Tmr* 21B2), which is available during normal shop hours.

POST OFFICE (*Tmr* 24E2) More a semi-permanent caravan, sited prior to the river bed, and open weekdays 0730-1400hrs.

SPORTS FACILITIES Almost every form of water sport known to man (and woman). Para-skiing has the added delight of not only being a participatory activity, but, on occasions, a (deadly) spectator sport. Rumour, only rumour, has hinted at certain unlicensed operators managing to smack this client into a hotel (which did not give way), 'used' that para-skier to cut a swathe through the massed beach umbrellas (with the result that both the participant and a sunbather expired), whilst yet other punter accidentally garroted a passer-by with the tow line! Who needs the Colosseum, Christians and lions? A suitably positioned Esplanade cocktail bar might allow 'a ringside' seat.

TAXIS (*Tmr* 22B/C2/3) Rank on the Main Square.

TELEPHONE NUMBERS & ADDRESSES

Doctor	Tel 91202
Municipal Tourist office (*Tmr* 20C2)	Tel 91139
Taxis (*Tmr* 22B/C2/3)	Tel 91465

TRAVEL AGENTS & TOUR OFFICES Numerous, with selected offices acting for this or that holiday companies. These offices include those of **V Tours** (*Tmr* 2B2), **Kardamena Travel & Exchange** (*Tmr* 3C/D2), and **Aranghi Travel/Rent-A-Car/Money Xchange** (*Tmr* 23D/E2). Most conduct foreign exchange transactions, whilst some have safe-deposit boxes.

Returning to the main route. From the Antimachia roundabout, the road to Kefalos is one of the most scenically boring it has been my misfortune to travel. The road narrows, initially between poor farmland, on the right, and heath, on the left, which countryside degenerates into scrubbly moorland, with the Army ever-present. Clumps of pines spasmodically edge the thoroughfare, their tortured shapes reflecting the wind-blown nature of the landscape. Prior to breasting the rise, high above Ag Stefanos, one or two lanes wander off to the left, down towards:

Paradise Beach (approx 35km from Kos) Also called 'Bubble Beach', due to the large amount of bubbles that filter-up through the clear blue seas, from the sea-bed. The steep, main track to the beach empties on to a series of serried, packed earth and hardcore surfaced car parks. Alongside the upper level is a restaurant, to fortify both the descending, and the ascending. The final approach is on foot. For once, the adjective paradise does not belie the long, lovely, crescent of sandy beach. It is only despoiled by sun umbrellas!

Where the main road crests a rise, above Ag Stefanos, is one of the most breathtaking and lovely views. Mt Latra rears up, in the middle distance, Nisiros island crouches darkly, on the far horizon, whilst on the immediate left is an incredible *Club Mediterranee* complex. Down below, close to the shore of the long, gently curving, sandy bay, is the islet of **Kastri**, topped off by a diminutive chapel, all set in a sparkling sea sprinkled with wind surfers. The development of this area has been rapid, and the area between the one-time hamlets of Ag Stefanos and Kamares is continuing to infill, with a rag-bag of hasty developments.

At **Ag Stefanos** there are sufficient accommodation possibilities, with *Rooms* at Maria Skevofilaka's costing 3000drs. Close to, the beach is rather disappointing, being more pebble than sand.

The **Kamares** waterfront has three tavernas, and the *Hotel Sydney* (Class D, tel 71286), where en suite singles cost 4970/5460drs & doubles 6680/7360drs. Beyond and around Kamares are* a filling station, many *Rooms* and a number of hotels. Kefalos settlement can be seen peeping over a towering hillside and, to the right, is a conspicuous, still functioning windmill.

In this case, is it are? No prizes, but I will send a signed photocopy of the flyleaf of Fowler/Partridge to the first answer, I adjudge the most amusing. That is unless I hear from Frank Delaney. Thinking about that, and with no disrespect to his august self, I would rather not have him read any of my books. It would only result in damning thunder-bolts of literary indictment, in respect of that which I laughingly refer to as prose. Without these thoroughly deserved rebukes, I would be able to continue to scribble, in my flawed, twilight world of naive illiteracy.

A very steep ascent and series of tight hairpin bends indicates the final approach to:

KEFALOS (40km from Kos) An appealing, hill-top village, which has greatly enlarged over recent years, but has yet to be totally ruined by the depredations of tourism. From a tight centre, it spreads out into dusty, sprawling surrounds. The to-be-recommended, traditional, carnation bedecked and brightly coloured *Kali Kardia Taverna* is to the right of the High St. A lunchtime meal here of 1 souvlaki, a Greek salad, and a beer costs about a 1000drs a head.

From Kefalos, a number of dirt tracks radiate out. These include an unmade 4km lane, past the aforementioned windmill, to **Limonas**, a small, man-made harbour with a tiny stretch of sand.

A 7/8km long road to **Ag Ioannis**, and the southern-tip of the island, switchbacks up, and up, and up, and then down, only to go up again. A section of the journey is through a fire devasted area that has left a swathe of blackened, petrified trees marching along the steep hillside. The views are truly amazing with the land falling away, comparatively gently, over a boulderous landscape to the coastline far below.

About 2km along the Ag Ioannis road, and a 6km stretch of good track branches off to the right, to the coast at **Ag Theologos**. Here is a golden, fine sand beach, often near deserted. At the top of the final descent to the shore is a rather strange, rudimentary, somewhat expensive taverna, run by a smart young man.

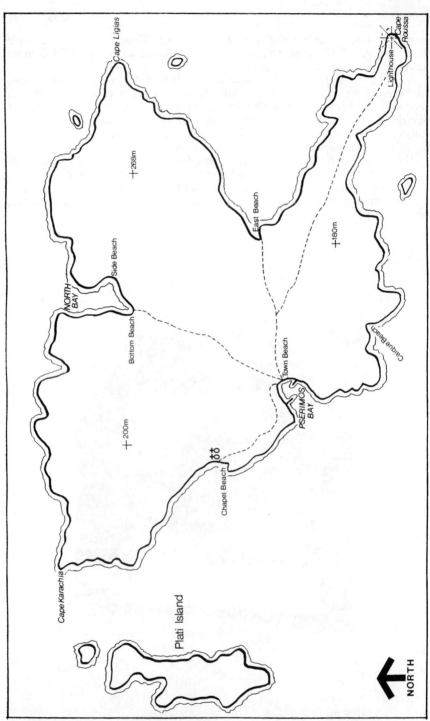

Illustration 23 Pserimos island

11 PSERIMOS ✻✻
Dodecanese Islands

FIRST IMPRESSIONS Fly-infested tavernas; goat-infested landscape; plastic-beaches; gun-toting hunters (in season).

LOCAL RELIGIOUS HOLIDAYS & FESTIVALS 14/15th Aug - a popular monastic and religious festival, which overwhelms the island's sparse facilities. Don't plan to make a visit either side of these dates.

VITAL STATISTICS Area 10sq km; population some 60.

GENERAL The large inter-island ferries plough past Pserimos. On the other hand, Pserimos is regularly serviced by a number of short haul excursion boats, from Kos Town and Mastichari (Kos), as well as Kalimnos island. The supposed tranquillity of the island is disturbed by the flood and ebb of day-trip tourists. Outside of these twice daily intrusions, the inhabitants and few 'long-stay' tourists relapse into a placid existence.

The only settlement, a collection of low-rise buildings, borders the backshore of the splendid, sandy beach at the bottom of Pserimos Bay - the 'Town Beach'. In strict contrast, the hamlet's surrounds are gloriously squalid. A couple of three-wheelers cart the supplies and rubbish about.

Visitors must not expect to find a bank, Post Office, or shops, although the lady next door to the kafeneion does stock a few jars of jam, some washing-up liquid, and other odds and ends, but her doors are usually closed. All provisions, including bread, are ferried in from Kalimnos island. Pserimos is desperately water-short, and the locals can be seen queuing-up at the communal standpipe, opposite the *Kafeneion O Manolas*, to fill the 'family-bucket', with the dribble that emanates from the tap.

The Town Beach is fine, golden sand, and is kept clean.

ARRIVAL BY EXCURSION BOAT Arrive from about 0930hrs onwards, and depart no later than 1600hrs. The sea voyages from Kos take 30/45 mins and cost about 2000drs, for the round-trip.

The 'scheduled', daily link with the outside world is the **FB Pserimos Express**, which arrives one hour after leaving Kalimnos. The boat is detailed as departing at 1600hrs, BUT this can be variable, sometimes being 1500hrs, and on other occasions being 1530hrs. The round trip costs 1000drs.

THE ACCOMMODATION & EATING OUT The various backshore enterprises may advertise involvement in the provision of both lodgings and victualling. Despite which, each business tends to concentrate on one or other of the activities. Rather than engage in a price-war, the proprietors gently 'rubbish' their competitor's services and supplies. For instance, one may hint of another's accommodation, that it is fine, but "...there is the possibility of electric shocks, whilst in the douche"! Mmmh.

Amongst the available are:

Pension/Taverna Niki-Ross Close to the boat-jetty, this establishment is fairly new. The owners are Niki and Ross. A double en suite bedroom costs about 3000/3500drs a night. The taverna 'bit' appears to be rather dormant.

Restaurant Andreas Also known as the *Snak Bar Golden Beash* (*sic*). Has red plastic chairs, and being the first eaterie, after disembarking from a boat, is 'day-tripper' popular. The smiley, gold-toothed mama is an active schlepper, as is her competitor at the purple seated *Kalo Kardia*, next door. Andreas' meals are large helpings and tasty. A meal, for two, of a Greek salad, 1 stuffed tomatoes, 1 lamb stew, a small bottle of retsina, a soda, 2 Greek coffees, 2 ouzos, bread & service, cost about 2800drs. A Coke and small Amstel costs 450drs.

Rooms/Taverna Kalo Kardia The friendly lady is not so 'pushy' as her 'oppo', and her son has reasonably good English. Prices for meals and bedrooms are in line with the others 'on the beach'.

Estiatorio/Rooms Pserimou Unfortunately, the Zorba-like Kapitan, Yannis, and his long-suffering wife, assisted by various hangers-on, appear to have handed over the management to an inquisitive Brit, from the north of England. He settles in for the summer months and has a fellow countryman as a helper. Now not so well patronised, except for flies and cats. The latter provide some entertainment whilst engaged in acrobatic, two-pawed swipes at the flies. Meals are (just) passable, with a lunchtime repast of 2 Greek salads, 1 tzatziki, beans & 2 tins of Amstel, costing 1600drs.
   Yannis made a name for the establishment by serving freshly caught fish, but apparently no more. He would also caique folk to Mastichari, on the north coast of Kos island.

Kafeneion O Manolas A rather 'locals-only' gathering place, especially popular with hunters who flock here to compare 'bags'.

Cafe-bar Themis They have the sun-bed and umbrella concession, and charge 350drs for a pair per day. The studiously serious daughter of the house is efficient and speaks clear school-learnt English. Her friendly mama and papa clean and cook, and tend to remain in the background, as their grasp of English is limited, and they are rather shy.

Pension/Taverna Tripolitis The *Tripolitis* is owned by Mr Saroukos, who organises very acceptable sustenance and simple rooms, and is sited close to the sea's edge.

Beach Walks The barren, dry, parched, scrubbly interior, and dusty, stony, rough tracks are not conducive to other than 'perspiring about' the settlement. Those readers who are absolutely determined to engage in these activities, may find the following route march descriptions of some interest. And the intrepid must not consider that anything is being hidden away, concealed from view as it were. Apart from the uninspiring countryside, the most common sights are goats, and hunters.
   Most of the island's other beaches are dirty shingle shores, badly polluted with seaborne rubbish and plastic, surrounded by rugged landscapes. Additionally, there is some evidence of 'wild camping'. They are visited by yachts, speed boats and trip boats, the latter usually accompanied by wafts of very loud pop music. They all have 'sweet water' wells for grazing animals.

East Beach About 35mins. Select the lane alongside the last taverna to the right (*Sbo*), and follow it, keeping the olive grove and church on the left.

Edge the grove around to the left, beyond which choose the path towards the saddle of the hill, and a burnt tree. The beach is down below.

North Bay About 30mins. From alongside the village water tap and *Estiatorio Pserimou*, take the 'road' north-east of the settlement, keeping left at the first fork, past a Boy Scouts campsite and a gate beyond. The next ½km threads through, and by, coops, huts, pens and stys, as well as beehives. It is interesting to observe the imaginative use to which the inhabitants put old, unwanted taverna chairs. They are positioned as stone wall topping, in an effort to goat-proof the enclosures. Presumably they are inedible, even to a goat, and have been usurped by the modern red and plastic jobs that now grace the appropriate tavernas, 'back in town'. Other non-biodegradable by-products are put to good use, with plastic beer crates being pressed into service as chicken hutches.

The 'formal' track terminates alongside the island rubbish tip. At a fork, the right-hand path ascends to a saddle of land between two hills, to descend to the distant bay. There is a small pier, and a couple of wells. Sadly this shore is almost completely covered in rubbish. Round to the right (*Fsw*), continuing along what remains of the path, advances to a less polluted, if difficult to access beach, on the east side of North Bay.

Chapel Beach About 35mins. Follow the last track from the west side of the Town Beach. Keeping a square blue hut to the left, stride along the enclosure walls, which is 'almost' paved for 200m. The path follows the contour of a hill, to eventually drop on to the beach backshore. The chapels can be seen, one hanging on to a cliff edge. The large caves at the south end are 'home' to goats and sheep, which dash about 'willy-nilly', when people approach. In addition to a pair of water wells, there are the foundations of some three buildings. This is an excellent location at which to collect pumice stones.

Caique Beach A small beach, only accessible by boat. One of the fishermen can be 'flagged down', after negotiations have established a fee basis.

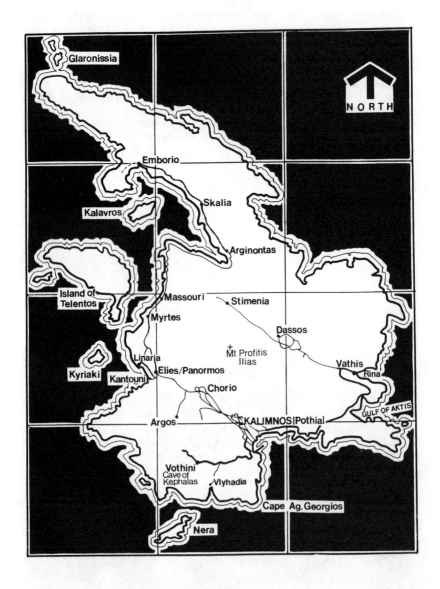

Illustration 24 Kalimnos island

13 KALIMNOS (Kalymnos, Calymnos) *****
Dodecanese Islands

FIRST IMPRESSIONS Large port town; barren mountains; azure blue sea; men, & more men; hunting dogs; mopeds, scooters & motorbikes.

SPECIALITIES Sponges; divers; honey.

LOCAL RELIGIOUS HOLIDAYS & FESTIVALS incl: 10th-20th April - Blessing fishing boats - Kalimnos Town; 27th July - Festival Ag Panteleimon.

VITAL STATISTICS Tel prefix 0243. The island is up to 21km long & 13km wide. Most of the 13,000 population live in or around the capital.

HISTORY Much as Kos.

GENERAL Geographically a large island. Due to the mountainous nature, and thus inaccessibility of much of the hinterland, Kalimnos appears to be smaller than it is... A bit Irish, I know.

Guide books, only a few years old, chatter on about the apparent poverty, the crippling effect of sponge diving, the unpreparedness of the island for tourism, the comparative peace and quiet, and more...

This is outdated twaddle. What is without doubt, is that the Kalimniots possess enterprise, ingenuity and adaptability. Qualities that stood them in good stead, during a period when the whole emphasis and thrust of their endeavours had to be altered. With the decline, and eventual collapse of the sponge diving industry, it was necessary to re-focus and find other avenues of business, work and wealth. It was also essential to face-up to the inevitable facts of a rapidly declining, and increasingly aged population. Fortunately, they did not idly resort (resort..., oh dear) to tourism, lying back and thinking of drachmae, as have so many other Aegean islanders, when faced with a similar problem. No, they diversified.

Naturally, tourism was taken on board, but as one of a number of props to the island's economy, and not as the sole source of income. Furthermore, the holiday industry was hived off, over on the west coast. Where, in most cases, emigration has proved a problem, the Kalimniots turned it to their advantage. Depopulation has not been allowed to break the backbone of enterprise and community spirit. Rather, the migrants have been treated as a profitable source of inward investment. The numbers who departed for the Antipodes have been sufficient to contribute a significant amount of invisible earnings to the island's exchequer, but not so many as to empty the place. It has to be admitted that there is a popular, if apocryphal, belief that there are more Kalimniots in Tasmania, than back at home. In addition, investment was made in building the renowned and eponymous **FB Nissos Kalymnos**, as it has been in fish farming. The evidence of the latter farms can be observed by the number of bulldozed tracks down to small coves, scattered around the island coastline. That is the reason for the presence of so many men, young and old, in addition to the prevailing ambiance of a thriving society.

One quality Kalimnos town does not have is peace and quiet, as the capital buzzes, and the air is rent by the scream of seemingly thousands of high powered, explosively noisy motorbikes. They appear to be everywhere, and no side-street can be considered safe from their intrusion, at any time of day

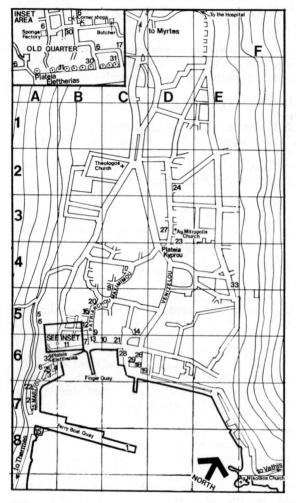

(Tmr)   = Town map reference
(Fsw)   = Facing seawards
(Sbo)   = Sea behind one
(Fbqbo) = Ferry-boat Quay behind one

Illustration 25 Kalimnos (Pothia) Port & Town

or night. There is supposed to be a ban on the night-time auditory assault.

I consider the island's hills rather too bare to be beautiful, except during the spring explosion of flowers, but individual areas are outstandingly lovely, and verdant. As for other islands, in this 'neck of the woods', early September may well experience persistently strong winds, far in excess of the Meltemi.

It is said that during the Italian occupation, the inhabitants painted their houses in the blue and white colours of the Greek flag. The idea was to keep alive their nationalistic aspirations, whilst at the same time infuriating their unwanted overlords. Even today a few island houses can still be seen with this colour scheme, as they can on the island of Karpathos. Stelios must be the island's saint's name, as is Spiros on Corfu island.

KALIMNOS (Pothia): capital town & port (Illus 25) Much larger, livelier and noisier than might be imagined. The quayside absolutely throbs at night, but with little evidence of tourism. In fact, much of old Kalimnos remains unsullied, with many of the traditional buildings and narrow lanes retained, and intact. It isn't a particularly attractive town, but is typically Greek, and a much more engaging place at which to stay, than the west coast tourist villages of, for instance, Kantouni, Myrtes or Massouri.

ARRIVAL BY FERRY Berth at the end of the large quay (*Tmr* 1C8). Arrivals have to walk down the long pier, before turning right towards the town. Taxis line-up, but few owners of accommodation meet 'the dockings'.

THE ACCOMMODATION & EATING OUT
The Accommodation Many of the private house *Rooms* are grouped in a small, maze-like area behind Plateia Eleftherias. The Esplanade hotels are rather hidden away behind the profuse cover of the roadside trees. As many of their signs are poorly illuminated, it is necessary to keep a sharp eye open.

The first accommodation possibilities, from the bottom of the Ferry-boat Quay, are almost immediately across 25th Martiou St, behind the central row of small garden plots dividing the road. They are to the right, and include *Rooms* (*Tmr* 2A7), three buildings south of the *Sirocco Bar* (*Tmr* 22A6/7). The name is obliterated by weather and time, even if the board is still attached to the modern verandah, of a building painted in an unattractive, matt brown wash, and where a double sharing the bathroom costs 2500/3000drs. Next door is another *Rooms*.

Hotel Olympic (*Tmr* 4A/B6) (Class C) Eleftherias Sq   Tel 28801
Directions: Right (*Fbqbo*) along the Esplanade, and on the corner of one of the noisiest positions in town.

The island's main hotel, and is clean and modern. All rooms have an en suite bathroom, with singles priced at 3250/4750drs & doubles 4200/6250drs.

Rather hidden away, behind the *Olympic*, is the:
Pension Patmos (*Tmr* 3A/B6/7)   Tel 29219
Directions: As above.

Simple, en suite double rooms, in quieter accommodation than the *Olympic* costs 3000/4000drs.

This area is speckled with signs for *Rooms*. Beyond the *Olympic*, the quay turns sharp right, at Eleftherias Sq, behind which is a tangle of extremely noisy lanes with *Rooms* (*Tmr* 6).

Hotel Thermae (*Tmr* 7B5/6) (Class C)   Tel 29425
Directions: From Plateia Eleftherias, continue east along the Esplanade (*Away from the Ferry-boat Quay*). The *Thermae* is above the *Kaiki Bar*.
An extremely clamorous location, and 'intelligence' received rather 'slags' the standards of cleanliness, the fixtures and fittings, as well as the lack of space. Double rooms, with en suite bathroom, cost 3000/4000drs.

Beyond the *Thermae*, is the lateral side-street of Patriarchou Maximimou, on to which turn left, and then left again into the 'maze' of 'Old Quarter' lanes. Beyond the Olympic office is the blue painted   building of the Sponge Treatment Factory (Inset).

Greek House   Tel 23752
Directions: As above, and, in front of the sponge factory, turn right. The *House* is 50m on and on the left, alongside a corner. There is a round sign.
The landlady speaks little English. Basic single rooms sharing the bathroom cost 1500drs a night & doubles 2500drs. At the top of the building are a pair of doubles, with mini en suite bathrooms, sharing a kitchen, with a fridge, and a large terrace, which cost 3000drs.

Back at the sponge factory, follow the signs for the Hotel Panorama, which lead past the:
Pension Katerina (Inset)   Tel 22186
Directions: As above.
A double, with self-catering facilities, costs 2500/3000drs. The landlady, Katerina Smaliou lives next door, and her establishment is recommended.

Immediately beyond *Pension Katerina*, pointers indicate the:
Hotel Panorama (*Tmr* 5A5) (Class C)   Tel 23138
Directions: As above.
The situation allows a great view out over the town, as well as a restricted glimpse of the sea. It is a much quieter and calmer situation than down on the 'jungle of the Esplanade'. A family run,   modern hotel, with small but clean, well furnished en suite bedrooms, each with a balcony. The bedrooms are cleaned daily, all the family speak good English, two 'ground floor' balconies are utilised as communal areas, where breakfast is taken and socialising takes place. A double costs 3000/4000drs, with a reasonable discount for guests staying a week or more. Breakfast is charged 500drs a head.

Beside Patriarchou Maximimou St are several hotels including the:
Hotel Evanic (*Tmr* 8B/C4/5) (Class C) P. Maximimou   Tel 22057
Directions: On the left (*Sbo*) beside a clamorous street.
All bedrooms are en suite, a single priced at 3160drs & doubles 4730drs.

At the more tranquil, far east end of the Esplanade, beyond the Ag Nikolaos Church (*Tmr* E/F8), is the brand new *Pension Panorama*.

The Eating Out There are dozens of cafe-bars lining the Esplanade, from Plateia Eleftherias (*Tmr* A/B6) to the Town police (*Tmr* 28C6) building. The waiters lie in wait to snare day-trippers (150drs for a Nes, 350drs for an ice cream, and a staggering 355drs for a can of Amstel). During the evening most of the Pothia males visit these coffee bars. It can be an unnerving experience for the ladies, as the local chaps tend to oggle tourist women.

Of the waterfront options, perhaps one of the best is the:
Cafeteria-bar Gove (*Tmr* 11B6)
Directions: Adjacent to Plateia Eleftherias, close to a bus stop, and with red chairs and small tables.
A most enjoyable breakfast of tea, coffee, a roll with butter & jam, and a large portion of delicious yoghurt, cost 800drs.

Whilst hereabouts, beside a corner, around the back of the *Hotel Olympic* (*Tmr* 4A/B6) is the:
Do Re Me Taverna
Directions: As above.
Admittedly not a traditional Hellenic eatery, but the food is good and the portions large. The owners speak excellent English. A meal for two of spaghetti bolognese, moussaka, 2 frappe coffees, ½ litre retsina, bread & service, cost about 2500drs.

In the main, the better waterfront eateries are beside the Esplanade, east of the Market (*Tmr* 19C/D6). By better, I mean cheaper, more traditional tavernas. Of these, the following are recommended:
Restaurant E Proikas (The Terrace) (*Tmr* C/D6)
Directions: Follow the directions of the faded signs. It is in an alley on the left side of the street opposite the church.
An excellent establishment, serving first rate food, from a tiny kitchen, cooked by a mama, called Maria, who is aided by friends. Diners can sit outside, on a large patio, beneath bamboo vines, or at the limited seating indoors. The place gets packed with local folk, and neighbours drop-by, in the evenings, to watch Greek TV 'soaps'. Service, not surprisingly, tends to deteriorate at about this time! A huge selection of pre-cooked dishes, enormous portions, reasonable quality and price, is matched by good, friendly service. A meal, for two, of 1 meat balls in avgolemono sauce, 1 lamb stew in tomato sauce with potatoes, 1 pea & meat pilaf, 2 x ½kg bottles retsina, 1 bottle of soda, bread & service, costs some 2500drs.

Towards the far, east end of the Esplanade is the **Psarotaverna Kampourakis**, flanked by two other popular establishments. Delicious mezes, and specialising in fresh fish. A tasty meal, for two, of a Greek salad, a tzatziki, a vlita, a souvlakia swordfish, a plate of octopus, a plate of roca (a hot raw herb), retsina, bread & service, cost 3000drs.

There are a number of greasy, but inexpensive, 'youth popular' souvlaki stalls spaced about the town.

THE A TO Z OF USEFUL INFORMATION
AIRLINE OFFICE (*Tmr* 12B5/6) The office is beside the narrow lane that branches   off   Patriarchou   Maximimou   St.   Open   Mon-Sat   between 0900-1600hrs. As yet there isn't an airport, but its completion is a continual 'threat'. The new runway can be seen on high ground above Kantouni, but the locals only shake their heads when the 1993 inaugeration date is mentioned.

BANKS The **National Bank** (*Tmr* 13B/C5/6) is situated beside the Esplanade, the **Commercial Bank** (*Tmr* 9B/C5/6) is on the right   (*Sbo*) of Patriarchou Maximimou St, and the **Ionian Bank** (*Tmr* 14C5/6) is close to the junction of the Esplanade and Venizelou St.

BEACHES A one and a half kilometre walk south from the harbour, along the Thermes road, leads to a small pebbly beach.

BICYCLE, SCOOTER & CAR HIRE There are a number of moped and scooter hire establishments. They are scattered around the side-streets, in the area behind Plateia Eleftherias (*Tmr* 30 Inset), as well as beside the Esplanade. These Esplanade proprietors, typified by the chap next door to The Marinos Food Centre (*Tmr* 21C5/6), tend to be a little sharp. They have a habit of quoting one rate, and attempting to charge another. The average daily rates start at about 1500drs. Another sleight-of-hand is for the firm's newest units to be put on display, but hirers are handed an older, clapped out version.

Scooter Hire Vassilis (*Tmr* 16B5)
Directions: On the left of Patriarchou Maximimou St, beyond the Commercial Bank, and on the other side of the street.
   One of the 'best in town'. A 2 seat moped costs 1500drs a day. Car hire has to be arranged through the travel agents. It is not unusual to see families of up to five astride a Vespa, or the hunting dogs draped in and overhanging pillion saddle boxes, or an admix of family and dogs.

BREAD SHOPS One **Baker** is in the side-street alongside, and prior to, the Ionian Bank (*Tmr* 14C5/6), with another (Inset *Tmr* 17) in the maze of streets behind Eleftherias Sq.

BUSES The service is quite extensive. The main terminus, or 'stasi' (*Tmr* 18C/D6) is behind the Market, but there are others, one beside the Esplanade, and another in Venizelou St. Conveniently, the timetables are pinned-up adjacent to the bus stop posts.

Bus timetable (Mid-season)
Kalimnos Town to Massouri, via Kantouni, Elies & Myrtes
Daily   0700 & then every 2 hours to 2100hrs
Return journey
Daily   0750 & then every 2 hours to 1950, 2130hrs.
One-way fare 100drs.
Kalimnos Town to Emborio, via Kantouni, Elies, Myrtes & Massouri
Mon/Wed/Fri   0800, 1600hrs
Return journey
Mon/Wed/Fri   0900, 1700hrs.
One-way fare 120drs.
Kalimnos Town to Vathis
Mon-Sat   0630, 1330, 1730hrs
Sun   0730, 1330, 1700hrs
Return journey
Daily   'Immediate'
One-way fare 200drs.

NOTE The schedules change from week to week, let alone year to year.

CINEMAS One.

COMMERCIAL SHOPPING AREA Labelled the 'City Hall' on the official map (well, actually 'Hity' Hall), the building is almost entirely taken up by the Market (*Tmr* 19C/D6). The stalls inside sell fruit, vegetables and meat.

Both sides of the Esplanade, in an easterly direction, are lined with trucks and stalls selling fish, flowers, and other offerings. At the other end of town (and the spectrum), towards Plateia Eleftherias, there is a frail old man, with his bicycle wheeled trolley, selling sunflower seeds. This reminds me of the island practice, for men and boys to wander round the bars, tavernas and restaurants selling bags of (overpriced) peanuts.

Most of the big stores and various shops are grouped along Venizelou St, and Plateia Kyprou. Beside Patriarchou Maximimou St are the **The Right Price Supermarket**, at No 2, in the area of the Commercial Bank (*Tmr* 9B/C5/6), and a **Supermarket** (*Tmr* 20B/C4/5). Beside the Esplanade is a most unusual, old-fashioned store, the **Marinos Food Centre** (*Tmr* 21C5/6). Despite its narrow front, it is surprisingly deep, once inside, with apparently everything for sale, including honey and yoghurt.

DISCOS Most of the action is at the seaside resorts, on the west coast.

FERRY-BOATS Dock at the top of the large quay (*Tmr* 1C8).
Ferry-boat timetable (Mid-season)

Day	Departure time	Ferry-boat	Ports/Islands of Call
Daily	0630hrs	Olimpios Apollon	Mastichari(Kos).
	0930hrs	Pserimos Express*	Pserimos.
	1530hrs	Olimpios Apollon	Mastichari(Kos).
	1930hrs	Olimpios Apollon	Mastichari(Kos).
Mon	0130hrs	Ialyssos/Kamiros	Kos, Rhodes.
	0600hrs	Nissos Kalymnos	Kos, Nisiros, Tilos, Simi, Rhodes, Kastellorizo.
	2245hrs	Ag Rafael	Kos, Rhodes.
Tue	0130hrs	Ialyssos/Kamiros	Kos, Rhodes.
	0300hrs	Ionian Sun	Kos, Rhodes.
	1200hrs	Ag Rafael	Leros, Patmos, Samos, Chios, Lesbos, Limnos, Kavala(M).
	1730hrs	Ialyssos/Kamiros	Leros, Patmos, Piraeus(M).
	1800hrs	Ionian Sun	Astipalaia, Tinos, Mykonos, Andros, Rafina(M).
Wed	0130hrs	Ialyssos/Kamiros	Kos, Rhodes.
	0730hrs	N. Kalymnos	Leros, Lipsos, Patmos, Angathonisi, Samos, Angathonisi, Patmos, Lipsos, Leros, Kalimnos.
	1730hrs	Ialyssos/Kamiros	Leros, Patmos, Piraeus(M).
Thur	0010hrs	Alceos	Kos, Rhodes.
	0130hrs	Ialyssos/Kamiros	Kos, Rhodes.
	0600hrs	N. Kalymnos	Astipalaia.
	1730hrs	Ialyssos/Kamiros	Leros, Patmos, Piraeus(M).
Fri	0130hrs	Ialyssos/Kamiros	Kos, Rhodes.
	0600hrs	N.Kalymnos	Kos, Nisiros, Tilos, Rhodes, Kastellorizo, Rhodes.
	1730hrs	Ialyssos/Kamiros	Leros, Patmos, Piraeus(M).
Sat	0130hrs	Ialyssos/Kamiros	Kos, Rhodes.
	0320hrs	Ionian Sun	Kos, Rhodes.
	1730hrs	Ialyssos/Kamiros	Leros, Patmos, Piraeus(M).
	1815hrs	Ionian Sun	Astipalaia, Mykonos, Tinos, Andros, Rafina(M).
Sun	0645hrs	N. Kalymnos	Leros, Lipsos, Patmos, Angathonisi, Samos, Angathonisi, Patmos, Lipsos, Leros, Kalimnos.
	1730hrs	Ialyssos/Kamiros	Leros, Patmos, Piraeus(M).

*The **FB Pserimos** Express departs daily, from in front of the *Olympic* (*Tmr* 4A/B6), arriving back at 1700hrs. The hour each way voyage costs a 1000drs return.

There are excursions every day, in the summer months, to Pserimos, and several days a week to Leros, Patmos and Kos. The excursion craft berth in the area of the quayside across from the *Olympic*. *See* Travel Agents & ...

Kalimnos Tours offers the following:
Turkey Sat/Sun EB Pride of Kalymnos Depart 0700hrs; return 2030hrs.
Leros   Sat EB Soula Depart (from Myrtes) 0900hrs; returns 1730hrs.
Patmos Tue EB Pride of Kalymnos Depart 0845hrs; returns 1830hrs.

Hydrofoil timetable
Daily   0645hrs   Kos
This craft returns from Kos, departing at 2015hrs.

FERRY-BOAT TICKET OFFICES For the best information make enquiries of one of the Travel Agents. To be recommended are: **DANE** (*Tmr* 32A6), which is rather concealed by the awnings of an adjacent kafeneion; and **Kalimnos Tours** (Tel 22036), closer to the Ferry-boat Quay. They open weekdays 0830-1300 & 1700-2030hrs. In the height of summer months, they open Saturday mornings, and Sundays in the busiest period.

HAIRDRESSERS The largest Ladies Hairdresser (*Tmr* 23D3/4) is the far side of Kyprou Sq, and on the right. Kourions, or men's barbers, are plentiful, especially in the streets one back from the Esplanade.

LAUNDRY There is a **Dry Cleaners** beyond Plateia Kyprou (*Tmr* D3/4).

MEDICAL CARE
Chemists & Pharmacies Plentiful, with three or four grouped together besideVenizelou St, in the area of the Ionian Bank (*Tmr* 14C5/6).
Dentist/Doctor Opposite each other, either side of Patriarchou Maximimou St.
Hospital A large facility alongside the Elies/Myrtes road, about 500m in the direction of Chorio.

NTOG (*Tmr* 25A6) More a Municipal Information shack, a tiny, chapel-like building, at the end of a neat path, set in a very small park, alongside the *Hotel Olympic*. On the edge of this particular garden there is a statue of a 'seated fellow' holding a trident. The staff speak excellent English and are very keen to help. They can advise in respect of the various transport schedules and timetables, as well as accommodation, in addition to the more usual hand-outs. The doors are open Mon-Fri 0830-1300 & 1500-2000hrs.

OTE (*Tmr* 24D2/3) The office is north of Plateia Kyprou, beyond Ag Mitropolis Church, and opens daily between 0730-2200hrs.

PETROL There are many filling stations situated around Plateia Kyprou, and beside the road to Chorio.

PLACES & EVENTS OF INTEREST
Ag Christos Church (*Tmr* 26C6) Sited alongside an imposing square, edged by a long municipal building, occupied by the Police and Customs offices,and a clock tower. This large church is not only strikingly beautiful, but has

attracted the interest of native and expatriate Greeks artists, mainly originating from Kalimnos, who have freely given of their time and energy to redecorate and refurbish the internal decorations and icons.

Municipal Museum (*Tmr* 33E4/5) Housed in the mansion of a former, wealthy Kalimniot family. A most noteworthy feature is the restored drawing room. Open Tue-Sun 0800-1400hrs. Admission is free.

Sponge Factory (Inset) The blue painted factory is in the maze of lanes spreading out behind Plateia Eleftherias, and is the last remaining example of a one-time thriving industry. The owner, Mr Gourlas, can converse in English and allows *ad hoc* tours, during which the processes of treating the sponges are explained. He is happiest if, those privileged to be shown round, purchase a keepsake, which is fair enough. A small sponge costs about 500drs.

Sponge Divers During the height of summer months, excursion boat tourists are treated to a charade in which a diver dons some fairly tatty looking diving gear, whilst standing on a stage, or more correctly the stern of a boat. In days of yore, in fact well into the 20thC, the divers achieved the depths necessary to harvest the crop, by tucking flat stones beneath their arms. Although most island men became divers, the profession was hazardous and often resulted in premature aging and crippling injuries.

Before treatment, the sponges are living, multi-cellular aquatic animals feeding by filtering sea-water through their many pores. Originally they could be picked up in the shallows, but hundreds of years of 'farming' forced the sponge divers deeper and deeper, and further and further afield. Eventually it became commonplace for the fleets to depart for the North African coast, towards the end of April, not to return until late in the summer. This routine led to feast days marking the departure and return of the fleet, a tradition which remains rooted in the festival celebrations still held today, and absorbed into the yearly pattern of life.

POLICE
Port (*Tmr* 15A7/8) Situated at the bottom of the Ferry-boat Quay.
Town (*Tmr* 28C6) Not to be bothered with tourist activity/enquiries.

POST OFFICE (*Tmr* 27D3) Positioned opposite Ag Mitropolis Church. Open weekdays between 0730-1400hrs.

TAXIS Taxis double-up as small mini-buses, stopping where and when hailed. There is a rank on the corner of the quay, almost opposite the *Hotel Olympic* (*Tmr* 4A/B6), and another, the main one, beside Plateia Kyprou (*Tmr* D3/4). This latter has a taxi office and a listed fare schedule. A sample is that to Myrtes, which costs 750drs.

TELEPHONE NUMBERS & ADDRESSES

Airline office (*Tmr* 12B5/6)	Tel 29265
Hospital	Tel 28851
Municipal Tourist office (*Tmr* 25A6)	Tel 23140
Police, Town (*Tmr* 28C6)	Tel 22100
Port police (*Tmr* 15A7/8)	Tel 29304
Taxi rank	Tel 28989

TRAVEL AGENTS & TOUR OFFICES Stelios Tours (*Tmr* 7B5/6, tel 28771) is beside the *Hotel Thermea*, and opens weekdays 0830-1300 & 1700-2030hrs, out of the busy summer months. During the summer months, they open Saturday mornings, and in the height of season activity they also open Sundays. One or three offices are gathered   together in the *Olympic Hotel* (*Tmr* 4A/B6) area of Plateia Eleftherias. *See* Ferry-boat Ticket Offices.

A popular, local'ish boat trip is to the **Caves of Kephalas** (or   Vothini). They are where the mythological god Zeus took sanctuary. The boats depart at 0930hrs for the stalagmite and stalactite sea caves, returning at 1700hrs, at a round-trip price of 2500drs.

ROUTE ONE

To Emborio (20½km) via Elies, Kantouni, Myrtes & Massouri The one-way systems that thread their way in and out of the north-west of Kalimnos Town, finally join together, beyond the Hospital. To the left, on a small hill set against the background of a much taller mountain, is the ruined **Castle Chrissocherias** (or Castle of the Knights), and three windmills. Within the castle walls are two very small churches. The location of the fort is typical of the medieval practice of making a secure place, a little inland from the coast, as a refuge from pillaging pirates.

Further on leads to:
CHORIO (2.8km from Kalimnos) Once the island's capital, and overlooked, to the right, by the glowering ruins of another castle and fortifications, amongst which are set a number of tiny churches. Several of these chapels are painted white, all over, and kept in good order. The backcloth is Mt Profitis Ilias. The 'Old Town' is now a village, with a few shops, a kafeneion, and some nicely painted, picturesque cottages beside the back lanes.

Back at the well-maintained main route, the road is attractively lined with fir trees, on both sides, almost all the way to:
ELIES or Panormos (5.4km from Kalimnos) At this settlement is a divergence of routes - left to Kantouni, right for Myrtes, and beyond.

The *Taverna Marino*, opposite a large, ethnic kafeneion on the right, is worth a visit. The proprietor prepares a delicious meal of traditional, roast stuffed lamb, which is served in the evenings, at a cost of 800drs. This is one of the only tavernas, here or anywhere else, to my knowledge, that serves this meal outside the Easter period. The rest of the super menu is interesting, well-cooked and reasonably priced.

From Elies, to the crest overlooking the sea, the pines give way to stately gum trees. To the left are two turnings. One is in Elies, the other, more clearly identifiable, half-way to Myrtes, descends to:

KANTOUNI (6.5km from Kalimnos) This unattractive resort village edges an unexpectedly long, sandy, if rather dirty and seaweed covered beach. The backshore is bordered by various establishments, which include cafe-bars, pensions, restaurants and the *Hotel Drossos* (Class C, tel 47518), the latter being rather set back.

Before the shore, the road divides - to the right to Linaria, and to the left to run out at the southern extremity of the beach. Unless I forget, surely the *Casa di Irene Restaurant*, with mini-golf, and a mini (often empty) swimming pool, deserves a mention! More especially, as the friendly couple appear to have modelled it on a Billy Butlin, pre-war holiday camp! The *Dionysus Taverna* comes mentioned 'in dispatches', and the *Sea & Sun Taverna*, just off the beach, is recommended for its excellent, if rather pricey menu.

Apart from the vehicle road round to Linaria, the shore extends northwards, past two chapels. At the far end of the beach, a concrete path continues on, skirting landward of an enormous rock, plonked down, firmly, on the surrounding terrain. On the way up, over and around this boulder, the path passes the *Cantina Rock & Blues Pub* and a chapel butted on to the side of a house, prior to spilling on to the shore at Linaria.

Returning to the fork in the road at Kantouni, alongside which is a sign for the 'Kantouni Hotel with swimming pool', turn right for:
LINARIA (7.5km from Kalimnos) A small square is set above the waterfront. Here is a sandy bit of shore, rather overrun with seaweed at the southern, 'big-rock' end. The square is more an irregular rhomboid, around which are a couple of bar/tavernas, some *Rooms*, a store and, across a small, steep lane, a block of apartments. The path curves away from the plateia, down to sea-level. It passes by a taverna, to a tiny, rectangular benzina harbour, beyond which is a small, boulderous, seaweed covered bay. It would appear the harbour is to be enlarged.
Round to the left (*Fsw*), towards the 'big-rock', is *Lanaria Rooms*, owned by a friendly, French speaking old couple. This is a popular pension, with double rooms sharing the bathroom, costing 3000drs a night. Guests have the use of a shared fridge, and a large, pleasant balcony facing out over the sea.

From Elies, the tree shaded road descends steeply by a turning left, signed:
MELIZACHAS (7km from Kalimnos) This is a really a suburb of Myrtes, and circles a small but pleasing fishing boat harbour. The 'village' doesn't have a shore, let alone a beach, but is rich in pensions, hotels, Rooms, and the *Grill House Ouzerie To Limanaki*. An establishment to try is the *Pension le Petit Paris*, if only for its Greco/French cuisine. Other possibilities include the *Hotel Australia* and the *Studios Fotini*. The latter is a clean, modern block of studios, which each have a shower, a fully equipped kitchen, and a large balcony, allowing views of Telentos island, at a cost of 3500drs per night. They are owned by a friendly man who spent of his life in Australia.

MYRTES (7.5km from Kalimnos) This seaside resort stretches along the main road, and marks an outbreak of pure, undiluted package holiday tourism. The reek of sun-tan oil pervades everything, and the Kosta character of the settlement is thoroughly evinced by the pizzerias, spaghetterias, music bars, pubs and discos. Whatever may be thought of the place, it affords splendid vistas of Telentos island.
The pretty, tree lined avenue is spanned by various establishments including the *Pub Kalidna*, *Hotels Myrties* (Class D, tel 47512), *Delfini* (Class C, tel 47514), with en suite singles priced at 3300/4300drs & doubles 4200/5300drs, many more hotels, and *Rooms*.
The Blue Island Travel Agency is invaluable for information and currency exchange, and scooter and vehicle hire is available. There is a public toilet. Babi, of *Babis Bar*, just behind the taxi rank, beside the 'square' of Myrtes, can be extremely friendly and helpful.
The most popular dining place is *Restaurant Nectar*, towards the beach. The popularity is easy to understand as tourists are targeted. To this end, there is an extensive, reasonably priced menu and good cuisine, accompanied by pleasant service. One bonus is that chips don't 'come with everything', unless requested. A meal, for two, of 1 garlic bread, 1 prawns wrapped in bacon, 1 chicken & walnuts, 1 steak with capers & mustard, 1 bottle red wine, bread & service, cost 3550drs. Good sized portions, nicely cooked, but not Greek!

Excursion and trip boats slip from the small fishing boat quay, with destination details pinned to boards on the approach to the pier. On the immediate right (*Fsw*), edging the grey, pebbly, not-so-clean, steeply shelving beach, is the *Restaurant Myrthies*. The friendly proprietor, whose establishment is extensively used by local hotel guests, speaks English and will answer a few questions, in respect of this and that. The meals are enjoyably palatable. Another contender in the Myrtes restaurant stakes is the *Restaurant Pythari*, run by a large, young, extremely enthusiastic American/Greek lady. She is trying to be a little different, whilst remaining Greek. The menu is imaginative, if westernised, and dishes include: pikileea - a large tray of hors d'oeuvre of beetroot, onion & yoghurt, aubergine & garlic, tuna & yoghurt, grated carrot, and potato salad; sofrito - stewed lamb with carrot, garlic & a touch of vinegar; and fried plaice with skordalia.

Apart from various excursion boat trips, which schedules include a connection to Xerokampos, Leros island, caiques make the short crossing to:
TELENTOS (Telendos) island More truly a sunken mountain, than an island, it was probably connected to Kalimnos, until an earthquake rent the two apart. There is almost certainly the remains of a submerged village in the channel. The mountain is supposed to resemble a royal lady, forever looking out to sea, in search of her long departed, equally regal lover. I can never achieve the state of mind required to conjure up this fanciful suggestion. Perhaps another bottle of retsina would help?
On the shore of Telentos, facing Kalimnos, is a small settlement with a couple of beaches, some tavernas, accommodation at three pensions, Roman remains and a medieval castle. There is no doubt that these ingredients should make for an almost ideal get-away location. And it is, out of the busy summer months, when day-trippers pour on and off the place. The caique that links Telentos island and Myrtes, operates every 30mins, between 0700-2400hrs. Locals use the service extensively, and the 10/15min crossing costs 300drs.
Close to the jetty is *Uncle Georges Pension Taverna* (Tel 47502). Nikos is the sole waiter. He speaks good English and has a great sense of humour, but at busy times the service can become extremely 'relaxed', if not almost non-existent. If this should prove irksome, there is an excellent taverna about a 100m distance, for which turn right (*Sbo*) after disembarking. Beyond a pigeon loft (a large white shed) are two waterside tavernas. The right-hand one (*Sbo*), with the starfish motif on its large window, provides excellent food and service, at favourable prices. Fresh fish is often available. Needless to say, it is well patronised by locals and other Greeks. Accommodation is available at *Demetrios Harinos* and *Cafe Festaria* (Tel 47401).
Behind the *Late Home Taverna* is a 'Beautiful Beach'. The island is only ¼ mile wide at this point, and a shadeless shore, with ten or so umbrellas, faces west. The approach displays 'No Nude Bathing' signs. Incidentally, all the so-called beaches are signposted, and have sun-beds and umbrellas.

Back on Kalimnos, the road north from Myrtes passes a house with **Rooms**, followed by *Niki's Guest House* and the *Why Not Pub* - why not indeed!

MASSOURI (8.5km from Kalimnos) Simply a continuation of Myrtes, if possibly more 'developed' and neater. Prominent are two 'pubs', *Smile* and *Paradise*, villas, hotels, tavernas, car & scooter hire, and the *Narcissus Disco*.
The beach, which is grey sand with a pebbly sea edge, can only be 'got at'

down a flight of steps. It goes without writing that the shore is 'equipped' with a beach bar, squatty toilet, windsurfers, sun-beds and umbrellas.

There can be little argument that neither Kantouni or Myrtes, nor Massouri, have anything to do with the age-old, sleepy, fishing boat shores of Greek tradition. Beaches whereon caiques are drawn-up on the first few metres, with the aid of ancient, weathered post winches. Shores whereon fishermen lie back, against the props of a beached boat, in the gloom of the shadows cast by the craft's superstructure. Beaches on which fisher-folk are surrounded by neat piles of nets, stretching the mesh of the weft and weave through their unshod toes, all the while threading the needle-shaped shuttle, in and out of the repairs. Beaches, on the tree shaded backshores of which are shacks of tavernas, around which scratch chickens, grazing goats, and one or two donkeys, tethered out of the scorching sun's rays. Not a sun-bed or umbrella in sight. Got the picture?

Once clear of Massouri, the situation alters quite dramatically. Not only are the worst excesses of tourism cast aside, but the countryside is transformed. The oleander edged road skirts the coast, allowing views of the yet distant villages of Skalia and Emborio. Down in some of the coves are fish farms.

The landscape becomes wilder and more dramatic, until the route runs down and alongside the clear waters of the gorgeous, fjord-like bay where is sited:

ARGINONTAS (12km from Kalimnos) This is more a two or three 'donkey droppings' hamlet, than a village. A handful of dwellings are spread about, in and around an olive grove, which edges the small, gently curving, pebbly, tree lined beach, at the end of the bay. A few sun-beds and umbrellas line the shore, which remains semi-deserted, even during the height of season invasions. There are three tavernas, one at each end of the beach and one set back, where enquiries can be made in respect of local accommodation.

Between Arginontas and Skalia are a number of cave-like depressions at the hillside bottom. Some host small, shady, sandy beaches, favoured by locals for a swim, whilst others are the provenance of fish farmers. The road snakes through hillsides, dotted with beehives, to **Skalia** (17km), where are only a sprinkling of buildings, and *Platanos Studio*, the siting of which allows great views. Callers to the hamlet are advised to bring the essentials!

EMBORIO (20½km from Kalimnos) This is more like the Greece about which I was prattling on, at the end of the Massouri entry. The spacious, old-world, clean but ethnic village fans out from a central, small, T-shaped quay. The latter 'shambles' into waters, edged by a fairly long, shallow, rubbish-free sweep of pebble beach, with a little sand, and prettily shaded by mature tamarisk trees. Some ancient sun-beds are laid out, whilst a fisherman is just as likely to be gutting and cleaning his catch, sprawled on the pier. Chickens and turkeys wander about the shore. Where the road runs out on the backshore, close to the quay and on the left (*Fsw*) is *O Emborio's Taverna*, with two clean toilets. If the (lack of) service here proves unacceptable, then across the way is the whitewashed building of the *Pension/Restaurant Themis*. The woodwork is picked-out in blue, and nice double bedrooms, with a balcony, cost 4000drs a night.

Probably the best Emborio establishment, is some 100m along the main street, on the left, indicated by a sign for *Harry's Pension/Taverna Paradise*

(Tel 47434). *Harry's* can be overlooked, as the building is about 50m up a path, and almost concealed by trees. The garden is delightful, as is the aptly named establishment. Apart from the pension's apartments, which cost 4000/5000drs a night, the meals served are most acceptable.

There are other *Rooms* in the village but, as they are not signed, it is necessary to ask around. Emborio is a lovely location and well worth the journey, although there are vestigial signs of new construction taking place. The number of skeletal structures on the hillside, to the left of the church, has increased. It is to be hoped that they remain uncompleted, and left to gradually blend into the landscape.

Do not be tempted to connect with **Stimenia** village, in an attempt to save backtracking along the route out from Kalimnos town. That is unless on foot, as the indicated track is no more than a path.

ROUTE TWO
To Vathis (8km) The initial stage of this route is remarkable, only for its unattractiveness. The Vathis road advances by the island's generating station, in the shadow of which is a full-blown boat repair yard, complete with a number of slipways, two small refineries, and the town's rubbish dump.

Further on are revealed a couple of small, indented, splendidly isolated, sandy bays. The first is small, popular, and reached from the road by way of a long, stair-like series of concrete steps. The second is accessed down an extremely rough, steep, unmetalled vehicle track, so 'difficult' that usually only locals make the journey, there and back up. The sea hereabouts is invitingly blue.

The road clings half-way up the side of arid and barren hills, the coast side of which slides boulderously into the sea down below. The Gulf of Aktis makes a very pleasant vista, even if the sea now does seem impenetrably black. The island of **Saronnisi** is in the foreground, with Pserimos island in the middle-distance, set against the backdrop of the Turkish mainland.

The road loops down to a plain. Here massed groves of oranges are enclosed in whitewashed, walled enclosures, through which the road slowly meanders to:

VATHIS or Rina (8km from Kalimnos) A very small, attractive port, stripped of all the non essentials. It is an extremely popular bay for yachtsmen, many boats remaining berthed, and at anchor, for long periods. The sea surges into the fjord-like inlet, which terminates at the narrow, squared-off harbour.

There are four restaurant/bars, the best of which is probably the one on the right (*Fsw*). To the left is the *Hotel Restaurant Galini* (Tel 31241), where en suite singles cost 2000drs & doubles 3500drs. Opposite the *Galini* is the new *Pension Manolis*, with clean, simple, en suite double rooms priced at 3500drs.

A small caique repair yard flanks the left-hand side (*Fsw*) of the little settlement and, on the right, a track edges the sea for eighty metres or so, with some small boats moored end-on to the bank. The path terminates alongside large steps, and a grand building that has been converted into a smart, 'candlelit dinner' restaurant, targeted at 'yachties'.

Inland of the harbour are one or two shops, stocking the basics. Onrequest, the water taxi **Katerina** ferries visitors to unspoiled beaches, only accessible by sea. This craft departs at 0900hrs, returning at 1300hrs. Prices are negotiable.

The lanes of the attractive valley behind Vathis, being very narrow, are sorted out into a one-way system. With the advent of the internal combustion engine, which has almost entirely superseded 'donkey power', this is an eminently sensible solution. The locals cannot always resist the temptation to take a short cut, the wrong way, which can prove exciting!

I have been advised that a Greek expatriate bought the first orange tree plants back from Palestine. But no one has been able to explain why the walls of the groves are almost substantial enough to be fortifications. Perhaps their stoutness was to assist villagers fight off marauding pirate attacks?

Half-way to **Dassos** village is a small hamlet complete with a kafeneion and a filling station.

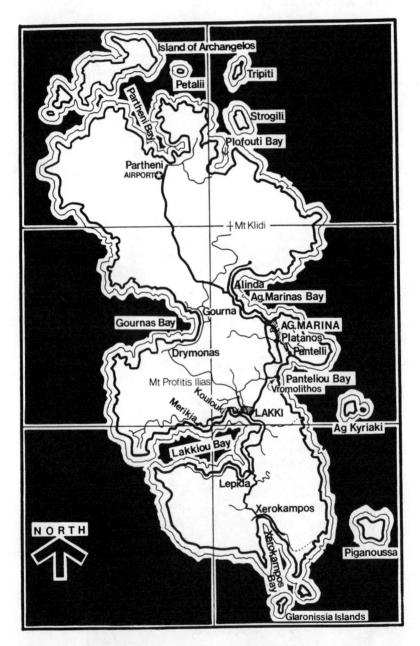

Illustration 26 Leros island

FIRST IMPRESSIONS Abandoned, 1930s Italianesque port buildings; palm trees; dusty; friendly 'natives'; few animals & little agriculture; fencing & barbed wire; green beehives; flat'ish; terrible postcards.

SPECIALITIES None, unless one takes account of the three mental hospitals, for which the island is now infamous, throughout the western world. Leros was also known as a place of exile - perhaps the two are connected!

LOCAL RELIGIOUS HOLIDAYS & FESTIVALS incl: Sunday before the Shrove Monday - Carnival; 26th Sept - Second World War commemoration, Lakki. It is widely regarded that, at carnival times, the islanders behave and dress in a manner dating back to ancient, pagan festivities.

VITAL STATISTICS Tel prefix 0247. The population of some 8,500 live on an island so savagely indented, that it resembles an ink blot. Leros is about 15km long and between 11½km & 1¼km wide.

HISTORY A Homeric island, much of its history is shared with the other Dodecanese, apart from a few notable exceptions. For instance, it is one of two or three islands where inheritances pass through the female line.

During the Second World War, Leros was the scene of a very bloody campaign in which some 5,000 British troops were cut down during German parachute assaults. The Italians, overmasters since 1912, had capitulated. The Allies moved to fill the vacuum but, unfortunately, failed to take Rhodes, from whence the Germans launched their devastating attack, on November 12th 1943. To help reinforce their troops, at the height of the most ferocious fighting, British HQ sent some 'chaps' from Samos. They arrived rather too late, and were themselves wiped out. The moving testament to this little-known campaign is a beautifully kept, tear-jerking war cemetery, close to Alinda village. Here are the graves of one hundred and seventy nine British, two Canadian and two South African servicemen.

In almost comic contrast, annually, on the 26th September, the Greeks honour thirty of their sailors, who also died during the Second World War. The day-long ceremony includes the attendance of as many naval ships as can be mustered, a military band, almost all the senior servicemen and church leaders in the region, national TV and radio crews, and the entire island population, plus many visitors. The centre of the jamboree is a commemorative stone, along the broad, Esplanade of Lakki Port. It appears that, during the war, the only operational Greek warship slipped into the bay, under the impression that fraternal forces were in occupation. This was a major misjudgement, as the crew found themselves staring down the gun barrels of a distinctly unfriendly and efficient, German shore-based gun crew. Whoops! A tourist may well be regaled with convoluted variations on this theme or, usually, more high-flown and romantic tales, but the above appears to be the gist of the matter. Travellers should arrive several days before the event, as there is little or 'no room at the inn' during the celebrations and festival.

The Colonels' junta (1967-1974), erected a bleak internment camp, at Partheni, which is still in evidence. It is now used by the military for more conventional purposes.

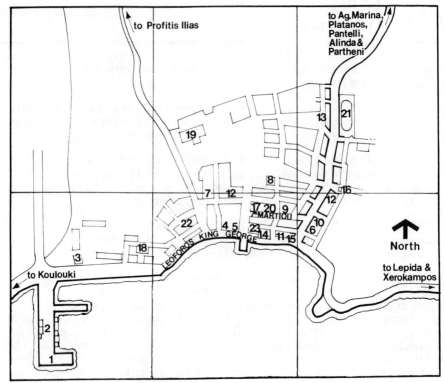

Tmr
1A2   Ferry-boat Quay
2A2   Cafe Bar/Leon Limani Bar/Municipal Tourist Office
3A2   Yacht Limani Restaurant
4B2   Restaurant Pizzeria
5B2   Snackbar Souvlakia
6C2   Cafe Bar
7B1/2 Hotel Miramare
8B1/2 Hotel Artemis
9B/C1/2 Hotel Katerina/Baker
10C2   National Bank
11B2   Rent-A-Car Leros
12C1/2 Giannos Rent Moto
13C1   Bread Shop
14B2   'Dead' Cinema
15B/C2 Kastis Travel & Shipping
16C1/2 Petrol
17B1/2 Post Office/Taverna O'Sostos
18A/B2 Port Police
19B1   Hospital
20B/C1/2 Public Toilets
21C1   Football Ground
22B2   Hairdresser Michael
23B2   Hotel Leros Palace - 'dead'

(Tmr)   = Town map reference
(Fsw)   = Facing seawards
(Sbo)   = Sea behind one
(Fbqbo) = Ferry-boat Quay behind one

Illustration 27 Lakki Port

GENERAL My first sight of Leros was, many years ago, from the aft deck of an old-time, inter-island ferry. I was rather mystified and curious about the strange, huge bay and port of Lakki. This impression does not dim over the years, even after closer familiarity. But do not be put-off - disembark, and explore. Even in the high season, Leros manages to maintain the ambiance of a simple Aegean island. Admittedly, there are package tourists, but in comparison to, say, Rhodes or Kos, this is a much simpler and quieter, more authentic location. Neither Leros, nor the inhabitants, have been overwhelmed, by the holiday companies, and remains more the habitat of the *cognoscenti*, than the mob.

LAKKI: main port (Illus 27) After the first acquaintanceship with Lakki, it comes as a surprise that the port is not the capital. Crumbling, Italian inspired buildings are spaced about the wide boulevard-like streets, and there is a hint, a sniff of town planning - a most alien concept to modern-day Greeks. But it is these very 'foreign' manifestations that explain why Lakki has not been honoured with 'senior settlement' status. The Italians were wholly responsible for the port's development, in conjunction with the massive harbour facilities across the bay. Lakki is a testament, that went horridly wrong, an almost grotesque, faded concrete monument to the Mussolini inspired, Italian dream of a Mediterranean Empire - a latter day Roman Kingdom, with grandiose buildings for the functionaries, envisaged as necessary to oversee the concept.

The islanders simply do not like the place, which is not surprising taking into account the architecture and layout. They are as dissimilar to the traditional, organic growth of 'your' average Greek town, as any mix of '1930s Italian Municipal' and a 'spaghetti-western' film set could possibly be.

Despite the appearance, this is no prohibition, speak-easy town - in fact it is difficult to find a lively taverna, let alone any semblance of night-life. But those who do not appreciate the strange delights of Lakki, should simply head for Pantelli, Alinda, or anywhere else, but this most odd location.

ARRIVAL BY AIR There is a regular Athens, 30 seat Dornier service to the rather bleak, tiny airstrip, close by the northern village of Partheni. The airport 'complex' is a small, box-like building, which triples-up as a bar, arrival/departure lounge, and baggage handling area. Reference to the latter subject, reminds me to comment further on the simple, but inefficient system 'installed' here. A trolley is wheeled out to the aircraft hold, the baggage tipped in, and the trolley wheeled back to the nissen hut - where the fun really starts. The Greeks' inability to queue is the root of the chaos, as passengers scramble, 'lucky-dip' fashion to unearth their bags. The luggage at the top falls to the bottom of the meshed-in pile, once someone has 'hit the jackpot' - only for the process to start all over again. If everybody were to form an orderly line, it would all take half the time - but this is Greece.

Taxis attend landings and departures, but buses of any shape are usually noticeable by their absence.

ARRIVAL BY FERRY The truly enormous Ferry-boat Quay (*Tmr* 1A2) is sited at the most westerly end of the equally wide Esplanade avenue. Some of the prairie-like space of the quay has been taken-up by a large split-level building (*Tmr* 2A2). On the ground floor of this is a large *Cafe-bar*, with a metered telephone on the counter. Ferry-boat tickets can be purchased here, which is recommended as some ferry-boat companies charge a 20% surcharge if tickets are purchased on board. Also located on the ground floor is the Municipal Tourist office, which might, or might not be open! The first floor hosts the open-air, smart *Leon Limani Bar*, a popular spot for locals to forgather at ferry-boat times. The staff appear to be predominantly Australian expatriates, and one of the waiter's might just pass round a Tupperware box of his mother's home-made cookies.

Arrivals will probably be offered accommodation on disembarking, whatever time of night the ferry arrives (and it is usually late in the night). If not, it is necessary to trudge down the long leg of the quay, passing by a mini-jetty for 'yachties', to the expansive Esplanade. There turn right (*Sbo*) past small parks and open spaces, to the centre of the development. This perambulation advances, curves and bends by various 'markers'. There is the *Yacht Limani Restaurant* (*Tmr* 3A2), whose owner may attempt to lure the unsuspecting into his lair. The place is popular with 'grotty' yachties and strapping 'deckies'. Further on are some buildings of an official demeanour, one containing the Customs officers, and another the 'Leros Lyceum'. Beyond the latter, are the first precursors of Lakki's cafe-bar society, more a number of bars from which rock music emanates. They are patronised by the 'cream' of the port's youth, idly sipping frappe coffees, and languidly keeping an eye on their particular moped, one of a pack propped-up outside.

THE ACCOMMODATION & EATING OUT

The Accommodation The generally accepted code of behaviour, for those not accosted on disembarking, or arriving very late, is to wander up to the hotel of their choice, grab a key, and sort the matter out with the proprietor, on the morrow. Unfortunately for *aficionados* of traditional C/D/E class Greek hotels, the *Hotel Leros Palace* (*Tmr* 23B2) appears to have closed down. This 'terminal' state is the fate of many an old-time accommodation - locked doors, cobwebbed, dusty and grime covered furniture, piled-up in the foyer, litter filling the corners of the loggia, scattered stacks of unopened mail, and old, sun-faded posters peeling off the walls. I hope the 'death' throes were quickly over. It is not as if Lakki can afford any diminishment in the number of opportunities available to the visitor.

Considering the port's pivotal position, it is surprising that there are so few hotels, and almost no pensions or *Rooms*. Taking into account the lack of enthusiasm for and about the place, perhaps it is to be expected.

Hotel Miramare (*Tmr* 7B1/2) (Class D)   Tel 22043
Directions: From the Ferry-boat Quay, right (*Fbqbo*) along the Esplanade and off to the left, on the right of the 'Hospital' street. Clearly visible from the waterfront, across some undeveloped land.

There is the hint of refurbishment, which would not be a 'half-bad' idea. At the moment, the establishment has a rather more family pension, 'great-aunts' atmosphere, than that attributable to a down-at-the-heel D class hotel. The bedrooms are crowded-out with a disparate and motley assembly of furniture, much of it possibly having been assembled from family attics. Guests intending to take their leave, either side of siesta, should ensure the formalities are out of the way, well before the fall of the sacred afternoon hours. Those who fail to so do, will find the place has assumed a 'Marie Celeste' emptiness. All bedrooms have en suite bathrooms, single rooms costing 2850/3100drs & doubles 3650/5050drs.

Hotel Katerina (*Tmr* 9B/C1/2) (Class E) 7th Martiou   Tel 22460
Directions: Two blocks back from the Esplanade, and within sight of the
Platanos main road 'out of town'.

Very clean rooms with small en suite bathrooms. A single costs about
3000drs & doubles 3000/5000drs. The 24 hours a day hot shower water often
only has sufficient 'energy' to dribble from the nozzle.

Hotel Artemis (*Tmr* 8B1/2) (Class C)   Tel 22416
Directions: Some five blocks back from the Esplanade, along the side-street
the far side of the 'dead' Cinema (*Tmr* 14B2).

A fresh'ish coat of paint has been applied. All bedrooms have en suite
bathrooms, with a single charged at 3000drs & doubles 4000drs. Beware, 'the
management' has a 'naughty' little habit of requesting rather more than the
official rates, by at least a 1000drs note.

The Eating Out If Lakki lacks breadth of accommodation, then eating places
are almost non-existent. A prominent contender in the 'grazing' stakes (I was
tempted to write 'steaks') is the:

Restaurant Pizzeria (*Tmr* 4B2)
Directions: In the west, or left-hand corner (*Sbo*) of a semi-derelict, Esplanade
bordering Italianesque block.

A barn-like 'greasy'ish spoon' with rotting, steel framed windows, and a
television set usually blaring away. It might be open, or shut! When in
business, the large, thick-set, but jolly proprietor, with a greasy apron, serves
passable food and stays open until the early hours. Mine host presents his
kitchen with a flourish, although I am not sure why. Mrs Beaton would
undoubtedly have suffered an attack of the vapours at the state of affairs.

More agreeable alternatives include:
Taverna O Sostos (*Tmr* 17B1/2)
Directions: In the same block, and adjacent to the Post Office, in a congenial,
tree shaded location.

Short Lakki may be in quantity, but *Sostos* makes up for this lack of
numbers, as it is a traditional taverna, the like of which one would hope to
find, on all and every Aegean island. Service is friendly and quick (except on
the busiest of occasions), with the Greek papa and the Swedish mama cooking,
whilst the son and daughter serve at the tables. The establishment's popularity
is validated by the number of locals observed tucking into, whatever is on
offer. A Greek salad is priced at 450drs, half a roasted chicken 1200drs
(straight-off the charcoal grill, and one of the tastiest sampled, anywhere), or
a large and succulent beef steak at the reasonable price of 900drs.

Snackbar Souvlakia (*Tmr* 5B2)
Directions: To one side of an Esplanade edging block of buildings.

Locally renowned for, either a 'pit-stop' snack, or a full-blown, 'chips-with-
everything', evening, family meal out - a 'take-away' giro pita (140drs) or a
plate of souvlaki (140drs), hot chips (150drs), tomato salad (200drs), tzatziki
(150drs) and a bottle of Amstel beer (220drs).

THE A TO Z OF USEFUL INFORMATION
AIRLINE OFFICE & TERMINUS *See* Platanos.

Aircraft timetable (Mid-season)
Leros to Athens
Daily   1100hrs
Return
Daily   0935hrs
One-way fare 15100drs; duration 65mins.

BANKS The National Bank (*Tmr* 10C2) is on the right (*Sbo*) of the Platanos main road, close to the junction with the Esplanade. The usual hours - Mon-Thur 0800-1400hrs & Fri 0800-1330hrs.

BEACHES None in the port. It is necessary to walk westward past the Ferry-boat Quay (*Tmr* 1A2), up and around the bluff above Lakki. This pleasantly wooded track proceeds, after 1km, to a tiny, tree lined lido at **Koulouki**. At this point, there is a snackbar and a very small, narrow strip of sandy beach. A further 1½km along the same stony track leads to **Merikia**. This is a rather strange, but pleasant area, by the sea's edge, set amongst a grove of trees, in which are a number of large, ruined buildings. The beach is narrow and covered in kelp.

BICYCLE, SCOOTER & CAR HIRE The closest, most easily located is:
Rent-A-Car Leros (*Tmr* 11B2)
Directions: Beside the Esplanade, close to the Platanos junction.
From a distance, this business resembles nothing more than a heap of roadside scrap metal. Closer inspection reveals that the agglomeration is nothing more than a disorderly collection of rusting bicycles and mopeds - for hire. Quantity, rather than quality, is the order of the day. The owner, despite having only one hand, manages to 'beat-start' and ride his steeds, whilst his daughter, who has a smattering of English, and her brother help out. Most running, and some 'not-so-running' repairs are carried-out by 'Mr Leros', on the pavement. From the latter vantage point, it is possible to fully appreciate just what an art-form is achieved in patching-up and restoring these two-wheeled transports. Bicycles cost 300drs a day, and mopeds 1000drs, with papa pronouncing 'special', at each and every occasion, whatever and whichever the equipment!

Giannagos Rent A Moto (*Tmr* 12C1/2) Directions: On the right of the Platanos road, immediately prior to the Argo filling station sign.
Similar prices to other firms, but the conveyances are of a better quality, and the scooters are Honda's which take two-up.

BOOKSELLERS More a foreign language newspaper (and video shop), close to the Cinema (*Tmr* 14B2).

BREAD SHOPS A **Baker** resides in the ground floor of the *Hotel Katerina*, whilst there is a **Bread shop** (*Tmr* 13C1), opposite the football ground, beside the Platanos road.

BUSES Rumours hint at this, and rumours hint at that, but fact is very difficult to establish.   Some suggest that they 'terminus' outside the   jewellers, immediately beyond the National Bank (*Tmr* 10C2), beside the Platanos road. It might be useful to note, that, as on the island of Kalimnos, taxis double-up as community mini-buses.

Bus timetable (If operating!)
Lakki Port to Xerokampos
Daily   0740, 0935, 1140, 1340, 1735, 2030hrs.
Lakki Port to Partheni via Vromolithos, Platanos, Ag Marina, Alinda.
Daily   0810, 1010, 1240, 1810, 2120hrs.

CINEMAS (*Tmr* 14B2) A magnificent art deco building (*Tmr* 14B2), but it might, or might not be closed!

COMMERCIAL SHOPPING AREA None. In fact there are few shops or stores, but no peripteros, cigarettes being sold from small kiosks.

FERRY-BOATS The ships dock at the large quay (*Tmr* 1A2).

Ferry-boat timetable (Mid-season)

Day	Departure time	Ferry-boat	Ports/Islands of Call
Mon	2130hrs	Ag Rafael	Kalimnos, Kos, Rhodes.
	2400hrs	Ialyssos/Kamiros	Kalimnos, Kos, Rhodes.
Tue	1315hrs	Ag Rafael	Patmos, Vathy(Samos), Chios, Lesbos, Limnos, Kavala(M).
	1830hrs	Ialyssos/Kamiros	Patmos, Piraeus(M).
	2400hrs	Ialyssos/Kamiros	Kalimnos, Kos, Rhodes.
Wed	0830hrs	Nissos Kalymnos	Lipsos, Patmos, Arki, Angathonisi.
	1830hrs	Ialyssos/Kamiros	Patmos, Piraeus(M).
	1955hrs	N. Kalymnos	Kalimnos, Kos.
	2400hrs	Ialyssos/Kamiros	Kalimnos, Kos, Rhodes.
Thur/Fri & Sat	1830hrs	Ialyssos/Kamiros	Patmos, Piraeus(M).
	2400hrs	Ialyssos/Kamiros	Kalimnos, Kos, Rhodes.
Sun	0815hrs	N. Kalymnos	Lipsos, Patmos, Pythagorion(Samos), Fournoi, Ag Kirikos(Ikaria).
	2400hrs	N. Kalymnos	Kalimnos.
	2400hrs	Ialyssos/Kamiros	Patmos, Piraeus(M).

Note, at this port in their schedules, ferry-boats might be several hours adrift.

From Ag Marina Port the following are available:
Excursion boats. At least once a week a craft connects Patmos/ Lipsos/Kos. Some five days a week a boat makes a Lipsos link.

Day	Departure time	Ports/Islands of Call
Mon/Wed/Thur/Fri/Sat	0930hrs*	Lipsos.
Sat	1100hrs+	Patmos, Lipsos, Kos.

*Arrives back at Ag Marina at 1700hrs. Return fare 2000drs.

+Costs 1800drs to Patmos/Lipsos and 3000drs to Patmos/Lipsos/Kos.

HYDROFOILS Ag Marina (possibly) hosts a summer months service:

Hydrofoil timetable

Thur/Fri	0930hrs	Patmos.
	1640hrs	Kos.
Sun	0930hrs	Patmos, Samos.
	1800hrs	Kos.

FERRY-BOAT TICKET OFFICES
Kastis Travel & Shipping (*Tmr* 15B/C2) King George Ave   Tel 22872
Directions: At the junction of the Esplanade and Platanos road.
Agent's for DANE Sea Lines, other ferry-boat companies, and Olympic Airways. The staff are helpful and the office opens Mon-Sat 0900-1230 & 1700-2030hrs, Sun 0900-1230hrs. Out of the height of season the doors may remain shut in the afternoons.

HAIRDRESSERS Michael Hairstyle (*Tmr* 22B2).

MEDICAL CARE
Chemists & Pharmacies A minimum of three.
Hospital (*Tmr* 19B1). To the side of the Profitis Ilias road.

MUNICIPAL TOURIST OFFICE *See* Arrival By Ferry.

OTE No office. One was constructed close to the *Restaurant Pizzeria* (*Tmr* 4B2), but, for the moment, it is derelict. *See* Arrival By Ferry.

PETROL One Filling station (*Tmr* 16 C1/2) is to the right (*Sbo*) of the Platanos road, prior to the football ground, as well as a number beside the Lakki-Platanos road.

POST OFFICE (*Tmr* 17B1/2) A large building alongside the thoroughfare that branches off the Esplanade, opposite the small finger pier, and on the corner with 7th Martiou St. Open Mon-Fri 0730-1400hrs.

POLICE Port (*Tmr* 18A/B2).

TAXIS The main rank is at the conjunction of the Esplanade and the Platanos road. A friendly bunch, many speaking 'grine'. Leros is an island from which the inhabitants flocked to Australia, over the years, only to return home, many years later, with a 'nest-egg' put-by, for the families old age. Meters are rarely used, drivers appearing to rely on a 'feel' for the fare level, and the ability of a client to pay! A typical fare from Lakki to the Airport is 1500drs.

TELEPHONE NUMBERS & ADDRESSES
Hospital (*Tmr* 19B1)	Tel 22351
Olympic Airways office	Tel 22844/24144; airport Tel 22777
Police	Tel 22221
Taxi rank	Tel 22550

TOILETS There is a public convenience (*Tmr* 20B/C1/2) at the right-hand side (*Sbo*) of the Post Office block.
Whilst 'moseying' about in this area, a circular, semi-derelict arcade, a perfect example of 1930s Italian Aegean architecture, is worth a look over.

TRAVEL AGENTS & TOUR OFFICES *See* Ferry-boat Ticket Offices.

EXCURSION TO LAKKI PORT SURROUNDS
Excursion to Platanos, (about 4km) Ag Marina & Pantelli From Lakki Port, the main road meanders through the hillsides, to the hub of the island. This is a collection of three villages, Platanos, Pantelli and Ag Marina, which straddle the western ridge of Mt Apeliki.

At a major fork in the main road, a left-hand turning leads directly over, and down to Ag Marinas Bay, emerging by a whacking great, leafy tree, in the middle of the road. At this junction, to the left advances to Alinda and Partheni, whilst to the right, a little to the west, is Ag Marina port.

Returning back to the aforementioned major fork, the right-hand turning by-passes the road to Pantelli, way down below, and curves along the ridge, past the small *Hotel To Rodon* (Class E, tel 22075), where all the bedrooms have en suite bathrooms, with a single priced at 2650/3300drs & doubles 3700/4550drs. Beyond *To Rodon* is:

PLATANOS: capital (3.5km from Lakki) (Illus 28) A hillside settlement, bestriding the saddle of a mountainside flank. To the north, the ground falls away sharply, in the direction of Ag Marina, whilst, to the south, the land tumbles down to the fishing hamlet of Pantelli. Platanos is dominated by a mountain top, Byzantine castle. The village radiates out from a pretty, small, workaday Main Square, gracefully shaded by a central plane tree. The almost disproportionately large Town Hall (*Tmr* 1B3/4) occupies one side of the plateia, whilst the rest is edged by bustling businesses, shops and stalls, and is jammed with 'ranked' taxis.

A visitor's approach will, more than likely, be along the busy, sometimes 'traffic continuous' 'High St', from the direction of Lakki. The **Doctor's** (*Tmr* 27A/B4), and the **Olympic Airways/Leros Travel** office (*Tmr* 2A/B4), are close to the sharp downhill bend, where the village is entered. The winding, narrow 'High St' is lined by shops, offices, as well as the occasional accommodation opportunity. For instance, opposite the Travel office, is *Rooms No 68* (*Tmr* 18A/B4, tel 22317), advertised by a yellow sign, visible from the street. The house is set high above the thoroughfare, allowing fine views, out over the town and bay. It is an imposing, neo-classical villa, with spacious, lofty, hand-painted ceilinged bedrooms. The proprietress is a young mother. She charges 3500drs per night for a double, some with en suite bathrooms, and 5000drs for a small, self-contained studio. Around the corner, past the junction with the road down to Pantelli, and to the left is a (Laskarina) **Travel Agent** (*Tmr* 7A/B4). Across the road are *Rosangelica Studios* (*Tmr* 6B4), a pool hall, and a **Baker** (*Tmr* 5B4). On the left, opposite the 'PT' dedicated *Hotel Elefteria*, is *Maria's Rooms & Studios* (*Tmr* 8A/B4). Beyond *Maria's*, the High St 'rushes' by a small square, with the 'hint' of a bus stop, and a taxi rank (Tel 23070/23340). Further along, on the left, is a **Supermarket** (*Tmr* 30B3/4), and the *Funny-Bunny Fast Food Restaurant*(!). This emporium of 'good taste' is 'done out' in the fashion of a McDonalds, and advertises 'food in the packet'. Quite hard on the heels of the latter, on the right, close to the Main Sq, is a **National Bank** (*Tmr* 4B3/4).

The Main Sq is a lively spot, apparently constantly circled by locals on mopeds, many of which have lost their silencers. Some thoughtful riders free-wheel down from castle area, round the square, and off towards Ag Marina, thus reducing the shattering noise levels, by a decibel or three. To the left of the square (*Town Hall behind one*) is the blue and white painted *Leros Club*, more a kafeneion, frequented and patronised by the elderly, wizened menfolk. Some choose to sit at the rickety deal tables, conveniently placed on the pavement. This vantage point allows that measured, leisurely observance of everyday life, so necessary to people the world over, but nowhere more a prerequisite, an essential lifeblood of life than in Greece. Half-left is a 'market' of fruit & vegetables shops, and a butcher, followed by a poky, but busy *Kafeneion*. This latter establishment is deservedly popular, serving a super souvlaki, with an egg mixed-in. It possesses a metered telephone, but a drawback is its hours of business. The cafe tends to shut at rather odd times, such as Saturday lunchtime, though is open from 1100hrs, through to 0200hrs! On the right-hand interior wall is an old, panoramic photograph *Panorama di Lero*. The picture details the castle, Ag Marina, Platanos and Pantelli. The proprietor explains that much of the old housing, on the upper castle slopes, was destroyed by bombing, during the Second World War.If found closed, the rather more modern, touristy *Cafe-bar/Rooms* next door serves a 'good souvlaki'. On the right is the *Bar O Pithari*, a source of loud rock music, and a haunt of local youth, most kitted out with dark sunglasses, even when in the darkest recesses of the *Pithari*!

Straight ahead, ascending the slope of the hillside (*Town Hall behind one*) is a rather 'squeezed-out' extension to the Main Square. This allows a choice of directions in which to head. To the half-left is a steeply ascending cul-de-sac, on the right of which is a **Dry Cleaners** (*Tmr* 26B/C3). To the right leads past the hairstylist **Michael's** (*Tmr* 12B/C3/4), and on up to the castle. To the left is a street, approximately paralleling the Ag Marina main road, which plummets past an island-wide publicised **Self-Service Laundry** (*Tmr* 11B/C3), as well as a hairdresser, butcher, and other shops.

Around to the left of the Town Hall (*Tmr* 1B3/4) is a narrow lane, on the right of which is a **Newspaper shop** (*Tmr* 10B3), selling some fairly ancient English magazines and newspapers. This alley wanders about, and to the right is a turning leading to 'squatty' Public toilets (*Tmr* 3B3).

The Kastro (Castle) The fortress can be reached, 'on wheels', by selecting the lane leading half-right from the small square, off the Main Square. This breaks into a rough track, which loops round behind the castle. One section runs along an extremely narrow, contour ridge, falling sharply and frighteningly away, either side of the path. For those on foot, and once again from the small square, a signpost indicates the steps that ascend, half-left through the piled-up houses, followed by an open area of hillside, prior to reaching the castle walls. The view is remarkable, but due to the presence of the Army, taking photographs is forbidden. Originally a Byzantine fort, it was taken over by the Knights. The church inside the entrance has been renovated. The castle is open daily between 0700-1900hrs.

Back at Platanos, from the Main Square, a road to the left (*Town Hall behind one*), hurtles down to the port of Ag Marina. The descent passes by a pharmacy, and, on the right, an **OTE & Post Office** (*Tmr* 9B3). The OTE is open Mon-Sat 0730-1500hrs and the Post Office weekdays 0800-1400hrs, the latter transacting foreign currency exchange. On the left are a dentist and *Rooms*. Opposite the Cathedral is a most interesting, if small museum. This is based on the possessions of a once important, wealthy island family, the Antonelli's, and is housed in the family farmhouse. Entrance costs 200drs. Amongst the pictures is one of the family (c 1900), when they had Egyptian connections, whilst another is of a kinsman who flew seaplanes for an Italian airline (c 1920-30). Two rooms contain exhibits of family belongings, embroidery, and other knick-knacks. All are carefully explained by a descendent, who acts as a caretaker.

A parallel lane steeply descends towards the port, from Platanos. About two-thirds of the way down, the two join, prior to:

AG MARINA: port (Illus 28) This was the original island harbour. Fortunately, the authorities have decided to preserve the tree lined port, which is a perfect example of its genre. Various boat trips and excursions remain based at Ag Marina, for details of which *See* Lakki. Despite the activity generated, there remains a quiet atmosphere, an overlay of genteel, if somewhat desolate abandonment. Certainly, there is little comparison with the rather more lively ambience of Alinda, or Pantelli.

From the far right (*Fsw*) of the waterfront, the Excursion boat Quay (*Tmr* 31B1/2) is at the east end. Moving to the left, the quay is followed by the venerable, stately building, which once housed the old Post Office. Also to the right of the Platanos road is the Port Square, around the environs of which are scattered: three travel agencies - **Kastis Travel** (Tel 22140), **Letec Tours** (Tel 23337) & **DRM Agency**; several tavernas, one being the *Taverna Ag Marina O Kostas* (*Tmr* 14B/C1/2), next door to a baker. Sample day rate charges levied by Kastis Travel are: bicycles 500drs; mopeds 1000drs; scooters 1500drs; and cars from 7000drs. The various travel firms are the 'font of wisdom' for all boat and excursion trip details. The owner of the *O Kostas* is the very polite, English speaking Kostas Stacianos. The taverna has check tablecloths, 'bum-numbing' chairs, and piped Greek music. Mr Kostas may offer an 'on the house' glass of Metaxa, and a plate of melon. A possibly too oily meal, for two, of a plate of chicken & chips (swimming in oil and fat), a Greek salad (good), a plate of black-eyed beans with onions & oil, a plate of mixed green beans, courgettes & potatoes in tomato sauce, a bottle of water, a small bottle of retsina, bread, and service, cost 2670drs.

Directly opposite the Agricultural Bank, which only deals with 'matters Greek', not exchange transactions, and along a narrow lane is a tiny *Cafe/Ouzerie/Souvlaki Bar*, where octopus is 'on the grill'. Yet another eatery is the *Italian Taverna*, easily identified by its red coloured chairs, and so nicknamed because the proprietor/cook is married to an Italian lady. The pleasant staff serve good food, particularly fish and Italian dishes, from a clean, modern kitchen. The taverna gets so busy, later in the evenings, that it is often impossible to order more than the main course. You have been warned, dine early, or order everything first time round.

The Taxi rank telephone number is 23340.

To left (*Fsw*) of the Platanos road is a Police station (*Tmr* 15B2), on the right, whilst on the left are not one, but two **Supermarkets** (*Tmr* 13A/B2 & 13A1/2). The road climbs gently upwards, with, to the right, a narrow, pretty, little lane. The latter wanders by a ruined seamill (*Tmr* 16A1), close to a promontory, then edges the sea, and a small beach to one hand, and quite grand houses on the other hand. The lane rejoins the road, which goes on to make a junction with the main Lakki to Alinda route.

Returning to Platanos, an aforementioned turning, to the left of the Lakki road, beyond the *Hotel Rosangelika*, runs down the right-hand side of a valley. This road passes by much waste ground, a doctor's, on the left, the *Disco Diana* (*Tmr* 17B5), and the surprisingly alpine, twee looking, package booked *Hotel Lavirinthos* (*Tmr* 19B5), next door to which is a *Rooms*. The thoroughfare bottoms out at:

PANTELLI (Pandeli): fishing hamlet (Illus 28) This lovely, 'picture-postcard' location is probably the island's most desirable resort. Despite some years of organised, if low-key tourist activity,   the overall impression is one of a relaxed, without-a-care, workaday ambiance, with fishermen leisurely going

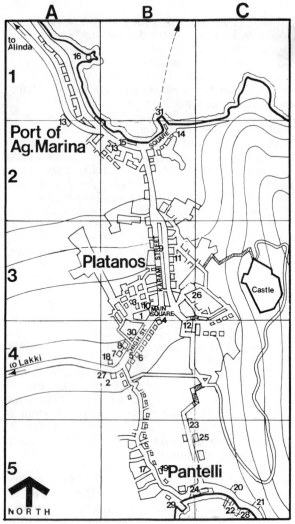

Illustration 28 Platanos, Ag Marina & Pantelli

about their daily round. In addition, Pantelli doesn't suffer from the traffic or general noise pollution that inflicts Platanos. On the other hand, it has not been so depopulated and emasculated of indigenous industry that it exudes the almost desolate air experienced at 'museum-piece' Ag Marina.

Visitors staying overnight might bear in mind that the early morning 'landing of the catch', involving some twenty or more fishermen, is usually a pretty noisy affair. Lodgers in the immediate vicinity of the piers might find their morning slumbers not a little disturbed.

Where the road from Platanos levels out, it curves sharply left past the *Taverna Taliro* (*Tmr* 29B5, where are served fish and salads), and along the backshore of a fine shingle, sandy but narrow beach. Between the two, a few young trees fight for survival, and the sea is crystal clear. Straight ahead is a small, but long rectangular block of buildings, around which the road bends, and in which are the slick'er, side-by-side *Tavernas Zorba* and *Sirtaki* (*Tmr* 24B/C5), both edging the steeply shelving foreshore.

Beyond the latter tavernas are manifestations of the village's more serious activity, namely the fishermen's caiques, moored haphazardly, but tidily, to ramshackle finger piers, which jut out from the ragged waterfront. Hereabouts is the *Taverna Drosia* (*Tmr* 22C5), opposite the *Pension Rosa* (*Tmr* 20C5). Following the bay round, leads to the 'old quarter', with, on the right, waterside fronting houses, the patios of which 'fall' into the sea. This is a lovely, 'in the middle of the action' locale, in amongst which are the *Pension Kavas* (*Tmr* 21C5) and *Taverna Maria* (*Tmr* 28C5). The *Kavas* has superb, almost A class accommodation, with en suite doubles priced at 3200/4000drs, including breakfast. The *Taverna Maria* 'comes' highly recommended, and faces out over the sea. A sign points the way between two whitewashed houses, to the entrance, on the waterfront side of the taverna. Round there is a small concrete raft 'of a terrace', on which are arranged tables and chairs. If inclement weather dictates, a covered lean-to, with windows overlooking the bay, keeps out the elements. The short, rotund, smiley, gold-toothed Maria and her husband run a most agreeable taverna, with attentive, friendly service. Having spent some time in Scandinavia, she has an extra fondness for those of a 'Swedish persuasion' - it sounds a bit like a deodorant induced illness. Perhaps it might indicate some form of immorality, similar to toe-sucking? It was a thought, and will date this entry. A meal, for two, of 2 Greek salads, a plate of kalamares, a bottle of Amstel beer, a soda, bread, service, and coffees, cost 1900drs - and Maria may insist on kissing diners, on their departure. Now, back to this 'Swedish persuasion'...!

Beyond *Maria's*, the track progresses by the *Tavernas Limani* and *Agrogiali*, as well as the *Bars Nectar* and *Savana*.

Back at the centre of the village, a lane ascends the middle of the valley, back towards Platanos. After 100m, on the right is a large hotel/cafeteria, followed by *Rooms* (*Tmr* 25B/C4/5) and *Rooms Aphroditi* (*Tmr* 23B/C4/5, tel 22103). The lane bends right, to run out at the bottom of a number of flights of steps. These connect with a street back to the south of Platanos, or the lane from Platanos to the castle. There is no way through, for wheeled transport, but should you have a donkey...!

ROUTE ONE
To Xerokampos via Lepida (5km) The road from Lakki Port skirts the enormous Bay of Lakkiou, past the tatty outskirts of the settlement, followed by pretty, tree lined countryside on the way to:

LEPIDA (1½km from Lakki) Once the Italian naval ordnance and repair yard. The area bordering the road is profusely tree planted and resembles a pre-war holiday camp. The Greeks have occupied part of the site, but have left most of the enormous, shoreside installations 'a-mouldering'.

The left-hand fork leads over the hillside to the spacious development of:
XEROKAMPOS (4½km from Lakki) The peaceable village, which absolutely 'dies' outside of the June-September months, spreads down past a to-be-recommended *Fish Taverna*, on the left, towards the sleepy, quiet, lovely bay. A few metres further on is a pebbly beach, stretching either side of a rustic backshore taverna, and the 'ferry' quay. A number of fishing caiques are moored to this small pier, as they are to the right of the taverna, with domestic ducks bobbing about amongst their hulls. The beach to the left (*Fsw*) is slightly kelpy, and the water muddy. There are *Rooms*, close to the beach, and a couple more cafe-tavernas. The cafe on the left, just before the right turn to the beach, has a metered phone, whilst the 'small pier' taverna serves good, basic food.

An added attraction is the arrival and departure of excursion boats, including a 'popular summer month's' connection to Myrtes, Leros island.

To the right of the village, as it is entered, or a ten minute walk from the beach, and on the ridge of a hill, is functional *Camping Leros* (Tel 23372). This is a quiet, shady, basic site, open June-September, and run by a Belgian woman, who speaks perfect English. The facilities include showers, toilets, cooking and washrooms, as well as a breakfast room and a BBQ. It costs 300drs to pitch a tent, and 500drs per head, per night.

The offshore **Glaronissia islands** make it appear that the bay is no more than an enormous lake, rather than a sea inlet

ROUTE TWO
To Alinda via Vromolithos (7km) From the main Lakki to Alinda road, an extremely sharp turning to the right, gives the impression of leaping into space, and very steeply inclines down to:

VROMOLITHOS (2km from Lakki) A backshore hamlet spread along a pretty, sheltered, curved bay. The tree edged and shaded beach is long and sandy, narrow to the right (*Fsw*) and pleasantly widening out to the left, where are a few benzinas moored to the shore. A scattering of businesses include the *Filoxinia Studios*, *Margaritas Rooms*, *Tony's Beach Studios*, a coffee bar, *Rooms Anastasios*, and *Frango's Restaurant*. *Frango's* is a highly rated, if sole dining establishment, serving 'the best food on the island'. A meal, for two, of 2 souvlaki (good size), a Greek salad, 1 kalamari, 4 Amstel beers, a Sprite, bread, a litre of water and service, costs about 3500drs.

Rooms Ginnis Anastasios (Tel 23247) is owned by a sister of *Rooms Kavos*, at Pantelli. The landlady has little English. The spacious double rooms are spotlessly clean, include the use of a fridge, have a balcony, with a splendid sea view (the sea is only some 6m distant), and plentiful hot water, all for a cost of 3500drs per night. Vromolithos is 'weekend-busy' with local families.

Beside the tree lined main road, that by-passes Platanos village, are some *Rooms*. At the junction with the Ag Marina road, the route to Alinda leads off to the left, around a large, central tree. This road undulatingly edges an attractive series of small coastal coves. *En route* passes by the *Taverna El*

Patio, which has a very large downstairs room, bordering the beach at the rear of the building. Despite the painfully slow service, that is slow even by the tardiest Greek standards, there is a variety of nicely cooked dishes that can be followed by ice-cream or a local gateau. About 200m beyond the *El Patio* is the *Hotel Athena*, opposite which is the *Restaurant Esperithes*. This establishment, behind a wall and up a flight of steps, serves an unusual, if comparatively expensive menu. The offerings include lamb fricasse, beef marengo, prawns, fresh fish, and so on.

A broad sweep of road, still adjacent to the water's edge, sweeps past an old kafeneion, and a hillock capped by a small chapel. Back at sea-level, on the left, is the peaceful, evocative, throat-catching, well-kept, but sadly little-visited British War Cemetery - no ouzos or Greek salad for these chaps. Those that do visit should read the War Graves Commission book, stowed away in one of the entrance gate piers. Next door is the cheapest, most Greek taverna on the island. It is a small building on some waste ground, with a few plastic tables and chairs outside. The owner is happy and likes everyone. A lunchtime 'pit-stop' of 4 Amstels, a Greek salad & bread cost 1200drs.

In complete contrast, the cemetery and taverna are followed by various disco-pubs, for the younger tourists, and cocktail bars, for the older set. The junction of the Partheni and Alinda roads is rather unexpected, with the route to Partheni a sharp turning off to the left. Continuing straight on, beside a pretty, tree lined, narrow, pebbly beach, from which wind surfers are hired, the road proceeds towards the spaced out development of:

ALINDA (7km from Lakki) A likable, if tourist location. Even out of the height of season, the slender shore is busy. The clear water bay is made up of numerous, small, fine shingle and sandy beaches. The inland side of the backshore 'Esplanade' hosts an admixture of spread out kafeneions, tavernas, restaurants, pensions, hotels and houses. Amongst these establishments is an eye-catching, seemingly deserted, castellated mansion, set in fairly large grounds, and presumably commissioned by a 'deranged' Italian, during that country's administration. It may sound as if the bay is already Kosta'd, but the expanse of slowly curving coastline is still able to cope with the present number of buildings.

Almost at the end of the bay, a small track drives to the left, up the hillside. Keeping to the right leads to the side-by-side *Pension Chrysoulla* and *Studio Nikita*, both owned by Mr Koumbaros, who is the proprietor of the *Hotel Katerina*, in Lakki Port. The *Chrysoulla* offers excellent accommodation, in a splendid setting, overlooking the bay, with the castle and villages of Platanos and Ag Marina forming a distant backdrop. To the rear are the dramatic slopes of Mt Klidi. Both the aforementioned pensions, and the next door *Angelika*, are surrounded by charming, flowery gardens. Fortunately, for those who share the innate belief that most 'things Greek' have an inevitable fallibility, I am delighted to report that the *Chrysoulla* is not without the occasional flaw. Be that as it may, it represents an unrivalled choice, with double rooms en suite priced at 3000drs. The adjacent apartments at the *Studio Nikita*, which has a basement bar, and is constructed around a swimming pool, costs 5000drs per night, for two people, and 7000drs, for three. The *Studio* is height-of-season popular with the Italians. Further to the right of this little complex, the brother of Mr Koumbaros has built the rather nice *Pension Angelika* (Tel 24610), with doubles at the 'going' rate. The brothers are genuine, friendly people, only too delighted to show prospects around, and then discuss the merits of their respective accommodations, over a coffee and home-made biscuits. The roosters are most effective, if inaccurate timekeepers. Alinda is rather mosquito-bound.

Before departing, the seafront road continues on past a taverna, a skeletal building, perhaps a hotel to-be, and local boats moored to the quayside. An unmade track proceeds beyond a very small bay, with a shingly beach, a chapel, an Army outpost, only to switchback by a second bay, larger than the first, and a fabulous looking house on the left. The track hereabouts peters out, alongside a small rubbish dump, becoming nothing more than a goat path. The path wanders down to a third, small, narrow but lovely bay, with a grove of trees. Here are some deserted dwellings and an old warehouse containing large wooden casks and stone troughs. This unofficial nudist beach is shingly sand. The donkeys tethered in the hills hereabouts have red tassels attached to their headbands.

ROUTE THREE
To Partheni via Alinda (12km) From the Alinda road junction, the concrete road is bordered by a 'litter' of new dwellings, being erected all over the place. The occasional, old agricultural shack and homestead, is hemmed-in by a morass of domestic animals.

GOURNA (10km from Lakki) The hamlet spreads round the mainly rocky but pretty bay. There is a small stretch of slender, pebble beach, and a chapel, idyllically set on an islet, close by the shore. There are no facilities. Wading through the shallows of the sea, gives access to an isolated cove. There it is possible to lounge the daylight hours away, set in a circle of mountains, edging the deepest sparkling blue sea imaginable.

A second turning towards Gourna leads through more homely - alright, downright scrubbly countryside, edged by hillbilly dwellings, all the way to a swampy looking rubbish tip.

The main road slopes northwards, gently past the airfield, for details of which *See* Arrival by Air, Lakki Port. From the airport, it is only a donkey trot along an unattractive approach to:
PARTHENI (12km from Lakki) Set in an inlet of Partheni Bay, the shores of which are somewhat marshy. The *raison d'etre* for the location is the large, Army base, once a concentration camp for the political prisoners of the Colonels' Junta. Keeping to the right leads to the lovely, clear waters of:

Plofouti Bay The boulderous, weedy and fine shingle seashore is edged by one lack-lustre, army personnel infested taverna, with an indifferent owner, and a few small caiques.

The situation seems to evoke a slightly foreboding atmosphere of quiet emptiness, a chilling evocation of the ghostly presence of spirits past. Were the Minoans here also?

FIRST IMPRESSIONS Ferries & cruise ships - moored to the quay, or anchored; tourists; neat farming country; bays & beaches; donkeys.

SPECIALITIES Religion.

LOCAL RELIGIOUS HOLIDAYS & FESTIVALS incl: 6th March - Festival in memory of the death of the Blessed Christodoulos, The Monastery; 21st May - Saint's day, The Monastery; 15th Aug - Festival of the Panaghia Church; 21st Oct - Festival to celebrate the return of the bones of the Blessed Christodoulos from Evia (Euboea). The Monastery celebrates the national holidays & religious festivals in very grand style. Star events are the Orthodox Easter and the 'Washing of the Feet', on Maundy Thursday.

VITAL STATISTICS Tel prefix 0247. The extremely indented island is 14km long & up to 8km wide. In excess of 2,000 of the overall population of 3,500 live in Skala Port and Chora.

HISTORY Unusually, for the Dodecanese islands, the history of Patmos does not mirror that of the others in the group. The reason lies in the Romans exiling St John the Divine to Patmos, in about AD 95. The saint experienced a revelation which, at the time, caused a 'bit of a stir' around the world. Some hundreds of years later, one of St John's admirers transcribed his 'memories' of the saint, but pirates kept the island clear of pilgrims until 1088. That was the year in which the Blessed Christodoulos received the sanction of the Orthodox Church to build a monastery on Patmos, in honour of St John. The fame of the religious order protected the fortified monastery, if not always the island, from the worst depredations of the various warmongers and overlords. The latter 'owners' included the Venetians, a Pope, the Turks, the Venetians briefly again, only for the Turks to take the island back, once more. The Turks lost possession, for a number of years, after the 1821-29 War of Independence, reclaimed it, to be followed by the Italians and Germans.

One of the reasons for the monastery's continued wealth and prosperity was that it owned a fleet of ships, even whilst, ostensibly, under the rule of the Turks. The ship's captains were in the habit of commissioning stylised, pendant jewellery symbolising their sailing vessels, with baubles hanging down to represent the keels. Some of these renowned pieces are displayed in the monastery museum, or treasury, which is more than can be said for the once great collection of books. Sadly, over the centuries, the library has been plundered by the learned, some of whose number were British scholars.

GENERAL Many guide books ramble on about the monastery's influence over the island's way of life, particularly in respect of moral standards. You know the sort of thing, the monks are a bit kill-joy, not allowing any loud music or discos, nor drunkenness after 'lights out'. More a general milieu of spirituality. This may well have been the case, in years gone-by, but is simply not so any more. Not even the most committed of religious cadres could have held back the effects of the merciless advance of the cruise ships, and their cargo of hedonistic passengers. Nowadays the sound of rock music has displaced the sonorous chants of religious ceremonies, the tinkle of cocktail

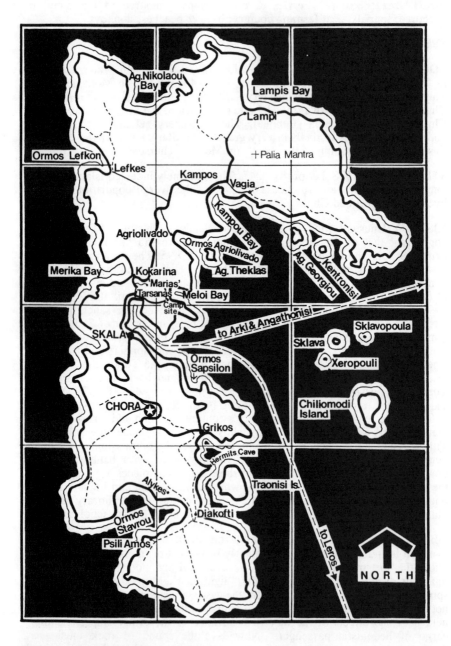

Illustration 29 Patmos island

glasses has replaced the bell-like clamour of holy censers. The influence of the liners is such that the traditional 'English breakfast' is Patmos styled - 'American'. It is pleasant to report, that beside Meloi beach is a sign 'On the Holy island of Patmos, there is no camping, and nuding (*sic*) is not allowed'. This board is hard-by the island campsite!

Some maintain that Patmos is one of the most beautiful of the Dodecanese islands, despite the surfeit, if not an avalanche of tourists. A most attractive geographical feature is that the heavily indented coastline has resulted in a disproportionately large number of bays. Unfortunately, few are outstanding. Another island-plus is that some of the inland villages are pleasingly characteristic, even new buildings observing the traditional architectural styles, despite their being constructed of precast concrete, not stone. A 'for-instance' is Kampos. A further joy is that the island's attractive and busy countryside is extremely neat. No parched fields, walled-in with flattened, rusting oil drums and discarded refrigerators, or washing machines. It has to be admitted that the seaside location of Grikos, conjures up visions of Mykonos, or Paros.

Despite, or perhaps because of these physical attractions, the island's economy is dominated by the cruise ships fun-loving, quaintly clothed clientele, who decant from and re-board the mother ship, in the fashion of giant flocks of starlings, at dawn and dusk.

The other noticeable invasion is home-grown, and occurs because of the island's importance to pilgrims of the Orthodox faith. The more religious visitors can easily be recognised, as they tend to travel in groups, on ship-borne coaches, and can be heard reciting sacred chants, or singing hymns.

Thus, the hard-pressed islanders, not only have to cope with the usual ebb and flow of island hopping travellers and package tour holiday-makers, but short-lived swarms of national and foreign visitors. The inhabitants require a lot of patience to cope with the ardours of these intrusive human invasions - but the money must help! To illustrate the extent of the 'blitzkrieg', at the height of the summer month madness, the liners literally queue, to wait their turn, in order to land their packed cargo of humans. One way to turn this phenomenon to one's advantage is to grab a convenient seat, and while away the hours, by simply watching the antics and inspecting the apparel of the hordes of passengers who disgorge from the giant floating palaces that serenely glide in and out of the bay.

Possibly due to the monastic presence, the citizens of Patmos do not appear to indulge, so wholeheartedly, in the otherwise unresistable impulse that seems to drive all right-thinking Hellenes to destroy all manner of wildlife. The result is that Patmos has a healthy number of feathered and furry creatures.

SKALA: port (Illus 30) The main settlement, and only island port, is bustling and extremely lively. The main body of the village spills off the edge of the enormous quay, dominating the south-east side of Skala. It almost appears that the locals have widened the alleys, lanes and waterfront, as well as pushed back the buildings, in order to allow the flow of even greater throngs of liner passengers. Even on a 'bad' day for liner visits, that is anything less than two or three, plenty of day-trip excursion boats arrive and drop-off deckfuls of 'happy', carefree visitors, from other tourist raddled islands. If this were not sufficient, Skala is a popular port of call for visiting yachts, and their crews. The regular infusions of hard, foreign currency, that swills about, ensures that the port, if not the island, is one of the most expensive throughout the Dodecanese.

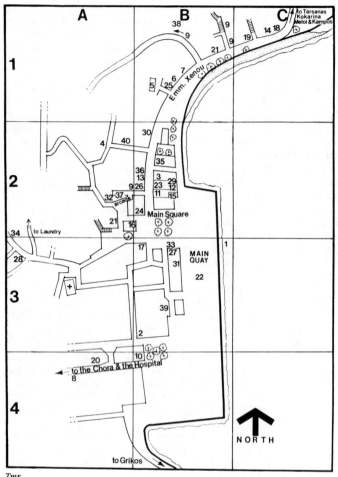

Tmr
1B/C3/4	Ferry-boat Quay	24A/B2	CA Ferry Agency
2A/B3/4	Hotel Rex/Patmos Rental	25B1	Fruit & Veg 'room'
3B2	Hotel Astoria	26A/B2	Agency A Konstantas
4A2	Hotel Rhodon	27B2/3	Post Office
5B1	Hotel Skala	28A3	OTE
6B1	Hotel Patmion	29B2	Astoria Travel
7B1	Hotel Chris	30A/B1/2	Cafe (with metered phone)
8A4	Rooms	31B3	Police Office/Town Hall/Information Office
9	Rooms To Let	32A2	Clinic/Doctor
10A/B3/4	Grigorys Grill	33B2/3	Taxi Rank
11B2	Cafe-bar Arion	34A2/3	Dentist
12B2	Restaurant	35B2	Restaurant Estiatorian
13A/B2	Kafeneion O'Pantelis (with telephone)	36A/B2	Estiatoria Pantelis
14C1	Cafe-bar Rebella	37A/B2	Public Toilets
15B2	Apollon Tours	38B1	Hotel Efi
16A/B2/3	National Bank	39B3	Tasos Rent A Car & Bikes
17A/B2/3	Kava Store/Ionian Bank Agent	40A/B2	Newspapers & Bookshop
18C1	Meltemi Bar		
19B/C1	Scooter & Bicycle Hire	(Tmr)	= Town map reference
20A3/4	Bookseller	(Fsw)	= Facing seawards
21	Bakers	(Sbo)	= Sea behind one
22B3	Bus Stop	(Fbqbo)	= Ferry-boat Quay behind one
23B2	Pharmacy		

Illustration 30 Skala port

ARRIVAL BY FERRY (*Tmr* 1B/C3/4) The ferry-boats and cruise liners berth towards the south end of the large, uneven sweep of concrete, on which are dotted about crash barriers. The boats are met by a veritable swarm of people, almost a biblical crush, many offering accommodation. And that includes the late arrivals, for Skala is a night-time docking for a number of scheduled ferry-boats. The rooms and hotel pedlars surge towards the disembarking passengers, in a disorganised rush, elbowing, pressing and pushing each other aside, whilst holding aloft their sign or placard, displaying the name of the particular establishment. Transport to a particular place is often in a car, on the roof of which is an illuminated sign bearing the name of the lodging. Yes!

THE ACCOMMODATION & EATING OUT
The Accommodation As pointed out, the human multitude that engulf the ferry-boat travellers include an almost frantic group of *Room* owners. They wildly compete for business, in an anxiety to fill their accommodation. There is plenty of choice, which can cope with all but the very busiest of times. The across the board, per night prices for a single bedroom, with en suite bathroom, is 2000/2500drs, a double bedroom, en suite in a private house is 3000/4000drs, and in a hotel 5500/6500drs. Guests may, or may not, have to partake in breakfast, which at Class B pensions costs about 500drs a head.

It really depends on a visitor's personal preferences, but I enjoy staying in private houses and getting involved, if only peripherally, in the day to day comings and goings of the household. Patmos is blessed with one of the best I have ever stayed in, that of:

Maria's Rooms   Tel 31480
Directions: Mrs Maria Papadatou's house is a fairly long walk from the quay. If a traveller is fortunate, one of her pretty, English speaking daughter's will 'possess' you, on disembarking, and lead the way to mother's. The fifteen minute hike, north of the port, skirts a small bay, proceeds past the generator station, and a small boatyard, to the tiny 'suburb' of Tarsanas. At the shallow end of the bay, the main road turns and rises, sharply to the left, at the outset of the climb, from the small plain, in the direction of Kampos. Where the road comes close to west coast Ormos Merika, in the environs called Kokarina, a narrow, unmade road tumbles off to the right. Maria's is on the right, set in a comparatively large, low-walled garden. If that sounds complicated, why not telephone?

An extremely pleasing double room, in this agreeable, almost squeaky-clean house, costs 3000/3600drs a night. The shared bathroom is excellent and use of the well equipped kitchen is part of the deal. As and when the few rooms are occupied, Maria, and her daughters, retire into a long, single storey shed, at the bottom of the garden. When Maria's accommodation is full, she directs people to her niece, Olga Vassilaki, just down the road. Maria, whose English is almost non-existent, is a lovely, if rather excitable hostess, and nothing is too much trouble for her. When guests arrive, leave, or when convenient, she will serve "Coffee, no charge".
Another small, but essential service that Maria can render is to telephone her contacts on Leros, if that island is the the next port of call.

On the way round to Tarsanas, beyond the generator station, a narrow lane to the left climbs a short distance to the:

Australis Pension   Tel 31576
Directions: As above, and a good looking establishment.
En suite double rooms are priced at 5000/5700drs.

A few yards further on, past the *Australis*, are some more **Rooms**. By keeping
to the shore-hugging road, beyond the Kampos turning, and alongside a petrol
station, slightly set back, is the:
Hotel Hellinis (Class C)   Tel 31275
Directions: As above.
All bedrooms are en suite, with a double costing 4900/6500drs.

Beyond the hotel, the concrete road climbs over the neck of the hillside, down
to lovely Ormos Meloi. The sandy beach, with some kelp in the shallow
water, is edged by trees. Apart from water skiing, wind surfing, and moored
caiques there is:
Rooms/Taverna Meloi   Tel 31888
Directions: As above, in a wonderful setting overlooking the beautiful and
tranquil bay, almost 'on the beach'.
Double rooms share the bathroom, at the very reasonable cost of 2000drs,
but the shower is in a lean-too outside, and the water is cold. But, at these
prices, perhaps all but the sensitive skinned will be able to put-up with this
minor, if chilling shortcoming. More especially if it is noted that a lever on
the side of the wall, near the shower, actuates a water heater! There's
knowledge for you.
Another reason to detail this establishment, is that the management's
philosophy is to cater (sorry) for the pockets of the nearby campers, not cruise
liner passengers. Admittedly, they are hardly likely to make it this far.
Whatever the objectives, the *Meloi* is quite possibly the best-value taverna on
the island. Clients must not expect a great deal of choice, or 'restaurant
sophistication', but the food is delicious and the waiters pleasant.

Close by is:
Patmos Flowers Camping   Tel 31821
Directions: As above.
An excellent, pretty campsite, popular with youngsters. The enthusiastic,
hard-working owner, Stefanos, lovingly presides over the operation, which is
situated on a small rise from the sea-lapped foreshore. The flower-filled, well
laid out site has room for 200 people. The plots are subdivided by welcome
screens of tall bamboo, whilst one area is afforded additional shade from the
sun, beneath a matt covered framework. The reception building has a mini-
market, there is an inexpensive cafe-bar, a clean, well equipped communal
block, with hot water showers, as well as toilets, washbasins and clothes
washing facilities. The bar stays open until 0300hrs, serving light snacks and
stocking cigarettes to sustain late night/early morning ferry-boat arrivals. As
is often the case, with solar heated supplies, the hot water doesn't last very
long, in the evenings. On occasions, the water supply to some sinks and
showers runs out completely, and the mini-markets' stocks are limited, and
more expensive than those 'in town'. The reception is adorned with an old-
fashioned trumpet gramophone. The site is open 15th May-15th October, and
rates are 700drs for an adult, or 1700drs a night for 2 adults and a tent.

Hotels in Skala Port include the:

Hotel Rex (*Tmr* 2A/B3/4) (Class D)   Tel 31242
Directions: Close to the outset of the Chora road.
Possibly the cheapest hotel 'in town'. The oldish, but spacious en suite bedrooms, cost from 1700drs for a single & from 3800drs for a double, increasing by about 1000drs a night, in the height of season months.

Whilst in this sector of 'the port', fairly close by is:
Rooms (*Tmr* 8A4) Tel 31369
Directions: On the left of the Chora road.
Bedrooms share, with mid-season doubles costing 5500drs. A further 200/300m along the Chora road are **Rooms** and apartments.

Back to the centre of the port, there are the:
Hotel Astoria (*Tmr* 3B2) (Class C)   Tel 31205
Directions: In a main quayside building, opposite the trip boat section. This is a noisy area due to the number of bars and restaurants hereabouts.
All bedrooms are en suite, with doubles priced at 4000/5700drs. 'Insider intelligence', or rumour, have it your own way, indicates that there is only an extremely slim chance of the *Astoria* being open, in 1993.

Hotel Rhodon (*Tmr* 4A2) (Class D)   Tel 31371
 Directions: From behind the *Estiatopian Restaurant* (Tmr 35B2), a lane proceeds westwards, and the hotel is on the right.
En suite doubles are charged 2500/5000drs.

Hotel Skala (*Tmr* 5B1) (Class B)   Tel 31343
Directions: Through an archway, left (*Fbqbo*) of the Esplanade.
All rooms have en suite bathrooms, with a single room priced at 4250/5600drs & doubles 5330/8035drs.

Hotel Patmion (*Tmr* 6B1) (B class pension) 34 Emm. Xenou   Tel 31313
Directions: Almost next door to the *Hotel Skala*, the building follows the curve of the waterfront.
An agreeable pension. Only double rooms, those sharing costing 2500/3000drs & those en suite charged at 3500/4500drs.

Hotel Chris (*Tmr* 7B1) (Class C)   Tel 31001
Directions: North and beside the Esplanade, alongside the unkempt grounds of an imposing house. In the ground floor is a disco-bar, almost always closed - so as not to disturb hotel guests?
The renovated hotel has clean, congenial bedrooms, all with en suite bathrooms. A single costs 3200/3800drs & doubles 4500/5000drs.

Hotel Efi (*Tmr* 38B1) (B class pension)   Tel 32500
Directions: Beyond the *Hotel Chris*, a turning branches off the Esplanade,which angles round the back of the *Chris*. The *Efi* is on the right, about 200m along the street.
New, efficient and clean. All bedrooms are en suite, those on the first and second floors are particularly recommended, with singles priced at 2530/3430drs & doubles 3520/5420drs.

Hotel Kastelli (*Tmr* A1) (B class pension)   Tel 31361
Directions: As for the *Hotel Efi*, but further on round, and situated behind the *Skala* (*Tmr* 5B1).

All bedrooms have en suite bathrooms, with a single priced at 2450/4650drs & doubles 3600/6250drs.

There are other *Rooms* spread throughout Skala (*Tmr* 9), with a clutch to the side of the northern Esplanade.

The Eating Out The swamp of visitors militates against there being many, if any traditional tavernas. The waterfront establishments fill-up with transient visitors, early in the evening. This is certainly one of those locations where it pays to depart the hub of the port. For instance, wander north, following the curve of the Esplanade. Immediately beyond the sharp bend in the road, close to the rather strange, railed-off tomb (*See* Places & Events...), and on the water's edge are a couple of most acceptable considerations. Of these, the *Taverna O Vrachos* serves good dishes and fresh fish at reasonable prices. Back at the port, probably the best of the 'affordable' choice is the:

Estiatoria O Pantelis (*Tmr* 36A/B2)
Directions: Situated in the street one back from the Esplanade, and on the left (*Fbqbo*), about 10m beyond the ferry-boat agent.
The restaurant has quite a large outside seating area, and is popular, if rarely overcrowded. The service supplied by the English speaking papa and his two daughters is speedy and efficient. The food is typical Greek taverna offerings, and the prices are reasonable - for Patmos that is! A meal, for two, of melitzanes & skordalia (aubergines & a 'sort of' garlic sauce), stuffed tomatoes, gigantes (beans), 2 Heineken beers, bread & service, cost 2480drs.
The *Restaurant Estiatorian* (*Tmr* 35B2) appears to be under the same 'management' as the *Pantelis*, as might be the adjacent *Kafeneion O Pantelis* (*Tmr* 13A/B2). The *Kafeneion* offers good value, and has a metered telephone.

Arion Cafe-bar (*Tmr* 11B2)
Directions: In the main, waterfront block.
The port's most popular waterfront bar, pumping out loud beat and rock music, 'a la Mykonos'. The interior is spacious and furnitured with heavy wooden tables and chairs. Small bottles of Becks beer cost 600drs, small ice-creams 450drs, and an espresso coffee 200drs. Beck beer! What is wrong with an Amstel?

It is reported that the *Ouzerie Moulos*, immediately prior to the OTE (*Tmr* 28A3), serves a tasty range of mezes, at fair prices.

At the outset of the Chora road is:
Grigorys Grill (*Tmr* 10A/B3/4)
Directions: As above, on the right, on the corner of the building.
A varied menu of national dishes, at comparatively reasonable prices. An English lady is the female of the partnership, and the atmosphere is more 'Kosta Brava', rather than Greek taverna!

As mentioned in The Accommodation section, the *Taverna Meloi* represents very good, if somewhat distant value.

THE A TO Z OF USEFUL INFORMATION
AIRLINE OFFICE The agent for Olympic Airways is Apollon Tours (*Tmr* 15B2). *See* Ferry-boat Ticket Offices.

BANKS The National Bank (*Tmr* 16A/B2/3) has a Main Sq office. Currency matters are negotiated at an external hatch and grill, on the right of the building. Open the usual hours, Mon-Fri 0800-1400hrs. The **Ionian Bank** is represented by the smart Kava drink store (*Tmr* 17A/B2/3) on the left (*Sbo*) of the Main Sq. The cashier of the latter is a thin, disinterested, very white skinned, aristocratic old man. As the staff of the National Bank exhibit the usual 'counter reluctance' vis-a-vis tourists piffling requirements, there is more chance of being served at the Kava, even during banking hours.

BEACHES A 'town beach' edges the tree lined Esplanade, from about the *Hotel Chris* (*Tmr* 7B1), as far round as the *Meltemi Bar* (*Tmr* 18C1). This is a sandy, but dirty and narrow shore. It borders a greenish sea, which laps a steeply shelving sea bottom. At the north end, the beach runs out on a small bluff, across from an incongruous, railed-off tomb (*See* Places & Events...).

BICYCLE, SCOOTER & CAR HIRE Our recommendation is **Moped Rental Tassos** (*Tmr* 39B3), to the left (*Sbo*) and one row back from the Town Hall (*Tmr* 31B3). A reliable moped, with a full tank, is charged 2000drs a day. There is at least one other scooter firm nearby, as is often the case. For instance, **Patmos Rental** (*Tmr* 2A/B3/4, tel 32203) is alongside the *Hotel Rex*. Not only does he hire 50cc Vespa's, at the market rate, but he changes travellers cheques, over the weekend, which can prove most handy, thank you. There are more firms 'going' north from the port, such as a Scooter & Bike outfit (*Tmr* 19B/C1), and **Navy Rent-A-Car.**

BOOKSELLERS An interesting **Book shop** (*Tmr* 20A3/4) is located 30m or so along the Chora road, on the right. A bonus is that they stock a selection of second-hand English books. There is a **Newspaper shop** (*Tmr* 40A/B2), selling magazines and books, beside the street leading towards the *Hotel Rhodon*. The poster publicity will assist in the search!

BREAD SHOPS A **Baker** (*Tmr* 21A/B2/3) is 'snuggled' away behind the National Bank. A couple of smart Bread shops, also sell pies and pastries. One is beside the Chora road, and the other (*Tmr* 21B1) alongside the Esplanade, beyond the *Hotel Chris*.

BUSES The Bus terminal (*Tmr* 22B3) is on the Esplanade, in front of the police station. Timetables of the comprehensive service are affixed to a large notice board, and are pinned-up in the foyer of most hotels/pensions.

Bus timetable
Skala Port to the Chora/Monastery
Daily   0740, 0915, 1115, 1130, 1200, 1330, 1530, 1730, 1930, 2040, 2130, 2230hrs
Return journey
Daily   0800, 1000, 1200, 1300, 1345, 1545, 1700, 1745, 2005, 2100, 2145, 2300hrs.
Skala Port to Kampos
Daily   0815, 1030, 1415, 1830hrs
Return journey
Daily   0840, 1100, 1500, 1900hrs
Skala Port to Grikos
Daily   0915, 1230, 1330, 1530, 1630, 1730, 2130, 2230hrs.

Grikos to the Chora
Daily 0945, 1245, 1645, 1950hrs
Return journey
Daily 0930, 1345, 1545, 1745, 1940, 2145hrs
There is a certain amount of ambiguity in these details!

COMMERCIAL SHOPPING AREA Stores and shops radiate out from the Main Square. Purveyors of goods and provisions are sufficient unto the shopping basket thereof, and include a Butcher and a Dairy. An unusual little number is the 'Fruits & Vegetables' room (*Tmr* 25B1) - yes a room .

DISCO Not so much a disco, more a profusion of music bars, amongst whose number is the *Meltemi Bar* (*Tmr* 18C1).

FERRY-BOATS & HYDROFOILS Both dock at the quayside (*Tmr* 1B/C3/4). The Port policeman (*Tmr* 31B3) is very helpful, and will produce a handwritten list, detailing not only the ferry-boats, but the islands at which they dock, as well as times. Well beyond the call of duty.

Ferry-boat timetable (Mid-season)

Day	Departure time	Ferry-boat	Ports/Islands of Call
Mon	2015hrs	Ag Rafael	Leros, Kalimnos, Kos, Rhodes.
	2300hrs	Ialyssos/Kamiros	Leros, Kalimnos, Kos, Rhodes.
Tue	0100hrs	Romilda	Mykonos, Syros, Piraeus(M).
	1430hrs	Ag Rafail	Samos, Chios, Lesbos, Limnos, Kavala(M).
	1500hrs	Chioni	Ikaria, Fourni, Samos.
	2000hrs	Ialyssos/Kamiros	Piraeus(M).
	2300hrs	Ialyssos/Kamiros	Leros, Kalimnos, Kos, Rhodes.
Wed	1030hrs	N. Kalymnos	Arki, Angathonisi, Samos.
	1300hrs	Chioni	Ikaria, Fourni, Samos.
	1745hrs	N. Kalymnos	Lipsos, Leros, Kalimnos, Kos, Rhodes.
	2000hrs	Ialyssos/Kamiros	Piraeus(M).
	2300hrs	Ialyssos/Kamiros	Leros, Kalimnos, Kos, Rhodes.
Thur	2000hrs	Ialyssos/Kamiros	Piraeus(M).
	2300hrs	Ialyssos/Kamiros	Leros, Kalimnos, Kos, Rhodes.
Fri	1500hrs	Chioni	Ikaria, Fourni, Samos.
	2000hrs	Ialyssos/Kamiros	Piraeus(M).
	2300hrs	Ialyssos/Kamiros	Leros, Kalimnos, Kos, Rhodes.
Sat	2000hrs	Ialyssos/Kamiros	Piraeus(M).
	2300hrs	Ialyssos/Kamiros	Leros, Kalimnos, Kos, Rhodes.
Sun	1000hrs	N. Kalymnos	Samos, Fourni.
	1100hrs	Romilda	Naxos, Paros, Piraeus(M).
	2000hrs	Ialyssos/Kamiros	Piraeus(M).
	2100hrs	N. Kalymnos	Lipsos, Leros, Kalimnos, Kos, Rhodes.

In addition there are any amount of daily excursion boat trips, many operating to a timetable, many not running on any day that a scheduled ferry-boat/hydrofoil is making the voyage. Note that the local, private enterprise inter-island craft are more costly and are subject to 'variation' - alright, alteration and cancellation, at the drop of an isobar. Furthermore they are contingent upon large-scale, year to year alterations and amendments, and are severely curtailed out of the tourist season - but what isn't?

An idea, a flavour of that on offer is as follows:
Patmos daily to: Leros; Kalimnos; Kos; & Samos; Lipsos; Arki & Marathi.
The Lipsos, Arki & Marathi excursions each cost 1800drs return.

Anna Express This craft is based on Lipsos. Despite the nomenclature, it is not necessarily the fastest boat, but undertakes the crossing from Patmos to Lipsos in about 45mins, at a fee of 1500drs, for the return trip. It daily departs Lipsos at 1600hrs, and slips from Patmos at 2300hrs.

Hydrofoil timetable (Mid-season)

Day	Departure time	Ports/Islands of Call
Tue/Fri	1600hrs	Leros, Kos.
Sun	1000hrs	Samos.
	1600hrs	Kos.

The information in respect hydrofoils can be extremely patchy! Apollon Tours (*Tmr* 15B2) should be able to assist - as they are the agents for the craft.
   In addition, there are Hydrofoil excursions, although it is difficult to spot the difference between scheduled and excursion voyages!
   They are rumoured to be as follows:

Day	Ports/Islands of Call
Tue/Fri	Rhodes.
Wed/Sat/Sun	Kos.
Sun	Samos.

One-way fare Patmos to: Leros 1900drs; Kos 2900drs; Rhodes 5800drs.

FERRY-BOATS & HYDROFOIL TICKET OFFICES CA Ferries Agency (*Tmr* 24A/B2), which steadfastly eschews displaying a sign, is agent for the **FB Nissos Kalymnos & Romilda**. Along the street is **Agency A Konstantas** (*Tmr* 26A/B2, tel 31314), agent for the **FB Ialyssos & Kamiros**. Facing the waterfront is **Apollon Tours** (*Tmr* 15B2, tel 31356/31324) who act for Ilio Lines, owners of the Hydrofoils.

LAUNDRY A well-signposted launderette is eight minutes walk up the twisting, stepped street, which is the last right-hand (*Sbo*) turning, prior to the OTE office (*Tmr* 28A3).

MEDICAL CARE
Chemists & Pharmacies A Pharmacy (*Tmr* 23B2) is beside the street off the Main Sq, that parallels, and is one back from the Esplanade.
Clinic/Doctor (*Tmr* 32A2) The medical office is up a flight of stairs, off an alley. Dr Christos Kirozis is in attendance. The surgery opens weekdays 0830-1200 & 1700-1900hrs and weekends, as posted.
Dentist (*Tmr* 34A2/3) Further along the 'OTE road'.
Hospital 2km on up the Chora road.

MUNICIPAL TOURIST OFFICE (*Tmr* 31B3) Not so much an NTOG, more a Town Hall run office, on the far side of the Italianesque block in which are located the police offices. Open standard weekday hours. Not only hands out leaflets, but changes currency and hires cars. Various information sheets are pinned to a notice board, affixed to one side of the Police station (*Tmr* 31B3). The officers are extremely helpful and friendly, with at least one speaking excellent English. Travellers waiting for a ferry can leave their luggage beneath the external stairs of the police station.

OTE (*Tmr* 28A3) Open weekdays 0830-2200hrs. The *Kafeneion* (*Tmr* 13A/B2) has a metered telephone, as does a *Cafe* (*Tmr* 30A/B1/2).

PETROL The one and only (Fina) filling station is beyond the *Hotel Hellinis*, on the northern outskirts of Skala.

PLACES & EVENTS OF INTEREST The railed off tomb, the other side of the road from the far end of the town beach, is (according to the attached plaque) the foundations of the baptistry of St John the Divine. *See* The Chora and Monastery, Route One.

I am indebted to a correspondent for the following notes in respect of Easter celebrations on the island.

"*Maundy Thursday* Patmos is especially renowned for the 'Niptiras' ceremony which takes place on this day. 'Niptiras' means 'basin', the rites being a re-enactment of Christ washing his disciples' feet, at the Last Supper. The ceremony begins about 1100hrs in the Lozia Square, Chora. As there are so many spectators, it is best to arrive early. The monks set out from the monastery, at about the stated time, and make their way through the lavender-strewn streets to perform the 90 minute ritual.

Good Friday (Megali Paraskevi) A day of deep mourning. The Lauds of Good Friday are sung in the main monastery church, at 0800hrs & 0900hrs. Laments are held at 0800hrs, both in the monastery and in the churches of Kambos and Skala. The most interesting spectacle of the day is perhaps the 'Epitafios', or funeral service, which is performed after the 1830hrs evening services. A funeral bier, covered with flowers, is carried through the streets, followed by the mourners clutching lighted candles.

Easter Saturday/Sunday Resurrection services are held in the monastery and at Kambos and Skala. It goes without saying, that those at the monastery are the most impressive. They commence a little before 1100hrs. At midnight the Resurrection is announced with the words 'Christos Anesti' (Christ is risen). This is the signal for an explosion of fireworks, all over Greece, and the priest passes the flame of life from the altar to the candles of the worshippers who, in turn, pass it on to the whole congregation. Afterwards the Lenten fast is broken and everyone makes their way home, or to a restaurant, to eat the Easter soup of 'maghiritsa' made from lambs' innards, flavoured with dill and lemon, and eggs dyed red, to symbolise the blood of Christ.

Easter Sunday All over the island, lambs are spit roasted. At the Police station and the Army camp, special celebrations are held, around lunchtime, to which everyone is welcome, to partake of a drink and a small plate of food.

In the Monastery the Service of Love (Agapi) is held at around 1400hrs, at which the Abbott gives a red egg a kiss and a blessing to all the children attending. Easter Tuesday This day, the icons and relics, from all over Patmos are carried to the Aghios Levias Sq, Chora, to be blessed. Subsequently the holy objects are taken to island homes, to transfer the blessings to them, and the occupants, for the coming year.

POLICE
Port The 'on the spot' officers occupy a quay building (*Tmr* 1B/C3/4), which they share with a bar.
Town (*Tmr* 31B3) The officers, and Port officials, are housed in a section of the Town Hall building.

POST OFFICE (*Tmr* 27B2/3) In the same Town Hall building as the Police offices, and open Mon-Fri between 0730-1400hrs.

TAXIS Rank (*Tmr* 33B2/3) alongside the Town Hall, on the edge of the Main Sq. A taxi to Chora costs about 600drs, one-way, and is well worth the price, as the walk is arduous - and takes some 85-90mins.   Incidental intelligence suggests that those foolhardy enough to contemplate such an imprudent course of action, should select the main road, and not the path. It may be longer, 'as the donkey flies', but the track is made hazardous by the many loose stones that litter the way. A taxi to Kampos, that is Upper Kampos, not the beach, also costs some 600drs, one way.

TELEPHONE NUMBERS & ADDRESSES

Clinic/Doctor (*Tmr* 32A2)	Tel 31577
Hospital	Tel 31211
Police, port (*Tmr* 31B3)	Tel 31231
Police, town (*Tmr* 31B3)	Tel 31100/31303
Taxi rank (*Tmr* 33B2/3)	Tel 31225
Town Hall (*Tmr* 31B3)	Tel 31235/31058

TOILETS There is an ethnic facility (*Tmr* 37A/B2) near to the Clinic.

TRAVEL AGENTS & TOUR OFFICES Apart from the Agents detailed under Ferry-boat Ticket Offices, **Astoria Travel** (*Tmr* 29B2, tel 21205/31208) peddles 'pure' travel agent activities. These include excursion boat and coach trips. Of the ferry-boat listings, the **Apollon** (*Tmr* 15B2) is the most travel agent orientated, also selling excursions, on land and water.

WATER TAXIS They are the most popular method of getting to and from the various beaches. The launches usually moor across from the *Arion Cafe-bar* (*Tmr* 11B2). Signs of destination and times are posted the night before, at about 2200hrs. The average return fare is 550drs.

ROUTE ONE To Psili Amos & Diakofti via Chora, the capital, & the Monastery of St John the Divine (some 6km) As the crow flies, the first section of the journey to Chora is about 2km. Following the looping, tree shaded road, the distance travelled measures about 3km. The route passes the **Monastery of the Apocalypse,** now a theological college, the Hospital, and the **Grotto of the Apocalypse,** where St John experienced the Revelation. The trees which line the road are pines, but these are supplanted by tall, elegant gum trees. The last kilometre is across shadeless, boulderous, granite terrain.

CHORA (Illus 31) The old town, or Chora, is totally subordinate to the monastery, which dominates the settlement. It is the quintessential Cycladean-style Chora. That is a maze of clean, whitewashed, narrow lanes, hemmed-in by medieval-tall houses and walls, and apparently deserted. I am advised that Chora is irresistibly reminiscent of San Marino, in Italy. On the other hand, I can never entirely erase images of those seemingly foresaken Mexican villages, as depicted in the 'Dirty Dozen' films, all expectancy, but no inhabitants, dogs or birds - they are there, but where?
　　Two signposts indicate totally conflicting directions to the Main Square, and there are a number of kafeneions and tavernas. Of these the *Restaurant Vangelis*, beside the Main Sq, serves a most acceptable, traditional meal, as does the *Taverna Vassilli*, bordering a small square, close to the monastery. There are some *Rooms* 'on the other side of the monastery', as well as an OTE on the right (*Facing the monastery/hill*) of the car park.

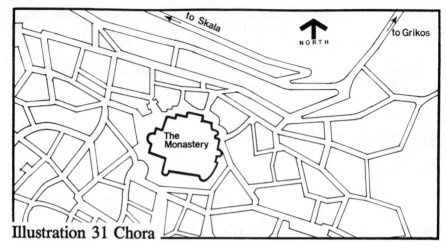

Illustration 31 Chora

Monastery of St John the Divine Entrance is free. The opening arrangements are as follows: Mon/Wed/Thur/Fri/Sat 0800-1400hrs; Tues 0800-1400 & 1600-1800hrs; and Sun 0800-1200 & 1600-1800hrs. On the other hand, a notice reads 'The above programme (the scheduled hours) is liable to change due to unscheduled visits of ships'. So even the monks genuflect to the whims and caprices of cruise liners!

The final approach, up which swarm hordes of tourists, is an ascending, cobbled slope. All around the monastery are a number of old vendors, stopping anyone who hesitates, in an attempt to sell them - something. They are cloaked in an air of quiet desperation, but are probably making a fortune.

At the main gate a 'kindly' soul 'loans out' pairs of trousers and or wrap-round skirts (not to one and the same person, you understand) for about 100drs. This reminds me to reiterate that it is not only good manners, but obligatory to dress with some decorum for a monastery visit. Every day a number of tourists seem determined to ignore this reasonable dictum. So trousers and shirts, or skirts and blouses are the order of the day, please. Photographers should note that the use of flash equipment is forbidden.

The fortified monastery is beautiful, extreme peaceful, allows stunning views, dominates the old capital town, and is a five star, 'fully operational' establishment. The vistas stretch as far as Samos to the north, Naxos to the west, Kos in the south, and Turkey to the east. Assuming they are open, both the Library and Museum are extremely interesting.

Contrary to a popular myth, the monastery does not control the production and sale of the island postcards and maps. Certainly the monks sell these items, but they are no different than are now available elsewhere.

The main road skirts the elevated town and continues on to Grikos (*See* Route Two). About ½km from Chora, a turning to the right, along an unmade, wide track (and keeping left) lurches to a rather unique, monastic, old stone road. This bends down the gentle hillside, leaving the hamlet of **Alykes** way below, on the right. The laid stone pathway finally disappears, reverting to flint track.

Stout shoes are order of the day. The large, pebble beach to the south of Alykes is set in a beautiful bay, but the foreshore is piled high with kelp and is rather rubbish littered.

At the far end of the curve of Ormos Stavrou is the absolutely lovely, sandy and tree edged shore of **Psili Amos**. This pure white, fine sand beach is (unofficially) the island's only nudist beach. It is a 'dashed' long walk, which can sensibly be avoided by taking the one hour water taxi from Skala.

A short walk, over the neck of land, to the east coast, leads to the peaceful **Diakofti** hamlet. The pleasing, large pebble foreshore is clean, and usually deserted. One fisherman's cottage edges the backshore. The sea-bed is slimy.

ROUTE TWO

To Grikos (3km) A 'standard' island road takes in Ormos Sapsilon, hardly a sunbathing bay, but there is a clean, slender, pebbly foreshore. For those who decide to walk, it is about a 45min hike, but there are scheduled buses and water taxis make the trip. From Chora proceed by the main Skala turning, straight on past the town, taking a left fork down to:

GRIKOS (3km from Skala) A tourist resort, with a sandy beach, all the water and sun activities required, as much accommodation as it is possible to squeeze in, and absolutely no Greek atmosphere!

The settlement edges a large, curving cove and the road runs out on the enclosed shores, bordering calm waters. On the backshore is *Stamatis Taverna*, and thirty paces away another beach restaurant, as well as a small quay. There are a number of ramshackle finger piers, to which boats and caiques are moored. The beach to the left, as well as the first section to the right, is rather dirty and very seaweedy. Further to the right, the fine shingle beach is clean, and a variety of water sports equipment is for hire.

The *Hotel Grikos* (B class pension, tel 31294/31167) is rather luxurious for such a location as Grikos. All its bedrooms have en suite bathrooms, with singles priced at 2250/3750drs & doubles 4750/6500drs. This hotel is one block back from the shore, and to the left, as are the *Panorama Apartments* (Class C, tel 31209) and *Hotel Xenia* (Class B, tel 31219). All the latter's bedrooms have en suite bathrooms, with singles costing 5000/6000drs & doubles 5330/8035drs. The management is of a mind to reduce these prices, when desperate for custom - and so they should! At the other end of the scale is the *Hotel Flisvos* (Class D, tel 31380).

An islet blocks out any broad seascapes, and gives the impression of joining-up with a foreground, narrow-necked isthmus. The latter terminates in a blob of rock, which is difficult to scale. Despite, or perhaps because of this it 'houses' a hermit's cave, facing seawards, a deep well, and some wall carvings. There is a suggestion that provisions are always 'in the larder' for any traveller who gains access. The views make the climb worthwhile.

ROUTE THREE To Kampos (5km) & other points north Close by *Maria's* house (*See* The Accommodation, Skala), at Kokarina, a track to the left leads down to a cramped, weedy beach. An old man has built a shack on the sea's edge, at the far end of the tiny bay.

Another 2km along the main route and a road to the right ends up 50m short of the beach at:
Ormos Agriolivado (4km from Skala) The last few steps must be made on foot. The first section of the beach is boulderous, with earth spoil forming small swamps, whilst the rest of the beach is shingly sand. Signs include 'No Camping, no nudism, The Police Station' and 'Please keep the place clean'.

The backshore is edged by tamarisk trees with whitewashed trunks. The building on the left (*Fsw*) is a small beach bar, and has a toilet. A house, further to the left, bears a sign reading 'No trespassing'. Somebody this-a-way is sign-happy!

About ½km further along the main road, a rough track to the left, resembling a summer-dry river-bed, tumbles down to the:
Lefkon Bay The access terminates on the foreshore of a rather horrid, shingly beach, covered with thick seaweed and edged by tamarisk trees. To the left is a jetty, overlooked by an imposing, hillside, but rather incongruous house, possibly of Italian design.

KAMPOS (5km from Skala) The upper, nice, quiet, clean, hilltop village has a cobbled square. One edge of the plateia is bordered by a church, whilst 'circling' are a couple of to-be-recommended tavernas, *Yiannis* and *Sarantis*. Sometimes live music is laid-on for weekend evenings. There is a store.
   A helpful sign indicates the direction for the various beaches, at this end of Patmos. To the left is an extremely steep, concreted track. This runs out above Upper Kampos, from whence there are some splendid views over the north-west part of the island.
   Back at the centre of the village, a road forks down the hillside to the right, and along the waterfront of a small bay, to:

Lower Kampos (Ormos Kampou) This beach is one of the island's most popular. It is an agreeable mix of sand, pebble and stone, on which are drawn-up quite a few caiques. Three tavernas, at least one of which will be open, look after the inner person. Facing the bay, the fishing boats are to the right, sunbathing benches (*sic*) and umbrellas to the left, as are the ski boat run and windsurfers. Accessible by water taxi, bus, or a 45min walk.

At the end of Ormos Kampou, and off to the right, is a precipitous gravel track. This leads up the hump of the hillside, and down the other side, to the coastal hamlet of:
VAGIA A small, shingly beach, off which are anchored fishing boats. A sign nailed to the bottom of a telegraph pole, on the crest of the approach road proclaims 'Rooms For Rend'. Probably the best of the island's beaches, and is a most acceptable, peaceful spot, with clear sea water, and one taverna.

The main road snakes on, up and around the small mountain of Palia Mantra, across a scenic landscape, to a steep, unmade track. The latter, continues on, and from hereabouts it is a short stretch, down to the right-hand end of Ormos Lampis, and the tiny hamlet of:
LAMPI (9km from Skala) The location is renowned for its beautiful multi-coloured stones, which make up much of the extremely clean, shingle beach. The occasional blob of tar spots the foreshore. There is some sand, adjacent to the far *Dolphin Taverna*, beyond a small jetty. The nearside, rather basic taverna has a pretty vine-covered garden, at the back of the building. Here are a few, single storey changing rooms, some simple double rooms for rent, at about 2500drs, and the owner serves a reasonably priced, if limited menu. A number of workmanlike fishing boats anchor in the bay.
   Lampi has one of the oldest island churches, the Church of Christos, built in the 16thC.

16 LIPSOS
Dodecanese Islands

FIRST IMPRESSIONS Quiet; signposting; beaches; dust; blue & white churches; sparklingly vivid town.

SPECIALITIES Hand woven carpets.

LOCAL RELIGIOUS HOLIDAYS & FESTIVALS incl: 24th Aug - Festival of the Madonna of Charos Chapel (when dried flowers in the building are supposed to spring to life).

VITAL STATISTICS Tel prefix 0247. The island is about 9km long and, at the narrowest point, only 1km wide. The population numbers about 650.

HISTORY Inextricably linked to Patmos, the monastery of which owned Lipsos, for some six hundred years, dating from Byzantine times.
   Some sources link the island with Calypso, seducer of Odysseus in the Odyssey. The name certainly echoes the enchantress' name. On the other hand, experts plump for Gozo, adjacent to Malta - sorry Lipsos!

GENERAL Lipsos is usually lumped together with the much smaller islands of Arki, Marathi and Angathonisi, as a day-trip possibility, at the end of a chapter about Patmos. In fact, although still relatively quiet, Lipsos is much more set on the road to development than the others. It should be visited, quickly, if the recent increase in tourist activity is anything to go by. Patmos is not the only source of day-trippers, as small craft arrive from Leros. Oh blow you winter winds! That sorts out the excursion boats, of which some two a day cross-over from Patmos, and one a day from Leros.
   The steady increase in tourism has resulted in a matching expansion of the number of pensions and tavernas, and Lipsos is reasonably popular with the yachting fraternity. Many islanders are engaged in fishing, despite which agriculture remains a buoyant pursuit.

LIPSOS (Lipsoi, Lipsi, Lipso): port & village (Illus 34) This is the only settlement. Considering its relatively small size, it is well organised, and at first sight, appears to be an attractive location, dominated by a Cycladean type, large, blue domed church. It is fair to write, that first impressions are probably rather flattering. From early morning, the port is enjoyably lively, with the day-to-day farming and fishing activities in full flow. In the busy summer months, the mid-morning arrival of day-trippers makes for a lot of activity. During the afternoon siesta, the place 'dies'. Once the 'invaders' have departed, Lipsos is gloriously quiet.

ARRIVAL BY FERRY Ferry-boats dock at the Ferry-boat Quay, which is around to the far left (*Sbo*) of the bay. On this quay is the *Ocean Cafe-bar*, and 'just off quay' are a 'spotting' of pensions, including the *Panorama*, and *Rooms*. Excursion craft moor up to the smaller quay (*Tmr* 1B3), in front of the *Calypso Hotel*.
   All arrivals are met by a motley collection of jeeps and trucks, with cab mounted wooden boards, indicating the name of the beach to which they will transport passengers. This 'assault' is based on the assumption that almost

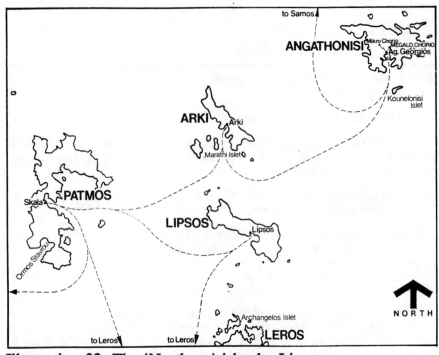

Illustration 32 The 'Northern' islands, Lipsos,
Arki, Marathi, & Angathonisi

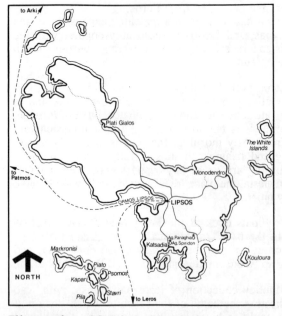

Illustration 33 Lipsos island

all visitors have disembarked, in order to visit one of the island's celebrated beaches. Travellers wishing to overnight should eschew this 'rash of trucks'. It will be necessary to walk 'into town', as owners of accommodation rarely attend a boat's docking. They simply lie in wait for trudging prospects.

The only 'out of town' accommodation is at Katsadia Beach. The 'trucks' are 'the' island's transport system, and punters who miss the first wave, which fill-up in minutes, will have to walk, although the vehicles reappear, later in the morning - 'to lurk'.

THE ACCOMMODATION & EATING OUT

The Accommodation The closest choice, rather depends at which quay a boat docks. Inland of the main Ferry-boat Quay, amongst some *Rooms*, is the:

Pension Panorama
Directions: As above.
A new building, in which clean, spacious bedrooms share the bathroom. Double room prices average 3500drs a night.

One of the adjacent possibilities is:
Rooms Matsouris
Directions: As above, and a couple of years old.
Owned by Nick and and his smiley wife Anna. The accommodation is kept spotlessly clean. Nick doesn't speak much English, but Anna's is adequate. He is a fisherman and sells his catch over on Patmos, as the prices are too low on Lipsos. Some of the bedrooms are more studios, with en suite shower, a fridge, gas ring, cutlery, crockery, and a nice balcony overlooking the harbour. The prices are the island average.

Behind the Excursion Boat Quay (*Tmr* 1B3) is the:
Hotel Calypso (*Tmr* 2A/B2/3) (Class D)   Tel 41242
Directions: As above.
The hotel/restaurant has undergone a rebuild. The Australian educated owner and his family are friendly and helpful. He does not seem to regard his accommodation as highly as he does the restaurant, and there are the occasional rumours in respect of whatever is 'next to godliness'! A double room en suite costs 3500drs a night.

Less expensive, but more basic accommodation is available at the *Pension* (*Tmr* 3A/B1/2) behind the *Calypso*. Further round, beyond the church, is the:
Pension Flisvos (*Tmr* 14D/E5/6)
Directions: As above, and on the right (*Fbqbo*).
Regarded as probably the best accommodation in Lipsos, and thus is very often full. The basic bedrooms share the bathroom, as well as a kitchen and balcony. A mid-season double costs 3000drs a night.

Another option is that belonging to 'Fat' Maria, whose *Rooms* are recommended (*See Restaurant Barbarossa*, The Eating Out).

The Eating Out A favourite watering-hole is the:
Ouzerie (*Tmr* 19A/B2/3).
Directions: Between the Excursion Boat Quay and the *Calypso*.
Rather more a store selling almost everything, with some tables and chairs outside. Well-patronised by the locals, performing the usual charade of shouting at each other and hurling playing cards at the table. Strangers are

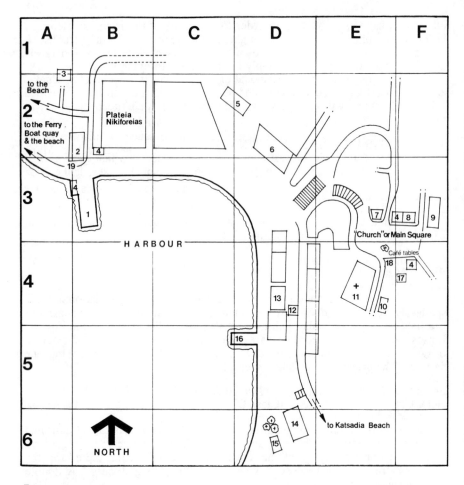

Tmr
1B3	Excursion-boat Quay
2A/B2/3	Calypso Hotel/Restaurant
3A/B1/2	Pension
4	Cafes
5C/D2	Taverna
6D2/3	Police Station
7E/F3	Post Office
8E3	Library
9F3	Town Hall/Museum/Tourist Office/Public Toilets
10E/F4	Clinic/Doctor
11E4	The Church
12D4/5	General Store
13D4	Fish Freezing Plant
14D/E5/6	Pension Flisvos
15D6	Fish Taverna
16C/D4/5	Fishing Boat Pier
17F4	Bakery
18E/F4	OTE
19A/B2/3	Ouzerie

(Tmr) = *Town map reference*
(Fsw) = *Facing seawards*
(Sbo) = *Sea behind one*
(Fbqbo) = *Ferry-boat Quay behind one*

Illustration 34 Lipsos Port

made welcome, and this is an excellent spot at which to drop in, for an ouzo and grilled octopus.

Restoran Barbarossa (*sic*)
Directions: West of the *Calypso*, on the top of the hill, between the Excursion Boat Quay and the town beach.

A rather ethnic 'restoran', run by 'Fat' Maria and uncle Billy. They are a charming pair and Billy is (rightly) proud of his cooking. Service is fitful. A meal of a tasty aubergine & courgettes, in tomato sauce, 1 fulsome Greek salad, a Pepsi, bread & service, cost 1850drs. Don't forget that 'Fat' Maria has accommodation.

Beside the Esplanade, and about 50m from the Ferry-boat Quay is the:
Taverna Kali Kardia
Directions: As above.

Similar prices and quality to the *Barbarossa*, if rather more touristy, with a nicely shaded terrace. The moustached mama loves to speak Italian, whilst the one-toothed papa, Vassileia Prasimou, who has very little English, but acceptable German, welcomes clients into their kitchen. Here, they wave their arms at whatever is on offer, and exclaim "Sit down, the waiter will come" - which he does, eventually! The tasty 'special omelette' is a spongy cross between a pre-cooked omelette and a pancake, rolled and stuffed with cooked vegetables. A simple meal of 1 Greek salad, a plate of octopus, a crown top retsina, bread & service, costs 1680drs.

Calypso Restaurant (*Tmr* 2A/B2/3)
Directions: *See* The Accommodation.

The waiters are quiet and friendly. There are two dining slots, a restaurant on the left (*Sbo*), for tourists, and a taverna on the right (*Sbo*) catering, in the main but not exclusively, for locals. Good quality food at reasonable prices.

There are a number of alternative dining choices, such as the: *Taverna O Theologos*, near to the *Calypso*, which serves only fresh fish at acceptable prices; *Taverna* (*Tmr* 5C/D2); and the *Fish Taverna* (*Tmr* 15D6), close to the *Pension Flisvos*. As a matter of interest the *Cafe-bar* (*Tmr* 4F4) beside the Main Square, and closest to the church, is owned by Dimitris, father of Dina, she of the *Taverna Miltos*, Fourni island (*See* GROC's Guide to the NE Aegean, for the panegyric).

THE A TO Z OF USEFUL INFORMATION
BANKS None. See Post Office.

BEACHES The trucks collect punters from the quays, and drive them to and from the selected location, at a return fare fee of 1000drs.
Town/Lendou Beach The nearest to the village, and a five minute walk, to the west of the *Hotel Calypso*. Follow the quayside as far as the *Restoran Barbarossa*, then cut across the dirt path to the track, which runs parallel and one back from the quay. This drops immediately to the sandy beach. The shore is sometimes spotted with tar, borders clear seas, and the backshore has some tree cover. This beach is one of the busiest, being closest to the port. It is likable enough, but is scattered with discarded building odds and ends. The fine sand runs beneath the sea and swimming is enjoyable. It is worth noting there are no 'outfalls' visible. During the busy season months, a kiosk opens,

selling refreshments, and hiring pedaloes. There are no sun-beds or umbrellas, possibly because it isn't the greatest shore on which to lie.

By the backshore is a 'no name dancing bar', which breaks into loud music, in the evenings, and, occasionally, in the afternoons. Further back is a pleasing looking *Rooms*.

Other island beaches include:

Monodendro A 40min walk to the north-east, and the unofficial nudist beach. Some would say it is the best beach.

Plati Gialos Beach A good hour's walk. A long and sandy shore.

Katsadia Beach *See* Route One.

BICYCLE, SCOOTER & CAR HIRE None, but enquiries, and the hint of remuneration, stands the chance of bringing forth a scooter.

BREAD SHOPS (*Tmr* 17F4) South of the Main Sq, and open daily. There is another one listed in Commercial Shopping.

COMMERCIAL SHOPPING AREA Apart from the **General store** (*Tmr* 12D4/5), where basic supplies are sold, there is a 'concentration' of possibilities, north of the Main Sq. These include a Hardware store, an Electrical shop/workshop, a 'Tourist' shop, with a few tatty glasses and other bits and pieces, in a very dusty window, two Fruit & Veg shops, a Butcher, and a Baker. There are several other small, 'ethnic' shops in the same area.

FERRY-BOATS The sole scheduled inter-island ferry that calls in is the **FB Nissos Kalymnos**, and then only twice a week.

Ferry-boat timetable (Mid-season)

Day	Departure time	Ferry-boat	Ports/Islands of Call
Wed	0915hrs	Nissos Kalymnos	Patmos, Arki, Angathonisi, Samos.
	1840hrs	Nissos Kalymnos	Leros, Kalymnos, Kos.
Sun	0900hrs	Nissos Kalymnos	Patmos, Samos, Fourni, Ikaria.
	2245hrs	Nissos Kalymnos	Leros, Kalymnos.

However, the island is daily linked, in the summer months, to Patmos, by at least two, if not three excursion boats. Of these the Anna Express is probably the least expensive, and certainly not the slowest. It departs for Patmos every afternoon at 1600hrs, slipping Skala quay, Patmos, at about 2300hrs. The voyage takes about 45min and costs some 1500drs, for the return fare.

The Maria Express runs a once-a-week excursion to Arki, Marathi and Angathonisi, in addition to its Leros and Patmos trips.

FERRY-BOAT TICKET OFFICES None. Tickets are purchased on board.

MEDICAL CARE (*Tmr* 10E/F4) The doctor's Clinic/Pharmacy, is across the way from the church. Consultations and dispensing takes place daily, mornings and early evenings, but not siesta time. It is not unknown for the doctor to pop round for a chat, drink, and informal examination.

MUNICIPAL TOURIST OFFICE (*Tmr* 9F3) Housed in the ground floor of the Town Hall, within the museum, but there is little for them to 'inform' about. Should the museum and Tourist office be closed, pop up the external stairs, to the Town Hall 'bit', and demand attention! The official hours are weekdays 0930-1330 & 1600-2000hrs, weekends 1000-1400hrs.

OTE (*Tmr* 18E/F4) The bare room, containing a couple of telephones, is opposite the church. Open weekdays between 0800-1500hrs.

PLACES & EVENTS OF INTEREST
Museum An extremely pleasing display is in the restored ground floor of the Town Hall, which also 'houses' the information desk. The limited exhibits include: finds from the ocean floor (encrusted vases and the like); sacred icons; church paraphernalia; a rather odd collection of jars of water, from various 'religious' locations, such as Mt Athos peninsula, brought together by the village priest; and costumes from Lipsos, and nearby islands.
The Monument There are 'field' reports of a huge monument, at the east side of the town, north of the road to Monodendro. It is silver painted, about 13m high, with a crown or flower on the top. The base is six-sided, with embossed on it - plaques, red badges, a red star, that looks like a crescent moon and star, and a cart wheel. It stands in a small, fenced-off olive grove. More information is needed!

POLICE (*Tmr* 6D2/3) The Police station is a large, square building at the bottom of the steps leading up to the Main Square. The one policeman is unfriendly, unhelpful and unwilling to dispense any information. Best to head for the Town Hall and Tourist office.

POST OFFICE (*Tmr* 7E/F3) Borders the Main Square, conducts currency exchange transactions, and open weekdays between 0730-1400hrs.

TAXIS None.

TELEPHONE NUMBERS & ADDRESSES
Police (*Tmr* 6D2/3)   Tel 41222/41209
Tourist office (*Tmr* 9F3)   Tel 41288

TOILETS A facility is in the ground floor of the Town Hall (*Tmr* 9F3)

Excursion to Katsadia Beach Rather than bump to Katsadia in a truck, it is reported to be more rewarding to make the journey on foot. This is about a 25min hike, through fertile countryside and over a hill, from whence the track drops down to a wide, picturesque bay, edged by the narrow, sandy beach. I think I will take the truck!

Despite being the most celebrated of the island's beaches, it is difficult to fathom out why? It is not particularly beautiful, it is only about 2m wide, and tends to become littered with tourists, and their rubbish. This crowding is due to the daily press of visitors, on day-excursion trips from the larger islands of Patmos and Leros. There is some tar, but the sea is lovely and clear.

The backshore, tatty, rather primitive *Dilaila Taverna & Rooms* is heavily promoted in the 'town', but is a 'bit of a rip-off'. A basic double bedroom costs about 2500drs a night, but there is no electricity and clients must draw their own water from a well. Very rustic!

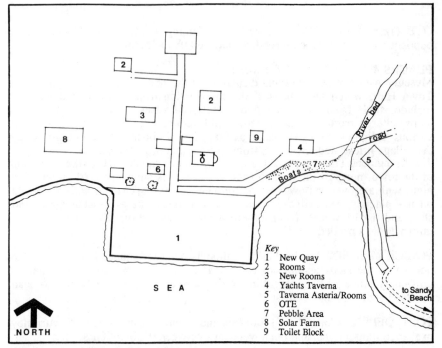

Illustration 35 Arki - Port Augusta

Key
1. New Quay
2. Rooms
3. New Rooms
4. Yachts Taverna
5. Taverna Asteria/Rooms
6. OTE
7. Pebble Area
8. Solar Farm
9. Toilet Block

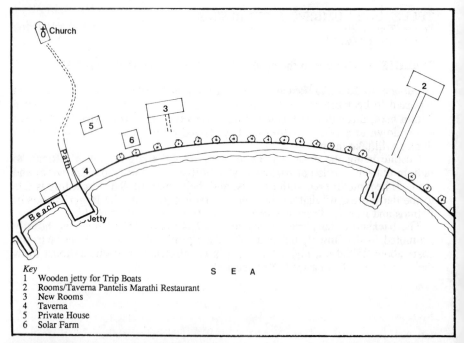

Illustration 36 Marathi Beach

Key
1. Wooden jetty for Trip Boats
2. Rooms/Taverna Pantelis Marathi Restaurant
3. New Rooms
4. Taverna
5. Private House
6. Solar Farm

ARKI The quiet, untouched island is about 5km long (north-west to south-east) and 1km in width, with a population of some 70. The tel prefix is 0247.

Gentle, hilly little Arki is covered with greenish scrub, but few trees. Fishing is the sole source of indigenous income, whilst fish, eggs, goats milk and cheese are the only island produced commodities. Everything else, including drinking water, has to be freighted in by ship. The only other source of income is that generated by the few tourists and visiting yachtsmen.

Port Augusta (Illus 35), the single settlement, is at the end of a small fjord, protected by the islands scattered about the entrance to the inlet. The houses are constructed of dry stone, without mortar.

Getting to and from Arki, in the summer, is not overly difficult. Apart from a once a week inter-island ferry (*See* Ferry-boats, Lipsos), there are daily excursions from Patmos and Leros, with a weekly boat from Lipsos.

The solar plant (*Tmr* 8), completed in 1984, provides electricity for the houses and businesses. To obtain accommodation, it is probably best to enquire of the taverna proprietors. More often than not, they are landlords of the *Rooms*. A for-instance is the *Taverna Asterias* (*Tmr* 5, tel 32371/VHF 12), owned by the most friendly and helpful Ilion Lentheris. His accommodation is the newly built block, on the outskirts of the port hamlet, just to one side of the road to the north. The en suite double rooms cost 3000drs.

The OTE (*Tmr* 6) is located in a small hut, in the garden of a house behind the New Quay. There is one telephone and a ship-to-shore VHF radio. The facility is open all day, until about midnight, as long as the friendly old lady, who oversee's the installation, is 'at home'.

The water of the harbour is murky and greenish, a pointer to where the settlement's effluent outfalls! There are a couple of beaches, one pebbly, one sandy, both to the south of the port, around at **Port Stretti Bay** and the coves which make it up. The closest is a pebble one, which is a scramble around the nearest headland. It is about 30m long.

A track from the port takes off up the hill to **Panaghia**, a cluster of tumbledown buildings, surrounding a blue and white church. One or two families still hang-on there.

If Arki sounds like a paradise, for those wishing to get away from it all, so it may be. There will be very few other visitors staying overnight. On the other hand, travellers intending to stay should bear in mind the facilities not available, as opposed to the other way around. A list may not go amiss. There is no 'town' beach, no drinking water 'on tap', no medical facilities, no Post Office, no shops or bakery, no transport, no policeman, no army outpost, not even a priest! Yes, it does sound good, doesn't it? And the locals are extremely hospitable. However, do not forget to pack a good book or three, any favourite provisions, a phrase book, and fly/mosquito repellent!

MARATHI (Marathos, Maranthi) (Illus 36) This low-lying, little islet is a super place to stay. That is as long as a visitor is seeking peace, comfort, good food, a long, sand and shingle beach, and clear seas in which to swim.

The natural harbour hosts fishing craft from nearby, bigger islands and is a popular stopping-off place for private yachts.

No inter-island ferry-boats include Marathi in their schedule. Not even the Dodecanese 'workship', the **FB Nissos Kalymnos** drops anchor. On the other hand, there are daily excursion boats from Patmos. Passengers should note that the voyage can be 'fraught', due to inclement weather causing a choppy sea state. Obviously the smaller craft 'wallow worst', but nothing that a change of dry clothes won't put right! Without doubt, whatever the conditions, the captain will excude calm aplomb, from the 'bridge'.

The original summer month resident family, who run the *Rooms Taverna Pantelis Marathi Restaurant* (*Tmr* 2) now have competition in the shape of the *Other Place Rooms Taverna* (*Tmr* 4). Was it ever thus in Greece? The *Pantelis* is pleasantly set in 'goat-free' gardens, and is a friendly family affair. The enterprising owner was originally from Arki, but speaks excellent 'Grine', as do his wife and sons, who also spent most of their lives in Australia. A tasty meal, for two, of Greek salad, moussaka, a couple of cans of Amstel, (delicious) bread and service, costs about 2000drs. Fish meals are excellent, but comparatively expensive. The taverna and rooms are clean and modern, with a double room en suite costing 3000/3800drs.

The equally popular *Other Place* edges the backshore, to the left-hand (*Sbo*) side of the waterfront. The narrow concrete terrace is shaded by a rush canopy and tamarisk trees. The establishment's acclaim is recognised by local house flies. They are probably not only attracted by the food, but the serried rows of dead hooded crows, pinned to the fence at the back, and the billy goat skulls, which adorn the tamarisk trees, at the front. This taverna is not quite so clean as the *Pantelis*. Their double rooms cost 3500drs, but only have cold water, and are in a separate block, adjacent to the taverna, also set in goat-free garden grounds.

Goats are an island 'event'. For instance, goat meat, with a plate of spaghetti, is on offer at the *Pantelis*, whilst the *Other Place* has the referred-to skulls 'prominent'. Apart from these manifestations, goats have eaten, chewed, bitten and nibbled some of the island bare. Cross-country hiking is made that little more difficult by the anti-goat stone walls that have been erected, and are topped-off with brush and thornwood. This is in a vain attempt to halt the wretched animals inexorable advance, and to stop them munching away at the rest of the island's vegetation, thus turning all of Marathi into a semi-desert.

From the far side of the *Other Place*, a goat track heads off towards a hillside, a derelict hamlet, and an apparently abandoned church. Descending the short distance, the other side of the hill, advances, over 'goat walls', to a rocky, windward shore.

18 ANGATHONISI (Angathonissi, Agathonisi, Gaidaros, Gaidharos) Dodecanese Islands

Angathonisi (Illus 37) is about 5km wide, and 2½km from top to bottom. The Tel prefix is 0247. Approximately 130 inhabitants populate this, the most northerly, desolate and remote of the Dodecanese islands.

Its rather isolated position, being 36km from Patmos, and 25km from Samos, makes the island almost too distant for the usual pack of day-trip excursion boats, which increasingly seem to settle, mindlessly on this, that, or the other location. Despite the inhabitants being denied these daily delights, they do not appear to consider themselves deprived. There is no sense of doom or gloom, more one of fortitude, with a population that has remained constant for many years. Most of the inhabitants are involved in fishing or shepherding, and notwithstanding its small size, the community is vibrant and surprisingly healthy. The most prolific crop is thorn, on the bush - hence the name, 'thorn island'.

It might not come as a surprise that Angathonisi is an ideal bolt-hole, for both the traveller wishing to escape the stresses of 20thC life, and the true lover of Greece. This is one of the few truly traditional, Greek island's of yesteryear, with hardly a tourist in sight. The pace (pace, what pace) of life is slow, very slow, the natives reserved, but sincere. Everything is truly Hellenic - siesta times, house decoration and furniture, and simple manners.

There are three island settlements - **Ag Georgios**, the port, and the two villages of **Megalo Chorio** and **Mikro Chorio**. Megalo Chorio is on the mountainside to the right (*Sbo*) of the port, and Mikro Chorio, with only a dozen or so inhabitants, is to the left. Both villages are linked to the harbour by a narrow concrete road. This is just wide enough to take the pick-up trucks, and those high-cabbed, three wheelers, which transport everything, including livestock, people, and the mail, up and down the hillsides. A track connects the two roads.

The scheduled ferry-boat, the (you've guessed it) **FB Nissos Kalymnos,** calls just one day a week, to scenes of great excitement and frantic activity. The usual harbourside activity is enlivened by the chaotic quay scenes, with most of the inhabitants attending the event. So, once disembarked, it's a week until the next craft docks. Fortunately, for those who are concerned, that they might not like the place, the Sunday boat arrives in the morning, to steam on to Samos, and then back to Fourni, and redock at Angathonisi, before proceeding to Patmos, Leros and Kalimnos - to return a week later. Thus, prospective 'Robinson Crusoe's' have most of a day to make up their mind if Angathonisi is for them, or not. Can't be bad. There are rumours in respect of height-of-the-season, twice weekly caique connections with Samos, to the north, as well as once weekly excursion craft to and from Lipsos and Patmos.

Accommodation is principally in Ag Georgios, where there are two *Pensions*, with five bedrooms each, as well as a few *Rooms* in private houses. Average per night, double room rates are 3000drs.

There are several port tavernas, catering mainly for 'yachties', as there are so few tourists, as well as a handy kafeneion, perched on the Ferry-boat Quay. The latter is a good bet for breakfast, where a Nes meh ghala costs 200drs.

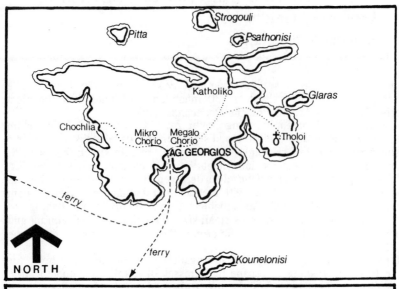

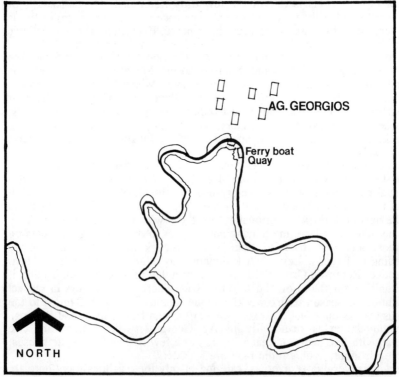

Illustration 37 Angathonisi island & Ag Georgios Port

Ginger-headed 'George the Sailor' owns the *Taverna*, set back from the track round the beach, where a meal, for two, of tzatziki, Greek salad, kalamares, retsina, bread and service, cost 1950drs.

The port beach is rather more a stretch of large pebble shore, which pebbles run on into the sea. Apart from sea and wind driven rubbish, some green slime and weed, there is evidence of tar. Mmmh! The lack of any sun-beds or umbrellas may not come as a surprise!

Just above Ag Georgios, at the beginning of the road to Megalo Chorio, is the island's Police station, which doubles up as an 'Army camp', housing a few soldiers, leisurely defending the 'realm'. The young, friendly and pleasant policeman 'trebles up' as port policeman and customs official. As he has some broken English, it is not a bad idea to make a friendly gesture, on arrival. Modern-speak would explain all this with some twaddle about body-language. I am suggesting visitors don't poke his eye out with a stick. I am not suggesting they fall about proffering gifts! Just a friendly wave, or twenty. Further up the same road is the generating station.

Although the pensions and tavernas are down at the harbour, most bona fida village life takes place in Megalo Chorio. Here is the island school, the doctor's surgery and pharmacy, the main church, and the two general stores. The latter stock a limited, but essential variety of foodstuffs, as all produce and supplies, including bread, have to be bought in by ship. There aren't any banks, nor a museum, OTE or Post Office. The island's well water is no good for drinking, and has to be tanker'd in from Samos.

Despite the basic lifestyle, there isn't a perception of life being unbearable for the inhabitants. In fact, once the initial wariness has worn off, they are friendly, helpful, hospitable and eager to show off the delights of Angathonisi. As no map is available, it is fortuitous that the locals willingly point enquirers in the right direction, for walks to nearby beaches or ruined settlements. A few words of Greek and the ability to disassociate oneself from 'the stein of lager' chappies is an invaluable assistance for any stay. A nod is as good as a teuton - whoops, a wink!

Artwork: Ted Spittles &
        Geoffrey O'Connell
Packaging: Willowbridge
        Publishing
Plans
& Maps: Graham Bishop &
        Geoffrey O'Connell
Typeset: Disc preparation
        Viv Grady & Willowbridge
        Publishing
Cover Preparation &
Printing: FotoDIRECT Ltd
Printers: The Bath Press